The LATTER RAIN

Using the
BOOK OF ISAIAH
As the Key to Unlock Bible Prophecies
That Are Relevant Today

The LATTER RAIN

Using the BOOK OF ISAIAH
As the Key to Unlock Bible Prophecies That Are Relevant Today

JAMES M. CONIS

FRANKLIN, WEST VIRGINIA

The Latter Rain
Copyright © 2010 James Mason Conis
All Rights Reserved
Design and layout by Mark Vermeulen
Storm photo © Tamara Kulikova
Drought photo © Anton Prado
No part of this book may be reproduced in any form whatsoever, without the prior written permission of the publisher, except in the case of brief passages embodied in critical reviews and articles where the title, author and ISBN accompany such review or article.

All opinions expressed herein are the author's alone and are not associated with any church or other organization.

All scripture references: King James Version of the Holy Bible, unless otherwise noted.

This book is an original publication of Castle Mountain Press.
Visit us at www.CastleMtPress.com

Library of Congress Cataloging-in-Publication Data
Conis, James M., 1960 -
  The Latter Rain: Using the book of Isaiah as the key to unlock bible prophesies that are relevant today / James M. Conis
    p. cm.
  ISBN: 978-0-9827108-0-7 Hardcover
  ISBN: 978-0-9827108-1-4 Softcover
  1. Isaiah 2. Latter Rain 3. Religion 4. Bible 5. Revelation 6. Prophecy
  Library of Congress Control No. 2010911332

Printed in the United States of America
10 9 8 7 6 5 4 3 2 1

I dedicate this book to my father, James Norman Conis. He has never lost hope in me, and has been a constant support and refuge through the tough times of my life. Without him, I feel certain this book would have never come to be. Thank you father!

Contents

Preface		ix
Chapter 1	Prophecy, Revelation, and Divine Inspiration	1
Chapter 2	Rain as a Symbolic Type	17
Chapter 3	Symbols and Types of the Book of Isaiah	24
Chapter 4	The Message of the Book of Isaiah	33
Chapter 5	The Book of Jeremiah and His Lamentations	56
Chapter 6	The Book of Ezekiel	88
Chapter 7	The Book of Daniel	127
Chapter 8	The Book of Psalms	134
Chapter 9	Joseph in Egypt	152
Chapter 10	Moses and the Exodus	178
Chapter 11	The New Testament	207
Chapter 12	The Mission of Jesus Christ	219
Chapter 13	Priesthood Authority	230
Chapter 14	The Revelation of St. John the Divine	257
Chapter 15	The Latter Rain	289

Preface

So I now seem to be able to lay it down as a general rule that whatever I perceive very clearly and distinctly is true. (...) And since I have no cause to think there is a deceiving God, and I do not even know for sure whether there is a God at all, any reason for doubt which depends simply on this supposition is a very slight and, so to speak, metaphysical one. But in order to remove even this slight reason for doubt, as soon as the opportunity arises I must examine whether there is a God, and, if there is, whether he can be a deceiver. For if I do not know this, it seems that I can never be quite certain about anything else.

René Descartes, French Philosopher
From his Third Meditation, *"The Existence of God"*

What is truth? And how can we perceive it? If we assume that René Descartes is correct, then "whatever I perceive very clearly and distinctly" can thus be assumed to be true. The exception to this rule would be if God could be a deceiver, then things could appear to be true and not be. However, I do not believe that God can be a deceiver, or he would cease to be God. Thus, God has given every man and woman the ability to perceive the truth when it is heard or felt. While we might still be led away by false assumptions based on incorrect information presented to us by others, I believe that if we sincerely seek counsel from God to know the truth of a thing, he will enlighten our minds to know the absolute truth of it.

It is important to make this issue clear because what I intend to do in this book is to uncover truth. I maintain that each individual that reads this book can and should call upon God in prayer to discover if these things have relevance in his or her life. I do not believe that God is a deceiver and, therefore, I do not believe that he will allow a person to read this book, or any other book for that matter, and somehow be led astray by falsehood. If the reader is truly a seeker of truth, and is willing to counsel with the Lord directly in his or her search for sound doctrine, the truth will become self-evident.

THE LATTER RAIN

Except for the discussion of a few historical facts and other references to current events, the majority of the content of this book comes directly from the Bible. Therefore, I ask you to please appeal to God if questions arise in your mind. "He that answereth a matter before he heareth it, it is folly and shame unto him." (Proverbs 18:13 King James Version) Likewise, "Be not hasty in thy spirit to be angry: for anger resteth in the bosom of fools." (Ecclesiastes 7:9) Therefore, I ask anyone who reads this book to honestly study it out and appeal to God for wisdom and understanding. To do otherwise leaves one vulnerable to the influences of every wind of doctrine espoused by men and devils.

Returning to the writings of Descartes cited above, I wish to make one thing completely clear right from the onset: I know that there is a God, and that he is a living being. He is our Father and we are created in his image. Furthermore, it is my sincere belief that if we are honest seekers of truth, he will make himself known unto us. If anything written in this book leads people closer to their God, then I will have accomplished my objective for writing it. My base assumption in presenting my findings in this book is that God himself will help the reader understand it, and comprehend the truth thereof.

This same process occurred for me. When my oldest daughter was in middle school some years ago, she asked me to explain to her the meaning of the Book of Isaiah contained in the Old Testament of the Bible. I did my best, but conceded to myself that I did not really know what Isaiah was trying to tell me. Later, a friend asked me questions about the meaning of the Book of Isaiah, which renewed my daughter's earlier challenge. I spent about two and a half months pouring through the text of this great work. Likewise, I spent much time in prayer, asking that the Lord might make known unto me the meaning and interpretation of these writings as they apply to me and those living in our day. During this period of time, there came a point where it seemed as though my mind became opened to understanding. The symbols and types brought forth by Isaiah suddenly appeared to make sense in a way I had never before imagined. This process occurred line upon line and precept upon precept as described in Isaiah 28:9-11, in that I received answers to certain questions I had posed to the Lord, and these answers then led me to ask new questions and so on. This process continued until I was more or less satisfied that Isaiah's message had indeed been revealed to me. I immediately proceeded to write down my impressions in the form of an essay which, at the time, I called, "A Personal Analysis of the Book of Isaiah."

When at last I presented this essay to my friends and family members, they all seemed to agree that my ideas were genuine and interesting. My sister was especially impressed, and encouraged me to seek publication for the work as an article in a religious journal of Theology. As I considered her suggestion, several months passed, and I continued to study the scriptures, picking up where I had left off at the end of Isaiah. Thus, I read the books of Jeremiah, Lamentations, Ezekiel, and Daniel. As I read these other books, the ideas and concepts I had gained from my study of Isaiah's writings began to repeat themselves over and over again. I came to the conclusion that the reason the Lord seemed to place so much emphasis on the Book of Isaiah throughout the other scriptures was

PREFACE

because Isaiah appeared to be a key to their understanding. Therefore, this is the major finding of this book, namely that the Book of Isaiah is an important key to understanding the meaning of not just Isaiah's writings, but of the entire Bible.

This discovery was a major epiphany in my life. It was at this point that I developed an overwhelming feeling that I should not just publish my findings about Isaiah as an article, but that I should put together a more extensive work, including ideas and concepts that I observed in various other books of the Bible. My objective in writing this book, therefore, is to share this amazing discovery with others, and to show how a better understanding of Isaiah has led me to see greater meaning in the other books of the Bible as well. While this is a more extensive work than the original article on Isaiah itself, it is still not all-encompassing. I am hopeful that others will gain from this work and apply it to their own study of the scriptures, bringing to light additional observations and insights that might help us all draw closer to the truth concerning the nature and will of God. Thus, with no further ado, I present to you my book, *The Latter Rain*, and may God bless you in your quest for truth wherever it may be found.

Sincerely,

James M. Conis

CHAPTER ONE

Prophecy, Revelation, and Divine Inspiration

Imagine a family seated around the dinner table, blessing the food and giving thanks. Or, you might see a small girl kneeling beside her bed at night, asking the Lord to bless her father to find work soon. Perhaps you might feel that even the unspoken yearnings in the heart of someone who is hurting inside may find their way to the Lord and appeal to his mercy and grace. No matter what opinion you have about God or religion, most people would still agree that those who attempt to communicate with God, do so through prayer. But, this brings up another question:

How Does God Communicate With Man?

This question requires a little more thought. We learn about such things from our parents, religious studies, or from reading and studying the scriptures. The Bible, for example, contains stories that demonstrate how God has communicated with his children on earth in the past. In fact, the Bible is often referred to as "the word of God" or "God's holy word." For some, his word stops with the Old Testament, including the Book of Genesis up through Malachi. For others, the word of God includes both the Old Testament and the New Testament. The New Testament relates the events associated with the life of Jesus Christ and his Apostles. Likewise, other faiths have written works (e.g. the Qur'an, the Aqdas, etc.) which they hold to be sacred communications from God through oracles on the earth. The men who wrote these books, which others consider to be holy, are usually considered to have been prophets. Thus, for many people, learning how God communicates with man begins through a study of what they consider to be Holy Scripture, written down by men that received revelation from God indicating things God felt were important for us to know. For example:

Amos 3:7

7 Surely the Lord God will do nothing, but he revealeth his secret unto his servants the prophets.

THE LATTER RAIN

This verse taken from the Old Testament is a message from God through the prophet Amos. If we accept that Amos was a true prophet, then his message would be something God wanted us to know. In this specific case, Amos is telling us that the Lord always uses prophets to communicate his messages and directions to his children on the earth. In fact, without them, God will do nothing. When you think of a prophet, you might first think of those that actually have books attributed to them in the Bible. The first five books of the Old Testament, for example, are attributed to Moses: Genesis, Exodus, Leviticus, Numbers, and Deuteronomy. Many books in the Bible actually bear the name of the author (e.g., Malachi) or the subject of the book (e.g., 1st and 2nd Kings tell of the succession of the Israelite kings). Books written by prophets thus contain information that is attributed as the will of God for man. Such information, generally known as prophecy or revelation, can be given for people living on the earth at the time it is received, but may also have meaning and importance to people living in future eras. Thus, revelation occurs when a person is inspired to say things, write things, or do things that are given him directly from the Holy Spirit of God.

The Bible is often referred to as the "Holy Bible" because it is recognized as a volume or library of holy books containing prophecies given to God's personal oracles living on the earth. The Book of Isaiah is presumed to contain the prophecies of the Lord's prophet Isaiah and the Book of Jeremiah the holy prophecies of the prophet Jeremiah. However, some prophets mentioned in the Bible either did not write down the revelations they received from God or, if they did, those revelations were not preserved and are lost. For example, Abraham is shown to have paid tithes to a man by the name of Melchisedec, as related in Chapter 14 of the Book of Genesis and again in Hebrews 7:

Hebrews 7:1-4
1 For this Melchisedec, king of Salem, priest of the most high God, who met Abraham returning from the slaughter of the kings, and blessed him;
2 To whom also Abraham gave a tenth part of all; first being by interpretation King of righteousness, and after that also King of Salem, which is, King of peace;
3 Without father, without mother, without descent, having neither beginning of days, nor end of life; but made like unto the Son of God; abideth a priest continually.
4 Now consider how great this man was, unto whom even the patriarch Abraham gave the tenth of the spoils.

Melchisedec must have also been a prophet, even though none of his writings are contained in the modern-day Bible. The Apostle Paul is making the point to the Hebrews that Melchisedec was even greater than Abraham, who, by the way, also has no book bearing his name in the Bible. In other words, there is no Book of Melchisedec, nor a Book of Abraham contained in the Bible. However, most would agree that both were holy men. Furthermore, there appears to be a difference between being a prophet and being prophetic. When Saul was anointed King of Israel by Samuel the prophet, the new king went forth and began to prophesy, even though he was not considered to be a prophet prior to that event.

1 Samuel 10:9-13
9 And it was so, that when he had turned his back to go from Samuel, God gave him another heart: and all those signs came to pass that day.

PROPHECY, REVELATION, AND DIVINE INSPIRATION

10 And when they came thither to the hill, behold, a company of prophets met him; and the Spirit of God came upon him, and he prophesied among them.
11 And it came to pass, when all that knew him beforetime saw that, behold, he prophesied among the prophets, then the people said one to another, What is this that is come unto the son of Kish? Is Saul also among the prophets?
12 And one of the same place answered and said, But who is their father? Therefore it became a proverb, Is Saul also among the prophets?
13 And when he had made an end of prophesying, he came to the high place.

Several pertinent issues relative to the subject of prophecy are described in the verses of 1 Samuel 10. First, we learn that Saul received the gift of prophecy after he was anointed king over Israel. In other words, the spirit of the Lord came down upon him and he was filled with the word of God unto prophesying. Many who had known him before noticed the change that came over Saul. We should note that even though Samuel was the head priest and prophet in Israel at the time, other men were considered to be prophets as well. "A company of prophets met him," referring to Saul, "and the Spirit of God came upon him, and he prophesied among them." These other men, who are not mentioned by name, were also prophets and capable of prophesying. They were capable of relaying messages from the Lord to the people living on the earth.

This spiritual outpouring occurs elsewhere in the scriptures. When Moses is advised by his father-in-law, Jethro, to select men to help judge Israel (Exodus 18:13-27), he chooses able men, and makes them heads over the people, rulers of thousands, rulers of hundreds, and so forth. Before this, Moses was deciding all cases, and it was wearing him out. These chosen judges appear to be temporal leaders. Later, Moses does likewise for spiritual matters. He selects 70 men to assist him in ministering to Israel, which sheds light on the subject of prophets and prophecy.

Numbers 11:24-30

24 And Moses went out, and told the people the words of the Lord, and gathered the seventy men of the elders of the people, and set them round about the tabernacle.
25 And the Lord came down in a cloud, and spake unto him, and took of the spirit that was upon him, and gave it unto the seventy elders: and it came to pass, that, when the spirit rested upon them, they prophesied, and did not cease.
26 But there remained two of the men in the camp, the name of the one was Eldad, and the name of the other Medad: and the spirit rested upon them; and they were of them that were written, but went not out unto the tabernacle: and they prophesied in the camp.
27 And there ran a young man, and told Moses, and said, Eldad and Medad do prophesy in the camp.
28 And Joshua the son of Nun, the servant of Moses, one of his young men, answered and said, My lord Moses, forbid them.
29 And Moses said unto him, Enviest thou for my sake? would God that all the Lord's people were prophets, and that the Lord would put his spirit upon them!
30 And Moses gat him into the camp, he and the elders of Israel.

This story shows that, like in the case of Saul, a man can receive the gift of prophecy whenever the spirit of the Lord descends upon him. Likewise, it shows that it does not matter where a man is located physically, the spirit of the Lord can still descend upon him and cause him to speak prophetically. Even though these 70 men became prophets, Moses still remained the head or lead prophet over Israel. Thus, there was still an order to the authority administered from God to the men in this situation. Finally, this passage shows Moses' particular view concerning who should be allowed to be a prophet. According to Moses, "would God that all the Lord's people were prophets, and that the Lord would put his spirit upon them!" And by all, he apparently means all. The gift of prophecy is not limited to men, at least not according to the scriptures. Several situations mentioned in the Bible confirm the existence of prophetesses. First of all, Miriam, the sister of Moses and Aaron, was considered to be a prophetess.

Exodus 15:20-21

20 And Miriam the prophetess, the sister of Aaron, took a timbrel in her hand; and all the women went out after her with timbrels and with dances.
21 And Miriam answered them, Sing ye to the Lord, for he hath triumphed gloriously; the horse and his rider hath he thrown into the sea.

Likewise, consider Miriam's encounter with the Lord as recorded in Numbers 12:

Numbers 12:4-5

4 And the Lord spake suddenly unto Moses, and unto Aaron, and unto Miriam, Come out ye three unto the tabernacle of the congregation. And they three came out.
5 And the Lord came down in the pillar of the cloud, and stood in the door of the tabernacle, and called Aaron and Miriam: and they both came forth.

Miriam was intimately acquainted with God. She conversed with him and was known of him. She was called to come forward and to be in the presence of the Lord, just like Moses. At various times, the Lord also spoke to the people using her as a means to convey his message (see Numbers 12:2). Miriam was a woman endowed with great spirituality, and a woman who was known as a prophetess by the people. Again, a person can have the spirit of prophecy and be very close to the Lord without necessarily being the main leader of Israel. This distinction exists here in the case of Miriam. Later, in the Book of Judges, we find a most interesting case where a prophetess not only exhibits the spirit of prophecy, but also serves as a judge in Israel.

Judges 4:4-9

4 And Deborah, a prophetess, the wife of Lapidoth, she judged Israel at that time.
5 And she dwelt under the palm tree of Deborah between Ramah and Beth-el in mount Ephraim: and the children of Israel came up to her for judgment.
6 And she sent and called Barak the son of Abinoam out of Kedesh-naphtali, and said unto him, Hath not the Lord God of Israel commanded, saying, Go and draw toward mount Tabor, and take with thee ten thousand men of the children of Naphtali and of the children of Zebulun?
7 And I will draw unto thee to the river Kishon Sisera, the captain of Jabin's army, with his chariots and his multitude; and I will deliver him into thine hand.
8 And Barak said unto her, If thou wilt go with me, then I will go: but if thou wilt not go with me, then I will not go.
9 And she said, I will surely go with thee: notwithstanding the journey that thou takest shall not be for thine honour; for the Lord shall sell Sisera into the hand of a woman. And Deborah arose, and went with Barak to Kedesh.

PROPHECY, REVELATION, AND DIVINE INSPIRATION

While Barak does not seem to mind being led by a female and even recognizes her ability to receive revelation from God, Deborah points out the shame that will come to Barak when Sisera, the captain of the enemy's forces, is ultimately killed by a woman rather than by Barak and his men. There is irony in the situation. Still, this story points out that women as well as men can be prophetic, and can use the inspiration they receive to be leaders in God's Kingdom on the earth. However, no accounts are found in the Bible of women being ordained to the priesthood by the laying on of hands. Therefore, Deborah's position as a judge was probably not a priesthood calling, but rather a functional position within the government structure of ancient Israel (as in Exodus 18:13-27).

The concept of priesthood authority will be revisited later, but for now let us define priesthood as the authority of God given to man to administer the ordinances and rites pertaining to God's Kingdom on the earth. God's Kingdom on the earth is also referred to in other terms such as Zion, Israel, His Church, and so forth. Here again, a distinction is made between being prophetic and of having priesthood authority. This very point is well-illustrated by the story of the next prophetess cited in the scriptures. Her name is Huldah, and she is mentioned in 2nd Kings in the Old Testament.

2 Kings 22:8-14

8 And Hilkiah the high priest said unto Shaphan the scribe, I have found the book of the law in the house of the Lord. And Hilkiah gave the book to Shaphan, and he read it.
9 And Shaphan the scribe came to the king, and brought the king word again, and said, Thy servants have gathered the money that was found in the house, and have delivered it into the hand of them that do the work, that have the oversight of the house of the Lord.
10 And Shaphan the scribe shewed the king, saying, Hilkiah the priest hath delivered me a book. And Shaphan read it before the king.
11 And it came to pass, when the king had heard the words of the book of the law, that he rent his clothes.
12 And the king commanded Hilkiah the priest, and Ahikam the son of Shaphan, and Achbor the son of Michaiah, and Shaphan the scribe, and Asahiah a servant of the king's, saying,
13 Go ye, enquire of the Lord for me, and for the people, and for all Judah, concerning the words of this book that is found: for great is the wrath of the Lord that is kindled against us, because our fathers have not hearkened unto the words of this book, to do according unto all that which is written concerning us.
14 So Hilkiah the priest, and Ahikam, and Achbor, and Shaphan, and Asahiah, went unto Huldah the prophetess, the wife of Shallum the son of Tikvah, the son of Harhas, keeper of the wardrobe; (now she dwelt in Jerusalem in the college;) and they communed with her.

The king did not say, "Go, enquire of Huldah the prophetess," but rather, "Go ye, enquire of the Lord for me." It appears that Hilkiah, the High Priest at the time, was not too certain of his own ability to receive revelation directly from God. Huldah, on the other hand, seems to have been a woman known for her ability to receive the word of the Lord, as we see in the next verses.

2 Kings 22:15-20

15 And she said unto them, Thus saith the Lord God of Israel, Tell the man that sent you to me,
16 Thus saith the Lord, Behold, I will bring evil upon this place, and upon the inhabitants thereof, even all the words of the book which the king of Judah hath read:

17 Because they have forsaken me, and have burned incense unto other gods, that they might provoke me to anger with all the works of their hands; therefore my wrath shall be kindled against this place, and shall not be quenched.
18 But to the king of Judah which sent you to enquire of the Lord, thus shall ye say to him, Thus saith the Lord God of Israel, As touching the words which thou hast heard;
19 Because thine heart was tender, and thou hast humbled thyself before the Lord, when thou heardest what I spake against this place, and against the inhabitants thereof, that they should become a desolation and a curse, and hast rent thy clothes, and wept before me; I also have heard thee, saith the Lord.
20 Behold therefore, I will gather thee unto thy fathers, and thou shalt be gathered into thy grave in peace; and thine eyes shall not see all the evil which I will bring upon this place. And they brought the king word again.

In the case of Huldah, I wish to make several points. First, even though a person is called and ordained to an office within the priesthood, apparently that is no guarantee that the spirit of prophecy will accompany that person due to calling alone. In verses 12 and 13 we see that "the king commanded Hilkiah the priest, and Ahikam the son of Shaphan, and Achbor the son of Michaiah, and Shaphan the scribe, and Asahiah a servant of the king's, saying, Go ye, enquire of the Lord for me, and for the people, and for all Judah, concerning the words of this book that is found..." Despite their authority due to their ecclesiastic positions of leadership, none of these men apparently thought themselves worthy or capable of inquiring of the Lord directly. Instead, they sought out Huldah, one possessing the spirit of prophecy. The corollary to this finding, however, is that Huldah, while being prophetic, was not ordained to nor did she hold an office in the priesthood of God.

The above passage also demonstrates the power of reading or hearing the scriptures for oneself. While there is some debate as to what book had been found (e.g., Deuteronomy), it was apparently a book of scripture, and the scriptures had not been read to Josiah as a child. He learned of the content when the book of the law was found and read to him by Shaphan the scribe. When he heard the many prophecies against Judah, which had apparently been ignored by his fathers before him, he suddenly realized the dangerous situation for him and his people. His reaction, therefore, was to have his assigned priest, Hilkiah, go and inquire of the Lord. Hilkiah did so, but only indirectly through the prophetess Huldah. My point is that Huldah evidently had the spirit of prophecy and had gained favor in the eyes of the Lord. Yet, despite her saintly status, her name seems to have been forgotten in comparison to other well-known women of the Bible: Sarah, Deborah, Rachael, Ruth, and so forth, which are all common names today.

Other prophetesses in the scriptures include Noadiah in Nehemiah 6:14. Except for being a prophetess, however, we unfortunately have *no idea* about anything else she did during her life. The list also includes Isaiah's wife (Isaiah 8:3), whose name is not mentioned; Anna in the New Testament who prophesied many things about Jesus Christ when he was brought to the temple by his parents as an infant; Mary the Mother of Jesus; and Mary Magdalene, who apparently was the first person to see the risen Lord. These situations teach us many things about the spirit of prophecy and how it functions. The spirit of prophecy, therefore, is a

PROPHECY, REVELATION, AND DIVINE INSPIRATION

gift given from God through the outpouring of his spirit. A person may gain the spirit of prophecy by studying the scriptures, and by humbly seeking the Lord in prayer. But, this gift is only received from the Lord directly.

I have perhaps over-emphasized the subject of women and prophecy. I do so, however, to show that the spirit of prophecy is open to all of God's children. He is not a respecter of persons, and can inspire a woman as well as a man. I hope this point is clear. While I showed in the case of Hilkiah the priest (in 2 Kings 22) that holding the priesthood of God is no guarantee that the spirit of prophecy will attend that person, evidently, one can receive the spirit of prophecy without necessarily being called to a specific office in the priesthood of God. The pouring out of the spirit of God on the family of Cornelius the Centurion in Acts 10 of the New Testament helped confirm Peter's recent dream. He thus saw that the Gospel of Jesus Christ should indeed be extended not only to the Jews, but also to the Gentiles and to all people who repent and humble themselves before the Lord.

> Acts 10:1-6
> 1 There was a certain man in Caesarea called Cornelius, a centurion of the band called the Italian band,
> 2 A devout man, and one that feared God with all his house, which gave much alms to the people, and prayed to God alway.
> 3 He saw in a vision evidently about the ninth hour of the day an angel of God coming in to him, and saying unto him, Cornelius.
> 4 And when he looked on him, he was afraid, and said, What is it, Lord? And he said unto him, Thy prayers and thine alms are come up for a memorial before God.
> 5 And now send men to Joppa, and call for one Simon, whose surname is Peter:
> 6 He lodgeth with one Simon a tanner, whose house is by the sea side: he shall tell thee what thou oughtest to do.

Cornelius was not a Jew, but a Gentile. Therefore, he did not hold the priesthood, was not baptized, and was thus not yet considered to be a member in the Church of God. We learn from the second verse that despite his worldly station, he was still a devout man, very generous, and most importantly, he prayed to God all the time. As a result, the Lord blessed him with the visit of an angel directing him to do specific things. Thus Cornelius received revelation directly from God.

> Acts 10:7-16
> 7 And when the angel which spake unto Cornelius was departed, he called two of his household servants, and a devout soldier of them that waited on him continually;
> 8 And when he had declared all these things unto them, he sent them to Joppa.
> 9 On the morrow, as they went on their journey, and drew nigh unto the city, Peter went up upon the housetop to pray about the sixth hour:
> 10 And he became very hungry, and would have eaten: but while they made ready, he fell into a trance,
> 11 And saw heaven opened, and a certain vessel descending unto him, as it had been a great sheet knit at the four corners, and let down to the earth:
> 12 Wherein were all manner of fourfooted beasts of the earth, and wild beasts, and creeping things, and fowls of the air.
> 13 And there came a voice to him, Rise, Peter; kill, and eat.
> 14 But Peter said, Not so, Lord; for I have never eaten any thing that is common or unclean.

15 And the voice spake unto him again the second time, What God hath cleansed, that call not thou common.
16 This was done thrice: and the vessel was received up again into heaven.

Like Cornelius, Peter was also a very devout man and one who prayed frequently. Unlike Cornelius, Peter was a Jew and held the priesthood. He had been instructed by Jesus directly while the Lord yet lived on the earth. In fact, Peter was selected by the Lord to be the lead Apostle and Head of the Church following the death and resurrection of Christ (Matthew 16:18). We see a similar situation as occurred with Cornelius in that Peter is now receiving direct revelation from God, albeit in the form of a dream rather than a visit by an angel. Let us see how these two situations tie together.

Acts 10:17-29
17 Now while Peter doubted in himself what this vision which he had seen should mean, behold, the men which were sent from Cornelius had made enquiry for Simon's house, and stood before the gate,
18 And called, and asked whether Simon, which was surnamed Peter, were lodged there.
19 While Peter thought on the vision, the Spirit said unto him, Behold, three men seek thee.
20 Arise therefore, and get thee down, and go with them, doubting nothing: for I have sent them.
21 Then Peter went down to the men which were sent unto him from Cornelius; and said, Behold, I am he whom ye seek: what is the cause wherefore ye are come?
22 And they said, Cornelius the centurion, a just man, and one that feareth God, and of good report among all the nation of the Jews, was warned from God by an holy angel to send for thee into his house, and to hear words of thee.
23 Then called he them in, and lodged them. And on the morrow Peter went away with them, and certain brethren from Joppa accompanied him.
24 And the morrow after they entered into Caesarea. And Cornelius waited for them, and had called together his kinsmen and near friends.
25 And as Peter was coming in, Cornelius met him, and fell down at his feet, and worshipped him.
26 But Peter took him up, saying, Stand up; I myself also am a man.
27 And as he talked with him, he went in, and found many that were come together.
28 And he said unto them, Ye know how that it is an unlawful thing for a man that is a Jew to keep company, or come unto one of another nation; but God hath shewed me that I should not call any man common or unclean.
29 Therefore came I unto you without gainsaying, as soon as I was sent for: I ask therefore for what intent ye have sent for me?

Here Peter was able to do something that was really odd for a Jew. Namely, according to the Jewish custom, it was unlawful for a Jew to meet with a Gentile, whom the Jews considered to be unclean. Because of his revelation from the Lord in the form of a dream, Peter, as the head prophet of the Lord's Church, was able to act on this matter with a high degree of certainty that it was indeed God's will for him to teach Cornelius and his family and friends. Let us now see the result of this interesting encounter.

Acts 10:30-38
30 And Cornelius said, Four days ago I was fasting until this hour; and at the ninth hour I prayed in my house, and, behold, a man stood before me in bright clothing,
31 And said, Cornelius, thy prayer is heard, and thine alms are had in remembrance in the sight of God.

PROPHECY, REVELATION, AND DIVINE INSPIRATION

32 Send therefore to Joppa, and call hither Simon, whose surname is Peter; he is lodged in the house of one Simon a tanner by the sea side: who, when he cometh, shall speak unto thee.
33 Immediately therefore I sent to thee; and thou hast well done that thou art come. Now therefore are we all here present before God, to hear all things that are commanded thee of God.
34 Then Peter opened his mouth, and said, Of a truth I perceive that God is no respecter of persons:
35 But in every nation he that feareth him, and worketh righteousness, is accepted with him.
36 The word which God sent unto the children of Israel, preaching peace by Jesus Christ: (he is Lord of all:)
37 That word, I say, ye know, which was published throughout all Judaea, and began from Galilee, after the baptism which John preached;
38 How God anointed Jesus of Nazareth with the Holy Ghost and with power: who went about doing good, and healing all that were oppressed of the devil; for God was with him.

Peter's main message was that Jesus is the Christ and the chosen Messiah that had been prophesied by all the holy prophets before him. Furthermore, the blessings of forgiveness and salvation offered through Jesus' infinite sacrifice were not limited to the Jews, but open to all that believed on him and accepted his baptism.

Acts 10:39-48
39 And we are witnesses of all things which he did both in the land of the Jews, and in Jerusalem; whom they slew and hanged on a tree:
40 Him God raised up the third day, and shewed him openly;
41 Not to all the people, but unto witnesses chosen before of God, even to us, who did eat and drink with him after he rose from the dead.
42 And he commanded us to preach unto the people, and to testify that it is he which was ordained of God to be the Judge of quick and dead.
43 To him give all the prophets witness, that through his name whosoever believeth in him shall receive remission of sins.
44 While Peter yet spake these words, the Holy Ghost fell on all them which heard the word.
45 And they of the circumcision which believed were astonished, as many as came with Peter, because that on the Gentiles also was poured out the gift of the Holy Ghost.
46 For they heard them speak with tongues, and magnify God. Then answered Peter,
47 Can any man forbid water, that these should not be baptized, which have received the Holy Ghost as well as we?
48 And he commanded them to be baptized in the name of the Lord. Then prayed they him to tarry certain days.

Peter, in his capacity as the lead prophet over the Church, received a tremendous revelation from the Lord through a vision during a dream. This revelation was received by Peter only, and led to a quantum change in the way the Church would conduct its missionary efforts from then on. Cornelius also received a great revelation even though he was not a Jew, not yet baptized, and not a holder of the priesthood at all. However, Cornelius' revelations from God were for him and his family, not for the Church as a whole. Cornelius received a great spiritual manifestation in the appearance of an angel to him, which subsequently led to the outpouring of the spirit of the Lord upon him and his household following Peter's visit to his home. Thus, we see that the Lord is indeed no respecter of persons, and he can and does bestow his spirit upon whomever he chooses.

Cornelius was fasting and praying to the Lord with great energy of soul prior to the manifestation of the spirit in his life. Was Cornelius in a sense a prophet in this given situation? I believe he was a prophet for his family and the members of his household over which he presided, while Peter was the Prophet for the Church as a whole and the members over whom he presided. Peter was ordained as an Apostle by Jesus Christ (John 15:16), thus receiving the priesthood. And, Peter became the leader of the Church and lead Apostle following the ascension of the risen Lord. Still, both Cornelius and Peter received the spirit of prophecy in order to guide their decisions and to lead those they were serving.

This example of an outpouring of the spirit also demonstrates the true purpose of priesthood power, which is to bless the lives of God's children living on the earth. Priesthood power is used to heal the sick, bless people for certain callings or missions, and most importantly, it is designed to administer the saving ordinances of God's Kingdom. By saving ordinances, I mean the outward observances that one must perform to receive salvation in the Kingdom of God at the time of final judgment. From the scriptures we know these would include such things as baptism and receiving the Holy Ghost (John 3:5). We also get the idea from the Bible that the priesthood administers ordinances performed in the temple of God as well. However, the things that occurred in the temple and the tabernacle are not clearly specified by the ancient records found in the Bible. Priesthood authority is essential if God's children are to progress and take the steps necessary to obtain eternal life.

What we learn from the scriptures about priesthood authority is that it is the authority and power of God given to men to act in his name. Unlike worldly power, priesthood power can only be used to bless others. A priesthood holder cannot lay his hands on his own head and pronounce a blessing on himself. He can only lay his hands on others and administer blessings on them. Let us examine some scriptures that shed light on the issue of priesthood authority, how it is received, and how it is administered.

Hebrews 5:1-6

1 For every high priest taken from among men is ordained for men in things pertaining to God, that he may offer both gifts and sacrifices for sins:
2 Who can have compassion on the ignorant, and on them that are out of the way; for that he himself also is compassed with infirmity.
3 And by reason hereof he ought, as for the people, so also for himself, to offer for sins.
4 And no man taketh this honour unto himself, but he that is called of God, as was Aaron.
5 So also Christ glorified not himself to be made an high priest; but he that said unto him, Thou art my Son, to day have I begotten thee.
6 As he saith also in another place, Thou art a priest for ever after the order of Melchisedec.

The above passage indicates that men are taken or selected to hold the priesthood, and cannot or should not take the honor unto themselves. Instead, they should receive it as Aaron did. Let us therefore look to see how Aaron was called. The Lord chose him to be the mouthpiece for Moses; Aaron did not choose his position. It was given to him by the Lord through Moses.

PROPHECY, REVELATION, AND DIVINE INSPIRATION

Exodus 4:10-16

10 And Moses said unto the Lord, O my Lord, I am not eloquent, neither heretofore, nor since thou hast spoken unto thy servant: but I am slow of speech, and of a slow tongue.
11 And the Lord said unto him, Who hath made man's mouth? or who maketh the dumb, or deaf, or the seeing, or the blind? have not I the Lord?
12 Now therefore go, and I will be with thy mouth, and teach thee what thou shalt say.
13 And he said, O my Lord, send, I pray thee, by the hand of him whom thou wilt send.
14 And the anger of the Lord was kindled against Moses, and he said, Is not Aaron the Levite thy brother? I know that he can speak well. And also, behold, he cometh forth to meet thee: and when he seeth thee, he will be glad in his heart.
15 And thou shalt speak unto him, and put words in his mouth: and I will be with thy mouth, and with his mouth, and will teach you what ye shall do.
16 And he shall be thy spokesman unto the people: and he shall be, even he shall be to thee instead of a mouth, and thou shalt be to him instead of God.

Aaron was called to his position in the priesthood by prophecy and by the communication of the Lord to Moses concerning His will on the matter. In fact, the Lord did not even approach Aaron about this matter, but allowed Moses to communicate his will to Aaron through prophecy. The Lord chose Aaron; Aaron did not take the position upon himself. Jesus Christ makes it clear who calls men to the priesthood in the Book of John in the New Testament.

John 15:16

16 Ye have not chosen me, but I have chosen you, and ordained you, that ye should go and bring forth fruit, and that your fruit should remain: that whatsoever ye shall ask of the Father in my name, he may give it you.

The Lord selects men to hold the priesthood and to serve in specific assignments by telling the current leader what his will is and who he desires to hold a position at that given moment. Unlike men, God is not swayed by physical appearance or worldly influence. This point is well-illustrated by the story in 1 Samuel 16, where Samuel is asked to ordain a new king to reign in Israel from among the sons of Jesse.

1 Samuel 16:1-13

1 And the Lord said unto Samuel, How long wilt thou mourn for Saul, seeing I have rejected him from reigning over Israel? fill thine horn with oil, and go, I will send thee to Jesse the Bethlehemite: for I have provided me a king among his sons.
2 And Samuel said, How can I go? if Saul hear it, he will kill me. And the Lord said, Take an heifer with thee, and say, I am come to sacrifice to the Lord.
3 And call Jesse to the sacrifice, and I will shew thee what thou shalt do: and thou shalt anoint unto me him whom I name unto thee.
4 And Samuel did that which the Lord spake, and came to Bethlehem. And the elders of the town trembled at his coming, and said, Comest thou peaceably?
5 And he said, Peaceably: I am come to sacrifice unto the Lord: sanctify yourselves, and come with me to the sacrifice. And he sanctified Jesse and his sons, and called them to the sacrifice.
6 And it came to pass, when they were come, that he looked on Eliab, and said, Surely the Lord's anointed is before him.
7 But the Lord said unto Samuel, Look not on his countenance, or on the height of his stature; because I have refused him: for the Lord seeth not as man seeth; for man looketh on the outward appearance, but the Lord looketh on the heart.

8 Then Jesse called Abinadab, and made him pass before Samuel. And he said, Neither hath the Lord chosen this.

9 Then Jesse made Shammah to pass by. And he said, Neither hath the Lord chosen this.

10 Again, Jesse made seven of his sons to pass before Samuel. And Samuel said unto Jesse, The Lord hath not chosen these.

11 And Samuel said unto Jesse, Are here all thy children? And he said, There remaineth yet the youngest, and, behold, he keepeth the sheep. And Samuel said unto Jesse, Send and fetch him: for we will not sit down till he come hither.

12 And he sent, and brought him in. Now he was ruddy, and withal of a beautiful countenance, and goodly to look to. And the Lord said, Arise, anoint him: for this is he.

13 Then Samuel took the horn of oil, and anointed him in the midst of his brethren: and the Spirit of the Lord came upon David from that day forward. So Samuel rose up, and went to Ramah.

The above reference covers several issues worthy of note. First, we see in verse seven that "the Lord seeth not as man seeth; for man looketh on the outward appearance, but the Lord looketh on the heart." His judgments are always just and true, while men are prone to be swayed and confused by appearances or other worldly attributes. Second, we see that David came out of nowhere. Samuel did not choose David to reign. Likewise, David did not choose himself to reign. David was chosen by prophecy directly from God when the spirit of the Lord inspired Samuel. While we are not told if David had any premonition about his being called as king, we can only imagine that he and his brothers and father were all surprised that David, the youngest son of a humble servant in Israel, would be chosen of the Lord to serve in such an important calling.

Finally, this passage shows the interplay between the fear of men and the fear of the Lord. Samuel is at first reluctant to go and anoint a new king because he fears that Saul will hear of it and be angry. The Lord belies that fear by telling him precisely what to do and how to go about it. When Samuel arrives at Bethlehem, the home town of David and his father Jesse, the scriptures indicate that the "elders of the town trembled exceedingly at his coming, and said, Comest thou peaceably?" Jesse and the elders of the town were wondering why the recognized prophet of God happened to come specifically to them. They wanted the reassurance that he had not come to curse them, or to administer some negative judgment from God upon them. It was as if God himself had come to call upon them, so great was their respect for the mantle of authority that rested upon Samuel the prophet.

Numbers 27:15-23

15 And Moses spake unto the Lord, saying,

16 Let the Lord, the God of the spirits of all flesh, set a man over the congregation,

17 Which may go out before them, and which may go in before them, and which may lead them out, and which may bring them in; that the congregation of the Lord be not as sheep which have no shepherd.

18 And the Lord said unto Moses, Take thee Joshua the son of Nun, a man in whom is the spirit, and lay thine hand upon him;

19 And set him before Eleazar the priest, and before all the congregation; and give him a charge in their sight.

20 And thou shalt put some of thine honour upon him, that all the congregation of the children of Israel may be obedient.

PROPHECY, REVELATION, AND DIVINE INSPIRATION

21 And he shall stand before Eleazar the priest, who shall ask counsel for him after the judgment of Urim before the Lord: at his word shall they go out, and at his word they shall come in, both he, and all the children of Israel with him, even all the congregation.
22 And Moses did as the Lord commanded him: and he took Joshua, and set him before Eleazar the priest, and before all the congregation:
23 And he laid his hands upon him, and gave him a charge, as the Lord commanded by the hand of Moses.

From this passage, we see how the calling that Moses held was passed on to the next generation. The Lord called Joshua to become the next prophet over Israel. It should be noted that Joshua received this calling by prophecy and by the laying on of hands by Moses. The practice of laying hands on the head of another to ordain, bless, or designate for a given mission or calling is seen in many places in the scriptures. For example, the Apostle Paul lays his hands on the heads of newly baptized members of the Church and gives them the Holy Ghost.

Acts 19:1-7

1 And it came to pass, that, while Apollos was at Corinth, Paul having passed through the upper coasts came to Ephesus: and finding certain disciples,
2 He said unto them, Have ye received the Holy Ghost since ye believed? And they said unto him, We have not so much as heard whether there be any Holy Ghost.
3 And he said unto them, Unto what then were ye baptized? And they said, Unto John's baptism.
4 Then said Paul, John verily baptized with the baptism of repentance, saying unto the people, that they should believe on him which should come after him, that is, on Christ Jesus.
5 When they heard this, they were baptized in the name of the Lord Jesus.
6 And when Paul had laid his hands upon them, the Holy Ghost came on them; and they spake with tongues, and prophesied.
7 And all the men were about twelve.

Besides baptism and the giving of the Holy Ghost to new disciples, the apostles also used the priesthood authority to ordain men when positions in the priesthood were open. In the New Testament, a replacement for Judas Iscariot was needed since he was no longer a member of the Twelve Apostles. Let us see how this was handled by the remaining apostles.

Acts 1:21-26

21 Wherefore of these men which have companied with us all the time that the Lord Jesus went in and out among us,
22 Beginning from the baptism of John, unto that same day that he was taken up from us, must one be ordained to be a witness with us of his resurrection.
23 And they appointed two, Joseph called Barsabas, who was surnamed Justus, and Matthias.
24 And they prayed, and said, Thou, Lord, which knowest the hearts of all men, shew whether of these two thou hast chosen,
25 That he may take part of this ministry and apostleship, from which Judas by transgression fell, that he might go to his own place.
26 And they gave forth their lots; and the lot fell upon Matthias; and he was numbered with the eleven apostles.

We see here that priesthood authority passes from one man to another, and those called are chosen by inspiration and by the word of the Lord to those already in authority. As we already read in Hebrews, "no man taketh this honour unto himself." Nor can this authority be purchased with money:

Acts 8:17-20
17 Then laid they their hands on them, and they received the Holy Ghost.
18 And when Simon saw that through laying on of the apostles' hands the Holy Ghost was given, he offered them money,
19 Saying, Give me also this power, that on whomsoever I lay hands, he may receive the Holy Ghost.
20 But Peter said unto him, Thy money perish with thee, because thou hast thought that the gift of God may be purchased with money.

The above example shows clearly that priesthood authority cannot be purchased with money. One's social standing, political power, education, and financial wealth seem to have no direct impact on who receives the priesthood power. A man must simply be called of God by those in authority to do so. The inspiration of the spirit indicating such a calling comes not to the man being ordained, but to those in the position of leadership over that man. We see that there appears to be some kind of division in the priesthood authority. Philip had the authority to baptize the newly converted persons he encountered; he did not have the authority to give them the Holy Ghost, which had not yet descended on any of them. When the apostles arrived, they apparently had a higher order of priesthood authority, and thus were able to lay their hands on the new converts and give them the Holy Ghost. We know that Jesus Christ was called to be a High Priest forever, after the order of Melchisedec. We can assume that the priesthood of Jesus is of the highest order, since Jesus Christ is considered a member of the Godhead. There appears to be another order of priesthood as well.

Hebrews 7:11
11 If therefore perfection were by the Levitical priesthood, (for under it the people received the law,) what further need was there that another priest should rise after the order of Melchisedec, and not be called after the order of Aaron?

It is not completely clear from the scriptures exactly how this distinction is set forth. Perhaps it is similar to how John the Baptist had a different priesthood from Jesus Christ, or how Aaron and the Levites after him seemed to have a different administrative authority from Moses and the subsequent lead prophets over Israel. The example of Simon trying to buy the priesthood authority brings up one last issue that we should mention concerning prophecy, revelation, and priesthood authority—this is the issue of false prophets and priestcraft. The scriptures are full of warnings against false prophets. Throughout the Old Testament, the children of Israel are warned about following those who were not called, but who teach things that are easy to follow and easy to hear. These false prophets teach easy things to the people in order to get gain and the praise of the world. The same warnings about false teachers and false prophets continue in the New Testament. Jesus Christ warns his disciples of false prophets several times throughout his mortal life.

PROPHECY, REVELATION, AND DIVINE INSPIRATION

Matthew 7:15-23

15 Beware of false prophets, which come to you in sheep's clothing, but inwardly they are ravening wolves.
16 Ye shall know them by their fruits. Do men gather grapes of thorns, or figs of thistles?
17 Even so every good tree bringeth forth good fruit; but a corrupt tree bringeth forth evil fruit.
18 A good tree cannot bring forth evil fruit, neither can a corrupt tree bring forth good fruit.
19 Every tree that bringeth not forth good fruit is hewn down, and cast into the fire.
20 Wherefore by their fruits ye shall know them.
21 Not every one that saith unto me, Lord, Lord, shall enter into the Kingdom of heaven; but he that doeth the will of my Father which is in heaven.
22 Many will say to me in that day, Lord, Lord, have we not prophesied in thy name? and in thy name have cast out devils? and in thy name done many wonderful works?
23 And then will I profess unto them, I never knew you: depart from me, ye that work iniquity.

Similar warnings are found throughout the scriptures. We need to understand that false priests and false prophets have always been a problem for the children of men. These men are not called of God, but set themselves up as such. However, instead of the having the welfare of the flock in mind, they call themselves to apparent positions of priesthood authority in order to get money and praise from the people. But, in the end, the Lord will not recognize their authority. Unfortunately, the saving ordinances that they practiced on behalf of the innocent and the naïve will not be valid either. Thus, we see why they are so dangerous to the Lord's plan of salvation.

Divine Inspiration

A final note of consideration concerns divine inspiration. In this case, I am referring to any type of inspiration that apparently comes from outside of the individual's own consciousness. I believe the Lord inspires men and women with respect to scientific, literary, artistic, musical, governmental, and other secular achievements. The Lord gives knowledge and understanding to those that earn it through their mental, physical, and spiritual efforts towards a certain goal.

We can see through the recorded history of the last 2,000 years that there has been a general outpouring of knowledge from above. What began in the Renaissance, or rebirth period, has continued to this day. Since the Lord is no respecter of persons, he will give knowledge to anyone who seeks it out. While a scientist, for example, may not be considered to be religious per se, he or she might attack a problem religiously. The problem consumes his or her waking hours until finally, something clarifies the issue, and he or she is able to see the solution. Once the scientist experiences this "ah ha" phenomenon, it may be surprising how simple the answer turns out to be. Such an inspiration might also come at a moment when the scientist is engaged in some other activity unrelated to scientific pursuit. Nonetheless, something acts as a catalyst to the mind, and he or she is suddenly "enlightened" with a new perspective of how to solve the problem. While scientists, composers, and so forth might not be religious, they nonetheless take the steps necessary to retrieve knowledge and understanding from the Lord. Through the rigor of their analysis and mental thought, their spirits are in a sense praying to the Lord for the answer, although not addressing God directly. They do it through their actions and ponderings.

The subject of secular achievement through divine inspiration may be intriguing, but it is not the principle subject of this book. I include it here to be thorough, but will hereafter limit my scope of analysis to that contained in the scriptures, and specifically to the prophecies and revelations pertaining to the Kingdom of God, its function and organization. We have seen from the scriptures that the spirit of prophecy comes from God directly, and can fall on anyone. Fasting, prayer and good works are often prerequisites to one receiving the spirit of prophecy. The terms revelation and prophecy are often used interchangeably. Revelation is the answer to one's question put to the Lord. Prophecy is something that in some way predicts the future, or declares a truth. In many instances in the scriptures, a revelation received by a servant of the Lord also carries with it an element of prophecy as well. With these fundamental doctrinal concepts now defined, let us proceed with our discussion and show what is meant by the term "the Latter Rain."

CHAPTER TWO

Rain As a Symbolic Type

The subject of prophets, the spirit of prophecy, and priesthood authority could occupy an entire book of its own. Adequate information has been set forth relevant to the question: "How does God communicate to his children on the earth?" We have learned that he has the ability to inspire men and women with the spirit of prophecy and, in so doing, he is able to speak to his people through these individuals or oracles. Revelation and inspiration can come in the form of thoughts and ideas, visitations by angels, dreams, or through the actions of other people. Prophets are not angels themselves, but are living human beings, and can be shown to have weaknesses and frailties like anyone else. They can even fall from grace and be rejected of the Lord. Still, when needed, they serve as the voice of the Lord in any given situation.

While anyone can receive the spirit of prophecy as dictated by the Lord, there still seems to be some order concerning the authority and organization of the priesthood of God as it pertains to the administration of the saving ordinances. In other words, while Cornelius' visions and revelations may have helped confirm Peter's intuition concerning his recent dream, Cornelius did not dictate to Peter the will of the Lord concerning the Church and the position it should take regarding the Gentiles. This decision was given to Peter alone, as the acting head of the Kingdom of God on the earth at that particular point in time.

Reviewing these stories from the Bible raises a critical question: Where are the prophets of God today? If God will do nothing without revealing his secrets to his servants the prophets, as we read in Amos 3:7, then where are the modern day prophets? Furthermore, why did scripture writing stop with the Book of Malachi in the Old Testament, and the Book of Revelation in the New Testament? These questions are relevant to the subject of this book and will be addressed in due course. First, let us turn our attention to the subject of "rain" and its use as a symbolic type in the writings of the Bible.

THE LATTER RAIN

If we accept the scriptures as the word of God as transmitted through his earthly oracles, the prophets, then we can look to them for meaning and understanding. Often, stories or parables given in the scriptures can have hidden meaning through the use of symbols and types. Some things in the scriptures are hard to understand without inquiring of the Lord for understanding. For example, Jesus was known to speak in parables.

Matthew 13:10-17
10 And the disciples came, and said unto him, Why speakest thou unto them in parables?
11 He answered and said unto them, Because it is given unto you to know the mysteries of the Kingdom of heaven, but to them it is not given.
12 For whosoever hath, to him shall be given, and he shall have more abundance: but whosoever hath not, from him shall be taken away even that he hath.
13 Therefore speak I to them in parables: because they seeing see not; and hearing they hear not, neither do they understand.
14 And in them is fulfilled the prophecy of Esaias, which saith, By hearing ye shall hear, and shall not understand; and seeing ye shall see, and shall not perceive:
15 For this people's heart is waxed gross, and their ears are dull of hearing, and their eyes they have closed; lest at any time they should see with their eyes, and hear with their ears, and should understand with their heart, and should be converted, and I should heal them.
16 But blessed are your eyes, for they see: and your ears, for they hear.
17 For verily I say unto you, That many prophets and righteous men have desired to see those things which ye see, and have not seen them; and to hear those things which ye hear, and have not heard them.

Jesus would tell stories that had a surface or obvious meaning, but also contained a hidden meaning that could only be perceived by meek and open-minded hearers. These hidden meanings had to be discerned by the listener through the spirit, or through an interpretation given by someone else that had the spirit of understanding and could thus explain the full impact of the story being told. Recall that Josiah, the King of Judah, asked Hilkiah to go and inquire of the Lord to understand the meaning of the things that had been read to him by Shasham the scribe. Hilkiah went to Huldah, who was then able to explain things more clearly. Ultimately, someone had to actually pray to the Lord to receive clear understanding.

This same thing occurs throughout the scriptures. Through his prophets, God is able to tell stories that have obvious instructional value. The same story or historical event, however, might also have meaning that is much broader and far-reaching. To really understand, the reader must learn to interpret the Lord's use of symbols and types in order to see these more subtle communications from the Lord. One such "type" found in the Bible is the reference to rain by the prophets. Let's examine how this symbolic type, "rain," is applied and how it is relevant to our current discussion.

The Former Rain and the Latter Rain

Deuteronomy 32:1-3
1 Give ear, O ye heavens, and I will speak; and hear, O earth, the words of my mouth.
2 My doctrine shall drop as the rain, my speech shall distil as the dew, as the small rain upon the tender herb, and as the showers upon the grass:
3 Because I will publish the name of the Lord: ascribe ye greatness unto our God.

RAIN AS A SYMBOLIC TYPE

When I first read this scripture in Deuteronomy many years ago, I was curious about the association of rain as mentioned in the scriptures as a symbolic reference to revelations and communications from God to man. As I examined this type further, I began to see that, in many places in the scriptures, the Lord would refer to periods of little or no communication from God as a period of drought. Likewise, he would also relate periods of abundant communications with his children as periods of heavy rain or periods of prosperity. Then, an even more peculiar observation was made. I looked up every scripture I could find that mentioned "rain," and I noticed that there were several verses of scripture that described the people receiving a "Former Rain," and then afterwards receiving a "Latter Rain." There were actually two major eras of rain spoken of in the scriptures. The corollary to this discovery is that the period in between these two major eras of rain would then constitute a period of drought or famine—no rain, or in other words, no prophets! Let us examine a few verses that demonstrate this point.

Deuteronomy 11:13-17
13 And it shall come to pass, if ye shall hearken diligently unto my commandments which I command you this day, to love the Lord your God, and to serve him with all your heart and with all your soul,
14 That I will give you the rain of your land in his due season, the first rain and the latter rain, that thou mayest gather in thy corn, and thy wine, and thine oil.
15 And I will send grass in thy fields for thy cattle, that thou mayest eat and be full.
16 Take heed to yourselves, that your heart be not deceived, and ye turn aside, and serve other gods, and worship them;
17 And then the Lord's wrath be kindled against you, and he shut up the heaven, that there be no rain, and that the land yield not her fruit; and lest ye perish quickly from off the good land which the Lord giveth you.

Clearly, the surface meaning is that the Lord can control the rain that actually falls on farms from the clouds, and that his power to do this impacts Israel's ability to feed and nourish itself with crops. However, applying the type derived from Deuteronomy 32, we can read the scripture again and imply a broader meaning to the above-mentioned verses. Namely, we can see that he will give the Former Rain period, where prophets are present on the earth, and the Latter Rain period where they are again present on the earth. But, if Israel fails to keep his commandments, then a famine period is predicted, separating these two great eras of spiritual prosperity.

Job 29:21-23
21 Unto me men gave ear, and waited, and kept silence at my counsel.
22 After my words they spake not again; and my speech dropped upon them.
23 And they waited for me as for the rain; and they opened their mouth wide as for the latter rain.

While this is Job speaking about his own counsels to his fellow men, it still relates the idea of speech dropping upon men like rain from heaven. Likewise, he mentions the idea of waiting for this "latter rain" with their mouths wide open, waiting to receive it.

THE LATTER RAIN

Psalm 72:4-9
4 He shall judge the poor of the people, he shall save the children of the needy, and shall break in pieces the oppressor.
5 They shall fear thee as long as the sun and moon endure, throughout all generations.
6 He shall come down like rain upon the mown grass: as showers that water the earth.
7 In his days shall the righteous flourish; and abundance of peace so long as the moon endureth.
8 He shall have dominion also from sea to sea, and from the river unto the ends of the earth.
9 They that dwell in the wilderness shall bow before him; and his enemies shall lick the dust.

"He shall come down like rain upon the mown grass: as showers that water the earth." In other words, his revelations to men will be like rain falling and making things prosper. Likewise, those that have not the revelations of God will "dwell in the wilderness." So, we see another type that bears mentioning—that being wilderness, dearth or famine. These descriptive symbols found in the scriptures are synonymous with a lack of prophets, revelation, or help from God.

Jeremiah 3:1-5
1 They say, If a man put away his wife, and she go from him, and become another man's, shall he return unto her again? shall not that land be greatly polluted? but thou hast played the harlot with many lovers; yet return again to me, saith the Lord.
2 Lift up thine eyes unto the high places, and see where thou hast not been lien with. In the ways hast thou sat for them, as the Arabian in the wilderness; and thou hast polluted the land with thy whoredoms and with thy wickedness.
3 Therefore the showers have been withholden, and there hath been no latter rain; and thou hadst a whore's forehead, thou refusedst to be ashamed.
4 Wilt thou not from this time cry unto me, My father, thou art the guide of my youth?
5 Will he reserve his anger for ever? will he keep it to the end? Behold, thou hast spoken and done evil things as thou couldest.

Here we learn that because of iniquity, "the showers have been withholden, and there hath been no latter rain." Likewise, we see Israel crying unto the Lord, "My father, thou art the guide of my youth?" This plea is in the form of a question. Israel is asking, "Why are you not guiding me now, when you used to guide me in my youth?"—or in the former times. Israel finds itself in the precarious position of being deprived of any prophetic guidance directly from the Lord.

Jeremiah 5:23-25
23 But this people hath a revolting and a rebellious heart; they are revolted and gone.
24 Neither say they in their heart, Let us now fear the Lord our God, that giveth rain, both the former and the latter, in his season: he reserveth unto us the appointed weeks of the harvest.
25 Your iniquities have turned away these things, and your sins have withholden good things from you.

The surface meaning is that rain in the appointed time has been withheld. Applying the symbolism we derived earlier, we see another meaning. Your sins have turned away the rain of revelation from heaven, and the voice of the prophet in its season.

Jeremiah 14:1-4, 21-22
1 The word of the Lord that came to Jeremiah concerning the dearth.
2 Judah mourneth, and the gates thereof languish; they are black unto the ground; and the cry of Jerusalem is gone up.

RAIN AS A SYMBOLIC TYPE

> 3 And their nobles have sent their little ones to the waters: they came to the pits, and found no water; they returned with their vessels empty; they were ashamed and confounded, and covered their heads.
> 4 Because the ground is chapt, for there was no rain in the earth, the plowmen were ashamed, they covered their heads.
> 21 Do not abhor us, for thy name's sake, do not disgrace the throne of thy glory: remember, break not thy covenant with us.
> 22 Are there any among the vanities of the Gentiles that can cause rain? or can the heavens give showers? art not thou he, O Lord our God? therefore we will wait upon thee: for thou hast made all these things.

This prophecy suggests a time when Judah is experiencing a dearth or famine. The heavens are sealed and no rain is forth coming. They even ask if there are any among the vanities of the Gentiles that can cause rain. Are there any among the people of the earth with the spirit of revelation? Judah is left to wait on the Lord. Their hope of the return of prophecy is expressed in Hosea as follows:

Hosea 6:3
> 3 Then shall we know, if we follow on to know the Lord: his going forth is prepared as the morning; and he shall come unto us as the rain, as the latter and former rain unto the earth.

Again, the prophet not only mentions rain, but he makes this curious reference to a Former Rain and a Latter Rain. If we look at the growing season experienced by farmers in the northern hemisphere today, is there really such a thing as a Former Rain and a Latter Rain? Clearly "April showers bring May flowers" and the hurricane season brings more rain in the fall in certain areas of the world, as does the change in temperatures accompanying the onset of the fall season. Likewise, in the Jerusalem area, two distinct rainy seasons exist. These examples show the obvious surface meaning of these verses that mention a former and a latter rain. To have a successful crop, farmers need rain throughout the summer as well, or a plan for irrigation. For this reason, the idea of a Former Rain and a Latter Rain stands out in my mind with respect to revelation from God to his children on earth.

Joel 2:21-24
> 21 Fear not, O land; be glad and rejoice: for the Lord will do great things.
> 22 Be not afraid, ye beasts of the field: for the pastures of the wilderness do spring, for the tree beareth her fruit, the fig tree and the vine do yield their strength.
> 23 Be glad then, ye children of Zion, and rejoice in the Lord your God: for he hath given you the former rain moderately, and he will cause to come down for you the rain, the former rain, and the latter rain in the first month.
> 24 And the floors shall be full of wheat, and the vats shall overflow with wine and oil.

Zechariah 10:1-2
> 1 Ask ye of the Lord rain in the time of the latter rain; so the Lord shall make bright clouds, and give them showers of rain, to every one grass in the field.
> 2 For the idols have spoken vanity, and the diviners have seen a lie, and have told false dreams; they comfort in vain: therefore they went their way as a flock, they were troubled, because there was no shepherd.

If he is asked to do so, the Lord will cause rain to come down for the children of Zion. He has already given them the Former Rain moderately, and he will eventually give the latter rain as well. In Zechariah, we see again the connection between rain and prophecy or prophets when we read, "they went their way as a flock, they were troubled, because there was no shepherd." To restate Zechariah 10:1-2, one might say, "Ask ye of the Lord prophecy again on the earth as in the ancient times, and inspire these modern prophets with the spirit of prophecy and understanding. For because of transgression and iniquity, Israel became as a lost flock, they were troubled, because there was no prophet."

James 5:7-8

7 Be patient therefore, brethren, unto the coming of the Lord. Behold, the husbandman waiteth for the precious fruit of the earth, and hath long patience for it, until he receive the early and latter rain.
8 Be ye also patient; stablish your hearts: for the coming of the Lord draweth nigh.

James the Apostle is asking the people to be patient like the farmer who waits for the early and latter rain, "for the coming of the Lord draweth nigh." The fact that this former and latter rain concept is repeated many times throughout the scriptures is like a spiritual light shining on an important issue to be examined. It is seen not only in the Old Testament, but in the New Testament as well. In both we see periods of rain divided by a period of no rain. In other words, the Holy Bible symbolically describes a time when prophets are no longer found on the earth. This famine era is a time when the children of Israel are left to themselves and are caught up in the vain beliefs, doctrines, and dogmas of the world.

By way of scriptural analysis, we see that such a period of dearth is indeed prophesied and expected, and, it is not just a minor event lasting a short time. It is a major event with significant consequences for the children of Israel, and for all God's children. This period of "prophecy famine" is real and clearly defined in the scriptures. Thus, the existence of prophets on the earth has not been one continuous history. Rather, there was the Former Rain period, when prophets received revelations and the people were guided by the counsels of God. Then the Lord withdrew from the earth, leaving men and women to interpret the scriptures for themselves. Finally, the scriptures predict a time when the Lord will open the heavens once more and the grand period of the Latter Rain will be ushered in. Please consider the following verse from the Book of Amos:

Amos 8:11-12

11 Behold, the days come, saith the Lord God, that I will send a famine in the land, not a famine of bread, nor a thirst for water, but of hearing the words of the Lord:
12 And they shall wander from sea to sea, and from the north even to the east, they shall run to and fro to seek the word of the Lord, and shall not find it.

The above reference leaves little room for misinterpretation. The Lord is declaring through the prophet Amos that he will send a famine in the land. Now this, in and of itself, is nothing new. Famines and periods of no rain are common occurrences in the Bible narrative. However, in this case, the Lord distinguishes this particular famine from other famines we have seen before. This is "not a famine of bread, nor a thirst for water, but of hearing the words of the LORD:

RAIN AS A SYMBOLIC TYPE

And they shall wander from sea to sea, and from the north even to the east, they shall run to and fro to seek the word of the LORD, and shall not find it." Thus, the famine spoken of here in Amos 8:11-12 is a famine of prophets and a famine of revelation.

Isaiah 3:1-2
1 For, behold, the Lord, the Lord of hosts, doth take away from Jerusalem and from Judah the stay and the staff, the whole stay of bread, and the whole stay of water,
2 The mighty man, and the man of war, the judge, and the prophet, and the prudent, and the ancient,

In the Book of Isaiah, we see this famine of hearing the words of the Lord predicted as well. Isaiah uses symbols and types to demonstrate the Lord's intention to withdraw from Israel, and to take away "the prophet, and the prudent, and the ancient" if Israel does not repent and return unto him.

The principal finding of this book is that the Book of Isaiah serves as a key to unlock this mystery and to bring it to light in a way that will clarify and enlighten. The Latter Rain/Former Rain symbolism has lain dormant in the scriptures, but has been there all along. These symbols and types have remained hidden because the surface meaning of how man interacts with rain and famine in normal life tends to be so accepted that the deeper meaning is missed. Only by piecing these doctrines together are we able to make the connection and see how the rain/revelation symbolism carries itself throughout the scriptures. In fact, it is ubiquitous. Once this symbolic code is perceived by the reader of the Book of Isaiah and this shift in thinking occurs, it becomes nearly impossible to miss it when reading other books in the Bible.

Isaiah uses the symbols of rain and famine to predict the occurrence of a major Spiritual Famine like we saw in Amos 8:11-12. He also develops a system of additional, supporting symbols and types that, combined with the rain analogy, give light and meaning to the rest of the scriptures contained in the Bible. This is why the Book of Isaiah is so important, and why I refer to it as the key to understanding Bible prophecies that are relevant today. The end result of this Isaiah symbolism is to show with a great degree of clarity that this great period of Spiritual Famine is, in fact, a reality of life. Some time shortly after the death and resurrection of Jesus Christ, the Lord withdrew from the earth, leaving no prophets, no priesthood authority, and no divine counsel.

Let us now begin a methodical analysis of various books of the Bible starting with Isaiah. Our goal is to find meaning and truth. I am looking for evidence to support the idea that God at some point decided to abandon the earth, leaving it void of prophets, priesthood, and authority. Likewise, if that is true, then we should also examine evidences regarding "the Latter Rain"—the period when such oracles are once again restored to the earth. Let us now see what Isaiah has to say on this important subject.

CHAPTER THREE

Symbols and Types of the Book of Isaiah

The writings of the Prophet Isaiah are apparently extremely important to the Lord. Isaiah is the prophet most frequently quoted by Jesus Christ during his life on the earth, as recorded in the New Testament. The Apostles Peter, John, and Paul cite verses from Isaiah, making him the most frequently quoted of all the Old Testament prophets. Despite the apparent importance of Isaiah's writings, the meaning of his prophecies has been the subject of much debate throughout the ages due to his use of types and symbols to convey his message. Isaiah's prophecies are written both for those living at the time of his mortal ministry (BC 740-701) and for those living in the latter days. Hence, the book cannot be read lightly or taken solely at face value. If we seek guidance from the Lord directly, his Spirit can help us see the meaning of the book and its importance to us today.

Of course, the interpretation of scripture is a personal matter. Scriptures can have different meanings, depending on the context of the reader and the personal circumstances that have caused the reader to search for meaning therein. The absolute or principal intended meaning of a verse or section of scriptures can also be elucidated with the help and insight provided by the Lord's servants, the prophets. For instance, when Jesus Christ spoke to the people from a ship while they listened on the shore (Matthew 13), he spoke in parables. Later, he explained the meaning of his parables to his disciples. Likewise, in attempting to understand Isaiah, one can refer to interpretations and meanings explained by the Savior through his prophets in scriptural references outside of the Book of Isaiah itself. In this way, we will attempt to understand the meaning of the Book of Isaiah and to apply that meaning to the other books of the Bible.

I will now list the major symbols and types as I see them, based on my study of the Book of Isaiah. By doing this up front, I hope to demonstrate how these types work together to convey the overall meaning that should be derived from Isaiah's writings. Through this process, the reader should begin to understand the significance of the Book of Isaiah.

SYMBOLS AND TYPES OF THE BOOK OF ISAIAH

Relevant Types and Symbols Identified in the Book of Isaiah:
1. **Water and Rain** = Word of God or revelation.
2. **Famine, Hunger, Drought, Wilderness, Desolation, or Darkness** = Period when revelation is not found on earth; a period of Spiritual Famine when no prophets are available to guide the people.
3. **The Sword** = Two different meanings: (a) The Sword of punishment, which is the onslaught of persecution and false doctrine that overcomes the inhabitants of Zion; (b) The Sword of the Lord, which is the Word of God as preached by the servants of the Lord in the Last Days.
4. **Zion** = Church/People/Nation of the Lord, characterized by righteousness and obedience to the Lord; also referred to as Israel.
5. **King of Assyria and his Kingdom** = Satan and his institutions and churches. False doctrines, traditions, and philosophies inspired by the devil.
6. **Joseph/Ephraim/Israel/Gentiles/Samaria** = the Ten Lost Tribes of Israel mixed with the Gentiles or the non-Israelite nations.
7. **Judah/David/Jesse/Jerusalem** = the Jews or the Tribe of Judah, which actually consists of the Two Tribes to the south (only tribe of Israel still identifiable today by the world in general).
8. **Egypt** = the Arm of Flesh, i.e., Man-made churches and organizations that feign divine authority. More specifically, churches develop to escape other churches deamed corrupt, or not of God. While serving as a temporary refuge, they nonetheless lack the true priesthood of God.
9. **Idols** = False beliefs, philosophies, and doctrines that are taken from the heathen traditions. Basically, anything that distracts men and women from finding the true doctrine of the Lord.
10. **Harlot** = Israel's turning from the true God to the false gods of the neighboring countries is represented as her becoming a harlot or an unfaithful wife (Isaiah 1:21).
11. **Vineyard** = the vineyard symbol represents Zion, or Israel.

Over the centuries, Isaiah's message has remained hidden, cloaked in symbolism. By identifying the meaning of these specific types, Isaiah's symbolic framework is revealed, and can be applied to other books of the Bible as well. Let us now examine each of these types in turn.

Water and Rain

In the previous chapter, we saw that the use of water, rain, dew, etc., to symbolize revelation is not isolated to the Book of Isaiah. Recall that this scriptural type was actually quite well-defined in the first two verses of Deuteronomy 32: "Give ear, O ye heavens, and I will speak; and hear, O earth, the words of my mouth. My doctrine shall drop as the rain, my speech shall distil as the dew, as the small rain upon the tender herb, and as the showers upon the grass." The Lord himself is referred to as the "fountain of living waters" or, in other words, the source of revelation and divine inspiration, as in Jeremiah 2:13. Isaiah uses this same imagery in his writings to convey meaning, as will be pointed out.

THE LATTER RAIN

Famine, Hunger, Drought, Wilderness, Desolation, or Darkness

In conjunction with the analogy of water and rain symbolizing the word of God unto man, the idea of famine or hunger is symbolic of the lack of God's word. Recall the verses found in the Book of Amos in the Old Testament:

> Amos 8:11-12
> 11 Behold, the days come, saith the Lord God, that I will send a famine in the land, not a famine of bread, nor a thirst for water, but of hearing the words of the Lord:
> 12 And they shall wander from sea to sea, and from the north even to the east, they shall run to and fro to seek the word of the Lord, and shall not find it."

This same imagery is repeated in Isaiah, and also includes the idea of a people wandering in the desert or wilderness. We will see that Isaiah makes references to the same point, using other symbolic types such as blindness and darkness versus the images of seeing clearly or encountering bright light.

The Sword

Isaiah uses the image or type of a "sword" in two different ways. First, the Lord allows the sword of justice (a negative type) to overtake Israel in the form of the king of Assyria and to drive the children of Israel into obscurity and darkness. This sword represents tyranny, opposition to truth, and persecution of the just. Much of Isaiah's writings seem almost gruesome in their prediction of Assyria's might being unleashed upon Israel.

In the end, however, the Lord promises us through the prophet Isaiah that "the sword of the Lord" (a positive type) will eventually be brought forth to avenge Israel from its ruthless captor, the king of Assyria. Instead of representing persecution and false doctrine, this sword type represents the word of God unto man, or the preaching of the Gospel through his disciples to those that stand in darkness.

Zion

As was pointed out in the previous section, the Kingdom of God on the earth is often referred to as "Zion." Words that are somewhat synonymous with Zion include the Church, Kingdom, Nation or Chosen People of the Lord. It can also at times be used to refer to a particular geographical location, like Jerusalem, if that is where the people of God are residing. The terms Israel and Zion are also at times interchangeable. For our purpose, let us merely note that the use of the term Zion is a reference to God's chosen people, and to the government or structure used to administer such a people. It is by definition a nation that is governed by the priesthood through the spirit of God which, in its fullest manifestation, would be found in the heart of each and every citizen of Zion.

The King of Assyria and His Kingdom

While many other symbolic types are used in the Book of Isaiah, a dominant theme presented by the prophet is the symbolic struggle between various entities within the narrative. Isaiah describes a nation known as Assyria, and its leader, the king of Assyria. This nation is a ruthless and powerful nation that, according to Isaiah, overcomes all other nations. In fact, the Lord uses Assyria to punish Israel for its wickedness and unfaithfulness unto the Lord.

> **Isaiah 10:5-6**
> 5 O Assyrian, the rod of mine anger, and the staff in their hand is mine indignation.
> 6 I will send him against an hypocritical nation, and against the people of my wrath will I give him a charge, to take the spoil, and to take the prey, and to tread them down like the mire of the streets.

The identity of the king of Assyria is made known in Isaiah, Chapter 14. In verse 12 it reads: "How art thou fallen from Heaven, O Lucifer, son of the morning! How art thou cut down to the ground, which didst weaken the nations!" Lucifer, the son of the morning, is a clear reference to Satan or the devil. In verses 16 and 17, we start to see the link between Satan and this character known as the king of Assyria, "They that see thee shall narrowly look upon thee, and consider thee, saying, Is this the man that made the earth to tremble, that did shake kingdoms; that made the world as a wilderness, and destroyed the cities thereof; that opened not the house of his prisoners?" Finally, in Isaiah 14:25, Isaiah refers to Satan as the Assyrian, saying, "That I will break the Assyrian in my land, and upon my mountains tread him under foot: then shall his yoke depart from off them, and his burden depart from off their shoulders."

Isaiah Chapter 14 describes Satan/Lucifer, who is an actual being and the enemy of all righteousness. In verse 25, Isaiah suddenly refers to him as the Assyrian. Therefore, the king of Assyria is not some future anti-Christ or mortal tyrant. Rather, references to the king of Assyria found in the Book of Isaiah are actually references to the devil himself, a spirit being. Likewise, references to the nation of Assyria represent the devil's dominions and institutions on the earth.

Ephraim and Judah

Ephraim and Judah are both represented in Isaiah. Ephraim, the son of Joseph who was sold into Egypt by his brethren, became symbolic of the ten tribes that broke away from Israel after the reign of Solomon. When Rehoboam, Solomon's son, succeeded Solomon to the throne, he increased the burdens on his subjects, which in turn led to the separation of Israel into two separate kingdoms. Jeroboam became the king of the Northern Ten Tribes, while Judah and Benjamin remained under the rule of Rehoboam until his death, and then under the rule of David's descendants from then on. The Northern Ten Tribes kept the name Israel, or went collectively by the name of Ephraim. Historically, when the Northern Ten Tribes were carried away into captivity around 721 BC, they were never recovered.

Judah remained a kingdom until about 587 BC, when it too was conquered and carried into captivity by the nation of Babylon. The tribe of Judah (Judah and Benjamin combined), unlike the northern tribes, was not completely lost to historical record. In fact, a remnant of Judah ultimately returned and rebuilt Jerusalem and remained until approximately 70 AD, when Jerusalem was again destroyed and the Jews scattered. Modern-day Jews are still identified with the tribe of Judah, and remain the only tribe of Israel visibly known to the world as a whole. The rest of the tribes of Israel have been dispersed and mixed with the nations of the world. Therefore, references in the scriptures to David, Jesse, Judah, or the Jews indicate the Southern Two Tribes through which the coming of the Messiah had been foretold. References to Joseph, Ephraim, Israel, the Lost Ten Tribes, or the Gentiles indicate the children of Israel from the Northern Ten Tribes that were carried away captive and mingled with the nations of the earth (the heathen or non-Israelite nations). At other points in the scriptures, the Lord simply refers to these two tribal entities by the name of their capital cities: Samaria for Ephraim and Jerusalem for Judah.

While the original twelve tribes that came out of the loins of Jacob were named and known in ancient Israel, the Lord ultimately narrows his interactions with Israel down to the two tribes, Ephraim and Judah. We will touch on this point further as we continue our discussion. It is important to have these concepts established early on, as the references we will be citing from the Bible generally refer to one of these two families. Let us look at a few examples of this two-family, or two-tribe relationship.

Jeremiah 33:24

24 Considerest thou not what this people have spoken, saying, The two families which the LORD hath chosen, he hath even cast them off? thus they have despised my people, that they should be no more a nation before them.

Ezekiel 37:21-22

21 And say unto them, Thus saith the Lord GOD; Behold, I will take the children of Israel from among the heathen, whither they be gone, and will gather them on every side, and bring them into their own land:
22 And I will make them one nation in the land upon the mountains of Israel; and one king shall be king to them all: and they shall be no more two nations, neither shall they be divided into two kingdoms any more at all:

Isaiah 11:11-13

11 And it shall come to pass in that day, that the Lord shall set his hand again the second time to recover the remnant of his people, which shall be left, from Assyria, and from Egypt, and from Pathros, and from Cush, and from Elam, and from Shinar, and from Hamath, and from the islands of the sea.
12 And he shall set up an ensign for the nations, and shall assemble the outcasts of Israel, and gather together the dispersed of Judah from the four corners of the earth.
13 The envy also of Ephraim shall depart, and the adversaries of Judah shall be cut off: Ephraim shall not envy Judah, and Judah shall not vex Ephraim.

This "two-tribe" concept is important to understand as we begin our analysis of the Book of Isaiah. At the time of Christ, only Judah held the full priesthood of God, having its capital at Jerusalem. While some refugees from Ephraim were perhaps present in Samaria at that same time period (see 2 Chronicles 15:9), it is clear from the New Testament that the religion of the Samaritans had been corrupted and was without authority (see John 4:20-22). In the end, however, both houses of Israel fell into a state of desolation as pertaining to the prophets of God.

SYMBOLS AND TYPES OF THE BOOK OF ISAIAH

Isaiah 8:14

14 And he shall be for a sanctuary; but for a stone of stumbling and for a rock of offence to both the houses of Israel, for a gin and for a snare to the inhabitants of Jerusalem.

Egypt

Egypt is also mentioned as a nation in the Book of Isaiah narrative. In Isaiah 31, the Lord reproves Israel for turning to Egypt for help against its enemies, instead of turning to the Lord himself. In Isaiah 20, the Lord shows that even Egypt, with all her chariots and worldly power, shall be overrun by Assyria and be ashamed. Thus, Egypt in this sense represents the arm of flesh, and the futility of relying on it as opposed to the arm of God. Finally, other minor nations are mentioned including Moab, Tyre, etc. These nations are all consumed and dispersed by Assyria.

In a spiritual sense, Egypt actually represents the man-made religions and institutions of the world that feign divine authority but do not truly possess it. A distinction exists between Assyria and Egypt. Assyria represents the churches and organizations developed through the direct inspiration of the devil. They are created to subjugate man and to pull us down, corrupting the correct order and function of the priesthood. They do so willfully, to get gain and the praise of the world. The Assyrian-type churches and organizations are used as a means of punishment for Israel, and are responsible for completely snuffing out the remaining prophets, priests, and disciples of the Lord's true church, namely Zion.

Egypt represents a class of churches and organizations that are created by well-meaning persons desiring to escape the grasp of tyranny found in the Assyrian-type faiths. They are indeed a source of refuge at first, and do much good in the world as they weaken the power of Satan and help people draw closer to the Lord. Unfortunately, the Egypt-type churches are man-made organizations. Instead of consulting directly with the Lord, the founders of these institutions do the best they can with what they see written in the scriptures. Since these churches are also lacking in direct authority from God (the true priesthood), they remain susceptible to the corruption of men. Over time, they too fall victim to the Assyrian, or Satan. In the end, they lose their initial benefit of drawing men and women to God, and instead do the same as the Assyrian-type churches. They create confusion and prevent the progress of those seeking the true and undefiled Church of God—which is missing from the earth.

I want to emphasize the important roll that the Egyptian sojourn plays in preparation for the restoration of the true Zion. The Egypt-type organizations were in most cases created with the best of intentions. While they may lack the priesthood authority, they nonetheless depart from the tyranny of the Assyrian-type organizations for a time. The mission of Jesus Christ as the Savior and promised Messiah is spread throughout the world by these churches and freedom of religion is ultimately espoused by many nations of the world. The environment of religious tolerance and freedom is developed in large part due to this movement away from tyranny, and toward freedom of thought. The Lord blesses those that worship him in sincerity of heart, no matter what organization they have chosen. Once Zion is restored, however, he has promised to send his messengers to seek out the honest in heart and lead them to the true fold of God.

Eventually, Satan is able to gain control over these man-made institutions and uses them to hinder the progress of the faithful servants of the Lord. They are left captives to the same false doctrines and unauthorized priesthood authority as existed under the rule of Assyria. The devil is able to do this because these man-made entities were formed without counseling with the Lord directly and lack priesthood authority. They ultimately serve only to get gain and worldly influence for those that lead such institutions. The Egyptian-type churches thus become a stumbling block for the humble and innocent who are deceived by the false doctrines and tenants espoused by such churches. The leaders of these man-made institutions will fight against Zion when it is finally reestablished.

The mighty difference between Zion and the false doctrines of the world is revelation. Zion will have prophets to guide her and direct her, directly from God. Revelation is new and alive. When it is available, it clarifies doctrine. It answers questions and eliminates disputes. In contrast, without prophets available, mankind has experienced confusion concerning doctrine, questions without answers, and many disputes about religion. Instead of asking God directly for guidance and understanding, man has relied on "learned men" to interpret the scraps of doctrine that can be gleaned from the available scriptures, which are the writings of dead prophets. These interpretations have served as manna and sustained our hope and faith in God, but have not satisfied us completely. They have only kept us alive as we have wandered through the wilderness of the Great Spiritual Famine. The true followers of God long for the Promised Land: A restored Zion and living prophets as existed in the ancient world.

Idols

The worship of idols is obviously a wicked practice that is often mentioned in the Bible. In fact, the Ten Commandments condemn this practice specifically:

Exodus 20:4-6
4 Thou shalt not make unto thee any graven image, or any likeness of any thing that is in heaven above, or that is in the earth beneath, or that is in the water under the earth:
5 Thou shalt not bow down thyself to them, nor serve them: for I the LORD thy God am a jealous God, visiting the iniquity of the fathers upon the children unto the third and fourth generation of them that hate me;
6 And shewing mercy unto thousands of them that love me, and keep my commandments.

Isaiah uses idol worship as a type. The worship of idols described in the Book of Isaiah represents the worship of something man-made, and it specifically means the worship of false doctrines, philosophies, and tenants. The mention of idol worship by Isaiah, and subsequently by other Bible prophets, has a double meaning. First, it describes the literal practice of worshiping statues or other man-made icons, which concept is readily understood by most. Secondly, the concept of worshiping idols symbolizes the worship of God through man-made doctrines, tenants, and traditions. This second meaning has the same damaging effect as the first.

SYMBOLS AND TYPES OF THE BOOK OF ISAIAH

Religions and other organizations created by man without the sanction and authority of God do not have the power to save their members, nor direction from the Lord in the form of revelation through true prophets. Anything that consumes our attention and focus, distracting us from the true Church of God, can be considered an idol. When people living on the earth finally recognize the futility of such organizations, they begin to search for the true Zion. The children of Israel finally recognize that they are entangled in these false organizations, as they compare it to the pure doctrine of Zion. Only then do they desire to let go of their former traditions and beliefs which were false. Isaiah describes this process in a descriptive manner.

> **Isaiah 30:22**
> 22 Ye shall defile also the covering of thy graven images of silver, and the ornament of thy molten images of gold: thou shalt cast them away as a menstruous cloth; thou shalt say unto it, Get thee hence.

We will also see in later discussions that, when leaving Egypt (which represents the worldly man-made churches), many of the first generation sought to return to the worship of idols. Likewise, in the last days, when Zion is restored to the earth and prophets again called, some of those that leave the world to come to Zion will desire to bring their worldly practices with them and, in some cases, return to their former faith and doctrine. Those that endure and cling to truth and rely on the spirit to guide them, will be led safely to the restored Zion and help others get there as well. The term "idol" as used by Isaiah thus has two meanings, one literal (a man-made statue or icon) and one spiritual (a man-made doctrine or tenant).

Harlot

This symbol is introduced in Isaiah 1:21: "How is the faithful city become an harlot!" It is again taken up in Isaiah 47, where Babylon is referred to as a woman who was once called, "The lady of kingdoms" (Isaiah 47:5). Jeremiah and Ezekiel later make great use of this symbolic type, showing both Ephraim and Judah as two unfaithful wives who play the harlot and forsake their good husband, the Lord God of Israel. John the Revelator likewise uses this image in the Book of Revelation.

Vineyard

Vineyards were common in ancient Israel. Isaiah uses the idea of a fortified and protected vineyard as a type to represent Israel, or the Kingdom of God on the earth. We will see in our subsequent discussion that, without the protection of the Lord, the vineyard does not prosper.

> **Isaiah 5:4-7**
> 4 What could have been done more to my vineyard, that I have not done in it? wherefore, when I looked that it should bring forth grapes, brought it forth wild grapes?
> 5 And now go to; I will tell you what I will do to my vineyard: I will take away the hedge thereof, and it shall be eaten up; and break down the wall thereof, and it shall be trodden down:

6 And I will lay it waste: it shall not be pruned, nor digged; but there shall come up briers and thorns: I will also command the clouds that they rain no rain upon it.
7 For the vineyard of the LORD of hosts is the house of Israel, and the men of Judah his pleasant plant: and he looked for judgment, but behold oppression; for righteousness, but behold a cry.

Instead of prospering, it is overrun and the Lord even withholds the "rain" so that the vineyard is no longer watered and nourished. Under these circumstances, the vineyard (Israel), becomes desolate. In verse seven, we see that "the vineyard of the Lord of hosts is the house of Israel, and the men of Judah his pleasant plant." Thus, the Lord himself defines this symbolic type for us through the prophet Isaiah.

Other Considerations

A few final points to consider when reading the Book of Isaiah are as follows:

1. The Lord is a merciful God. He does not delight in bloodshed, nor does he desire that his children should be lost or condemned. On the contrary, he desires to gather them and to protect them. In the name of justice, those who forsake his Atonement and transgress his statutes must ultimately suffer the consequences of their sins. We see this concept from the very beginning of the Book.

    Isaiah 1:18
    18 Come now, and let us reason together, saith the Lord: though your sins be as scarlet, they shall be as white as snow; though they be red like crimson, they shall be as wool.

    The Lord repeats such pleas again and again throughout the entire book, "For all this his anger is not turned away, but his hand is outstretched still" as in Isaiah 10:4. While he is not pleased with the actions of the wicked, he is always ready to receive the repentant unto him.
2. Isaiah's writings are not chronological per se. In other words, the same event might be described several times throughout the book.
3. Isaiah uses different types and symbols to emphasize events. The same event might be described using different types or analogies at different points in the book.

CHAPTER FOUR

The Message of the Book of Isaiah

The Book of Isaiah begins by introducing the concept that the once favored and chosen people of the Lord, Israel, have rejected the Lord as their God, and gone astray from the true Gospel. To retrieve his people from their wicked state, the Lord decrees that he will chasten his people, and bring judgment upon them, while at the same time extending his arm in mercy to all those who will repent. This chastisement occurs by the Lord withdrawing from his people, and leaving them subject to the king of Assyria, who is thereby allowed to conquer the entire world.

Once this conquest is complete, and the people of the Lord again begin to call on him for help, the Lord promises that he will once again gather his people unto him. Zion breaks forth once more upon the earth, and begins to march forth against the forces of Assyria, which have the chosen people of the Lord under subjugation. Zion prospers and enlarges her borders until at last it fills the whole earth, and the Lord himself returns and possesses his rightful throne at the head of his chosen people, Israel.

Application of this Symbolic Plot to Real Life

On a surface level, it is tempting to look for the king of Assyria to be manifested in the image of some future tyrannical leader. We might imagine such a man to rise in power, and to begin to conquer the earth, nation by nation, until he has vanquished the entire earth under his dominion. In fact, many historical leaders may have indeed had this as their ultimate political goal, e.g., Hitler, etc. In the history of the world, there has never been a single nation that has been successful in taking over the entire world. There have been many vast and powerful empires rise up. However, each in turn has ultimately reached a limit to its dominion, and each has ultimately fallen from power and either been eliminated completely or greatly diminished. Therefore, the symbolic nation of Assyria spoken of in Isaiah has no historical basis. It must, therefore, be a future nation that will rise up, or representative of something spiritual. As has been stated earlier, the king of Assyria is not a future king, but rather Satan. It follows that Assyria is the kingdom of the devil, and his institutions and dominion over the earth.

What Isaiah is really saying is that the Lord will at some point allow Satan to overcome the entire earth, spiritually speaking, such that true prophets are no longer found on the earth, true religion is lost, and the priesthood authority to perform the saving ordinances is unavailable. This period of time we shall refer to as a period of apostasy. An apostasy is defined as "an abandoning of what one has believed in, as a faith, cause, or principles" (Webster's New World Collegiate Dictionary, Fourth Edition, Wiley Publishing, Cleveland, 2007). For the purposes of our present discussion, an apostasy would be a falling away from or the creation of a defiled form of an originally true religion. This great period of apostasy is a period when the true form of government and organization originally found in Zion fell away and became corrupted, lacking the power and authority of the priesthood and the revelation from God to his prophets to administer the ordinances and blessings of such an organization.

Period of Apostasy

Isaiah uses multiple types, symbols and images to describe the fall of the true Gospel into a state of apostasy—namely famine, drought, wilderness, desolation, and so forth. This fall into Spiritual Famine is also symbolically represented as the Lord's people being overcome by the "nation" of Assyria. Let us examine several examples of this falling away of the Lord's people:

Isaiah 1:7-9

7 Your country is desolate, your cities are burned with fire: your land, strangers devour it in your presence, and it is desolate, as overthrown by strangers.
8 And the daughter of Zion is left as a cottage in a vineyard, as a lodge in a garden of cucumbers, as a besieged city.
9 Except the LORD of hosts had left unto us a very small remnant we should have been as Sodom, and we should have been like unto Gomorrah.

Here the symbol of desolation is used to describe the state of Spiritual Famine that befalls Israel and, except for the Jews and perhaps the nation state of Israel (the very small remnant), no other part of Israel remains recognizable today by the world in general.

Isaiah 3:1-3

1 For, behold, the Lord, the LORD of hosts, doth take away from Jerusalem and from Judah the stay and the staff, the whole stay of bread, and the whole stay of water.
2 The mighty man, and the man of war, the judge, and the prophet, and the prudent, and the ancient,
3 The captain of fifty, and the honourable man, and the counsellor, and the cunning artificer, and the eloquent orator.

Isaiah uses the images of drought and famine in the first verse, and then clarifies the symbolic meaning by indicating that even the prophet will be removed from Israel.

THE MESSAGE OF THE BOOK OF ISAIAH

Isaiah 5:5-7, 13-14

5 And now go to; I will tell you what I will do to my vineyard: I will take away the hedge thereof, and it shall be eaten up; and break down the wall thereof, and it shall be trodden down:
6 And I will lay it waste: it shall not be pruned, nor digged; but there shall come up briers and thorns: I will also command the clouds that they rain no rain upon it.
7 For the vineyard of the LORD of hosts is the house of Israel, and the men of Judah his pleasant plant: and he looked for judgment, but behold oppression; for righteousness, but behold a cry.
13 Therefore my people are gone into captivity, because they have no knowledge: and their honourable men are famished, and their multitude dried up with thirst.
14 Therefore hell hath enlarged herself, and opened her mouth without measure: and their glory, and their multitude, and their pomp, and he that rejoiceth, shall descend into it.

In this case, Isaiah uses a vineyard type to symbolically represent Israel, which is made completely clear in verse seven. The Lord shows that he has not only broken down the wall of protection around the vineyard, but he has also shut the heavens, "that it rain no more upon it." Israel's honorable men are "famished, and their multitude dried up with thirst." The above passage describes a period of time when Israel has no prophets to receive God's word. Likewise, the people receive no inspiration from God. In verse 14, we again see that in reality it is hell (the kingdom of the devil) that has enlarged itself—another key to the identity of Assyria and its king.

Isaiah 6:11-13

11 Then said I, Lord, how long? And he answered, Until the cities be wasted without inhabitant, and the houses without man, and the land be utterly desolate,
12 And the LORD have removed men far away, and there be a great forsaking in the midst of the land.
13 But yet in it shall be a tenth, and it shall return, and shall be eaten: as a teil tree, and as an oak, whose substance is in them, when they cast their leaves: so the holy seed shall be the substance thereof.

These verses describe not only desolation or Spiritual Famine, but the idea of a tenth returning, and still being eaten up. Historically, while most of the tribes of Israel were lost after about 587 BC, the tribe of Judah (with Benjamin mixed in with it) or about a tenth of Israel returned and reestablished Jerusalem, and they had prophets until after the coming of Christ in the flesh. Shortly thereafter, even this remnant was "eaten," yet "the holy seed shall be the substance thereof." Hence, the lineages of Judah and Ephraim are important to the Lord's plan.

Isaiah 7:17

17 The LORD shall bring upon thee, and upon thy people, and upon thy father's house, days that have not come, from the day that Ephraim departed from Judah; even the king of Assyria.

Isaiah 8:5-8

5 The LORD spake also unto me again, saying,
6 Forasmuch as this people refuseth the waters of Shiloah that go softly, and rejoice in Rezin and Remaliah's son;
7 Now therefore, behold, the Lord bringeth up upon them the waters of the river, strong and many, even the king of Assyria, and all his glory: and he shall come up over all his channels, and go over all his banks:

> 8 And he shall pass through Judah; he shall overflow and go over, he shall reach even to the neck; and the stretching out of his wings shall fill the breadth of thy land, O Immanuel.

In these verses, Isaiah introduces the king of Assyria. He shows that since the "people refuseth the waters of Shiloah" (or the revelations and prophets of Christ), instead he will allow Satan to have power and dominion over all the earth (a period of apostasy). Here the water analogy is used to show that men will receive revelation from Satan rather than God because they chose it.

Isaiah 26:13-14
> 13 O LORD our God, other lords beside thee have had dominion over us: but by thee only will we make mention of thy name.
> 14 They are dead, they shall not live; they are deceased, they shall not rise: therefore hast thou visited and destroyed them, and made all their memory to perish.

Isaiah again suggests the identity of the king of Assyria and his nation. Satan and his angels were cast down to the earth prior to their birth. Thus, they are spirits and "shall not live; they are deceased," and will not rise in the resurrection, but will remain spirits throughout all eternity. Even the vilest of historical figures, including Hitler, Herod, Cain, and so forth, will eventually come forth and be resurrected—although they only come forth at the last resurrection prior to the judgment. The 15th verse of Acts 24 of the New Testament makes this point fairly clear: "And have hope toward God, which they themselves also allow, that there shall be a resurrection of the dead, both of the just and unjust." Both the just and the unjust will eventually rise in the resurrection. The king of Assyria is not a living political leader, but rather Satan himself—a being of spirit, not flesh and blood. This is not a dual prophecy either. The idea—that a future tyrannical leader will be born into mortality and take over the entire world—is a misinterpretation of this concept. Instead, without prophets to guide us, it is as if we are drunk or asleep, and Satan has control over all the earth.

Isaiah 29:9-10
> 9 Stay yourselves, and wonder; cry ye out, and cry: they are drunken, but not with wine; they stagger, but not with strong drink.
> 10 For the LORD hath poured out upon you the spirit of deep sleep and hath closed your eyes: the prophets and your rulers, the seers hath he covered.

Here again, Isaiah is very plain in showing that the period of Spiritual Famine, which he predicts, is a period when no prophets are found on the earth.

Isaiah 32:13-15
> 13 Upon the land of my people shall come up thorns and briers; yea, upon all the houses of joy in the joyous city:
> 14 Because the palaces shall be forsaken; the multitude of the city shall be left; the forts and towers shall be for dens for ever, a joy of wild asses, a pasture of flocks;
> 15 Until the spirit be poured upon us from on high, and the wilderness be a fruitful field, and the fruitful field be counted for a forest.

Again, a period is described when desolation will reign, and it will remain thus, "until the spirit be poured upon us from on high, and the wilderness be a fruitful field." Israel will remain in a state of Spiritual Famine until the Lord again calls a prophet upon the earth, and gives his revelation again to the children of men.

Isaiah 51:17-19

17 Awake, awake, stand up, O Jerusalem, which hast drunk at the hand of the LORD the cup of his fury; thou hast drunken the dregs of the cup of trembling, and wrung them out.
18 There is none to guide her among all the sons whom she hath brought forth; neither is there any that taketh her by the hand of all the sons that she hath brought up.
19 These two things are come unto thee; who shall be sorry for thee? desolation, and destruction, and the famine, and the sword: by whom shall I comfort thee?

"There is none to guide her among all the sons whom she hath brought forth" would seem to mean that there are no prophets from the seed of Jacob. They are left with desolation and famine and so forth—again symbolic of apostasy.

Isaiah 59:9-11

9 Therefore is judgment far from us, neither doth justice overtake us: we wait for light, but behold obscurity; for brightness, but we walk in darkness.
10 We grope for the wall like the blind, and we grope as if we had no eyes: we stumble at noonday as in the night; we are in desolate places as dead men.
11 We roar all like bears, and mourn sore like doves: we look for judgment, but there is none; for salvation, but it is far off from us.

Isaiah 60:2

2 For, behold, the darkness shall cover the earth, and gross darkness the people: but the LORD shall arise upon thee, and his glory shall be seen upon thee.

In these verses in chapters 59 and 60, instead of famine, Isaiah uses the analogy of darkness to represent the period of apostasy. They have no eyes because they have no prophets. They are left to themselves to find their own way like a blind man groping for a wall to lean against. "Darkness shall cover the earth, and gross darkness the people."

Isaiah 64:10-12

10 Thy holy cities are a wilderness, Zion is a wilderness, Jerusalem a desolation.
11 Our holy and our beautiful house, where our fathers praised thee, is burned up with fire: and all our pleasant things are laid waste.
12 Wilt thou refrain thyself for these things, O LORD? wilt thou hold thy peace, and afflict us very sore?

Wilderness and desolation are synonymous with Spiritual Famine, or a falling away from the true Gospel, and the removal of prophets and revelation from the earth. The last question leads us to our next subject. When will the Lord intervene, and reinstate Zion again on the earth? When will he begin his fight against Assyria and its dominions? From our earlier discussion, we know that it is when the children of Israel turn to the Lord and seek counsel from Him directly.

If not to the Lord, where else does Israel go for help? In the Book of Isaiah narrative, they go down to Egypt for help. In doing so, they disappoint the Lord, and he again delays his coming forth among them. Let us examine a few verses that spell out this dynamic, and then try to interpret the meaning of this symbolism.

Isaiah 2:22

22 Cease ye from man, whose breath is in his nostrils: for wherein is he to be accounted of?

Isaiah 3:5-8

5 And the people shall be oppressed, every one by another, and every one by his neighbour: the child shall behave himself proudly against the ancient, and the base against the honourable.
6 When a man shall take hold of his brother of the house of his father, saying, Thou hast clothing, be thou our ruler, and let this ruin be under thy hand:
7 In that day shall he swear, saying, I will not be an healer; for in my house is neither bread nor clothing: make me not a ruler of the people.
8 For Jerusalem is ruined, and Judah is fallen: because their tongue and their doings are against the LORD, to provoke the eyes of his glory.

In Isaiah 2, the Lord counsels his children not to seek counsel from man. Yet we see from Isaiah 3 that not only is Jerusalem ruined and Judah fallen, but instead of seeking help from the Lord, the general tendency is to seek one's brother to rule over them. Israel wants to get out from under the tyranny and oppression of Satan, but instead of seeking the Lord directly, men seek counsel among themselves and form their own doctrines and creeds, churches and institutions. This reliance on man is often referred to as "the arm of flesh," and Isaiah uses the nation of Egypt to illustrate the vanity of relying on the arm of flesh.

Isaiah 31:1-3

1 WOE to them that go down to Egypt for help; and stay on horses, and trust in chariots, because they are many; and in horsemen, because they are very strong; but they look not unto the Holy One of Israel, neither seek the LORD!
2 Yet he also is wise, and will bring evil, and will not call back his words: but will arise against the house of the evildoers, and against the help of them that work iniquity.
3 Now the Egyptians are men, and not God; and their horses flesh, and not spirit. When the LORD shall stretch out his hand, both he that helpeth shall fall, and he that is holpen shall fall down, and they all shall fail together.

The arm of flesh concept is evident here when Isaiah says, "the Egyptians are men, and not God; and their horses flesh and not spirit." "But they look not unto the Holy One of Israel, neither seek the Lord!"

Isaiah 30:1-7

1 WOE to the rebellious children, saith the LORD, that take counsel, but not of me; and that cover with a covering, but not of my spirit, that they may add sin to sin:
2 That walk to go down into Egypt, and have not asked at my mouth; to strengthen themselves in the strength of Pharaoh, and to trust in the shadow of Egypt!
3 Therefore shall the strength of Pharaoh be your shame, and the trust in the shadow of Egypt your confusion.
4 For his princes were at Zoan, and his ambassadors came to Hanes.
5 They were all ashamed of a people that could not profit them, nor be an help nor profit, but a shame, and also a reproach.
6 The burden of the beasts of the south: into the land of trouble and anguish, from whence come the young and old lion, the viper and fiery flying serpent, they will carry their riches upon the shoulders of young asses, and their treasures upon the bunches of camels, to a people that shall not profit them.
7 For the Egyptians shall help in vain, and to no purpose: therefore have I cried concerning this, Their strength is to sit still.

THE MESSAGE OF THE BOOK OF ISAIAH

The Lord is disappointed with Israel for seeking the arm of flesh over the arm of the Lord. We see that they carry their treasures to "a people that shall not profit them." Once Israel and Judah have been conquered by Assyria, some will seek refuge in "Egypt" or the arm of flesh. They will carry their treasures (the scriptures and doctrines) into a country that cannot profit them since they do not have the true authority of God to act in his name. They lack the authorized priesthood of God, and thus the saving ordinances performed by these man-made institutions "shall not profit them." In other words, a baptism performed without the proper authority will not count in the great Day of Judgment. Yet the humble believers in Christ who innocently accept these unauthorized ordinances are at least still trying, with the best of intentions perhaps, to reestablish the former glory of ancient Zion. Unfortunately they do so without seeking the Lord himself.

Isaiah 30:9-14

9 That this is a rebellious people, lying children, children that will not hear the law of the LORD:
10 Which say to the seers, See not; and to the prophets, Prophesy not unto us right things, speak unto us smooth things, prophesy deceits:
11 Get you out of the way, turn aside out of the path, cause the Holy One of Israel to cease from before us.
12 Wherefore thus saith the Holy One of Israel, Because ye despise this word, and trust in oppression and perverseness, and stay thereon:
13 Therefore this iniquity shall be to you as a breach ready to fall, swelling out in a high wall, whose breaking cometh suddenly at an instant.
14 And he shall break it as the breaking of the potters' vessel that is broken in pieces; he shall not spare: so that there shall not be found in the bursting of it a sherd to take fire from the hearth, or to take water withal out of the pit.

After Assyria has conquered Israel, and driven it into a state of apostasy, there will be an attempt to re-establish the Church of God, but it will be a man-made Church, albeit based on the treasures left over from the former times. They will "say to the seers, See not; and to the prophets, Prophesy not unto us right things, and cause the Holy One of Israel to cease from before us." Isaiah prophesies that the false doctrine of Assyria will be so awful and perverse that it will ultimately break into pieces, or many different churches, doctrines, and religions; yet "there shall not be found in the bursting of it a sherd to take fire from the hearth, or to take water withal out of the pit." Although the original falsehood is broken up into various pieces, the new churches are based on the arm of flesh and not brought forth by God himself. They do not "hold water." They do not have prophets or divine revelation from God directly. Therefore, in the end, these new churches are eventually overrun by Assyria as well. They may have started with the best of intentions by persons desiring to do the right thing before God, but they cannot save man from his lost and fallen state since they lack the authority and power of the Priesthood of the Lamb.

Isaiah 20:4-6

4 So shall the king of Assyria lead away the Egyptians prisoners, and the Ethiopians captives, young and old, naked and barefoot, even with their buttocks uncovered, to the shame of Egypt.
5 And they shall be afraid and ashamed of Ethiopia their expectation, and of Egypt their glory.

THE LATTER RAIN

6 And the inhabitant of this isle shall say in that day, Behold, such is our expectation, whither we flee for help to be delivered from the king of Assyria: and how shall we escape?

Isaiah 30:15-18

15 For thus saith the Lord GOD, the Holy One of Israel; In returning and rest shall ye be saved; in quietness and in confidence shall be your strength: and ye would not.
16 But ye said, No; for we will flee upon horses; therefore shall ye flee: and, We will ride upon the swift; therefore shall they that pursue you be swift.
17 One thousand shall flee at the rebuke of one; at the rebuke of five shall ye flee: till ye be left as a beacon upon the top of a mountain, and as an ensign on an hill.
18 And therefore will the LORD wait, that he may be gracious unto you, and therefore will he be exalted, that he may have mercy upon you: for the LORD is a God of judgment: blessed are all they that wait for him.

Here we get the feeling of a fugitive fleeing from his captors. As they flee from falsehood and oppression, they come closer and closer to the truth. However, since each subsequent religion is still based on the precepts of men, the Lord waits until someone finally calls upon his name directly before restoring Zion to the earth. When this new prophet finally addresses the Lord directly, the Lord will reveal himself to him, and thus end the long dearth that has wasted the earth.

Isaiah 30:19-25

19 For the people shall dwell in Zion at Jerusalem: thou shalt weep no more: he will be very gracious unto thee at the voice of thy cry; when he shall hear it, he will answer thee.
20 And though the Lord give you the bread of adversity, and the water of affliction, yet shall not thy teachers be removed into a corner any more, but thine eyes shall see thy teachers:
21 And thine ears shall hear a word behind thee, saying, This is the way, walk ye in it, when ye turn to the right hand, and when ye turn to the left.
22 Ye shall defile also the covering of thy graven images of silver, and the ornament of thy molten images of gold: thou shalt cast them away as a menstruous cloth; thou shalt say unto it, Get thee hence.
23 Then shall he give the rain of thy seed, that thou shalt sow the ground withal; and bread of the increase of the earth, and it shall be fat and plenteous: in that day shall thy cattle feed in large pastures.
24 The oxen likewise and the young asses that ear the ground shall eat clean provender, which hath been winnowed with the shovel and with the fan.
25 And there shall be upon every high mountain, and upon every high hill, rivers and streams of waters in the day of the great slaughter, when the towers fall.

To summarize, Ephraim and Judah are both overcome by Satan when the Lord withdraws his presence from them because of their iniquity. A period of complete apostasy covers the whole earth. Men will, however, seek to rebuild the fallen Zion by taking the treasures of the Jews (the scriptures and doctrines) and formulating churches of men. These churches will splinter into many sects and creeds, but there will be a refining process that ultimately leads to the point where someone from the House of Israel finally calls upon the Lord directly for help in understanding religion. We see this same concept repeated throughout Isaiah, for example in Isaiah 42 we read:

Isaiah 42:22

22 But this is a people robbed and spoiled; they are all of them snared in holes, and they are hid in prison houses: they are for a prey, and none delivereth; for a spoil, and none saith, Restore.

The use of the word "Restore" in the above verse is quite significant. When something is restored, it is returned to its original form. It is not merely tweaked or improved incrementally, but it is completely reestablished as it was before. Likewise, Isaiah 42:22 indicates that someone on earth has to question the current state of religion. Someone needs to say: "Restore." Zion cannot come out of Assyria by merely fleeing to Egypt, but must be led out directly by God. Any church formed by coming out of a corrupt religion having no divine authority will itself remain corrupt. Therefore, the only true solution is for a new prophet to seek the Lord directly, and to receive the perfect doctrines and authority to act in his name on earth. Only then can it be said for sure that Zion is reborn again on the earth.

Isaiah 41:25-29
25 I have raised up one from the north, and he shall come: from the rising of the sun shall he call upon my name: and he shall come upon princes as upon morter, and as the potter treadeth clay.
26 Who hath declared from the beginning, that we may know? and beforetime, that we may say, He is righteous? yea, there is none that sheweth, yea, there is none that declareth, yea, there is none that heareth your words.
27 The first shall say to Zion, Behold, behold them: and I will give to Jerusalem one that bringeth good tidings.
28 For I beheld, and there was no man; even among them, and there was no counselor, that, when I asked of them, could answer a word.
29 Behold, they are all vanity; their works are nothing: their molten images are wind and confusion.

These verses in Isaiah seem to indicate that a man "from the north" (perhaps a descendant from the Northern Ten Tribes) will at some point be raised up by the Lord, and will go forth and call upon the name of the Lord directly. He will seek knowledge from the Lord and with that knowledge he will begin the reversal of fortune for Israel. Thus, the Lord will finally "give one to Jerusalem that bringeth good tidings," after the long period where "there was no man; even among them, and there was no counselor, that, when I asked of them, could answer a word." Thus, a new prophet will be called forth in the latter days that will begin to put an end to the vanity and confusion of the dark ages of Spiritual Famine.

Return of Zion

Isaiah uses several types and symbols to represent the restoration of the true and living Gospel to the earth in the latter times. The first two concepts are: (1) that of waking up from sleep, and (2) that of loosening the bands that hold one bound.

Isaiah 52:1-2
1 AWAKE, awake; put on thy strength, O Zion; put on thy beautiful garments, O Jerusalem, the holy city: for henceforth there shall no more come into thee the uncircumcised and the unclean.
2 Shake thyself from the dust; arise, and sit down, O Jerusalem: loose thyself from the bands of thy neck, O captive daughter of Zion.

Isaiah 51:9-11
9 Awake, awake, put on thy strength, O arm of the LORD; awake, as in the ancient days, in

the generations of old. Art thou not it that hath cut Rahab, and wounded the dragon?
10 Art thou not it which hath dried the sea, the waters of the great deep; that hath made the depths of the sea a way for the ransomed to pass over?
11 Therefore the redeemed of the LORD shall return, and come with singing unto Zion; and everlasting joy shall be upon their head: they shall obtain gladness and joy; and sorrow and mourning shall flee away.

The idea of waking up from a deep sleep is further developed in Isaiah 29, where Isaiah points out that the Lord is the one that has caused the deep sleep to come upon Israel.

Isaiah 29:9-14

9 Stay yourselves, and wonder; cry ye out, and cry: they are drunken, but not with wine; they stagger, but not with strong drink.
10 For the LORD hath poured out upon you the spirit of deep sleep, and hath closed your eyes: the prophets and your rulers, the seers hath he covered.
11 And the vision of all is become unto you as the words of a book that is sealed, which men deliver to one that is learned, saying, Read this, I pray thee: and he saith, I cannot; for it is sealed:
12 And the book is delivered to him that is not learned, saying, Read this, I pray thee: and he saith, I am not learned.
13 Wherefore the Lord said, Forasmuch as this people draw near me with their mouth, and with their lips do honour me, but have removed their heart far from me, and their fear toward me is taught by the precept of men:
14 Therefore, behold, I will proceed to do a marvelous work among this people, even a marvellous work and a wonder: for the wisdom of their wise men shall perish, and the understanding of their prudent men shall be hid.

Verse ten above suggests that the type or symbol of a "deep sleep" actually means "a people without prophets and seers to guide them"—namely during a period of Spiritual Famine. Therefore, it would follow that the restoration of Zion back to the earth in the latter days would be accompanied by the Lord's calling of a new prophet to guide his people. It should be noted that verses 11 and 12 seem to suggest that there may be a conflict between this newly-called prophet and the learned men of the earth at the time of the restoration. This new prophet, when he is called forth, will likely cause much controversy, and he will probably be greatly opposed by the established religious orders of the day. That which is done by him will be "a marvelous work and a wonder."

Isaiah 44:1-4

1 YET now hear, O Jacob my servant; and Israel, whom I have chosen:
2 Thus saith the LORD that made thee, and formed thee from the womb, which will help thee; Fear not, O Jacob, my servant; and thou, Jesurun, whom I have chosen.
3 For I will pour water upon him that is thirsty, and floods upon the dry ground: I will pour my spirit upon thy seed, and my blessing upon thine offspring:
4 And they shall spring up as among the grass, as willows by the water courses.

Isaiah 29:24

24 They also that erred in spirit shall come to understanding, and they that murmured shall learn doctrine.

Those that join themselves to the restored Zion of the last days will not only have access to the spirit to better interpret the writings of the ancient prophets, but they will most likely receive new knowledge as well. The Old Testament and the New Testament will no doubt be a part of the scriptural library of the modern-day Zion. If a new prophet or prophets are called, we should assume that these new prophets will help clarify and interpret the meaning found in the scriptures. The soundness of the doctrine of the restored Zion will be increased and fortified. If we accept the counsel of the Savior Jesus Christ: "Wherefore by their fruits ye shall know them" (Matthew 7:20), then the new doctrine might well be the fruits of the newly-called prophet or prophets in the latter days.

Isaiah 22:8-11
8 And he discovered the covering of Judah, and thou didst look in that day to the armour of the house of the forest.
9 Ye have seen also the breaches of the city of David, that they are many: and ye gathered together the waters of the lower pool.
10 And ye have numbered the houses of Jerusalem, and the houses have ye broken down to fortify the wall.
11 Ye made also a ditch between the two walls for the water of the old pool: but ye have not looked unto the maker thereof, neither had respect unto him that fashioned it long ago.

Adhering to the analogy between water and revelation, we see that, prior to the great period of Spiritual Famine, revelation was gathered from the "old pool" and it is used to sustain a belief in the Gospel of Jesus Christ. This refers to the Bible, since it contains the words of the ancient prophets, or the "old pool" or "old revelations." If the old pool corresponds to the Former Rain period, then we should expect to receive a "new pool"—a new collection of revelation descending from heaven during the period of the Latter Rain. While many people in the world respect the Bible, they do not look unto the "maker thereof, neither had respect unto him that fashioned it long ago." Instead they seek counsel among men.

Isaiah 8:19
19 And when they shall say unto you, Seek unto them that have familiar spirits, and unto wizards that peep, and that mutter: should not a people seek unto their God? for the living to the dead?

Throughout time, it has been a general tendency for people to accept deceased prophets, but it is much more difficult for them to accept living prophets. For example, at the time of Christ, the Jews gladly accepted the Old Testament scriptures as being holy, and they looked to the prophets such as Moses as being true prophets. But, many of them rejected John the Baptist, Jesus Christ, and his disciples. They never imagined that the actions, prophecies, and deeds of Jesus Christ and his disciples would ever be considered scripture. This same phenomenon might be present when Zion is restored in the last days. The clarification of the doctrines contained in the Bible, enhanced by personal revelation, in a sense creates a sure path to the true and newly restored Gospel. Isaiah represents this concept as the establishment of a highway leading out of Assyria and into Zion.

Isaiah 11:16
16 And there shall be an highway for the remnant of his people, which shall be left, from Assyria; like as it was to Israel in the day that he came up out of the land of Egypt.

Isaiah 30:21
21 And thine ears shall hear a word behind thee, saying, This is the way, walk ye in it, when ye turn to the right hand, and when ye turn to the left.

Isaiah 35:3-10
3 Strengthen ye the weak hands, and confirm the feeble knees.
4 Say to them that are of a fearful heart, Be strong, fear not: behold, your God will come with vengeance, even God with a recompence; he will come and save you.
5 Then the eyes of the blind shall be opened, and the ears of the deaf shall be unstopped.
6. Then shall the lame man leap as an hart, and the tongue of the dumb sing: for in the wilderness shall waters break out, and streams in the desert.
7 And the parched ground shall become a pool, and the thirsty land springs of water: in the habitation of dragons, where each lay, shall be grass with reeds and rushes.
8 And an highway shall be there, and a way, and it shall be called The way of holiness; the unclean shall not pass over it; but it shall be for those: the wayfaring men, though fools, shall not err therein.
9 No lion shall be there, nor any ravenous beast shall go up thereon, it shall not be found there; but the redeemed shall walk there:
10 And the ransomed of the LORD shall return, and come to Zion with songs and everlasting joy upon their heads: they shall obtain joy and gladness, and sorrow and sighing shall flee away.

After their long period of Spiritual Famine and bondage under the tyrant king of Assyria, the Lord of Hosts prepares a way for them to return and be gathered in unto Zion. It is a sure way. The way out of Assyria is sound doctrine—and those who follow it "though fools, shall not err therein." Personal revelation will thus abound in the latter days, guiding the faithful along their path through life.

Isaiah 12:3
3 Therefore with joy shall ye draw water out of the wells of salvation.

Isaiah 28:9-11
9 Whom shall he teach knowledge? And whom shall he make to understand doctrine? Them that are weaned from the milk, and drawn from the breasts.
10 For precept must be upon precept, precept upon precept; line upon line, line upon line; here a little, and there a little:
11 For with stammering lips and another tongue will he speak to this people.

These verses show the process whereby the Lord will lead his people along. It is precept upon precept, line upon line. Those who truly learn to recognize God's promptings in this manner are those that are "weaned from the milk." As one studies the Old Testament and the New Testament, the true followers of Christ receive the milk and have some understanding of the Gospel Plan from the milk of their previous religious experience. It is as if they have been given a bottle to feed them, and they develop and prepare themselves to receive more doctrine. Eventually, however, the individual must begin to learn doctrine directly from the Lord himself, through personal study and prayer.

The scriptures teach men and women to pray and as they do, the Lord's promptings distill upon their minds as the dew from Heaven. Those that diligently search the scriptures and pray directly to the Lord for help in solving problems and answering questions will be lead line upon line, and precept upon precept, until they encounter the restored Gospel, or Zion. In this way they are lead on

THE MESSAGE OF THE BOOK OF ISAIAH

the highway provided by the Lord for the dispersed of Israel, who are mingled among the nations of the world and held captive by Assyria.

Isaiah 42:16

16 And I will bring the blind by a way that they knew not; I will lead them in paths that they have not known: I will make darkness light before them, and crooked things straight. These things will I do unto them, and not forsake them.

Isaiah 43:18-20

18 Remember ye not the former things, neither consider the things of old.
19 Behold I will do a new thing; now it shall spring forth; shall ye not know it? I will even make a way in the wilderness, and rivers in the desert.
20 The beast of the field shall honour me, the dragons and the owls; because I give waters in the wilderness, and rivers in the desert, to give drink to my people, my chosen.

The chosen people of the Lord will recognize the new doctrines and revelations that spring forth. They will harken to the voice of the Lord's chosen prophets whom he shall call in the latter days. Finally, they will be guided by their own personal revelation that leads them along and brings them safely into the fold of God, or into Zion.

The Sword of the Lord

Isaiah uses imagery to illustrate the coming forth of Zion upon the earth, and the overthrow of Assyria, or kingdom of Satan, that has been allowed to overcome the entire earth during the period of the Great Famine. This process is symbolized in the Book of Isaiah by showing Zion as a fierce army marching forth in an offensive battle, gaining strength and power as it goes forward.

Isaiah 14:24-27

24 The Lord of hosts hath sworn, saying, Surely as I have thought, so shall it come to pass; and as I have purposed, so shall it stand:
25 That I will break the Assyrian in my land, and upon my mountains tread him under foot: then shall his yoke depart from off them, and his burden depart from off their shoulders.
26 This is the purpose that is purposed upon the whole earth: and this is the hand that is stretched out upon all nations.
27 For the Lord of hosts hath purposed, and who shall disannul it? And his hand is stretched out, and who shall turn it back?

Isaiah 10:24-34

24 Therefore thus saith the Lord God of hosts, O my people that dwellest in Zion, be not afraid of the Assyrian: he shall smite thee with a rod, and shall lift up his staff against thee, after the manner of Eqypt.
25 For yet a very little while, and the indignation shall cease, and mine anger in their destruction.
26 And the Lord of hosts shall stir up a scourge for him according to the slaughter of Midian at the rock of Oreb: and as his rod was upon the sea, so shall he lift it up after the manner of Egypt.
27 And it shall come to pass in that day, that his burden shall be taken away from off thy shoulder, and his yoke from off thy neck, and the yoke shall be destroyed because of the anointing.
28 He is come to Aiath, he is passed to Migron; at Michmash he hath laid up his carriages:
29 They are gone over the passage: they have taken up their lodging at Geba; Ramah is afraid; Gebeah of Saul is fled.
30 Lift up thy voice, O daughter of Gallim: cause it to be heard unto Laish, O poor Anthoth.

31 Madmenah is removed; the inhabitants of Gebim gather themselves to flee.
32 As yet shall he remain at Nob that day: he shall shake his hand against the mount of the daughter of Zion, the hill of Jerusalem.
33 Behold, the Lord, the Lord of hosts, shall lop the bough with terror: and the high ones of stature shall be hewn down, and the haughty shall be humbled.
34 And he shall cut down the thickets of the forest with iron, and Lebanon shall fall by a might one.

Here we are given the impression that the Lord's army is coming forth to "break the yoke" that the Assyrian has placed upon the chosen people of the Lord during the period of Great Famine. The Lord is marching forth with his forces from place to place, and as he does, the people are stirred up, and desire to flee away.

Isaiah 13:1-5

1 THE burden of Babylon, which Isaiah the son of Amoz did see.
2 Lift ye up a banner upon the high mountain, exalt the voice unto them, shake the hand, that they may go into the gates of the nobles.
3 I have commanded my sanctified ones, I have also called my mighty ones for mine anger, even them that rejoice in my highness.
4 The noise of a multitude in the mountains, like as of a great people; a tumultuous noise of the kingdoms of nations gathered together: the LORD of hosts mustereth the host of the battle.
5 They come from a far country, from the end of heaven, even the LORD, and the weapons of his indignation, to destroy the whole land.

The Lord assembles his army to go against the established nations. I wish to make clear that the army described in these verses is not a wicked force, but an army assembled by the Lord himself. He has called his "sanctified ones," and his "mighty ones." In verse four, we see plainly that it is the Lord of Hosts that has called this group of righteous soldiers to battle. Now, let us see what this righteous army does to those they encounter.

Isaiah 13:6-22

6 Howl ye; for the day of the LORD is at hand; it shall come as a destruction from the Almighty.
7 Therefore shall all hands be faint, and every man's heart shall melt:
8 And they shall be afraid: pangs and sorrows shall take hold of them; they shall be in pain as a woman that travaileth: they shall be amazed one at another; their faces shall be as flames.
9 Behold, the day of the LORD cometh, cruel both with wrath and fierce anger, to lay the land desolate: and he shall destroy the sinners thereof out of it.
10 For the stars of heaven and the constellations thereof shall not give their light: the sun shall be darkened in his going forth, and the moon shall not cause her light to shine.
11 And I will punish the world for their evil, and the wicked for their iniquity; and I will cause the arrogancy of the proud to cease, and will lay low the haughtiness of the terrible.
12 I will make a man more precious than fine gold; even a man than the golden wedge of Ophir.
13 Therefore I will shake the heavens, and the earth shall remove out of her place, in the wrath of the LORD of hosts, and in the day of his fierce anger.
14 And it shall be as the chased roe, and as a sheep that no man taketh up: they shall every man turn to his own people, and flee every one into his own land.
15 Every one that is found shall be thrust through; and every one that is joined unto them shall fall by the sword.
16 Their children also shall be dashed to pieces before their eyes; their houses shall be spoiled, and their wives ravished.

THE MESSAGE OF THE BOOK OF ISAIAH

17 Behold, I will stir up the Medes against them, which shall not regard silver; and as for gold, they shall not delight in it.
18 Their bows also shall dash the young men to pieces; and they shall have no pity on the fruit of the womb; their eye shall not spare children.
19 And Babylon, the glory of kingdoms, the beauty of the Chaldees' excellency, shall be as when God overthrew Sodom and Gomorrah.
20 It shall never be inhabited, neither shall it be dwelt in from generation to generation: neither shall the Arabian pitch tent there; neither shall the shepherds make their fold there.
21 But wild beasts of the desert shall lie there; and their houses shall be full of doleful creatures; and owls shall dwell there, and satyrs shall dance there.
22 And the wild beasts of the islands shall cry in their desolate houses, and dragons in their pleasant palaces: and her time is near to come, and her days shall not be prolonged.

In Isaiah 13, Babylon is synonymous with Assyria. They are both the kingdom and dominion of the devil. This chapter describes a fierce and gory battle in which the Lord's army is ruthless and cruel. For example, in verse 16 it says, "Their children also shall be dashed to pieces before their eyes; their houses shall be spoiled and their wives ravished." Again in 18, "Their bows also shall dash the young men to pieces; and they shall have no pity on the fruit of the womb; their eye shall not spare children." This scene of carnage might at first glance make God seem like an angry and mean God that takes pleasure in bloodshed, and who enjoys war and the spoils of war. The net result, however, is that the Lord's army is victorious and completely overthrows Babylon. Verse 20 makes this clear, "It shall never be inhabited, neither shall it be dwelt in from generation to generation..." Despite this overwhelming victory by the Lord's army, the cruelty and barbaric practices described in this overthrow are somewhat disturbing to those who prefer a kind, merciful God, which would be symbolized by the life of Jesus Christ when he was upon the earth.

This dilemma can be overcome when we realize that the war waged by the armies of Zion against Assyria or Babylon is not a physical war, but rather a spiritual battle. We miss this because we are too focused on the idea of war in the physical sense. This is how dual prophecy hides the meaning from those that would alter or remove such works from the scriptures. Once we realize that the prophet Isaiah is using the horrors of war to describe the conversion of souls, Isaiah's meaning is clarified at last. The Lord is after the spiritual conversion of the sinner, and the gathering of his lost children to himself.

Isaiah 2:1-5
1 THE word that Isaiah the son of Amoz saw concerning Judah and Jerusalem.
2 And it shall come to pass in the last days, that the mountain of the LORD's house shall be established in the top of the mountains, and shall be exalted above the hills; and all nations shall flow unto it.
3 And many people shall go and say, Come ye, and let us go up to the mountain of the LORD, to the house of the God of Jacob; and he will teach us of his ways, and we will walk in his paths: for out of Zion shall go forth the law, and the word of the LORD from Jerusalem.
4 And he shall judge among the nations, and shall rebuke many people: and they shall beat their swords into plowshares, and their spears into pruninghooks: nation shall not lift up sword against nation, neither shall they learn war any more.
5 O house of Jacob, come ye, and let us walk in the light of the LORD.

Here we see that "the mountain of the Lord's house shall be established in the top of the mountains, and shall be exalted above the hills, and all nations shall flow unto it." And later, "for out of Zion shall go forth the law, and the word of the Lord from Jerusalem." What is it that goes forth out of Zion? It is "the word of the Lord" that shall go forth from Zion, and it will cause people to "beat their swords into plowshares, and their spears into pruning hooks: nation shall not lift up sword against nation, neither shall they learn war any more." Hence, it is the clear intention of the Lord, and of the nation of Zion, to do away with war, not to delight in it. The flow of the word of the Lord unto the nations shall have the effect of a two-edged sword that cuts to the very center of the soul.

> Isaiah 30:31
> 31 For through the voice of the Lord shall the Assyrian be beaten down, which smote with a rod.

> Isaiah 5:26-29
> 26 And he will lift up an ensign to the nations from far, and will hiss unto them from the end of the earth: and, behold, they shall come with speed swiftly:
> 27 None shall be weary nor stumble among them; none shall slumber nor sleep; neither shall the girdle of their loins be loosed, nor the latchet of their shoes be broken:
> 28 Whose arrows are sharp, and all their bows bent, their horses' hoofs shall be counted like flint, and their wheels like a whirlwind:
> 29 Their roaring shall be like a lion, they shall roar like young lions: yea, they shall roar, and lay hold of the prey, and shall carry it away safe, and none shall deliver it.

In these passages, we learn that the Lord will beat down the Assyrian "through the voice of the Lord." The army of the Lord is really his legion of disciples or missionaries, which will come from afar with great speed. When it says that their arrows are sharp and all their bows bent, it means these servants are well-prepared. They have the word of God on the tip of their tongues, and their knowledge of the scriptures is well-developed and ready to be used to convert those held captive by the kingdom of Assyria. They are filled with the spirit of the Lord, which inspires them in the very moment they need it.

The key point is that "they shall roar like young lions: yea, they shall roar, and lay hold of the prey, and shall carry it away safe, and none shall deliver it." What lion is there on the earth that will "carry it away safe?" Most lions in nature will kill and devour their prey, but here we see that these young lions "carry it away safe." Isaiah uses the lion as a symbol of a missionary possessing the power of the Lord in his speech, and when one is "taken" by the power of the true doctrine, they are carried away "safe." This same concept is repeated elsewhere.

> Isaiah 19:22
> 22 And the Lord shall smite Egypt: he shall smite and heal it: and they shall return even to the Lord, and he shall be intreated of them, and shall heal them.

How can the Lord smite and yet heal? It is because the sword of the Lord is his word, and his true doctrine, that cuts asunder the doctrines of men (Egypt), as well as the doctrines of the devil (Assyria). Thus, he clarifies the doctrines floating around in the world among the many institutions and organizations.

THE MESSAGE OF THE BOOK OF ISAIAH

Isaiah 14:2
2 And the people shall take them, and bring them to their place: and the house of Israel shall possess them in the land of the Lord for servants and handmaids: and they shall take them captives, whose captives they were; and they shall rule over their oppressors.

Once Zion is again established and begins to flow forth into the earth, those that are converted and join this restored church will begin to have influence on their friends, associates, and family members that are still members of other institutions and organizations of men. Assyria, which has kept men and women from the truth, will lose members to Zion. Though Assyria will oppose the advance of Zion, it will be to no avail.

Isaiah 29:7-8
7 And the multitude of all the nations that fight against Ariel, even all that fight against her and her munition, and that distress her, shall be as a dream of a night vision.
8 It shall even be as when an hungry man dreameth, and, behold, he eateth; but he awaketh, and his soul is empty: or as when a thirsty man dreameth, and, behold, he drinketh; but he awaketh, and, behold, he is faint, and his soul hath appetite: so shall the multitude of all the nations be, that fight against mount Zion.

Remember that Ariel here means Jerusalem, or Zion. Those from other religions that oppose the true doctrine of the restored Church of God will do so to their own detriment. In the end, they will think that they are in the Church of God, but when they awaken in the hereafter, they will see that they were mistaken. It will be like a dream that they had eaten, yet when they awaken they are still hungry; or that they drank, and awaken with a severe thirst.

The point here is to show that the warfare of the Lord is a spiritual warfare. In the cruel descriptions of Isaiah 13 above, when the Lord shall "destroy the sinners thereof out of it" it is because he will convert the sinner, and heal him. When "their children also shall be dashed to pieces before their eyes," it means that the children of a family shall join the true Church and their parents will see it as a horrible thing—like they have been dashed to pieces before their eyes.

Isaiah 31:8-9
8 Then shall the Assyrian fall with the sword, not of a mighty man; and the sword, not of a mean man, shall devour him: but he shall flee from the sword, and his young men shall be discomfited.
9 And he shall pass over to his strong hold for fear, and his princes shall be afraid of the ensign, saith the LORD, whose fire is in Zion, and his furnace in Jerusalem.

The same idea is brought forth here. Those held captive in the false doctrines of the world "shall flee from the sword (or the true doctrine of the Lord), and his young men shall be discomfited." In other words, a man's children shall join the restored Church of Christ, and the father will oppose them. Yet, later even the father himself might be taken by the true doctrine. Thus, mighty Zion advances through the earth, sparing neither the young nor the old.

Isaiah 30:27-31
27 Behold, the name of the LORD cometh from far, burning with his anger, and the burden thereof is heavy: his lips are full of indignation, and his tongue as a devouring fire:
28 And his breath, as an overflowing stream, shall reach to the midst of the neck, to sift the nations with the sieve of vanity: and there shall be a bridle in the jaws of the people, causing them to err.

29 Ye shall have a song, as in the night when a holy solemnity is kept; and gladness of heart, as when one goeth with a pipe to come into the mountain of the LORD, to the mighty One of Israel.
30 And the LORD shall cause his glorious voice to be heard, and shall shew the lighting down of his arm, with the indignation of his anger, and with the flame of a devouring fire, with scattering, and tempest, and hailstones.
31 For through the voice of the LORD shall the Assyrian be beaten down, which smote with a rod.

The preaching of the word of God is what ultimately breaks down Assyria and annihilates the sinner out of the earth, not swords, bombs, or other conventional weapons of war.

Isaiah 52:7
7 How beautiful upon the mountains are the feet of him that bringeth good tidings, that, publisheth peace; that bringeth good tidings of good, that publisheth salvation; that saith unto Zion, Thy God reigneth!

Jesus Christ is the God that reigneth. He is Jehovah, the God of both the Old and New Testaments, and he is the Savior of the World. Zion is his Kingdom and dominion, and Israel his chosen people. The central message of the Book of Isaiah is really the remission of sins, and salvation through the gift and power of the Savior, Jesus Christ.

Isaiah 9:6
6 For unto us a child is born, unto us a son is given: and the government shall be upon his shoulder: and his name shall be called Wonderful, Counsellor, The mighty God, The everlasting Father, The Prince of Peace.

Isaiah 28:16
16 Therefore thus saith the Lord God, Behold, I lay in Zion for a foundation a stone, a tried stone, a precious corner stone, a sure foundation: he that believeth shall not make haste.

Isaiah 43:25
25 I, even I, am he that blotteth out thy transgressions for mine own sake, and will not remember thy sins.

Isaiah 50:6
6 I gave my back to the smiters, and my cheeks to them that plucked off the hair: I hid not my face from shame and spitting.

When Jesus Christ came to the earth in the meridian of time, the Israelites were expecting a military and political leader that would free Israel from bondage and reestablish the nation of Israel as an autonomous kingdom. When questioned by Pilate concerning the nature of his Kingdom: "Jesus answered, My Kingdom is not of this world: if my Kingdom were of this world, then would my servants fight, that I should not be delivered to the Jews: but now is my Kingdom not from hence" (John 18:36). This is a key issue to bear in mind when reading Isaiah. The battles and conflicts depicted in Isaiah are seemingly out of character for the Lord Jesus Christ, until one makes the connection that they are figurative and represent the spiritual cleansing of the earth through the preaching of the word of God.

THE MESSAGE OF THE BOOK OF ISAIAH

This is not to say that religious wars and actual bloodshed involving the establishment of Zion or the return of the Jews to Jerusalem in the latter days will not also occur. Nor does it mean that the Lord will not physically slay the wicked that fight against Zion. Certainly there will be such conflicts. The narrative brought forth and developed throughout the Book of Isaiah is figurative, not literal. The king of Assyria is allowed to overcome the whole earth and have dominion over every nation: this is a figurative event that describes Satan's temporary triumph over the Church of God, or Zion—namely, the period of the Great Famine when no prophets or seers are found upon the earth. Isaiah makes it clear that the Lord allowed this to happen. The king of Assyria is thus used by the Lord to punish Israel for its many sins and iniquities. Furthermore, Isaiah makes it fairly clear that once a prophet is called and Zion springs forth again on the earth, it will never again fall back into a state of apostasy.

Isaiah 13:19-20

19 And Babylon, the glory of kingdoms, the beauty of the Chaldees' excellency, shall be as when God overthrew Sodom and Gomorrah.
20 It shall never be inhabited, neither shall it be dwelt in from generation to generation: neither shall the Arabian pitch tent there; neither shall the shepherds make their fold there.

Isaiah 37:33-35

33 Therefore thus saith the LORD concerning the king of Assyria, He shall not come into this city, nor shoot an arrow there, nor come before it with shields, nor cast a bank against it.
34 By the way that he came, by the same shall he return, and shall not come into this city, saith the LORD.
35 For I will defend this city to save it for mine own sake, and for my servant David's sake.

Isaiah 54:7-10

7 For a small moment have I forsaken thee; but with great mercies will I gather thee.
8 In a little wrath I hid my face from thee for a moment; but with everlasting kindness will I have mercy on thee, saith the LORD thy Redeemer.
9 For this is as the waters of Noah unto me: for as I have sworn that the waters of Noah should no more go over the earth; so have I sworn that I would not be wroth with thee, nor rebuke thee.
10 For the mountains shall depart, and the hills be removed; but my kindness shall not depart from thee, neither shall the covenant of my peace be removed, saith the LORD that hath mercy on thee.

Just as the Lord swore in the time of Noah that a flood would never again come upon the earth to destroy it, likewise, the period of the Great Spiritual Famine will only occur once. Once restored in the latter times, the Kingdom of Zion shall never be overcome again, but shall roll forth upon the earth until it consumes all falsehood and the Lord himself comes to rule and reign in righteousness. We can have complete confidence that the succession of prophets leading Zion forward through time will continue forever with Jesus Christ himself as the head.

We have observed and noted several types and symbols, which we can now look for in the many other books that make up the Holy Bible. First and foremost is the concept of water being symbolic of revelation. Such references include rain, dew, rivers, streams, fountains, etc. When water is brought forth and present in Israel, this represents a period where prophets are found in Zion, and the priesthood authority of God is also present and active in its execution among the children of men. Zion will not only have prophets to guide and direct her paths during periods when rain is abundant, but the people will receive personal revelation as well.

In contrast, during periods of dearth or famine, when no rain is had and the rivers are dried up, Zion is not found on the earth. The people faint without prophets to guide and direct them, and they are left to fend for themselves, being supported only by the manna of the scriptures left over from former periods of time when prophets were found on the earth. This same symbolic representation extends itself to a lack of food and the resulting hunger as well as a lack of water and the resulting thirst. Therefore, we will look for this same type of symbolism as we continue our study of the Bible.

The second principle symbolic type brought forth in Isaiah's writings deals with the idea of war and opposition. The king of Assyria is introduced as a mighty tyrannical leader who is allowed by God to consume and subject all the nations of the earth to his dominion and power. Because of transgression and wickedness, Israel is no exception to this cursed prediction. Isaiah foretells the overthrow of Zion by the devil and his agents, leading to a long period of captivity for God's chosen people as they are dispersed and held captive by this evil power. We saw that this battle between Zion and the devil is a spiritual conflict and not an actual physical war. The horrific scenes described in the scriptures are symbolic of the spiritual struggle that we experience here on earth. We will look for other references outside of Isaiah that show a tyrannical power being allowed to conquer all nations.

We will see that the Lord's prophets often mention Israel being overcome by both the sword and the famine. The sword in this case represents the persecution and false doctrines that beat down the children of Israel and lead them away from the truth. This sword is wielded by Satan, the ultimate tyrant king, as personified in the character of the king of Assyria. Repeatedly, we will see that those that survive the sword will be taken by the famine "until there are none to bury the dead." Those that are not overcome by the false doctrines and persecution will ultimately be overcome because of the withdrawal of the Lord's servants, the prophets. Without living prophets to guide and clarify, the good people of the earth cannot help being led astray into the way of falsehood.

Isaiah 51:18-19

18 There is none to guide her among all the sons whom she hath brought forth; neither is there any that taketh her by the hand of all the sons that she hath brought up.
19 These two things are come unto thee; who shall be sorry for thee? desolation, and destruction, and the famine, and the sword: by whom shall I comfort thee?

The subjection of Israel to bondage under the wicked king of Assyria, or the devil, leads to the dark period of Spiritual Famine. Historically, it is not necessarily ironic that the period of time following the mortal ministry of Jesus Christ on the earth is often referred to as the Dark Ages. This imagery points to another important symbolic representation found in Isaiah, namely, the use of light and darkness to convey the presence or absence of God's influence on the earth, respectively. For example, Isaiah 9:2 says, "The people that walked in darkness have seen a great light: they that dwell in the land of the shadow of death, upon them hath the light shined." This too is a type that we can look for in other books of the Bible as we move forward in our discussion. All of these major symbolic types were employed by Isaiah to prophesy of an event that would befall man during the middle period of the earth's history. In this manner, the Book of Isaiah serves as a key to unlock Bible prophesies that are relevant today.

The Stated Mission of Isaiah

Isaiah 49:1-4

1 LISTEN, O isles, unto me; and hearken, ye people, from far; The LORD hath called me from the womb; from the bowels of my mother hath he made mention of my name.
2 And he hath made my mouth like a sharp sword; in the shadow of his hand hath he hid me, and made me a polished shaft; in his quiver hath he hid me;
3 And said unto me, Thou art my servant, O Israel, in whom I will be glorified.
4 Then I said, I have laboured in vain, I have spent my strength for nought, and in vain: yet surely my judgment is with the LORD, and my work with my God.

From Isaiah 49, we learn that Isaiah was called from the womb for a specific purpose that is important to the Lord. Furthermore, we see that Isaiah's testimony will serve as a sharp sword, but that, apparently for years, his testimony remains hidden through the use of symbolic rhetoric. While some feel this refers to all of Israel due to the wording in verse three, "Thou art my servant, O Israel," it is actually referring to Isaiah personally. Isaiah the prophet is the one that is hid in the shadow of the Lord's hand. The meaning of his writings will have the effect of a polished shaft, hidden in the quiver of the Lord. The true meaning of Isaiah's message has been reserved for these the last days, and for the period of the Latter Rain. The idea of Isaiah's message being withheld for a period of time can be seen in the following citation:

Isaiah 6:8-12

8 Also I heard the voice of the Lord, saying, Whom shall I send, and who will go for us? Then said I, Here am I; send me.
9 And he said, Go, and tell this people, Hear ye indeed, but understand not; and see ye indeed, but perceive not.
10 Make the heart of this people fat, and make their ears heavy, and shut their eyes; lest they see with their eyes, and hear with their ears, and understand with their heart, and convert, and be healed.
11 Then said I, Lord, how long? And he answered, Until the cities be wasted without inhabitant, and the houses without man, and the land be utterly desolate,
12 And the LORD have removed men far away, and there be a great forsaking in the midst of the land.

Even Isaiah himself asks the Lord: "How long?" The Lord responds that it will be until "the land be utterly desolate." From our previous analysis, we know that wilderness and desolation are types describing the Great Spiritual Famine period. Isaiah's intended meaning is withheld from the people until the last days. So much time passes between the day he wrote the Book of Isaiah until it is finally brought to light that even Isaiah himself questions whether his work has been wrought in vain. It frustrates the prophet that no one is able to perceive the meaning of his writings since the Lord is withholding his precious rain of revelation.

> Isaiah 48:16-19
>
> 16 Come ye near unto me, hear ye this; I have not spoken in secret from the beginning; from the time that it was, there am I: and now the Lord GOD, and his Spirit, hath sent me.
> 17 Thus saith the LORD, thy Redeemer, the Holy One of Israel; I am the LORD thy God which teacheth thee to profit, which leadeth thee by the way that thou shouldest go.
> 18 O that thou hadst hearkened to my commandments! then had thy peace been as a river, and thy righteousness as the waves of the sea:
> 19 Thy seed also had been as the sand, and the offspring of thy bowels like the gravel thereof; his name should not have been cut off nor destroyed from before me.

Isaiah's message has always been before man, but now the Lord God and his Spirit is sending Isaiah's message forth to guide the children of Israel home. Had their fathers been righteous and not rejected the prophets, the entire dark period of Spiritual Famine could have been avoided. In the next verses, we see Isaiah's purpose reiterated, thanks to the understanding of the symbolic keys which we have previously defined.

> Isaiah 49:5-6
>
> 5 And now, saith the LORD that formed me from the womb to be his servant, to bring Jacob again to him, Though Israel be not gathered, yet shall I be glorious in the eyes of the LORD, and my God shall be my strength.
> 6 And he said, It is a light thing that thou shouldest be my servant to raise up the tribes of Jacob, and to restore the preserved of Israel: I will also give thee for a light to the Gentiles, that thou mayest be my salvation unto the end of the earth.

Herein, we see that Isaiah's special mission is to "raise up the tribes of Jacob, and to restore the preserved of Israel." Furthermore, the Lord says to Isaiah in verse six, "I will also give thee for a light to the Gentiles, that thou mayest be my salvation unto the end of the earth." Therefore, Isaiah's mission is closely linked to the restoration of the children of Israel to their former greatness, and their closeness to the Lord. Isaiah also seems to have a special calling to communicate not only to the Jews, but even more specifically to the Gentiles, or non-Jews, to clarify doctrine and lead them to truth.

> Isaiah 49:7-10
>
> 7 Thus saith the LORD, the Redeemer of Israel, and his Holy One, to him whom man despiseth, to him whom the nation abhorreth, to a servant of rulers, Kings shall see and arise, princes also shall worship, because of the LORD that is faithful, and the Holy One of Israel, and he shall choose thee.
> 8 Thus saith the LORD, In an acceptable time have I heard thee, and in a day of salvation have I helped thee: and I will preserve thee, and give thee for a covenant of the people, to establish the earth, to cause to inherit the desolate heritages;
> 9 That thou mayest say to the prisoners, Go forth; to them that are in darkness, Shew yourselves. They shall feed in the ways, and their pastures shall be in all high places.
> 10 They shall not hunger nor thirst; neither shall the heat nor sun smite them: for he that hath mercy on them shall lead them, even by the springs of water shall he guide them.

THE MESSAGE OF THE BOOK OF ISAIAH

Once the code of symbolic types found in Isaiah is made clear, the testimony of Isaiah suddenly has the effect of calling Jacob's offspring out of darkness. From our previous analysis, we know that springs of water means they will be guided by personal revelation toward the true doctrine of the Lord. Likewise, he will restore the priesthood and call forth new servants to administer the ordinances of salvation. Prophets shall again be called forth, having power and authority given them directly from God, and they will once again speak the will of God to his children on the earth. For this reason, the Book of Isaiah has a powerful purpose. It has been kept hidden to protect it from being altered by those wishing to corrupt the right ways of the Lord. But, "in an acceptable time," Isaiah is able to clearly indicate to the readers of the Bible just what has been predicted, and why it came to pass.

The Book of Isaiah is a critical link to understanding the ancient scriptures, leading the reader of the Bible to an important paradigm shift in his thinking. Rather than viewing God's dealings with man as one unbroken chain of events, we can now see that, as predicted, there was the Former Rain period when God was actively engaged in the affairs of men and women through his servants, the prophets. During the middle period, the Lord withdraws his prophets and revelation from the earth, leading to a great period of famine when man is left to himself to interpret doctrine, and the devil thus has complete dominion over the earth. Finally, the time comes for the glorious dispensation of the Latter Rain, when Zion is restored to the earth by the Lord. Prophets are again called, and the literal gathering of Israel begins, leading up to the Second Coming of Jesus Christ. Let us now look for this important message in other books of the Bible.

CHAPTER FIVE

The Book of Jeremiah and His Lamentations

Applying the information we gathered from Isaiah, we may now approach the Book of Jeremiah, as well as his Book of Lamentations, and look for similar references, types, and symbols. Let us first start with the concept of the kingdom of Assyria. Jeremiah mentions both Assyria and Babylon in his writings. While historical records show Assyria to have actually conquered the Northern Ten Tribes of Ephraim, and later for Babylon to have actually conquered Judah and carried it captive, the symbolic meaning of these events runs much deeper. Jeremiah refers to both of these nations as enemies of Israel and Judah, but he uses them interchangeably. Applying our key to this type from Isaiah, we may cease to focus on the original physical calamity that befell Israel and Judah. Instead, we may assume that when Jeremiah mentions Babylon or Assyria, it is a dual prophecy. His principle meaning for the reader in the last days is that Assyria and Babylon both represent the kingdom of the devil—his churches and institutions. Let us examine the text for examples of such references.

Assyria, Babylon, and Apostasy

Jeremiah 2:14-19

14 Is Israel a servant? is he a homeborn slave? why is he spoiled?
15 The young lions roared upon him, and yelled, and they made his land waste: his cities are burned without inhabitant.
16 Also the children of Noph and Tahapanes have broken the crown of thy head.
17 Hast thou not procured this unto thyself, in that thou hast forsaken the LORD thy God, when he led thee by the way?
18 And now what hast thou to do in the way of Egypt, to drink the waters of Sihor? or what hast thou to do in the way of Assyria, to drink the waters of the river?
19 Thine own wickedness shall correct thee, and thy backslidings shall reprove thee: know therefore and see that it is an evil thing and bitter, that thou hast forsaken the LORD thy God, and that my fear is not in thee, saith the Lord GOD of hosts.

In verses 14 and 15 above, we see early on in the Book of Jeremiah that Israel is spoiled and appears to be living now as a servant or slave. He is "spoiled," and his enemies have "made his land waste: his cities are burned without inhabitant." The ancient event is literal, while the event impacting our day is spiritual. In verse 18, we see to whom Israel has become a slave: Egypt and Assyria. In verse 16, we see that even the crown of his head is broken. The breaking of the crown on the head of Israel suggests that not only has Israel been driven into falsehood and spoiled, but the succession of its kings has also been broken or interrupted.

Jeremiah 2:36

36 Why gaddest thou about so much to change thy way? thou also shalt be ashamed of Egypt, as thou wast ashamed of Assyria.

Jeremiah 4:5-13

5 Declare ye in Judah, and publish in Jerusalem; and say, Blow ye the trumpet in the land: cry, gather together, and say, Assemble yourselves, and let us go into the defenced cities.
6 Set up the standard toward Zion: retire, stay not: for I will bring evil from the north, and a great destruction.
7 The lion is come up from his thicket, and the destroyer of the Gentiles is on his way; he is gone forth from his place to make thy land desolate; and thy cities shall be laid waste, without an inhabitant.
8 For this gird you with sackcloth, lament and howl: for the fierce anger of the LORD is not turned back from us.
9 And it shall come to pass at that day, saith the LORD, that the heart of the king shall perish, and the heart of the princes; and the priests shall be astonished, and the prophets shall wonder.
10 Then said I, Ah, Lord GOD! surely thou hast greatly deceived this people and Jerusalem, saying, Ye shall have peace; whereas the sword reacheth unto the soul.
11 At that time shall it be said to this people and to Jerusalem, A dry wind of the high places in the wilderness toward the daughter of my people, not to fan, nor to cleanse,
12 Even a full wind from those places shall come unto me: now also will I give sentence against them.
13 Behold, he shall come up as clouds, and his chariots shall be as a whirlwind: his horses are swifter than eagles. Woe unto us! for we are spoiled.

Jeremiah repeats the imagery of Judah being spoiled. His lands are made desolate, and his cities laid waste, without inhabitant. When he repeats the phrase, "without inhabitant," we get the feeling that no one, not one single soul, will survive this siege. This is consistent with Isaiah's description of Assyria conquering the entire world while Zion is reduced to nothing. However, it is not consistent with the literal events: the northern conquest of Israel by the Assyrians, or the southern conquest of Judah by Babylon.

From Jeremiah 4:7 above, we see who is doing the figurative conquering of Judah and Jerusalem. It is the same tyrant king that overcame Ephraim in the Book of Isaiah, "the destroyer of the Gentiles [or Ephraim] is on his way; he is gone forth from his place to make thy land desolate; and thy cities shall be laid waste, without an inhabitant." The Prophet Jeremiah is telling the Jews that they too will fall from grace, and lose the authority and power they hold, just as did their brethren to the north (Ephraim). Isaiah calls the devil the king of Assyria, while Jeremiah refers to him as the king of Babylon. They are the same being, Satan. We miss this spiritual meaning when our minds are too fixed on the ancient physical siege that was waged against these two principal families of Israel, Ephraim and Judah.

THE LATTER RAIN

Jeremiah 4:20

20 Destruction upon destruction is cried; for the whole land is spoiled: suddenly are my tents spoiled, and my curtains in a moment.

Jeremiah 6:22-26

22 Thus saith the LORD, Behold, a people cometh from the north country, and a great nation shall be raised from the sides of the earth.
23 They shall lay hold on bow and spear; they are cruel, and have no mercy; their voice roareth like the sea; and they ride upon horses, set in array as men for war against thee, O daughter of Zion.
24 We have heard the fame thereof: our hands wax feeble: anguish hath taken hold of us, and pain, as of a woman in travail.
25 Go not forth into the field, nor walk by the way; for the sword of the enemy and fear is on every side.
26 O daughter of my people, gird thee with sackcloth, and wallow thyself in ashes: make thee mourning, as for an only son, most bitter lamentation: for the spoiler shall suddenly come upon us.

Jeremiah serves as the voice of warning to Jerusalem. He warns them that they are about to be spoiled. The spoil and the waste come as a contradiction to what the wicked prophets and priests in Israel have told the people. In contrast to Jeremiah's prophecies, we will see in the following verses that the false prophets of his time were predicting that Israel would remain at peace.

Jeremiah 14:13-16

13 Then said I, Ah, Lord GOD! behold, the prophets say unto them, Ye shall not see the sword, neither shall ye have famine; but I will give you assured peace in this place.
14 Then the LORD said unto me, The prophets prophesy lies in my name: I sent them not, neither have I commanded them, neither spake unto them: they prophesy unto you a false vision and divination, and a thing of nought, and the deceit of their heart.
15 Therefore thus saith the LORD concerning the prophets that prophesy in my name, and I sent them not, yet they say, Sword and famine shall not be in this land; By sword and famine shall those prophets be consumed.
16 And the people to whom they prophesy shall be cast out in the streets of Jerusalem because of the famine and the sword; and they shall have none to bury them, them, their wives, nor their sons, nor their daughters: for I will pour their wickedness upon them.

Here, Jeremiah not only mentions the sword, but also famine. He states that, contrary to the word of the false prophets in Israel, the Lord will allow Israel to be overcome and swallowed up by an attacking enemy. This would therefore correspond to the sword of justice we saw from Isaiah, namely persecution and false teachings. He also states that the survivors of the sword will perish by famine. We saw from the writings of Isaiah that the symbolic representation of famine would mean that revelation and direction from the Lord would cease—no prophets, no priesthood, no guidance. As he stated earlier that Israel would be without inhabitant, here he states the same thing by saying in verse 16 that the victims of the famine and the sword will "have none to bury them." The victory of this enemy is complete and all-encompassing, allowing no small pocket of Israel to remain. While an actual famine is described in the Book of Jeremiah, and Jerusalem is actually destroyed by Babylon and the children of Israel carried away captive, the symbolic representation of these historical events is of even greater significance.

THE BOOK OF JEREMIAH AND HIS LAMENTATIONS

During the historically recorded siege (the carrying away of the Jews into Babylon), the priesthood was preserved as manifested through prophets and priests that lived in Babylon during this period (e.g., Daniel). During the symbolic siege, however (the spiritual siege on Judah by Satan and his servants), no one is left at all who holds the priesthood or who receives revelation from God. Thus, the historical event has a great symbolic significance.

Jeremiah 21:7

7 And afterward, saith the LORD, I will deliver Zedekiah king of Judah, and his servants, and the people, and such as are left in this city from the pestilence, from the sword, and from the famine, into the hand of Nebuchadrezzar king of Babylon, and into the hand of their enemies, and into the hand of those that seek their life: and he shall smite them with the edge of the sword; he shall not spare them, neither have pity, nor have mercy.

Even those that appeared to be spared for a moment are ultimately swallowed up by the king of Babylon. Again, we need to differentiate between the historic events being described and the spiritual overthrow that occurs later. The actual event becomes a type of the spiritual event, or dual prophecy. Because they would not have the Lord to be their King, they will be given over to this evil king, who Jeremiah represents as Nebuchadnezzar, king of Babylon, and who Isaiah represented as the king of Assyria. They are one and the same. They both represent the devil. Their kingdoms represent the devil's churches, organizations, and false doctrines. During the great period of apostasy that covers the entire earth, the literal descendants of Israel will be made to serve as slaves and prisoners to this evil, conquering nation, contrary to the predictions of the false prophets of Jeremiah's day.

Jeremiah 28:12-14

12 Then the word of the LORD came unto Jeremiah the prophet, after that Hananiah the prophet had broken the yoke from off the neck of the prophet Jeremiah, saying,
13 Go and tell Hananiah, saying, Thus saith the LORD; Thou hast broken the yokes of wood; but thou shalt make for them yokes of iron.
14 For thus saith the LORD of hosts, the God of Israel; I have put a yoke of iron upon the neck of all these nations, that they may serve Nebuchadnezzar king of Babylon; and they shall serve him: and I have given him the beasts of the field also.

Lamentations 1:8-11

8 Jerusalem hath grievously sinned; therefore she is removed: all that honoured her despise her, because they have seen her nakedness: yea, she sigheth, and turneth backward.
9 Her filthiness is in her skirts; she remembereth not her last bend; therefore she came down wonderfully: she had no comforter. O LORD, behold my affliction: for the enemy hath magnified himself.
10 The adversary hath spread out his hand upon all her pleasant things: for she hath seen that the heathen entered into her sanctuary, whom thou didst command that they should not enter into thy congregation.
11 All her people sigh, they seek bread; they have given their pleasant things for meat to relieve the soul: see, O LORD, and consider; for I am become vile.

Jeremiah is completely clear, and reiterates this point over and over again. The king of Babylon will come and destroy this land. In the Lamentations of Jeremiah, Chapter 1, verse ten, it is further clarified. Jeremiah, referring to Jerusalem, states, "The adversary hath spread out his hand upon all her pleasant things: for she hath seen that the heathen entered into her sanctuary." In other words, Satan inspired unauthorized men to take the pleasant things of Israel or Jerusalem (the scriptures, ceremonies, ordinances, and traditions), and to pervert them in order to usurp power and dominion over the inhabitants of the world. Again, we witness the historical event of the Babylonian captivity, yet also see it as a type of the more profound event, the conquering of Zion by Babylon (the kingdom of the devil).

Jeremiah 50:17-20
17 Israel is a scattered sheep; the lions have driven him away: first the king of Assyria hath devoured him; and last this Nebuchadrezzar king of Babylon hath broken his bones.
18 Therefore thus saith the LORD of hosts, the God of Israel; Behold, I will punish the king of Babylon and his land, as I have punished the king of Assyria.
19 And I will bring Israel again to his habitation, and he shall feed on Carmel and Bashan, and his soul shall be satisfied upon mount Ephraim and Gilead.
20 In those days, and in that time, saith the LORD, the iniquity of Israel shall be sought for, and there shall be none; and the sins of Judah, and they shall not be found: for I will pardon them whom I reserve.

In these verses, Jeremiah mentions both Assyria and Babylon as being conquering nations. In the above verses, the Lord tells us through the prophet Jeremiah that "Israel is a scattered sheep," and that Assyria and Babylon are the culprits. Assyria destroys and scatters Ephraim to the north, while Babylon destroys and conquers Judah to the south. From the Isaiah analysis, we are able to understand that both Assyria and Babylon represent the kingdom of the devil. While the true priesthood and authority from God will remain with Judah for a time even after the Ten Northern Tribes are spoiled and lost, ultimately, even Judah will enter a state of apostasy as well. The prophets and true Church of God ultimately disappear from the earth entirely.

Fortunately, the Lord also reveals through Jeremiah that he will not forsake his people forever. Ultimately, he will return and bring them again to Zion. Therefore, the Lord allowed Assyria and Babylon to spoil first Ephraim and then Judah as a punishment for their wickedness. He promises, however, to one day reestablish or restore Zion to the earth. At that point, when Zion sprouts forth again, he will begin to fight against the devil and his doctrines and institutions.

Jeremiah 51:25-26
25 Behold, I am against thee, O destroying mountain, saith the LORD, which destroyest all the earth: and I will stretch out mine hand upon thee, and roll thee down from the rocks, and will make thee a burnt mountain.
26 And they shall not take of thee a stone for a corner, nor a stone for foundations; but thou shalt be desolate for ever, saith the LORD.

Just as the apostasy was complete, covering the whole earth, so will the restoration of Zion be complete when the Lord is done. Zion will spring up suddenly, begin to roll forth, and ultimately fill the earth with the true doctrine of God. The inhabitants of Assyria and Babylon will be thrust through by the sword of the Lord. Applying the Isaiah analysis, we recall that the sword of the

Lord is his word or the true doctrines of restored Zion. Thus, a person adhering to false doctrines and false religion will be thrust through by the truth and either be converted over to Zion, or remain in opposition to the true Gospel. Either way, in the end, the Lord himself will reign over Zion, which will have converted the entire earth over to a state of righteousness. This period of restoration and gathering in of the Lost Sheep of Israel represents the great dispensation of the Latter Rain, and will occur prior to the Second Coming of the Lord Jesus Christ.

Rain, Wilderness, Water, Famine

(Revelation Ceases and then Resumes Again)

We now turn our attention to Jeremiah's use of the symbol or type: water or rain. We learned from Isaiah and other citations in the Bible that when the Lord mentions rain or water in the scriptures, he is often referring to revelation, prophets, the true priesthood, and inspiration from God. In contrast, references to wilderness, famine, or desolation indicate periods when revelation, prophets, and priesthood authority from God are not found.

Jeremiah 10:13

13 When he uttereth his voice, there is a multitude of waters in the heavens, and he causeth the vapours to ascend from the ends of the earth; he maketh lightnings with rain, and bringeth forth the wind out of his treasures.

Like Isaiah, Jeremiah again establishes this symbolic type. We see clearly from Jeremiah 10:13 that references to water, vapor, rain, dew, etc., are really referring to the voice of the Lord coming forth upon the earth to inspire and guide man by sending the "waters in the heavens" and "the wind out of his treasures." The precipitation of this heavenly water thus represents God's revelation to man.

Jeremiah 2:12-13

12 Be astonished, O ye heavens, at this, and be horribly afraid, be ye very desolate, saith the LORD.
13 For my people have committed two evils; they have forsaken me the fountain of living waters, and hewed them out cisterns, broken cisterns, that can hold no water.

Jeremiah 2:30

30 In vain have I smitten your children; they received no correction: your own sword hath devoured your prophets, like a destroying lion.

What are the two evils committed by the Lord's people? First they have forsaken the Lord himself, or the true source of revelation and divine inspiration. The Lord God of Israel refers to himself as "the fountain of living waters." By rejecting the Lord's true prophets and killing them and driving them off, Israel is thus rejecting the true source of "living water." Once Zion is overcome by false doctrine and false priesthood and driven into a state of world-wide apostasy, the false leaders, prophets and priests create churches and institutions that are "broken." A cistern is generally defined as a large storage container designed to collect rain as it falls so that it can be used later during periods of no rain. Thus, the churches of men formed during this period are constructed based on their interpretation of the "old" revelations given to the deceased prophets, as contained

THE LATTER RAIN

in the Bible. However, without true and living prophets that receive guidance from "the fountain of living waters" in order to interpret the writings of deceased prophets, these false churches are unable to save their members. They lack the authority and revelation from God directly.

Jeremiah 3:3-4
3 Therefore the showers have been withholden, and there hath been no latter rain; and thou hadst a whore's forehead, thou refusedst to be ashamed.
4 Wilt thou not from this time cry unto me, My father, thou art the guide of my youth.

Here, Jeremiah shows that due to unfaithfulness, Israel is forsaken and "the showers have been withholden." While the Lord God was indeed Israel's "guide of my youth," without actual revelation from God to a living prophet, the Lord's chosen people are left to wander to and fro on the earth without his guidance. Furthermore, verse three introduces the term "latter rain," indicating that it hath been withheld. When we combine the ideas of Israel being guided in its youth by the Lord himself, and then hewing for itself "broken cisterns" during the period of apostasy when no "true and living" prophets are available to guide the people, the concept of a Latter Rain gives hope that eventually the Lord will again call a prophet on the earth to restore Zion. In the meantime, without rain, nothing can grow in the once fruitful ground.

Jeremiah 4:3
3 For thus saith the LORD to the men of Judah and Jerusalem, Break up your fallow ground, and sow not among thorns.

Jeremiah 4:26-29
26 I beheld, and, lo, the fruitful place was a wilderness, and all the cities thereof were broken down at the presence of the LORD, and by his fierce anger.
27 For thus hath the LORD said, The whole land shall be desolate; yet will I not make a full end.
28 For this shall the earth mourn, and the heavens above be black: because I have spoken it, I have purposed it, and will not repent, neither will I turn back from it.
29 The whole city shall flee for the noise of the horsemen and bowmen; they shall go into thickets, and climb up upon the rocks: every city shall be forsaken, and not a man dwell therein.

In the above verses, the Lord asks the men of Judah to break up their dormant ground. In other words, the land in which no fruits have been growing. Nothing has been happening. The Prophet Jeremiah sees that "the fruitful place" becomes a wilderness, "and all the cities thereof were broken down." Furthermore, the Lord said, "The whole land shall be desolate." Not just a part of the land, but the "whole" land. Yet, the Lord "will not make a full end." This statement gives hope and indicates that the Lord has not forsaken Israel forever. Before the "full end" of the world, the Lord God of Israel will again turn to Israel and Judah and gather them in from the four corners of the earth. During the Dark Ages of the period of apostasy, "every city [of Zion] shall be forsaken, and not a man dwell therein." Until the "latter rain" comes, no one can be found that belongs to the true Church or religion of God.

THE BOOK OF JEREMIAH AND HIS LAMENTATIONS

Jeremiah 5:12-18

12 They have belied the LORD, and said, It is not he; neither shall evil come upon us; neither shall we see sword nor famine:
13 And the prophets shall become wind, and the word is not in them: thus shall it be done unto them.
14 Wherefore thus saith the LORD God of hosts, Because ye speak this word, behold, I will make my words in thy mouth fire, and this people wood, and it shall devour them.
15 Lo, I will bring a nation upon you from far, O house of Israel, saith the LORD: it is a mighty nation, it is an ancient nation, a nation whose language thou knowest not, neither understandest what they say.
16 Their quiver is as an open sepulchre, they are all mighty men.
17 And they shall eat up thine harvest, and thy bread, which thy sons and thy daughters should eat: they shall eat up thy flocks and thine herds: they shall eat up thy vines and thy fig trees: they shall impoverish thy fenced cities, wherein thou trustedst, with the sword.
18 Nevertheless in those days, saith the LORD, I will not make a full end with you.

Jeremiah 5:30-31

30 A wonderful and horrible thing is committed in the land;
31 The prophets prophesy falsely, and the priests bear rule by their means; and my people love to have it so: and what will ye do in the end thereof?

Jeremiah 6:8-10

8 Be thou instructed, O Jerusalem, lest my soul depart from thee; lest I make thee desolate, a land not inhabited.
9 Thus saith the LORD of hosts, They shall throughly glean the remnant of Israel as a vine: turn back thine hand as a grapegatherer into the baskets.
10 To whom shall I speak, and give warning, that they may hear? behold, their ear is uncircumcised, and they cannot hearken: behold, the word of the LORD is unto them a reproach; they have no delight in it.

The people desire for the prophets to "become wind" and to "prophesy falsely," such that "the word is not in them." "My people love to have it so." Evidently, they desire this because the true prophets are continuously prophesying against the people, saying that both the sword and the famine will come upon them. Therefore, the Lord declares that the words of Jeremiah will become as a fire and the people wood. They will all be devoured by these predicted calamities (the sword of false doctrine and the famine of having prophets no longer available). The Lord and his "soul depart from thee." While this terrible event of the Lord withdrawing his prophets and saving ordinances from the people will cover the whole earth for a long period of time, in verse 18 we again see the Lord's mercy in that he will not end the earth while they are in this state of apostasy. The hope still exists for a Latter Rain to come and shower the earth with the "living water" or revelation of God.

Jeremiah 5:23-24

23 But this people hath a revolting and a rebellious heart; they are revolted and gone.
24 Neither say they in their heart, Let us now fear the LORD our God, that giveth rain, both the former and the latter, in his season: he reserveth unto us the appointed weeks of the harvest.

With the understanding that references to water or rain are really referring to revelation from God to actual living prophets, we see here that Jeremiah is making a differentiation between "the Former Rain," when God led his people in olden times through living, breathing prophets, and "the latter rain," when God will restore Zion to the earth, and once again speak to the inhabitants of the earth through "living" prophets, just as in times past. A great distinction exists between receiving guidance in real time from living prophets, and attempting to apply the wisdom of man to interpret the words of dead or deceased prophets. The words of God are like fire in the mouth of his true prophets, devouring false doctrines and the ideas of men like dried wood.

At the time of Jeremiah's prophecies, the Lord is about to withdraw his presence from Israel entirely, thus leaving the chosen people of the Lord stuck in the period of the Great Famine in the land. They become stuck between the period of the Former Rain and the period of the Latter Rain that will come in the latter days.

> **Jeremiah 8:13-14**
> 13 I will surely consume them, saith the LORD: there shall be no grapes on the vine, nor figs on the fig tree, and the leaf shall fade; and the things that I have given them shall pass away from them.
> 14 Why do we sit still? assemble yourselves, and let us enter into the defensed cities, and let us be silent there: for the LORD our God hath put us to silence, and given us water of gall to drink, because we have sinned against the LORD.

Instead of the living water, the Lord has allowed them to taste "water of gall," or the revelation and inspiration of the devil. Because they have sinned against the Lord in desiring his withdrawal, they are left completely alone without guidance or direction from God. Instead, they are persecuted and driven by the institutions of men.

> **Jeremiah 9:9-16**
> 9 Shall I not visit them for these things? saith the LORD: shall not my soul be avenged on such a nation as this?
> 10 For the mountains will I take up a weeping and wailing, and for the habitations of the wilderness a lamentation, because they are burned up, so that none can pass through them; neither can men hear the voice of the cattle; both the fowl of the heavens and the beast are fled; they are gone.
> 11 And I will make Jerusalem heaps, and a den of dragons; and I will make the cities of Judah desolate, without an inhabitant.
> 12 Who is the wise man, that may understand this? and who is he to whom the mouth of the LORD hath spoken, that he may declare it, for what the land perisheth and is burned up like a wilderness, that none passeth through?
> 13 And the LORD saith, Because they have forsaken my law which I set before them, and have not obeyed my voice, neither walked therein;
> 14 But have walked after the imagination of their own heart, and after Baalim, which their fathers taught them:
> 15 Therefore thus saith the LORD of hosts, the God of Israel; Behold, I will feed them, even this people, with wormwood, and give them water of gall to drink.
> 16 I will scatter them also among the heathen, whom neither they nor their fathers have known: and I will send a sword after them, till I have consumed them.

Here we see that the period of apostasy covers all people, and covers the whole earth such that no one can escape it. When the Lord allows his people to be overrun by falsehood, "the land perisheth and is burned up like a wilderness, that none passeth through." As cited before, because of their disobedience and unfaithfulness, the Lord vows to "give them water of gall to drink," as opposed to that which would have come from the "fountain of living waters" had they desired it. Due to their wickedness, the Lord not only scatters them among the heathen, but he sends a sword after them, till they are all consumed.

Jeremiah 9:25-26

25 Behold, the days come, saith the LORD, that I will punish all them which are circumcised with the uncircumcised;
26 Egypt, and Judah, and Edom, and the children of Ammon, and Moab, and all that are in the utmost corners, that dwell in the wilderness: for all these nations are uncircumcised, and all the house of Israel are uncircumcised in the heart.

Here we see that when the period of apostasy is in full force on the earth, then it will not matter one bit whether a man is circumcised or not. There becomes no difference between the children of Israel and the heathen, who already worship falsehood without revelation from God through living prophets. While the men of Israel may still be circumcised physically, they are uncircumcised in the heart. Hence, the withdrawal of the Lord is from all people and from all nations on the earth. He is nowhere to be found.

Jeremiah 10:19-22

19 Woe is me for my hurt! my wound is grievous: but I said, Truly this is a grief, and I must bear it.
20 My tabernacle is spoiled, and all my cords are broken: my children are gone forth of me, and they are not: there is none to stretch forth my tent any more, and to set up my curtains.
21 For the pastors are become brutish, and have not sought the LORD: therefore they shall not prosper, and all their flocks shall be scattered.
22 Behold, the noise of the bruit is come, and a great commotion out of the north country, to make the cities of Judah desolate, and a den of dragons.

While Jeremiah occasionally mentions Assyria and its conquering of Israel (the Northern Ten Tribes), he is more focused on Judah (the Southern Two Tribes) because he is living during the time of their being carried away into Babylon. While Isaiah mainly refers to Assyria and Jeremiah mainly to Babylon, figuratively speaking, these nations are one and the same. They refer to the kingdom of the devil, and their kings represent Satan himself.

Jeremiah 10:25

25 Pour out thy fury upon the heathen that know thee not, and upon the families that call not on thy name: for they have eaten up Jacob, and devoured him, and consumed him, and have made his habitation desolate.

Jeremiah 12:10-12

10 Many pastors have destroyed my vineyard, they have trodden my portion under foot, they have made my pleasant portion a desolate wilderness.
11 They have made it desolate, and being desolate it mourneth unto me; whole land is made desolate, because no man layeth it to heart.
12 The spoilers are come upon all high places through the wilderness: for the sword of the LORD shall devour from the one end of the land even to the other end of the land: no flesh shall have peace.

THE LATTER RAIN

Here, Jeremiah refers to Jacob as having been devoured and consumed, which gives the sense that all of the tribes of Israel (the sons of Jacob) are scattered. This seems to be a correct assumption seeing that "the Lord shall devour from one end of the land even to the other end of the land: no flesh shall have peace."

Jeremiah 13:13-17
13 Then shalt thou say unto them, Thus saith the LORD, Behold, I will fill all the inhabitants of this land, even the kings that sit upon David's throne, and the priests, and the prophets, and all the inhabitants of Jerusalem, with drunkenness.
14 And I will dash them one against another, even the fathers and the sons together, saith the LORD: I will not pity, nor spare, nor have mercy, but destroy them.
15 Hear ye, and give ear; be not proud: for the LORD hath spoken.
16 Give glory to the LORD your God, before he cause darkness, and before your feet stumble upon the dark mountains, and, while ye look for light, he turn it into the shadow of death, and make it gross darkness.
17 But if ye will not hear it, my soul shall weep in secret places for your pride; and mine eye shall weep sore, and run down with tears, because the LORD's flock is carried away captive.

Jeremiah 13:24
24 Therefore will I scatter them as the stubble that passeth away by the wind of the wilderness.

These verses in Chapter 13 of Jeremiah are significant for several reasons. First, they show that all the leaders of former Israel will be filled with drunkenness—the kings, the priests, the prophets, and all the inhabitants. We see again that when the Lord withdraws his presence from Israel, not one person is left that can "see straight." They are all drunk and stumble in the darkness.

Second, this theme of darkness is very similar to the concept of "living water" versus "water of gall" or "rain" versus "famine." The Lord is the light of the earth, and he shines in the darkness. In the above verses, he indicates that, during the period of apostasy or "dark ages," even though "ye look for light, he turn it into shadow of death, and make it gross darkness." While men seek for truth in the religions around them, nothing available to them on the earth during this period of time has any light in it. It cannot save, since it has not the authority from God to perform the saving ordinances. Its leaders are not appropriately authorized of God, so they cannot guide the people properly. This does not mean that all the leaders of these organizations are without good intentions, or that they never receive inspiration to help others. However, without the proper authority, they are limited in what they can do for others.

Finally, in Jeremiah 13:17, we see the concern and love that the Lord has for his people. Although he has given the children of Israel more than adequate warning of his pending withdrawal from their presence, the Lord's "soul shall weep in secret places for your pride; and mine eye shall weep sore, and run down with tears, because the LORD's flock is carried away captive." The sadness is accentuated by the fact that the Lord must weep in secret places, for he is gone into hiding. He is only giving his chosen people that which they have desired. They desired habitation with the heathen, and in sadness and bitterness of soul, the Lord finally goes away and weeps for his scattered flock.

THE BOOK OF JEREMIAH AND HIS LAMENTATIONS

Jeremiah 14:1-6
1 The word of the LORD that came to Jeremiah concerning the dearth.
2 Judah mourneth, and the gates thereof languish; they are black unto the ground; and the cry of Jerusalem is gone up.
3 And their nobles have sent their little ones to the waters: they came to the pits, and found no water; they returned with their vessels empty; they were ashamed and confounded, and covered their heads.
4 Because the ground is chapt, for there was no rain in the earth, the plowmen were ashamed, they covered their heads.
5 Yea, the hind also calved in the field, and forsook it, because there was no grass.
6 And the wild asses did stand in the high places, they snuffed up the wind like dragons; their eyes did fail, because there was no grass.

In the first verse cited above, the word dearth means "famine." This becomes clear from the context that follows in the subsequent verses. The children born in the subsequent generations after Zion has fallen away will seek to draw water from the wells left by their fathers, however, when they get to the pits, they find no water therein, and thus "they return with their vessels empty." The famine is so severe that the "ground is chapt, for there was no rain in the earth." They seek to find the truth from the scriptures and traditions left by their fathers, but without the divine guidance from truly inspired and living prophets, none of these children can understand completely how to find their God. They learn to partake in what seems like worship and what seems like religion, but it has no substance, and worst of all, it lacks the power to heal their souls through the saving ordinances of the holy priesthood.

Jeremiah 14:13-16
13 Then said I, Ah, Lord GOD! behold, the prophets say unto them, Ye shall not see the sword, neither shall ye have famine; but I will give you assured peace in this place.
14 Then the LORD said unto me, The prophets prophesy lies in my name: I sent them not, neither have I commanded them, neither spake unto them: they prophesy unto you a false vision and divination, and a thing of nought, and the deceit of their heart.
15 Therefore thus saith the LORD concerning the prophets that prophesy in my name, and I sent them not, yet they say, Sword and famine shall not be in this land; By sword and famine shall those prophets be consumed.
16 And the people to whom they prophesy shall be cast out in the streets of Jerusalem because of the famine and the sword; and they shall have none to bury them, them, their wives, nor their sons, nor their daughters: for I will pour their wickedness upon them.

As in previous citations of these same verses, the false prophets have prophesied lies to the people saying all is well. They promise the people of Israel that the sword and the famine will not reach them. Yet we know that Jeremiah disagrees with this opinion, and sees instead a terrible scene in which "the people to whom they prophesy shall be cast out in the streets of Jerusalem because of the famine and the sword." The saddest thing of all is that the children of these wicked Israelites are the ones that really pay the price for their parents' transgressions, "for I will pour their wickedness upon them." The subsequent generations will have the wickedness of their fathers and mothers poured upon them. They suffer greatly for the decisions that ancient Israel made to reject the prophets.

THE LATTER RAIN

Jeremiah 16:4
4 They shall die of grievous deaths; they shall not be lamented; neither shall they be buried; but they shall be as dung upon the face of the earth: and they shall be consumed by the sword, and by famine; and their carcases shall be meat for the fowls of heaven, and for the beasts of the earth.

Remember that the Lord does not desire to withdraw his prophets from the earth. During this awful period of dearth, the Lord again laments that it must be so.

Jeremiah 14:17-22
17 Therefore thou shalt say this word unto them; Let mine eyes run down with tears night and day, and let them not cease: for the virgin daughter of my people is broken with a great breach, with a very grievous blow.
18 If I go forth into the field, then behold the slain with the sword! And if I enter into the city, then behold them that are sick with famine! Yea, both the prophet and the priest go about into a land that they know not.
19 Hast thou utterly rejected Judah? hath thy soul lothed Zion? why hast thou smitten us, and there is no healing for us? we looked for peace, and there is no good; and for the time of healing, and behold trouble!
20 We acknowledge, O Lord, our wickedness, and the iniquity of our fathers: for we have sinned against thee.
21 Do not abhor us, for thy name's sake, do not disgrace the throne of thy glory: remember, break not thy covenant with us.
22 Are there any among the vanities of the Gentiles that can cause rain? or can the heavens give showers? art not thou he, O LORD our God? therefore we will wait upon thee: for thou hast made all these things.

These verses not only show the Lord's lament over the suffering of his people, but they also recognize that the Lord had at one point made a covenant with Israel, and with Judah and his companions. The Lord is reminding the fallen of his people that they must remember this covenant, and that they must not seek for a solution from "among the vanities of the Gentiles" for they cannot "cause rain." Instead, the Lord is waiting for the time when the descendants of the fallen tribes of Israel will finally look to the true source of inspiration, the Lord God himself. At some point, someone must cease from accepting the traditions and ideas propagated by man from one generation to the next concerning religion. There must come a day when someone among all the inhabitants of the earth actually looks to the Lord himself for divine inspiration and guidance.

Jeremiah 16:19-21
19 O LORD, my strength, and my fortress, and my refuge in the day of affliction, the Gentiles shall come unto thee from the ends of the earth, and shall say, Surely our fathers have inherited lies, vanity, and things wherein there is no profit.
20 Shall a man make gods unto himself, and they are no gods?
21 Therefore, behold, I will this once cause them to know, I will cause them to know mine hand and my might; and they shall know that my name is The LORD.

These verses reiterate the same concept. At some point, someone from among the Gentiles is able to recognize that what he sees in the scriptures and what he sees around him in the form of organized religion is not the same thing. The confusion will ultimately drive him to seek the Lord directly for clarification, at which point the Lord "will cause them to know mine hand and my might; and they shall know that my name is The Lord." The whole idea here is that either because of pride, ignorance, wickedness, or just plain indifference, people living during the dark period of apostasy are somehow content to trust in the arm of flesh, or in the vain religions and ideas that exist around them. They believe their parents and follow their traditions and beliefs. If they do happen to disagree with their parents' ideas on religion, instead of asking God directly, they either join themselves with the church or belief of a friend, or in some cases start their own system of belief based on what they have learned from the available scriptures. Still others allow their faith to wax cold due to the confusion, and they stop trying to find God in the religions of the day. In each of these cases, the missing link is direct communication with God for his opinion on the matter. When the truth comes to them, they dismiss it and settle for the status quo.

Jeremiah 17:5-8

5 Thus saith the LORD; Cursed be the man that trusteth in man, and maketh flesh his arm, and whose heart departeth from the LORD.
6 For he shall be like the heath in the desert, and shall not see when good cometh; but shall inhabit the parched places in the wilderness, in a salt land and not inhabited.
7 Blessed is the man that trusteth in the LORD, and whose hope the LORD is.
8 For he shall be as a tree planted by the waters, and that spreadeth out her roots by the river, and shall not see when heat cometh, but her leaf shall be green; and shall not be careful in the year of drought, neither shall cease from yielding fruit.

When we seek inspiration from the Lord directly, we are promised we shall be "as a tree planted by the waters." We will soak up the knowledge from the Lord as he distills his ideas and guidance into our hearts and into our minds. In contrast, if we only seek opinions from man, or from our friends, family members, and so forth, then we have no such promise. Because people were not taught to seek the Lord and instead rendered over to falsehood, many people stumbled in their way. Tradition or not, until a man or woman is able to see clearly the confusion, and seek clarification from God directly, the period of the Spiritual Famine continues and is prolonged on the earth.

Jeremiah 18:15-17

15 Because my people hath forgotten me, they have burned incense to vanity, and they have caused them to stumble in their ways from the ancient paths, to walk in paths, in a way not cast up;
16 To make their land desolate, and a perpetual hissing; every one that passeth thereby shall be astonished, and wag his head.
17 I will scatter them as with an east wind before the enemy: I will shew them the back, and not the face, in the day of their calamity.

These churches, religions, faiths and institutions all practice a form of ceremony or worship, but none of them have properly authorized prophets to guide and direct them, straight from the mouth of the Lord himself. Their practices and observances, whatever form they may take, in the end are like "burning incense to vanity, and they have caused them to stumble in their ways from the ancient paths."

THE LATTER RAIN

Jeremiah 18:21
21 Therefore deliver up their children to the famine, and pour out their blood by the force of the sword; and let their wives be bereaved of their children, and be widows; and let their men be put to death; let their young men be slain by the sword in battle.

Jeremiah 34:22
22 Behold, I will command, saith the LORD, and cause them to return to this city; and they shall fight against it, and take it, and burn it with fire: and I will make the cities of Judah a desolation without an inhabitant.

Jeremiah 23:20-21
20 The anger of the LORD shall not return, until he have executed, and till he have performed the thoughts of his heart: in the latter days ye shall consider it perfectly.
21 I have not sent these prophets, yet they ran: I have not spoken to them, yet they prophesied.

Ultimately someone must come along who finally questions the state of religion enough to cause a reversal of fortune for the dispersed and forsaken children of the covenant. From Jeremiah 23:20-21, we get the feeling that it will occur at some point in the latter days. The "latter days" would thus be distinguished from the "former days," or the "latter rain" from the "Former Rain." The term "latter days" refers to the period of time close to the Second Coming of Jesus Christ. Likewise, most people would agree that prior to Christ's Second Coming, the gathering of Israel must take place. My question is, therefore, gathered from what? My response would be that they are gathered from falsehood and oppression. Hence, I propose that the terms "latter days," "last times," and "latter rain" go hand in hand.

According to the Lord's scriptures, the only way to know for sure the truth of anything is to ask Heavenly Father directly. We should not ask our parents, our spouse, or our friends. We must appeal to God directly through prayer, and we must do so with faith, truly believing that he is able to answer our sincere prayer. Only in this manner can an individual be sure whether a new doctrine is of God or not. If we do not ask God directly, but instead seek help from the arm of flesh, we then have no promise of obtaining the truth.

Jeremiah 42:15-16
15 And now therefore hear the word of the LORD, ye remnant of Judah; Thus saith the LORD of hosts, the God of Israel; If ye wholly set your faces to enter into Egypt, and go to sojourn there;
16 Then it shall come to pass, that the sword, which ye feared, shall overtake you there in the land of Egypt, and the famine, whereof ye were afraid, shall follow close after you there in Egypt; and there ye shall die.

Remember from our analysis of Isaiah that Egypt refers to churches and organizations developed by men. While it may be true that the men that developed them had good intentions, and may have even been inspired by God to leave their religion of birth, they fail to receive the complete seal of approval of the Lord. In other words, in both Isaiah, and now in Jeremiah, reference to the act of fleeing to Egypt, in order to get out of or away from Assyria or Babylon, is a reference to a man-made church or institution that was created to get away from another church or organization that seemed to be founded by the devil. At the very least, the founder and first members of the new faith feel inspired that theirs is a better or closer interpretation of the word of God, as contained in the Bible, than that held by the former church from which they are fleeing.

The only problem, as we see in Jeremiah 42:15-16, above, is that fleeing to Egypt is only a very temporary solution. Unless a religion is founded directly from God himself such that he calls new prophets and restores his priesthood and authority completely therein, the newly formed religion, while perhaps protesting something incorrect in its predecessor, will eventually be overcome by all the detestable things of the former religion. In other words, the devil will be given dominion over the works of men, while he can never have dominion over the works of God.

Jeremiah 44:2-6

2 Thus saith the LORD of hosts, the God of Israel; Ye have seen all the evil that I have brought upon Jerusalem, and upon all the cities of Judah; and, behold, this day they are a desolation, and no man dwelleth therein,
3 Because of their wickedness which they have committed to provoke me to anger, in that they went to burn incense, and to serve other gods, whom they knew not, neither they, ye, nor your fathers.
4 Howbeit I sent unto you all my servants the prophets, rising early and sending them, saying, Oh, do not this abominable thing that I hate.
5 But they hearkened not, nor inclined their ear to turn from their wickedness, to burn no incense unto other gods.
6 Wherefore my fury and mine anger was poured forth, and was kindled in the cities of Judah and in the streets of Jerusalem; and they are wasted and desolate, as at this day.

Jeremiah 44:11-14

11 Therefore thus saith the LORD of hosts, the God of Israel; Behold, I will set my face against you for evil, and to cut off all Judah.
12 And I will take the remnant of Judah, that have set their faces to go into the land of Egypt to sojourn there, and they shall all be consumed, and fall in the land of Egypt; they shall even be consumed by the sword and by the famine: they shall die, from the least even unto the greatest, by the sword and by the famine: and they shall be an execration, and an astonishment, and a curse, and a reproach.
13 For I will punish them that dwell in the land of Egypt, as I have punished Jerusalem, by the sword, by the famine, and by the pestilence:
14 So that none of the remnant of Judah, which are gone into the land of Egypt to sojourn there, shall escape or remain, that they should return into the land of Judah, to the which they have a desire to return to dwell there: for none shall return but such as shall escape.

If we take Egypt to mean the arm of flesh from our Isaiah analysis, or in other words, man-made religions, then the Lord is saying to Israel in the above verses that even if churches are formed and developed in order to "flee" from the falsehood of the day, unless the new church is brought forth by the Lord himself, it will do no good to flee there. The sword and the famine will follow them into Egypt and overcome them. In the end, they will have become like unto the church from which they left, having false priesthood and no truly-called prophets to guide and instruct them directly from the Lord.

Jeremiah 45:4

4 Thus shalt thou say unto him, The LORD saith thus; Behold, that which I have built will I break down, and that which I have planted I will pluck up, even this whole land.

THE LATTER RAIN

Jeremiah 51:14-17

14 The LORD of hosts hath sworn by himself, saying, Surely I will fill thee with men, as with caterpillers; and they shall lift up a shout against thee.
15 He hath made the earth by his power, he hath established the world by his wisdom, and hath stretched out the heaven by his understanding.
16 When he uttereth his voice, there is a multitude of waters in the heavens; and he causeth the vapours to ascend from the ends of the earth: he maketh lightnings with rain, and bringeth forth the wind out of his treasures.
17 Every man is brutish by his knowledge; every founder is confounded by the graven image: for his molten image is falsehood, and there is no breath in them.

During the period of the "Former Rain" the Lord established or built Zion and bestowed upon it prophecy and revelation through his servants the prophets. However, "that which I have built will I break down, and that which I have planted I will pluck up, even this whole land." The Zion that he established anciently is plucked up or removed from the earth, "even this whole land." From there, the inhabitants of the earth are left to wander to and fro seeking true religion, but not finding it. No more prophets are alive to receive revelations from God, and no one holds the priesthood authority for the performance of the saving ordinances. Zion is truly and utterly wasted.

In Jeremiah 51:17, we see that, rather than turning to the Lord directly for answers, those found in this period of no rain still prefer to worship man-made idols. "Every man is brutish by his knowledge; every founder is confounded by the graven image: for his molten image is falsehood, and there is no breath in them." Here, Jeremiah shows that while the Lord has plenty of revelation stored up in the heavens to send down upon the earth, men form "molten images" instead and worship them. What is the molten image Jeremiah describes? It is "falsehood" and there is no breath in it.

Jeremiah summarizes his prophecies concerning Israel in the form of his Lamentations. He laments that which is to befall Israel. Let us see for ourselves what he has to say.

Lamentations 1:19

19 I called for my lovers, but they deceived me: my priests and mine elders gave up the ghost in the city, while they sought their meat to relieve their souls.

The priesthood is lost to the earth since the priests and the elders who held the priesthood have all "given up the ghost"—they have all been killed off or died with no one chosen "by prophecy" to take their place.

Lamentations 2:9, 14

9 Her gates are sunk into the ground; he hath destroyed and broken her bars: her king and her princes are among the Gentiles: the law is no more; her prophets also find no vision from the LORD.
14 Thy prophets have seen vain and foolish things for thee: and they have not discovered thine iniquity, to turn away thy captivity; but have seen for thee false burdens and causes of banishment.

Not only do her prophets "find no vision from the Lord" (no rain), but the kings of Israel are also lost "among the Gentiles." Those that are left and claim to lead the people "have seen vain and foolish things for thee," and they have not "turned away thy captivity."

Lamentations 2:16-17

16 All thine enemies have opened their mouth against thee: they hiss and gnash the teeth: they say, We have swallowed her up: certainly this is the day that we looked for; we have found, we have seen it.
17 The LORD hath done that which he had devised; he hath fulfilled his word that he had commanded in the days of old: he hath thrown down, and hath not pitied: and he hath caused thine enemy to rejoice over thee, he hath set up the horn of thine adversaries.

During the dark ages of Spiritual Famine, it would appear that the adversary has "swallowed her up," referring to the Kingdom of God on the earth, or Zion. Why has this come about? It occurred because the people desired it. They rejected and killed the prophets, and even the son of God himself. Within a few years after the ascension of the Lord, all the apostles are gone as well. This martyrdom occurred because the Lord allowed it to happen in fulfillment "of his word that he had commanded in the days of old." Thus, we can see that the period of the Great Famine is in fact foretold by the prophets of old, and is meant to cover the entire earth.

Lamentations 3:1-11

1 I am the man that hath seen affliction by the rod of his wrath.
2 He hath led me, and brought me into darkness, but not into light.
3 Surely against me is he turned; he turneth his hand against me all the day.
4 My flesh and my skin hath he made old; he hath broken my bones.
5 He hath builded against me, and compassed me with gall and travail.
6 He hath set me in dark places, as they that be dead of old.
7 He hath hedged me about, that I cannot get out: he hath made my chain heavy.
8 Also when I cry and shout, he shutteth out my prayer.
9 He hath inclosed my ways with hewn stone, he hath made my paths crooked.
10 He was unto me as a bear lying in wait, and as a lion in secret places.
11 He hath turned aside my ways, and pulled me in pieces: he hath made me desolate.

Lamentations 3:44

44 Thou hast covered thyself with a cloud, that our prayer should not pass through.

Lamentations 4:4

4 The tongue of the sucking child cleaveth to the roof of his mouth for thirst: the young children ask bread, and no man breaketh it unto them.

Even when the children ask for knowledge and understanding, no one is left on the earth that can give it to them.

Lamentations 4:9-14

9 They that be slain with the sword are better than they that be slain with hunger: for these pine away, stricken through for want of the fruits of the field.
10 The hands of the pitiful women have sodden their own children: they were their meat in the destruction of the daughter of my people.
11 The LORD hath accomplished his fury; he hath poured out his fierce anger, and hath kindled a fire in Zion, and it hath devoured the foundations thereof.
12 The kings of the earth, and all the inhabitants of the world, would not have believed that the adversary and the enemy should have entered into the gates of Jerusalem.

13 For the sins of her prophets, and the iniquities of her priests, that have shed the blood of the just in the midst of her,
14 They have wandered as blind men in the streets, they have polluted themselves with blood, so that men could not touch their garments.

Jeremiah again shows that the iniquity of the fathers and mothers of Zion has become a great blight to their children who must now suffer the consequences. With the famine well upon them, they must "pine away, stricken through for want of the fruits of the field." Jeremiah makes it clear that it was indeed the will of the Lord to allow Zion to be overcome and vanquished completely. "The Lord hath accomplished his fury; he hath poured out his fierce anger, and hath kindled a fire in Zion, and it hath devoured the foundations thereof."

Even more significant is the next verse: "The kings of the earth, and all the inhabitants of the world, would not have believed that the adversary and the enemy should have entered into the gates of Jerusalem." Is not this the case today? The idea is so terrible and so diabolical (the complete overthrow of the true religion of God), no one left on the earth even considers this Spiritual Famine an actual possibility. The conspiracy of the devil is so complete, they are unaware that indeed Zion hath fled into the wilderness. Instead, they seek for truth among the rubble, and for understanding among the interpretations of men. The final chapter of Lamentations summarizes well the plight of the children of Zion.

Lamentations 5:1-22
1 Remember, O LORD, what is come upon us: consider, and behold our reproach.
2 Our inheritance is turned to strangers, our houses to aliens.
3 We are orphans and fatherless, our mothers are as widows.
4 We have drunken our water for money; our wood is sold unto us.
5 Our necks are under persecution: we labour, and have no rest.
6 We have given the hand to the Egyptians, and to the Assyrians, to be satisfied with bread.
7 Our fathers have sinned, and are not; and we have borne their iniquities.
8 Servants have ruled over us: there is none that doth deliver us out of their hand.
9 We gat our bread with the peril of our lives because of the sword of the wilderness.
10 Our skin was black like an oven because of the terrible famine.
11 They ravished the women in Zion, and the maids in the cities of Judah.
12 Princes are hanged up by their hand: the faces of elders were not honoured.
13 They took the young men to grind, and the children fell under the wood.
14 The elders have ceased from the gate, the young men from their musick.
15 The joy of our heart is ceased; our dance is turned into mourning.
16 The crown is fallen from our head: woe unto us, that we have sinned!
17 For this our heart is faint; for these things our eyes are dim.
18 Because of the mountain of Zion, which is desolate, the foxes walk upon it.
19 Thou, O LORD, remainest for ever; thy throne from generation to generation.
20 Wherefore dost thou forget us for ever, and forsake us so long time?
21 Turn thou us unto thee, O LORD, and we shall be turned; renew our days as of old.
22 But thou hast utterly rejected us; thou art very wroth against us.

In this eloquent lamentation, Jeremiah displays the longing that the children of Zion have to be recovered and brought again into the safe harbor. When they finally recognize that Zion is desolate, they can then ask the Lord in humility: "dost thou forget us for ever, and forsake us so long time?" Then and only then (when they realize that there has indeed been a great Spiritual Famine) can they ask the right questions and seek the right response from the Lord. "Turn thou us unto thee, O Lord, and we shall be turned; renew our days as of old."

A Highway Out of Falsehood

Once this change has come, and the descendants of the tribes of Israel that are scattered throughout the earth begin to seek the truth from the true source, then the Lord will begin to lead them back to Zion. First he must restore Zion, and then he will guide the seekers of truth to it as if they are on a special highway. This image of there being a holy pathway leading out of Assyria, Babylon and Egypt was first brought forth in Isaiah. Jeremiah also uses this type to show how the Lord will guide his people toward truth and away from falsehood in the last days—or in the days of the "Latter Rain."

Jeremiah 6:16-17
16 Thus saith the LORD, Stand ye in the ways, and see, and ask for the old paths, where is the good way, and walk therein, and ye shall find rest for your souls. But they said, We will not walk therein.
17 Also I set watchmen over you, saying, Hearken to the sound of the trumpet. But they said, We will not hearken.

The Lord instructs his children to "ask for the old paths" and ultimately, once he has reestablished Zion on the earth, he even sets up watchmen to direct them. Many, however, will not walk in the right path, but prefer to walk in their own pathways.

Jeremiah 10:23
23 O LORD, I know that the way of man is not in himself: it is not in man that walketh to direct his steps.

Jeremiah 18:15
15 Because my people hath forgotten me, they have burned incense to vanity, and they have caused them to stumble in their ways from the ancient paths, to walk in paths, in a way not cast up;

Here, Jeremiah shows that, left to himself, man is unable to direct himself in the right path. He needs guidance from above. Even when they try their best by looking at the remaining scriptures of the dead prophets, they are unable to find the true path but "burn incense to vanity" and stumble in their eternal progress. Ultimately, when they approach the Lord with the right attitude, and in a state of humility rather than false pride, the Lord will guide them straight way in the good path, close by the waters of inspiration and revelation from him directly.

Jeremiah 31:9
9 They shall come with weeping, and with supplications will I lead them: I will cause them to walk by the rivers of waters in a straight way, wherein they shall not stumble: for I am a father to Israel, and Ephraim is my firstborn.

Ephraim and Judah Play the Harlot

As has been stated earlier, the two separate kingdoms, Ephraim to the north and Judah to the south, were both in turn carried away captive by hostile nations that spoiled and scattered them. Ephraim was the first to be taken, being scattered by Assyria in 721 BC and never being recovered as a recognizable people in historical records. Thus comes the term often used in Theology as "the ten lost tribes." Judah, on the other hand, though invaded and spoiled by Babylon, still remained a recognized people. While many of the people of Judah were also killed, scattered and dispersed, the prophets of God and his holy priesthood remained intact and continued in force during the captivity in Babylon. A small remnant of Judah was eventually allowed to return and rebuild Jerusalem and its surrounding cities. Finally, Judah was crushed as a nation in 70 AD, and the temple of Solomon destroyed. From that time forward, the remaining descendants of Judah, or the Jews, have migrated or been dispersed throughout the world, albeit maintaining their physical and historical link to Judah, and their divine identity as the "chosen people of the Lord." Like Isaiah, Jeremiah continues to refer to the people of the Lord according to this division: Israel or Ephraim to the north and Judah or the Jews to the south. In fact, he refers to them as sisters; sisters having played the harlot.

Jeremiah 3:6-11
6 The LORD said also unto me in the days of Josiah the king, Hast thou seen that which backsliding Israel hath done? she is gone up upon every high mountain and under every green tree, and there hath played the harlot.
7 And I said after she had done all these things, Turn thou unto me. But she returned not. And her treacherous sister Judah saw it.
8 And I saw, when for all the causes whereby backsliding Israel committed adultery I had put her away, and given her a bill of divorce; yet her treacherous sister Judah feared not, but went and played the harlot also.
9 And it came to pass through the lightness of her whoredom, that she defiled the land, and committed adultery with stones and with stocks.
10 And yet for all this her treacherous sister Judah hath not turned unto me with her whole heart, but feignedly, saith the LORD.
11 And the LORD said unto me, The backsliding Israel hath justified herself more than treacherous Judah.

The theme of the two sisters, Israel and Judah, playing the harlot is completely consistent with our previous discussion. The message is the same, even though the analogy is different. Instead of showing them as two nations being overrun by outside invaders, the Lord through Jeremiah refers to them as two sisters who have defiled themselves through adultery—first Israel, then Judah. The adultery spoken of here, however, is an affair with other gods. This leads to their subsequent divorce from the Lord, who is herein represented as the husband to them both. Just as Israel, or the Northern Kingdom, was the first to be carried away captive by Assyria in a literal sense, Israel (or Ephraim) was also the first to fall into a state of apostasy towards God. Likewise, the authorized priesthood for the performance of saving ordinances was lost. Due to her iniquity, the Lord had no choice but to "put her away." The period of time during which no prophets are found in Israel is represented in three different ways: captivity to a tyrant king, passing through a famine of hearing the words of the Lord, and now, the period of divorcement from one's righteous husband.

THE BOOK OF JEREMIAH AND HIS LAMENTATIONS

Jeremiah 7:10-15

10 And come and stand before me in this house, which is called by my name, and say, We are delivered to do all these abominations?
11 Is this house, which is called by my name, become a den of robbers in your eyes? Behold, even I have seen it, saith the LORD.
12 But go ye now unto my place which was in Shiloh, where I set my name at the first, and see what I did to it for the wickedness of my people Israel.
13 And now, because ye have done all these works, saith the LORD, and I spake unto you, rising up early and speaking, but ye heard not; and I called you, but ye answered not;
14 Therefore will I do unto this house, which is called by my name, wherein ye trust, and unto the place which I gave to you and to your fathers, as I have done to Shiloh.
15 And I will cast you out of my sight, as I have cast out all your brethren, even the whole seed of Ephraim.

Jeremiah 13:19

19 The cities of the south shall be shut up, and none shall open them: Judah shall be carried away captive all of it, it shall be wholly carried away captive.

In her turn, the southern sister, Judah, followed after the ways of her sister Israel: refusing and killing the true and living prophets, while holding to and seeking after falsehood and idolatry. In fact, the above verses seem to indicate that Judah may have been even worse than her sister before her: "The backsliding Israel hath justified herself more than treacherous Judah." What are the things that Judah has done to anger the Lord and to defile her from Him? Let us examine Jeremiah 29 to answer this question:

Jeremiah 29:4-5

4 Because they have forsaken me, and have estranged this place, and have burned incense in it unto other gods, whom neither they nor their fathers have known, nor the kings of Judah, and have filled this place with the blood of innocents;
5 They have built also the high places of Baal, to burn their sons with fire for burnt offerings unto Baal, which I commanded not, nor spake it, neither came it into my mind:

They have worshipped other gods, and have even sacrificed their own children to these false gods. They have slain the innocent to get gain, including the prophets and servants of the Lord. The Lord ultimately decides to give them over to their vanity and falsehood altogether. Judah worshiped false gods and followed after the vain practices and ceremonies of the neighboring pagan nations, including human sacrifices, offering their infant sons to Baal. These vile practices, along with the rejection of the true prophets that tried to warn them, left the Lord with no other choice than to withdraw from them and leave them to themselves—subject to the kingdom and dominion of the devil. The prophet Jeremiah teaches us here that, whereas Israel and Judah were once a united kingdom with the Lord as their guide, they are now divided into two kingdoms, both of which have been dispersed or put away by the Lord. In the latter days, however, the hope remains of finally reuniting these two fallen sisters.

Jeremiah 3:18

18 In those days the house of Judah shall walk with the house of Israel, and they shall come together out of the land of the north to the land that I have given for an inheritance unto your fathers.

THE LATTER RAIN

> **Jeremiah 31:6-9**
> 6 For there shall be a day, that the watchmen upon the mount Ephraim shall cry, Arise ye, and let us go up to Zion unto the LORD our God.
> 7 For thus saith the LORD; Sing with gladness for Jacob, and shout among the chief of the nations: publish ye, praise ye, and say, O LORD, save thy people, the remnant of Israel.
> 8 Behold, I will bring them from the north country, and gather them from the coasts of the earth, and with them the blind and the lame, the woman with child and her that travaileth with child together: a great company shall return thither.
> 9 They shall come with weeping, and with supplications will I lead them: I will cause them to walk by the rivers of waters in a straight way, wherein they shall not stumble: for I am a father to Israel, and Ephraim is my firstborn.

In verse six, the watchmen upon mount Ephraim represent new prophets called from lineage of Ephraim, who are the first to break the silence of the famine period. While much emphasis is placed on the importance of Judah as the tribe through which the Messiah would be born, here we are also reminded of the importance of Ephraim to the Lord—"Ephraim is my firstborn." Ephraim, or the dispersed Ten Tribes, at some point in the latter days will spring forth and become recognized again. From the above verses we learn that Ephraim will be the first to return to Zion, although ultimately "Judah shall walk with the house of Israel" as well.

> **Jeremiah 31:28**
> 28 And it shall come to pass, that like as I have watched over them, to pluck up, and to break down, and to throw down, and to destroy, and to afflict; so will I watch over them, to build, and to plant, saith the LORD.

> **Jeremiah 33:7-8**
> 7 And I will cause the captivity of Judah and the captivity of Israel to return, and will build them, as at the first.
> 8 And I will cleanse them from all their iniquity, whereby they have sinned against me; and I will pardon all their iniquities, whereby they have sinned, and whereby they have transgressed against me.

While the kingdom and dominion of the devil is allowed to have full reign over the earth for a long period of time, the day ultimately arrives when the Lord will return from his long departure and once again gather his people. He will begin to "disquiet the inhabitants of Babylon."

> **Jeremiah 5:10,18**
> 10 Go ye up upon her walls, and destroy; but make not a full end: take away her battlements; for they are not the LORD's.
> 18 Nevertheless in those days, saith the LORD, I will not make a full end with you.

Because of the iniquity and unfaithfulness of Ephraim and Judah, the Lord might have been justified in ending his work entirely. He could have ceased to strive with the children of men, and given them up for good. However, we learn from these verses in Jeremiah 5 that the Lord in his mercy has decided not to make a full end, but to ultimately allow a way for their escape after a period of chastisement.

THE BOOK OF JEREMIAH AND HIS LAMENTATIONS

Zion Will Return

From our study of the writings of Isaiah, we saw that "this is a people robbed and spoiled; they are all of them snared in holes, and they are hid in prison houses: they are for a prey, and none delivereth; for a spoil, and none saith, Restore." Eventually, someone must say, "Restore!" (Isaiah 42:22). Only then will Zion be reestablished on the earth. Instead of merely looking to others on the earth for advice, this restoring prophet would actually turn to God directly in prayer. From this event, the Lord begins the last dispensation of the earth—the dispensation of the fullness of times.

Ephesians 1:10
10 That in the dispensation of the fulness of times he might gather together in one all things in Christ, both which are in heaven, and which are on earth; even in him:

This final period could also rightly be known as the period of the Latter Rain. It is characterized by the return of living prophets of God. The leaders of Zion in this final dispensation receive the Spirit of Prophecy directly from the Lord to once again clarify doctrine, receive revelations about specific questions and issues, and to guide the dispersed children of Israel back into the true fold of God.

Jeremiah 3:14-15
14 Turn, O backsliding children, saith the LORD; for I am married unto you: and I will take you one of a city, and two of a family, and I will bring you to Zion:
15 And I will give you pastors according to mine heart, which shall feed you with knowledge and understanding.

Lamentations 3:31-32
31 For the Lord will not cast off for ever:
32 But though he cause grief, yet will he have compassion according to the multitude of his mercies.

Jeremiah 12:14-16
14 Thus saith the LORD against all mine evil neighbours, that touch the inheritance which I have caused my people Israel to inherit; Behold, I will pluck them out of their land, and pluck out the house of Judah from among them.
15 And it shall come to pass, after that I have plucked them out I will return, and have compassion on them, and will bring them again, every man to his heritage, and every man to his land.
16 And it shall come to pass, if they will diligently learn the ways of my people, to swear by my name, The LORD liveth; as they taught my people to swear by Baal; then shall they be built in the midst of my people.

The Lord here promises that once Zion is reestablished he will provide teachers for the people. The people will, little by little, begin to be freed from the bondage of Assyria and the prison of Babylon. They will begin to recognize the truth when they hear it taught, and be carried away safe into the true fold of God again.

Jeremiah 30:17-24
17 For I will restore health unto thee, and I will heal thee of thy wounds, saith the LORD; because they called thee an Outcast, saying, This is Zion, whom no man seeketh after.

18 Thus saith the LORD; Behold, I will bring again the captivity of Jacob's tents, and have mercy on his dwellingplaces; and the city shall be built upon her own heap, and the palace shall remain after the manner thereof.
19 And out of them shall proceed thanksgiving and the voice of them that make merry: and I will multiply them, and they shall not be few; I will also glorify them, and they shall not be small.
20 Their children also shall be as aforetime, and their congregation shall be established before me, and I will punish all that oppress them.
21 And their nobles shall be of themselves, and their governor shall proceed from the midst of them; and I will cause him to draw near, and he shall approach unto me: for who is this that engaged his heart to approach unto me? saith the LORD.
22 And ye shall be my people, and I will be your God.
23 Behold, the whirlwind of the LORD goeth forth with fury, a continuing whirlwind: it shall fall with pain upon the head of the wicked.
24 The fierce anger of the LORD shall not return, until he have done it, and until he have performed the intents of his heart: in the latter days ye shall consider it.

Jeremiah says that "In the latter days ye shall consider it." He promises the city that was wasted "shall be builded upon her own heap." The leader of this restored Zion (their prophet) "shall proceed from the midst of them; and I will cause him to draw near, and he shall approach unto me: for who is this that engaged his heart to approach unto me?" When this restoration occurs, it will occur because someone had sufficient faith to actually "approach" God directly. He does not rely on the traditions of men, but asks God directly. This new prophet then becomes the governor in Zion, with the Lord directing his decisions and actions as in times past. With a prophet finally available to guide them, the children of Israel shall once again "be as aforetime," or as they were during the period of the Former Rain (Jeremiah 30:20 above).

Jeremiah 31:31-34

31 Behold, the days come, saith the LORD, that I will make a new covenant with the house of Israel, and with the house of Judah:
32 Not according to the covenant that I made with their fathers in the day that I took them by the hand to bring them out of the land of Egypt; which my covenant they brake, although I was an husband unto them, saith the LORD:
33 But this shall be the covenant that I will make with the house of Israel; After those days, saith the LORD, I will put my law in their inward parts, and write it in their hearts; and will be their God, and they shall be my people.
34 And they shall teach no more every man his neighbour, and every man his brother, saying, Know the LORD: for they shall all know me, from the least of them unto the greatest of them, saith the LORD: for I will forgive their iniquity, and I will remember their sin no more.

When the restoration occurs, men "shall teach no more every man his neighbor, and every man his brother," as they did during the period of Spiritual Famine. With a true prophet and authorized servants to teach the people, the truth and wisdom of the Lord can freely flow to those held captive in falsehood. Likewise, the spirit of the Lord will itself begin to distill in the hearts and minds of those that accept Zion and come unto her. "After those days, saith the Lord, I will put my law in their inward parts, and write it in their hearts; and will be their God, and they shall be my people."

THE BOOK OF JEREMIAH AND HIS LAMENTATIONS

Jeremiah 32:37-42

37 Behold, I will gather them out of all countries, whither I have driven them in mine anger, and in my fury, and in great wrath; and I will bring them again unto this place, and I will cause them to dwell safely:
38 And they shall be my people, and I will be their God:
39 And I will give them one heart, and one way, that they may fear me for ever, for the good of them, and of their children after them:
40 And I will make an everlasting covenant with them, that I will not turn away from them, to do them good; but I will put my fear in their hearts, that they shall not depart from me.
41 Yea, I will rejoice over them to do them good, and I will plant them in this land assuredly with my whole heart and with my whole soul.
42 For thus saith the LORD; Like as I have brought all this great evil upon this people, so will I bring upon them all the good that I have promised them.

Spiritual Battle, Not Physical Warfare

In Isaiah, we saw the sword and the famine used to describe the demise of Zion. We showed that these terms were figurative rather than literal. If the sword in this sense means persecution and falsehood, and the famine means the withdrawal of the Lord's true prophets, then the "pestilence" spoken of in verse 36 above would represent the state of confusion that results from this combination of misfortune. The children of Israel born during the Great Famine period have so much religious confusion swirling about them that it is nearly impossible to make sense of anything for certain—unless, of course, they call on God directly. Only then will God return and build Judah and Israel again.

Jeremiah 33:7

7 And I will cause the captivity of Judah and the captivity of Israel to return, and will build them, as at the first.

Jeremiah 33:14

14 Behold, the days come, saith the LORD, that I will perform that good thing which I have promised unto the house of Israel and to the house of Judah.

What is that "good thing" which the Lord has promised? It is the restoration of Zion, and the gathering of his lost and fallen people from among the nations where they have been driven.

Jeremiah 46:27-28

27 But fear not thou, O my servant Jacob, and be not dismayed, O Israel: for, behold, I will save thee from afar off, and thy seed from the land of their captivity; and Jacob shall return, and be in rest and at ease, and none shall make him afraid.
28 Fear thou not, O Jacob my servant, saith the LORD: for I am with thee; for I will make a full end of all the nations whither I have driven thee: but I will not make a full end of thee, but correct thee in measure; yet will I not leave thee wholly unpunished.

While he promises not to make a full end of Zion, but to restore it and reestablish it once more upon the earth, he does in fact say that he "will make a full end of all the nations whither I have driven thee." By the time the Lord has finished his gathering process, the falsehood and vanity that has captivated the world will ultimately be completely defeated and driven to nothing. The knowledge and wisdom of the Lord will fill the whole earth.

THE LATTER RAIN

Jeremiah 50:4-8

4 In those days, and in that time, saith the LORD, the children of Israel shall come, they and the children of Judah together, going and weeping: they shall go, and seek the LORD their God.
5 They shall ask the way to Zion with their faces thitherward, saying, Come, and let us join ourselves to the LORD in a perpetual covenant that shall not be forgotten.
6 My people hath been lost sheep: their shepherds have caused them to go astray, they have turned them away on the mountains: they have gone from mountain to hill, they have forgotten their restingplace.
7 All that found them have devoured them: and their adversaries said, We offend not, because they have sinned against the LORD, the habitation of justice, even the LORD, the hope of their fathers.
8 Remove out of the midst of Babylon, and go forth out of the land of the Chaldeans, and be as the he goats before the flocks.

Gradually, the faithful seekers of truth will begin their return unto Zion. They will question doctrine and seek counsel and direction. The Lord will guide them safely home. He does this by choosing servants and teachers after his own heart, and by prompting and teaching them with thoughts and ideas that distill in the hearts of his people as they hear the truth.

Jeremiah 50:9-15

9 For, lo, I will raise and cause to come up against Babylon an assembly of great nations from the north country: and they shall set themselves in array against her; from thence she shall be taken: their arrows shall be as of a mighty expert man; none shall return in vain.
10 And Chaldea shall be a spoil: all that spoil her shall be satisfied, saith the LORD.
11 Because ye were glad, because ye rejoiced, O ye destroyers of mine heritage, because ye are grown fat as the heifer at grass, and bellow as bulls;
12 Your mother shall be sore confounded; she that bare you shall be ashamed: behold, the hindermost of the nations shall be a wilderness, a dry land, and a desert.
13 Because of the wrath of the LORD it shall not be inhabited, but it shall be wholly desolate: every one that goeth by Babylon shall be astonished, and hiss at all her plagues.
14 Put yourselves in array against Babylon round about: all ye that bend the bow, shoot at her, spare no arrows: for she hath sinned against the LORD.
15 Shout against her round about: she hath given her hand: her foundations are fallen, her walls are thrown down: for it is the vengeance of the LORD: take vengeance upon her; as she hath done, do unto her.

A surface reading of these passages would have us think that a great and horrible battle will ensue in the last days that will be bloody and fierce. It will be the Lord's armies that are the cruelest of all. However, when we apply our understanding from our study of Isaiah, we can remember that the sword of the Lord is his word—or in other words, his true doctrine and true religion. An army from the "north countries" refers to Ephraim. Thus, in verse nine above, when we read that the Lord's armies "shall set themselves in array against her; from thence she shall be taken: their arrows shall be as of a mighty expert man; none shall return in vain," we should realize that this is really describing the legion of the Lord's missionaries and teachers from the Tribe of Ephraim going forth into the world. While they may be unlearned as to the understanding and wisdom of the world, they are armed with the wisdom and knowledge from God. Their "arrows shall be as of a mighty expert man." This same imagery was given in Isaiah 5.

THE BOOK OF JEREMIAH AND HIS LAMENTATIONS

Isaiah 5:26-29

26 And he will lift up an ensign to the nations from far, and will hiss unto them from the end of the earth: and, behold, they shall come with speed swiftly:
27 None shall be weary nor stumble among them; none shall slumber nor sleep; neither shall the girdle of their loins be loosed, nor the latchet of their shoes be broken:
28 Whose arrows are sharp, and all their bows bent, their horses' hoofs shall be counted like flint, and their wheels like a whirlwind:
29 Their roaring shall be like a lion, they shall roar like young lions: yea, they shall roar, and lay hold of the prey, and shall carry it away safe, and none shall deliver it.

"Whose arrows are sharp, and all their bows bent." In other words, the Lord's disciples of the Latter Rain period are prepared. They have studied the word of the Lord and are prepared to deliver the message of a restored Zion. "They shall roar, and lay hold of the prey, and shall carry it away safe, and none shall deliver it." Again, I ask the question, what lion is there that carries its prey away safe? In contrast to the young lions of Zion who carry away safe, the lions of Assyria and Babylon attack Zion and drive it into a state of apostasy and desolation. Thus, it can be said that the king of Assyria "hath broken his bones" (done great harm).

Jeremiah 50:17-20

17 Israel is a scattered sheep; the lions have driven him away: first the king of Assyria hath devoured him; and last this Nebuchadrezzar king of Babylon hath broken his bones.
18 Therefore thus saith the LORD of hosts, the God of Israel; Behold, I will punish the king of Babylon and his land, as I have punished the king of Assyria.
19 And I will bring Israel again to his habitation, and he shall feed on Carmel and Bashan, and his soul shall be satisfied upon mount Ephraim and Gilead.
20 In those days, and in that time, saith the LORD, the iniquity of Israel shall be sought for, and there shall be none; and the sins of Judah, and they shall not be found: for I will pardon them whom I reserve.

Verse 17 supports the two-phase concept by which Zion fell into a state of desolation. First, Assyria took Israel (Ephraim) away. Then later, Judah falls to Nebuchadnezzar of Babylon. In the end, however, as the dispersed people of Israel begin to return to Zion, they do so through repentance and humbling of their souls. They are refreshed and have a renewed sense of purpose and being, for the Lord has pardoned their transgressions and filled them with his spirit.

Jeremiah 50:24-25

24 I have laid a snare for thee, and thou art also taken, O Babylon, and thou wast not aware: thou art found, and also caught, because thou hast striven against the LORD.
25 The LORD hath opened his armoury, and hath brought forth the weapons of his indignation: for this is the work of the Lord GOD of hosts in the land of the Chaldeans.

Jeremiah 50:29-32

29 Call together the archers against Babylon: all ye that bend the bow, camp against it round about; let none thereof escape: recompense her according to her work; according to all that she hath done, do unto her: for she hath been proud against the LORD, against the Holy One of Israel.
30 Therefore shall her young men fall in the streets, and all her men of war shall be cut off in that day, saith the LORD.
31 Behold, I am against thee, O thou most proud, saith the Lord GOD of hosts: for thy day is come, the time that I will visit thee.

32 And the most proud shall stumble and fall, and none shall raise him up: and I will kindle a fire in his cities, and it shall devour all round about him.

Here we get the feeling that as this fledgling religion gains strength, the Lord ultimately begins to open up his whole "armoury, and hath brought forth the weapons of his indignation." What are the weapons of the Lord's armory? They are truth and righteousness. They are living prophets that confound the wisdom of the world. They are the Lord's messengers that teach with the authority of God, and are backed up by the power and might of the Holy Spirit of truth. When prophets exist again upon the earth, we should expect the words of the prophets to come forth in the form of scripture as in the times of old. These new writings will thus serve as strong evidence of the divinity of the Lord's new Zion, and it will cut through falsehood and false doctrine like a mighty two-edged sword.

Jeremiah 50:35-43
35 A sword is upon the Chaldeans, saith the LORD, and upon the inhabitants of Babylon, and upon her princes, and upon her wise men.
36 A sword is upon the liars; and they shall dote: a sword is upon her mighty men; and they shall be dismayed.
37 A sword is upon their horses, and upon their chariots, and upon all the mingled people that are in the midst of her; and they shall become as women: a sword is upon her treasures; and they shall be robbed.
38 A drought is upon her waters; and they shall be dried up: for it is the land of graven images, and they are mad upon their idols.
39 Therefore the wild beasts of the desert with the wild beasts of the islands shall dwell there, and the owls shall dwell therein: and it shall be no more inhabited for ever; neither shall it be dwelt in from generation to generation.
40 As God overthrew Sodom and Gomorrah and the neighbour cities thereof, saith the LORD; so shall no man abide there, neither shall any son of man dwell therein.
41 Behold, a people shall come from the north, and a great nation, and many kings shall be raised up from the coasts of the earth.
42 They shall hold the bow and the lance: they are cruel, and will not shew mercy: their voice shall roar like the sea, and they shall ride upon horses, every one put in array, like a man to the battle, against thee, O daughter of Babylon.
43 The king of Babylon hath heard the report of them, and his hands waxed feeble: anguish took hold of him, and pangs as of a woman in travail.

The same is not true for the rulers in Babylon who experience a drought "upon her waters; and they shall be dried up: for it is the land of graven images, and they are mad upon their idols." In other words, the Lord does not speak to them. As we recall from Jeremiah 10:4: "Every man [in Babylon] is brutish in his knowledge: every founder is confounded by the graven image: for his molten image is falsehood, and there is no breath in them." The molten images of today are "falsehood" and incorrect doctrines.

Jeremiah 50:33-34, 44-46
33 Thus saith the LORD of hosts; The children of Israel and the children of Judah were oppressed together: and all that took them captives held them fast; they refused to let them go.
34 Their Redeemer is strong; the LORD of hosts is his name: he shall throughly plead their cause, that he may give rest to the land, and disquiet the inhabitants of Babylon.

THE BOOK OF JEREMIAH AND HIS LAMENTATIONS

44 Behold, he shall come up like a lion from the swelling of Jordan unto the habitation of the strong: but I will make them suddenly run away from her: and who is a chosen man, that I may appoint over her? for who is like me? and who will appoint me the time? and who is that shepherd that will stand before me?
45 Therefore hear ye the counsel of the LORD, that he hath taken against Babylon; and his purposes, that he hath purposed against the land of the Chaldeans: Surely the least of the flock shall draw them out: surely he shall make their habitation desolate with them.
46 At the noise of the taking of Babylon the earth is moved, and the cry is heard among the nations.

Assyria will try to keep its people hostage, but it will be in vain. Little by little, Babylon the Great will lose its grip on the children of Israel held captive. For "their Redeemer is strong; the Lord of hosts is his name." Since the Lord himself is engaged in this great and last battle to convert souls to the true religion of God, the Lord's doctrine becomes so strong and so sensible that "surely the least of the flock shall draw them out"—even the greenest, and most naïve disciple will be as a mighty man among them. When the person investigating this new doctrine goes to the Lord to understand what has been preached to him, the Lord himself will speak directly to his soul. The spirit of God will convert him and bring him safely to Zion.

The Lord of Hosts asks the question in Jeremiah 50:44: "who is a chosen man, that I may appoint over her? for who is like me? and who will appoint me the time? and who is that shepherd that will stand before me?" In other words, where is a man that is worthy to be my chosen prophet, through whom I may restore Zion again to the earth? Such a man is needed so that God can visit his people and restore them to their former place. Without the symbolic clues we gleaned from our study of the Book of Isaiah, we would only see a great scene of some future war. We would view the Lord God of Israel as a cruel and blood-thirsty God. Just as we saw in Isaiah, the text of Jeremiah might also seem gruesome and horrifying if we were to take them as literal battles played out in the future and being waged between soldiers in the field.

Isaiah 30:31

31 For through the voice of the Lord shall the Assyrian be beaten down, which smote with a rod.

Indeed, this scene of carnage seems cruel. Isaiah serves as a key to explain that this is not the true intent of the Lord. The dual prophecy accounts for the physical warfare that occurred anciently, but also for the spiritual warfare that is waged to win over the dispersed of Israel, thus healing them through the pleasing word of the Lord. Again, his sword is not a literal sword, but his sword is his word, his voice, and the spirit of truth. When the Lord or one of his servants smites a person with truth, that person is slain as a member of Babylon, but is reborn into the true Zion of God. Jeremiah also makes this same distinction in Jeremiah 51. Here he shows that while the founders of the churches of men worship falsehood as their molten images, "the portion of Jacob is not like them."

Jeremiah 51:17-24

17 Every man is brutish by his knowledge; every founder is confounded by the graven image: for his molten image is falsehood, and there is no breath in them.

18 They are vanity, the work of errors: in the time of their visitation they shall perish.
19 The portion of Jacob is not like them; for he is the former of all things: and Israel is the rod of his inheritance: the LORD of hosts is his name.
20 Thou art my battle axe and weapons of war: for with thee will I break in pieces the nations, and with thee will I destroy kingdoms;
21 And with thee will I break in pieces the horse and his rider; and with thee will I break in pieces the chariot and his rider;
22 With thee also will I break in pieces man and woman; and with thee will I break in pieces old and young; and with thee will I break in pieces the young man and the maid;
23 I will also break in pieces with thee the shepherd and his flock; and with thee will I break in pieces the husbandman and his yoke of oxen; and with thee will I break in pieces captains and rulers.
24 And I will render unto Babylon and to all the inhabitants of Chaldea all their evil that they have done in Zion in your sight, saith the LORD.

The portion of Jacob is not falsehood, but truth and restored priesthood authority. The descendants of former Israel who discover that Zion is again in their midst, thus begin to join with her again—casting off the traditions and practices that have held them bound for generations. With these faithful servants, the Lord will "break in pieces the nations, and with thee will I destroy kingdoms." He will undermine the false teachings held by the churches of the world—churches that hold men and women captive to falsehood.

Zion Will Not Fall Again

Once Zion springs up, it will never again go into a state of desolation. While Babylon will be utterly wasted and completely wiped out, Zion will remain forever more. Individuals may lose faith and fall away, but as a collective nation or church, the true priesthood of God will never again be removed from the earth. Isaiah first introduced this concept in reference to the waters of Noah:

Isaiah 54:7-10

7 For a small moment have I forsaken thee; but with great mercies will I gather thee.
8 In a little wrath I hid my face from thee for a moment; but with everlasting kindness will I have mercy on thee, saith the LORD thy Redeemer.
9 For this is as the waters of Noah unto me: for as I have sworn that the waters of Noah should no more go over the earth; so have I sworn that I would not be wroth with thee, nor rebuke thee.
10 For the mountains shall depart, and the hills be removed; but my kindness shall not depart from thee, neither shall the covenant of my peace be removed, saith the LORD that hath mercy on thee.

The Lord was adamant about his decision to withdraw his Church and Kingdom from the earth. But he is just as firm in his resolve to protect and prosper Zion in the last days. He promises that Zion will never be taken away again. The Lord reiterates this same promise in the writings of Jeremiah:

Jeremiah 31:40

40 And the whole valley of the dead bodies, and of the ashes, and all the fields unto the brook of Kidron, unto the corner of the horse gate toward the east, shall be holy unto the LORD; it shall not be plucked up, nor thrown down any more for ever.

THE BOOK OF JEREMIAH AND HIS LAMENTATIONS

Zion shall not be "thrown down any more for ever." This not only shows the promise that Zion or the true Church of God will never again fall into a state of apostasy, but it demonstrates that, at one point, indeed Zion was "thrown down." There was a famine in the land of hearing the words of the Lord.

Jeremiah 50:35-39

35 A sword is upon the Chaldeans, saith the LORD, and upon the inhabitants of Babylon, and upon her princes, and upon her wise men.
36 A sword is upon the liars; and they shall dote: a sword is upon her mighty men; and they shall be dismayed.
37 A sword is upon their horses, and upon their chariots, and upon all the mingled people that are in the midst of her; and they shall become as women: a sword is upon her treasures; and they shall be robbed.
38 A drought is upon her waters; and they shall be dried up: for it is the land of graven images, and they are mad upon their idols.
39 Therefore the wild beasts of the desert with the wild beasts of the islands shall dwell there, and the owls shall dwell therein: and it shall be no more inhabited for ever; neither shall it be dwelt in from generation to generation.

Once the truth takes hold and marches forth throughout the earth, the false doctrines and half-truths that had blinded the children of men will be done away forever. The above statement could also be written another way. If Babylon "shall be no more inhabited for ever; neither shall it be dwelt in from generation to generation," that means that it will never have the power to overthrow Zion again. The members of the Lord's Church during the period of the Latter Rain can be certain and remain confident that the truly-called and ordained prophets and leaders of the restored Zion will never be allowed to lead her into another situation where God's authority would again be lifted from the earth. On an individual basis, some called servants may slip away from the truth, but the Lord himself will intervene in such matters and take such false leaders out of their midst.

We see that the types and symbols brought forth in the Book of Isaiah are found in the Book of Jeremiah as well. While Jeremiah might refer to the kingdom of the devil as Babylon and Isaiah calls it Assyria, they are one and the same. Hence, the knowledge of the types and symbols developed through our analysis of the Book of Isaiah has helped us better understand the message found in the writings of Jeremiah the Prophet (the Book of Jeremiah and Lamentations). Let us now see if these same types and symbols are present in the next book of the Old Testament—the Book of Ezekiel.

CHAPTER SIX

The Book of Ezekiel

The Book of Ezekiel immediately takes up the same imagery described in Isaiah and Jeremiah—that of war and military conflict. In Ezekiel, however, two attacking nations are mentioned, not just one.

Assyria and Babylon: A Siege Against Israel

Ezekiel 4:1-3

1 Thou also, son of man, take thee a tile, and lay it before thee, and pourtray upon it the city, even Jerusalem:
2 And lay siege against it, and build a fort against it, and cast a mount against it; set the camp also against it, and set battering rams against it round about.
3 Moreover take thou unto thee an iron pan, and set it for a wall of iron between thee and the city: and set thy face against it, and it shall be besieged, and thou shalt lay siege against it. This shall be a sign to the house of Israel.

As with Isaiah and Jeremiah, the concept of Jerusalem being besieged and overrun is quickly taken up by Ezekiel. Like the other Old Testament writers, he does not limit the attack to just the sword, but also mentions the famine and the pestilence.

Ezekiel 6:11-14

11 Thus saith the Lord GOD; Smite with thine hand, and stamp with thy foot, and say, Alas for all the evil abominations of the house of Israel! for they shall fall by the sword, by the famine, and by the pestilence.
12 He that is far off shall die of the pestilence; and he that is near shall fall by the sword; and he that remaineth and is besieged shall die by the famine: thus will I accomplish my fury upon them.
13 Then shall ye know that I am the LORD, when their slain men shall be among their idols round about their altars, upon every high hill, in all the tops of the mountains, and under every green tree, and under every thick oak, the place where they did offer sweet savour to all their idols.
14 So will I stretch out my hand upon them, and make the land desolate, yea, more desolate than the wilderness toward Diblath, in all their habitations: and they shall know that I am the LORD.

Here in Ezekiel 6, we not only see what is coming upon Judah, but also why the Lord is allowing it to happen. "Alas for all the evil abominations of the house of Israel!" As we saw in the other books already discussed, no one will survive this siege. In fact, even those that ultimately remain after the work begins will be overcome eventually by "the famine," which we know from our previous analysis refers to the lack of direct revelation from God through his true prophets.

Ezekiel 7:1-8

1 Moreover the word of the LORD came unto me, saying,
2 Also, thou son of man, thus saith the Lord GOD unto the land of Israel; An end, the end is come upon the four corners of the land.
3 Now is the end come upon thee, and I will send mine anger upon thee, and will judge thee according to thy ways, and will recompense upon thee all thine abominations.
4 And mine eye shall not spare thee, neither will I have pity: but I will recompense thy ways upon thee, and thine abominations shall be in the midst of thee: and ye shall know that I am the LORD.
5 Thus saith the Lord GOD; An evil, an only evil, behold, is come.
6 An end is come, the end is come: it watcheth for thee; behold, it is come.
7 The morning is come unto thee, O thou that dwellest in the land: the time is come, the day of trouble is near, and not the sounding again of the mountains.
8 Now will I shortly pour out my fury upon thee, and accomplish mine anger upon thee: and I will judge thee according to thy ways, and will recompense thee for all thine abominations.

As was the case with Isaiah and Jeremiah, Ezekiel also warns that the Lord will soon "recompense upon thee all thine abominations." For their continual disobedience, the Lord is promising through Ezekiel that "the day of trouble is near."

Ezekiel 7:9-15

9 And mine eye shall not spare, neither will I have pity: I will recompense thee according to thy ways and thine abominations that are in the midst of thee; and ye shall know that I am the LORD that smiteth.
10 Behold the day, behold, it is come: the morning is gone forth; the rod hath blossomed, pride hath budded.
11 Violence is risen up into a rod of wickedness: none of them shall remain, nor of their multitude, nor of any of theirs: neither shall there be wailing for them.
12 The time is come, the day draweth near: let not the buyer rejoice, nor the seller mourn: for wrath is upon all the multitude thereof.
13 For the seller shall not return to that which is sold, although they were yet alive: for the vision is touching the whole multitude thereof, which shall not return; neither shall any strengthen himself in the iniquity of his life.
14 They have blown the trumpet, even to make all ready; but none goeth to the battle: for my wrath is upon all the multitude thereof.
15 The sword is without, and the pestilence and the famine within: he that is in the field shall die with the sword; and he that is in the city, famine and pestilence shall devour him.

According to the above narrative, not one soul survives this terrible and all-encompassing siege against Judah. The Lord is completely clear on this matter, stating that "none of them shall remain, nor of their multitude, nor of any of theirs: neither shall there be wailing for them." The devastation and destruction of Israel will be so severe that no one will even be left to mourn their loss. Historically, we know that, from a physical standpoint, Israel was not completely wiped out such that no one was left. Some refugees from the scattered Ten Tribes of the north remained in Samaria, although their religion was corrupted. Likewise, the Jews (or the Southern Kingdom) remain a body of people recognized by the world as having their lineage directly from the Tribe of Judah. While we do not know the precise fate of the Northern Ten Tribes or where they are now, they were not all killed from a physical standpoint, and their descendants must therefore still be found on the earth. We can again see that the image of a complete annihilation of Israel is not a literal and physical decree from the Lord, but refers to the complete and utter withdrawal of the Lord's servants, the true and authorized prophets, and a complete withdrawal of the Lord's priesthood from the earth. This idea is further established in the following verses:

> **Ezekiel 7:20-27**
> 20 As for the beauty of his ornament, he set it in majesty: but they made the images of their abominations and of their detestable things therein: therefore have I set it far from them.
> 21 And I will give it into the hands of the strangers for a prey, and to the wicked of the earth for a spoil; and they shall pollute it.
> 22 My face will I turn also from them, and they shall pollute my secret place: for the robbers shall enter into it, and defile it.
> 23 Make a chain: for the land is full of bloody crimes, and the city is full of violence.
> 24 Wherefore I will bring the worst of the heathen, and they shall possess their houses: I will also make the pomp of the strong to cease; and their holy places shall be defiled.
> 25 Destruction cometh; and they shall seek peace, and there shall be none.
> 26 Mischief shall come upon mischief, and rumour shall be upon rumour; then shall they seek a vision of the prophet; but the law shall perish from the priest, and counsel from the ancients.
> 27 The king shall mourn, and the prince shall be clothed with desolation, and the hands of the people of the land shall be troubled: I will do unto them after their way, and according to their deserts will I judge them; and they shall know that I am the LORD.

As we saw in Chapter 6 of Ezekiel, the prophet not only describes what is going to happen to Israel, but he also tells us why it is going to happen—because of their iniquity. Israel shall be left to drift without counsel and understanding from the Lord's servants, the prophets. "The law shall perish from the priest," in that the authority of God will be taken away. Ultimately, without true prophets and priests to guide the people, "My face will I turn also from them, and they shall pollute my secret place: for the robbers shall enter into it, and defile it." Men will attempt to carry on the traditions started by the children of Israel, but without the divine authority or inspiration from God. They will merely interpret that which they find remaining in the scriptures, but not with direct access to God himself. Why will this happen? Because "the land is full of bloody crimes, and the city is full of violence." Israel not only adopted many of the pagan practices from the nations around them, but they did so while still feigning to believe in the living God of Israel. The Lord's displeasure with this form of hypocrisy is evident in the following verses.

> **Ezekiel 8:17-18**
> 17 Then he said unto me, Hast thou seen this, O son of man? Is it a light thing to the house of Judah that they commit the abominations which they commit here? for they have filled the

land with violence, and have returned to provoke me to anger: and, lo, they put the branch to their nose.
18 Therefore will I also deal in fury: mine eye shall not spare, neither will I have pity: and though they cry in mine ears with a loud voice, yet will I not hear them.

Here, the Lord expresses his amazement at how the children of Israel can "fill the land with violence," and still "return to provoke me to anger." Again, the idea of hypocrisy is felt in these verses. Because of this audacity on the part of the people, the Lord expresses his need to correct them harshly by withdrawing his presence from them.

Ezekiel 9:1-11
1 He cried also in mine ears with a loud voice, saying, Cause them that have charge over the city to draw near, even every man with his destroying weapon in his hand.
2 And, behold, six men came from the way of the higher gate, which lieth toward the north, and every man a slaughter weapon in his hand; and one man among them was clothed with linen, with a writer's inkhorn by his side: and they went in, and stood beside the brasen altar.
3 And the glory of the God of Israel was gone up from the cherub, whereupon he was, to the threshold of the house. And he called to the man clothed with linen, which had the writer's inkhorn by his side;
4 And the LORD said unto him, Go through the midst of the city, through the midst of Jerusalem, and set a mark upon the foreheads of the men that sigh and that cry for all the abominations that be done in the midst thereof.
5 And to the others he said in mine hearing, Go ye after him through the city, and smite: let not your eye spare, neither have ye pity:
6 Slay utterly old and young, both maids, and little children, and women: but come not near any man upon whom is the mark; and begin at my sanctuary. Then they began at the ancient men which were before the house.
7 And he said unto them, Defile the house, and fill the courts with the slain: go ye forth. And they went forth, and slew in the city.
8 And it came to pass, while they were slaying them, and I was left, that I fell upon my face, and cried, and said, Ah Lord GOD! wilt thou destroy all the residue of Israel in thy pouring out of thy fury upon Jerusalem?
9 Then said he unto me, The iniquity of the house of Israel and Judah is exceeding great, and the land is full of blood, and the city full of perverseness: for they say, The LORD hath forsaken the earth, and the LORD seeth not.
10 And as for me also, mine eye shall not spare, neither will I have pity, but I will recompense their way upon their head.
11 And, behold, the man clothed with linen, which had the inkhorn by his side, reported the matter, saying, I have done as thou hast commanded me.

In this symbolic passage, Ezekiel himself expresses concern over this "destruction" which the Lord has caused to come upon the whole land. He asks the specific question, "Ah Lord GOD! wilt thou destroy all the residue of Israel in thy pouring out of thy fury upon Jerusalem?" Ezekiel, while a prophet, is still rather amazed at the Lord's approach. He questions the Lord like one who questions a parent as to whether the punishment prescribed for a child is much too severe. Still, the Lord reminds Ezekiel of the extent of the perverseness and the crimes they have committed. They commit these great crimes against themselves and their God, saying, "The Lord hath forsaken the earth, and the LORD seeth not." In the end, the Lord does forsake the earth, withdrawing his prophets and priesthood authority. "And as for me also, mine eye shall not spare, neither will I have pity, but I will recompense their way upon their head." After years and generations of killing the prophets and casting them out from among them, the children of Israel finally are given that which they have desired of the Lord by their actions—a complete withdrawal of his prophets.

> **Ezekiel 11:9-12**
> 9 And I will bring you out of the midst thereof, and deliver you into the hands of strangers, and will execute judgments among you.
> 10 Ye shall fall by the sword; I will judge you in the border of Israel; and ye shall know that I am the LORD.
> 11 This city shall not be your caldron, neither shall ye be the flesh in the midst thereof; but I will judge you in the border of Israel:
> 12 And ye shall know that I am the LORD: for ye have not walked in my statutes, neither executed my judgments, but have done after the manners of the heathen that are round about you.

While the children of Israel may desire to remain in Jerusalem, we learn from the above passage that they will not do so. They will be cast out and smitten and driven, and the Lord will ultimately "deliver you into the hands of strangers, and will execute judgments among you." Why is this going to happen? "For ye have not walked in my statutes, neither executed my judgments, but have done after the manners of the heathen that are round about you."

> **Ezekiel 11:13-21**
> 13 And it came to pass, when I prophesied, that Pelatiah the son of Benaiah died. Then fell I down upon my face, and cried with a loud voice, and said, Ah Lord GOD! wilt thou make a full end of the remnant of Israel?
> 14 Again the word of the LORD came unto me, saying,
> 15 Son of man, thy brethren, even thy brethren, the men of thy kindred, and all the house of Israel wholly, are they unto whom the inhabitants of Jerusalem have said, Get you far from the LORD: unto us is this land given in possession.
> 16 Therefore say, Thus saith the Lord GOD; Although I have cast them far off among the heathen, and although I have scattered them among the countries, yet will I be to them as a little sanctuary in the countries where they shall come.
> 17 Therefore say, Thus saith the Lord GOD; I will even gather you from the people, and assemble you out of the countries where ye have been scattered, and I will give you the land of Israel.
> 18 And they shall come thither, and they shall take away all the detestable things thereof and all the abominations thereof from thence.
> 19 And I will give them one heart, and I will put a new spirit within you; and I will take the stony heart out of their flesh, and will give them an heart of flesh:
> 20 That they may walk in my statutes, and keep mine ordinances, and do them: and they shall be my people, and I will be their God.
> 21 But as for them whose heart walketh after the heart of their detestable things and their abominations, I will recompense their way upon their own heads, saith the Lord GOD.

Again we see the concern exhibited by the Prophet Ezekiel when he realizes the judgment which the Lord has decreed upon the inhabitants of Jerusalem and upon the nation of Israel. Amazed at the extent of the punishment, Ezekiel exclaims, "Ah Lord GOD! wilt thou make a full end of the remnant of Israel?" In an answer to this humble and loving plea on the part of the Lord's servant

Ezekiel, the Lord begins to hint at the ultimate mercy which he shall show unto his people in the latter days. While the scattering and destruction of Israel will be complete and all-encompassing in terms of the Lord's withdrawal, we are able to see from the above verses that, in the end, the Lord will not leave his people in their lost and fallen state. He will "gather them" out from the people where they have been scattered, and he will "take the stony heart out of their flesh, and will give them a heart of flesh: That they may walk in my statutes, and keep mine ordinances, and do them: and they shall be my people, and I will be their God."

Ezekiel 12:20-28

20 And the cities that are inhabited shall be laid waste, and the land shall be desolate; and ye shall know that I am the LORD.
21 And the word of the LORD came unto me, saying,
22 Son of man, what is that proverb that ye have in the land of Israel, saying, The days are prolonged, and every vision faileth?
23 Tell them therefore, Thus saith the Lord GOD; I will make this proverb to cease, and they shall no more use it as a proverb in Israel; but say unto them, The days are at hand, and the effect of every vision.
24 For there shall be no more any vain vision nor flattering divination within the house of Israel.
25 For I am the LORD: I will speak, and the word that I shall speak shall come to pass; it shall be no more prolonged: for in your days, O rebellious house, will I say the word, and will perform it, saith the Lord GOD.
26 Again the word of the LORD came to me, saying,
27 Son of man, behold, they of the house of Israel say, The vision that he seeth is for many days to come, and he prophesieth of the times that are afar off.
28 Therefore say unto them, Thus saith the Lord GOD; There shall none of my words be prolonged any more, but the word which I have spoken shall be done, saith the Lord GOD.

We learn that the children of Israel really understood the meaning of the prophecies that had been spoken against them. However, they still chose to remain in their state of wickedness, hypocrisy, and rebellion against God, saying that "The vision that he seeth is for many days to come, and he prophesieth of the times that are afar off." We get the sense that the Lord was also irritated by what he saw as a people sinning against great knowledge, unlike the heathen who were sinning out of ignorance and tradition.

Ezekiel 17:11-15

11 Moreover the word of the LORD came unto me, saying,
12 Say now to the rebellious house, Know ye not what these things mean? tell them, Behold, the king of Babylon is come to Jerusalem, and hath taken the king thereof, and the princes thereof, and led them with him to Babylon;
13 And hath taken of the king's seed, and made a covenant with him, and hath taken an oath of him: he hath also taken the mighty of the land:
14 That the kingdom might be base, that it might not lift itself up, but that by keeping of his covenant it might stand.
15 But he rebelled against him in sending his ambassadors into Egypt, that they might give him horses and much people. Shall he prosper? shall he escape that doeth such things? or shall he break the covenant, and be delivered?

THE LATTER RAIN

The Lord suggests that Israel has done grievous things that have led to its capture, destruction, and ultimate captivity. First, they have broken the covenant which they made with the Lord by worshipping other Gods and by breaking the commandments of the Lord. Secondly, they have in a sense, "made an oath" with the king of Babylon to serve him. However, once they become servants to Babylon and realize that the Lord is no longer with them, instead of returning to the Lord for help, they seek help from Egypt. As was the case in the books of Isaiah and Jeremiah, the Lord gives a strict warning about seeking assistance from Egypt or the hand of flesh: "Shall he prosper? shall he escape that doeth such things? or shall he break the covenant, and be delivered?"

Ezekiel 17:16-21

16 As I live, saith the Lord GOD, surely in the place where the king dwelleth that made him king, whose oath he despised, and whose covenant he brake, even with him in the midst of Babylon he shall die.
17 Neither shall Pharaoh with his mighty army and great company make for him in the war, by casting up mounts, and building forts, to cut off many persons:
18 Seeing he despised the oath by breaking the covenant, when, lo, he had given his hand, and hath done all these things, he shall not escape.
19 Therefore thus saith the Lord GOD; As I live, surely mine oath that he hath despised, and my covenant that he hath broken, even it will I recompense upon his own head.
20 And I will spread my net upon him, and he shall be taken in my snare, and I will bring him to Babylon, and will plead with him there for his trespass that he hath trespassed against me.
21 And all his fugitives with all his bands shall fall by the sword, and they that remain shall be scattered toward all winds: and ye shall know that I the LORD have spoken it.

As the Lord liveth, he shall surely cut off Israel from being a nation. Nor will it do any good for them to seek help from Pharaoh and from Egypt. Just as in the Book of Isaiah, Ezekiel shows that he "will bring him to Babylon," although Isaiah described it as being overrun by Assyria. It is the same event. Babylon and Assyria represent the same thing, the kingdom of the devil. Once men discover the awfulness of being subject to the kingdom of the devil and his false doctrines, they will attempt to escape it by constructing churches and organizations of their own, but they will not seek the Lord directly in these undertakings. While a man may seek to escape from the king of Babylon, or from the devil, by creating his own new church, "he will not escape," and the church which he creates will not have the power to save him.

Ezekiel 19:1-9

1 Moreover take thou up a lamentation for the princes of Israel,
2 And say, What is thy mother? A lioness: she lay down among lions, she nourished her whelps among young lions.
3 And she brought up one of her whelps: it became a young lion, and it learned to catch the prey; it devoured men.
4 The nations also heard of him; he was taken in their pit, and they brought him with chains unto the land of Egypt.
5 Now when she saw that she had waited, and her hope was lost, then she took another of her whelps, and made him a young lion.
6 And he went up and down among the lions, he became a young lion, and learned to catch the prey, and devoured men.

7 And he knew their desolate palaces, and he laid waste their cities; and the land was desolate, and the fulness thereof, by the noise of his roaring.
8 Then the nations set against him on every side from the provinces, and spread their net over him: he was taken in their pit.
9 And they put him in ward in chains, and brought him to the king of Babylon: they brought him into holds, that his voice should no more be heard upon the mountains of Israel.

Here the Lord again divides the Kingdom of Israel into its two chief parts, Joseph and Judah, and he refers to them metaphorically as two young lions. At first, both of these lions are terrible and mighty, passing through the land and devouring men. However, consistent with what we have seen in other prophesies, Joseph is carried away captive first. The Northern Ten Tribes are lumped together as one group for the most part, being referred to collectively as "Joseph," "Ephraim," or "Israel," depending on the context. In terms of geography, this group of tribes is also referred to as Samaria, it being the former capital city of the Northern Ten Tribes that separated themselves from Judah after the reign of King Solomon ended.

We know that this first lion is referring to Joseph because of the language that is used in the narrative: "The nations also heard of him; he was taken in their pit, and they brought him with chains unto the land of Egypt." It was Joseph with his coat of many colors, the eleventh son of Jacob and first-born of Rachael that was thrown into a pit by his brethren, who then sold him to merchants that were passing by. Ultimately, these merchants "brought him with chains unto the land of Egypt." This identifies the first lion as referring to Joseph, who was sold into Egypt, and to his descendants and offspring, and collectively to the Northern Ten Tribes of Israel. The Northern Ten Tribes were the first to be dispersed, scattered, and lost from the sight of the world.

Next, we see that, in the absence of her first young lion, Joseph, the mother of Israel puts her hope in a second young lion, which also "learned to catch the prey, and devour men." This second lion also has a moment of greatness and glory, but is ultimately taken by the nations of the world, who "spread their net over him: he was taken in their pit. And they put him in ward in chains, and brought him to the king of Babylon: they brought him into holds, that his voice should no more be heard upon the mountains of Israel." We see that even this second lion, Judah, is ultimately overcome by Babylon, and the kingdom of the devil is given complete dominion over the whole earth once Joseph and Judah are both driven into captivity and desolation.

Ezekiel 21:24-27

24 Therefore thus saith the Lord GOD; Because ye have made your iniquity to be remembered, in that your transgressions are discovered, so that in all your doings your sins do appear; because, I say, that ye are come to remembrance, ye shall be taken with the hand.
25 And thou, profane wicked prince of Israel, whose day is come, when iniquity shall have an end,
26 Thus saith the Lord GOD; Remove the diadem, and take off the crown: this shall not be the same: exalt him that is low, and abase him that is high.
27 I will overturn, overturn, overturn, it: and it shall be no more, until he come whose right it is; and I will give it him.

The sword of the king of Babylon will be allowed to completely overthrow the children of Israel, and there shall be none to escape. Whether it refers to the kingdom of Assyria, the kingdom of Babylon, or the kingdom of the devil, it is the same. Because of the gross wickedness of the children of Israel in committing murder and whoredom, and in worshipping false gods and sacrificing their own children to heathen gods, and in killing and driving off the true prophets, the Lord curses them by withdrawing his presence from them and taking his priesthood from the earth.

Egypt Will Not Protect Israel

As we saw before, Israel does not escape the king of Babylon despite a desperate attempt on its part to derive help from Egypt. If our analysis of the Book of Isaiah holds true, we should recall that references to Israel's attempts to find safety in Egypt are really referring to man's attempts to reestablish truth on the earth by creating churches of men. While they recognize that the church they are leaving is not correct, they fail to receive priesthood authority directly from God. These new churches of men flourish for a season, but are then overrun by the king of Babylon. Only a full restoration will reestablish Zion upon the earth. Only a living prophet can do it: one who calls on the Lord directly and receives direction and authority to act in his name.

> Ezekiel 29:19-21
>
> 19 Therefore thus saith the Lord GOD; Behold, I will give the land of Egypt unto Nebuchadrezzar king of Babylon; and he shall take her multitude, and take her spoil, and take her prey; and it shall be the wages for his army.
> 20 I have given him the land of Egypt for his labour wherewith he served against it, because they wrought for me, saith the Lord GOD.
> 21 In that day will I cause the horn of the house of Israel to bud forth, and I will give thee the opening of the mouth in the midst of them; and they shall know that I am the LORD.

The Lord will "give the land of Egypt unto Nebuchadrezzar king of Babylon; and he shall take her multitude, and take her spoil, and take her prey." Zion will be overthrown in a two-step process. First, Joseph or the Northern Ten Tribes, will fall into apostasy, followed by Judah, or the Southern Two Tribes. Eventually, the captives in Babylon will desire to escape, and will begin forming churches and organizations that they feel better match the ideal church described in the Old and New Testaments. This is what is meant by fleeing to Egypt or seeking help from Egypt. Furthermore, Isaiah, Jeremiah, and Ezekiel all show that seeking refuge through the aid of Egypt is vain. All three prophets show that the devil will ultimately "take the prey" from Egypt and overrun the man-made institutions, filling them with false doctrine, pomp and unauthorized priesthood observances. In verse 21 above, we see that the springing forth of new churches, albeit man-made, will be a precursor to the eventual restoration of the true Zion to the earth. "In that day will I cause the horn of the House of Israel to bud forth, and I will give thee the opening of the mouth in the midst of them; and they shall know that I am the LORD." At some point, in the last days, the Lord will again call a prophet on the earth, and Zion shall "bud forth." This new prophet will be a gift unto the children of men when he "opens [his] mouth in the midst of them; and they shall know that I am the LORD."

> **Ezekiel 30:10-12**
> 10 Thus saith the Lord GOD; I will also make the multitude of Egypt to cease by the hand of Nebuchadrezzar king of Babylon.
> 11 He and his people with him, the terrible of the nations, shall be brought to destroy the land: and they shall draw their swords against Egypt, and fill the land with the slain.
> 12 And I will make the rivers dry, and sell the land into the hand of the wicked: and I will make the land waste, and all that is therein, by the hand of strangers: I the LORD have spoken it.

Ezekiel 30 shows that while the Egypt-type churches that spring up may originally have been created with the best of intentions by men, and through the inspiration of God telling them that something was wrong in Babylon, in the end, these churches are overcome by the king of Babylon. When the Lord says, "I will make the rivers dry, and sell the land into the hand of the wicked: and I will make the land waste, and all that is therein, by the hand of strangers: I the LORD have spoken it," we get the feeling that without a duly-called prophet to guide them, these man-made organizations—while well-meaning in their conception—are nonetheless overrun by the cunning craftiness of the devil, and cannot save their members since they lack the properly-authorized priesthood from God to perform the saving ordinances.

> **Ezekiel 32:11-13**
> 11 For thus saith the Lord GOD; The sword of the king of Babylon shall come upon thee.
> 12 By the swords of the mighty will I cause thy multitude to fall, the terrible of the nations, all of them: and they shall spoil the pomp of Egypt, and all the multitude thereof shall be destroyed.
> 13 I will destroy also all the beasts thereof from beside the great waters; neither shall the foot of man trouble them any more, nor the hoofs of beasts trouble them.

If the Lord did indeed withdraw from the earth for a time, taking his Church and priesthood with him, the only way for Zion to be restored to the earth is to have the same organization and priesthood put back on the earth in its original form. This can only occur through a prophet or prophets who receive authority and guidance from God directly, and transmit these revelations to others. The message of these modern prophets will penetrate the hearts of their listeners, being accompanied by the spirit of God which testifies of all truth. Anything less than this can only be viewed as another interpretation of the Bible record, lacking the ultimate power and authority required for true salvation.

False Prophets in Ancient Israel

> **Ezekiel 13:1-9**
> 1 And the word of the LORD came unto me, saying,
> 2 Son of man, prophesy against the prophets of Israel that prophesy, and say thou unto them that prophesy out of their own hearts, Hear ye the word of the LORD;
> 3 Thus saith the Lord GOD; Woe unto the foolish prophets, that follow their own spirit, and have seen nothing!

4 O Israel, thy prophets are like the foxes in the deserts.
5 Ye have not gone up into the gaps, neither made up the hedge for the house of Israel to stand in the battle in the day of the LORD.
6 They have seen vanity and lying divination, saying, The LORD saith: and the LORD hath not sent them: and they have made others to hope that they would confirm the word.
7 Have ye not seen a vain vision, and have ye not spoken a lying divination, whereas ye say, The LORD saith it; albeit I have not spoken?
8 Therefore thus saith the Lord GOD; Because ye have spoken vanity, and seen lies, therefore, behold, I am against you, saith the Lord GOD.
9 And mine hand shall be upon the prophets that see vanity, and that divine lies: they shall not be in the assembly of my people, neither shall they be written in the writing of the house of Israel, neither shall they enter into the land of Israel; and ye shall know that I am the Lord GOD.

Here we learn that false prophets were among the people of Israel, and they were predicting peace and prosperity. The Lord is angry with them, and through Ezekiel he is telling them that such false prophecies are vanity and lies. The Lord states clearly that he is against such false prophets. Ultimately, these false teachers lead the children of Israel away into falsehood.

Ezekiel 13:10-16
10 Because, even because they have seduced my people, saying, Peace; and there was no peace; and one built up a wall, and, lo, others daubed it with untempered morter:
11 Say unto them which daub it with untempered morter, that it shall fall: there shall be an overflowing shower; and ye, O great hailstones, shall fall; and a stormy wind shall rend it.
12 Lo, when the wall is fallen, shall it not be said unto you, Where is the daubing wherewith ye have daubed it?
13 Therefore thus saith the Lord GOD; I will even rend it with a stormy wind in my fury; and there shall be an overflowing shower in mine anger, and great hailstones in my fury to consume it.
14 So will I break down the wall that ye have daubed with untempered morter, and bring it down to the ground, so that the foundation thereof shall be discovered, and it shall fall, and ye shall be consumed in the midst thereof: and ye shall know that I am the LORD.
15 Thus will I accomplish my wrath upon the wall, and upon them that have daubed it with untempered morter, and will say unto you, The wall is no more, neither they that daubed it;
16 To wit, the prophets of Israel which prophesy concerning Jerusalem, and which see visions of peace for her, and there is no peace, saith the Lord GOD.

The false prophets that rose up in Israel prior to the Great Famine period evidently were prophesying things that were easy to hear and pleasant to believe. The "building of a wall with untempered mortar" seems to refer to the development of a code of conduct and observances that, when followed, would protect them from being overcome by the adversary. The idea of "daubing" the protective wall with untempered mortar suggests that these false traditions and observances were added to from time to time, and from one generation to the next. These traditions came forth from false teachers and unauthorized priests—not from the Lord directly. They cannot protect Israel from the siege which has been pronounced upon her, and the great nation will be taken and scattered. While the Lord seems to be referring to the time prior to his withdrawal from Israel, this daubing and wall building continues during the Spiritual Famine period, as men try to construct a way of life that will lead them to salvation but is not based on divine inspiration through a living prophet. When the truth finally does come, many will still resist the message of the restoration, though it will be a very lovely song.

Ezekiel 33:31-33

31 And they come unto thee as the people cometh, and they sit before thee as my people, and they hear thy words, but they will not do them: for with their mouth they shew much love, but their heart goeth after their covetousness.
32 And, lo, thou art unto them as a very lovely song of one that hath a pleasant voice, and can play well on an instrument: for they hear thy words, but they do them not.
33 And when this cometh to pass, (lo, it will come,) then shall they know that a prophet hath been among them.

Rain, Water, Famine, Drought, Desolation

Ezekiel 1:28

28 As the appearance of the bow that is in the cloud in the day of rain, so was the appearance of the brightness round about. This was the appearance of the likeness of the glory of the Lord. And when I saw it, I fell upon my face, and I heard a voice of one that spake.

Consistent with our findings in Isaiah and Jeremiah, Ezekiel continues the symbolic association of moisture and rain with the presence of revelation from God and true doctrine. Even in the first chapter of his writings, Ezekiel makes this association clear, comparing the presence and glory of the Lord to that of a rainbow "in the day of rain." To make this point clearer, he says, "And when I saw it," meaning the glory of the Lord, "I fell upon my face, and I heard a voice of one that spake." Ezekiel defines a day of rain as one in which the glory of the Lord is present, and one in which a prophet of the Lord can hear the voice of the Lord through revelation. Revelation not only relieves one's thirst, but also one's hunger and want for bread.

Ezekiel 4:9-17

9 Take thou also unto thee wheat, and barley, and beans, and lentiles, and millet, and fitches, and put them in one vessel, and make thee bread thereof, according to the number of the days that thou shalt lie upon thy side, three hundred and ninety days shalt thou eat thereof.
10 And thy meat which thou shalt eat shall be by weight, twenty shekels a day: from time to time shalt thou eat it.
11 Thou shalt drink also water by measure, the sixth part of an hin: from time to time shalt thou drink.
12 And thou shalt eat it as barley cakes, and thou shalt bake it with dung that cometh out of man, in their sight.
13 And the LORD said, Even thus shall the children of Israel eat their defiled bread among the Gentiles, whither I will drive them.
14 Then said I, Ah Lord GOD! behold, my soul hath not been polluted: for from my youth up even till now have I not eaten of that which dieth of itself, or is torn in pieces; neither came there abominable flesh into my mouth.
15 Then he said unto me, Lo, I have given thee cow's dung for man's dung, and thou shalt prepare thy bread therewith.
16 Moreover he said unto me, Son of man, behold, I will break the staff of bread in Jerusalem: and they shall eat bread by weight, and with care; and they shall drink water by measure, and with astonishment:
17 That they may want bread and water, and be astonied one with another, and consume away for their iniquity.

What an amazing image! The children of Israel shall eat their defiled cakes, and bread that has been prepared with dung in it. And they shall do it "among the Gentiles, whither I will drive them." This imagery suggests that during the Dark Ages of apostasy, when the devil has total control over the religions of the world due to the withdrawal of the Lord and the lack of prophets to guide the people, the children of Israel will be forced to nourish themselves with a defiled and polluted form of bread. This bread spoken of is a defiled and polluted form of revelation. It may look like regular bread. It may be based on the former scriptures available to men at the time, but it will nonetheless be prepared with "dung that cometh out of men," or with "cow's dung for man's dung." They are religions based on the Bible, but formed from the ideas of men, not God. Finally, the Lord makes it clear in verse 16 what he intends by this symbolism: "Behold, I will break the staff of bread in Jerusalem: and they shall eat bread by weight, and with care; and they shall drink water by measure, and with astonishment: That they may want bread and water, and be astonied one with another, and consume away for their iniquity." The Lord made this same pronouncement in the Book of Isaiah, Chapter 3, as we may recall:

Isaiah 3:1-8

1 For, behold, the Lord, the LORD of hosts, doth take away from Jerusalem and from Judah the stay and the staff, the whole stay of bread, and the whole stay of water,
2 The mighty man, and the man of war, the judge, and the prophet, and the prudent, and the ancient,
3 The captain of fifty, and the honourable man, and the counsellor, and the cunning artificer, and the eloquent orator.
4 And I will give children to be their princes, and babes shall rule over them.
5 And the people shall be oppressed, every one by another, and every one by his neighbour: the child shall behave himself proudly against the ancient, and the base against the honourable.
6 When a man shall take hold of his brother of the house of his father, saying, Thou hast clothing, be thou our ruler, and let this ruin be under thy hand:
7 In that day shall he swear, saying, I will not be an healer; for in my house is neither bread nor clothing: make me not a ruler of the people.
8 For Jerusalem is ruined, and Judah is fallen: because their tongue and their doings are against the LORD, to provoke the eyes of his glory.

What does it mean then to take away "the whole stay of bread, and the whole stay of water?" It means that the Lord will remove from them "the judge, and the prophet," "For Jerusalem is ruined, and Judah is fallen: because their tongue and their doings are against the LORD, to provoke the eyes of his glory." This theme is repeated over and over again throughout the scriptures. Recall, as well, the words of Amos the Old Testament prophet we read at the onset of this book:

Amos 8:11-12

11 Behold, the days come, saith the Lord GOD, that I will send a famine in the land, not a famine of bread, nor a thirst for water, but of hearing the words of the LORD:
12 And they shall wander from sea to sea, and from the north even to the east, they shall run to and fro to seek the word of the LORD, and shall not find it.

I cannot imagine how this concept of a Spiritual Famine period could be stated more clearly: "they shall run to and fro to seek the word of the LORD, and shall not find it." They shall not find it because it is nowhere to be found. No prophets are left on the earth, and men and women are left to themselves and subject to the falsehoods and doctrines of the devil. Thus, the devil has been given full dominion over the entire earth according to prophecy. During this period, in terms of church organization, the Lord literally does nothing.

Amos 3:7
7 Surely the Lord GOD will do nothing, but he revealeth his secret unto his servants the prophets.

Without a duly-called prophet, he will continue to do nothing. He is still mindful of his children, and blesses those that seek righteousness, but without a prophet on the earth, his children are severely limited as to how much progress they can make on the earth. The prophet Ezekiel continues this same line of reasoning as he makes reference to the pestilence, famine, and the sword which will shortly overcome Zion and take her.

Ezekiel 5:14-17
14 Moreover I will make thee waste, and a reproach among the nations that are round about thee, in the sight of all that pass by.
15 So it shall be a reproach and a taunt, an instruction and an astonishment unto the nations that are round about thee, when I shall execute judgments in thee in anger and in fury and in furious rebukes. I the LORD have spoken it.
16 When I shall send upon them the evil arrows of famine, which shall be for their destruction, and which I will send to destroy you: and I will increase the famine upon you, and will break your staff of bread:
17 So will I send upon you famine and evil beasts, and they shall bereave thee; and pestilence and blood shall pass through thee; and I will bring the sword upon thee. I the LORD have spoken it.

Without the keys of understanding developed from our study of Isaiah and Amos, we would miss the real message of these verses. We would see it as a famine of no rain. Clearly, there were periods of actual physical famine in Israel. During the reign of King Ahab, Elijah caused a famine to come upon the land that lasted for three and a half years. During the time that Joseph was sold into Egypt, he interpreted the dream of Pharaoh to mean that seven years of prosperity would be followed by seven years of famine, and it was so, even according to his interpretation. However, the famine spoken of in the above verses is something different. Applying our keys of interpretation from Isaiah, we can see that they are referring to a time when the people of the earth are without true and living prophets to guide them.

Ezekiel 14:12-21
12 The word of the LORD came again to me, saying,
13 Son of man, when the land sinneth against me by trespassing grievously, then will I stretch out mine hand upon it, and will break the staff of the bread thereof, and will send famine upon it, and will cut off man and beast from it:
14 Though these three men, Noah, Daniel, and Job, were in it, they should deliver but their own souls by their righteousness, saith the Lord GOD.
15 If I cause noisome beasts to pass through the land, and they spoil it, so that it be desolate, that no man may pass through because of the beasts:

16 Though these three men were in it, as I live, saith the Lord GOD, they shall deliver neither sons nor daughters; they only shall be delivered, but the land shall be desolate.
17 Or if I bring a sword upon that land, and say, Sword, go through the land; so that I cut off man and beast from it:
18 Though these three men were in it, as I live, saith the Lord GOD, they shall deliver neither sons nor daughters, but they only shall be delivered themselves.
19 Or if I send a pestilence into that land, and pour out my fury upon it in blood, to cut off from it man and beast:
20 Though Noah, Daniel, and Job, were in it, as I live, saith the Lord GOD, they shall deliver neither son nor daughter; they shall but deliver their own souls by their righteousness.
21 For thus saith the Lord GOD; How much more when I send my four sore judgments upon Jerusalem, the sword, and the famine, and the noisome beast, and the pestilence, to cut off from it man and beast?

The above verses show how determined the Lord is to actually withdraw from his chosen people. His mind is so made up that even if Noah, Daniel, and Job were present, their righteousness would not prevent him from withdrawing his prophets and priesthood from the earth. The impending annihilation through the sword and famine is a symbolic pronouncement that will come to pass. By the time Ezekiel was alive and communicating the will of the Lord, nothing save true and complete repentance could have stopped this terrible judgment from being fulfilled.

Ezekiel 15:1-8
1 And the word of the LORD came unto me, saying,
2 Son of man, What is the vine tree more than any tree, or than a branch which is among the trees of the forest?
3 Shall wood be taken thereof to do any work? or will men take a pin of it to hang any vessel thereon?
4 Behold, it is cast into the fire for fuel; the fire devoureth both the ends of it, and the midst of it is burned. Is it meet for any work?
5 Behold, when it was whole, it was meet for no work: how much less shall it be meet yet for any work, when the fire hath devoured it, and it is burned?
6 Therefore thus saith the Lord GOD; As the vine tree among the trees of the forest, which I have given to the fire for fuel, so will I give the inhabitants of Jerusalem.
7 And I will set my face against them; they shall go out from one fire, and another fire shall devour them; and ye shall know that I am the LORD, when I set my face against them.
8 And I will make the land desolate, because they have committed a trespass, saith the Lord GOD.

Here, the Lord compares ancient Zion to a vine tree. He shows that while they were not profitable "to do any work" due to their iniquity and transgressions, they will be even less profitable to the people of the earth after they have passed through the judgment, or the "fire hath devoured it, and it is burned." The Lord will "set his face against them. And I will make the land desolate, because they have committed a trespass, saith the Lord GOD."

Ezekiel 19:10-14
10 Thy mother is like a vine in thy blood, planted by the waters: she was fruitful and full of branches by reason of many waters.
11 And she had strong rods for the sceptres of them that bare rule, and her stature was exalted among the thick branches, and she appeared in her height with the multitude of her branches.

12 But she was plucked up in fury, she was cast down to the ground, and the east wind dried up her fruit: her strong rods were broken and withered; the fire consumed them.
13 And now she is planted in the wilderness, in a dry and thirsty ground.
14 And fire is gone out of a rod of her branches, which hath devoured her fruit, so that she hath no strong rod to be a sceptre to rule. This is a lamentation, and shall be for a lamentation.

While "planted by the waters: she was fruitful and full of branches by reason of many waters." In other words, when she had living prophets among her, Israel was fruitful, due to the many revelations and visions given to those prophets to guide her in the ways of righteousness. When the kings of Israel were righteous and looked to the prophets for guidance and direction, Israel became a strong and mighty nation among the other nations of the world. When the Lord withdrew his prophets, his priesthood, and his presence from Israel, then Israel became "planted in the wilderness, in a dry and thirsty ground. And fire is gone out of a rod of her branches, which hath devoured her fruit, so that she hath no strong rod to be a sceptre to rule." Not only is Israel scattered and the prophets removed from her presence, but even the lineage of the kings is lost, and she has "no strong rod to be a sceptre to rule." They are left to wander to and fro in the land among the Gentiles and the heathen, not knowing what to do about their lost and fallen state.

Ezekiel 22:23-31
23 And the word of the LORD came unto me, saying,
24 Son of man, say unto her, Thou art the land that is not cleansed, nor rained upon in the day of indignation.
25 There is a conspiracy of her prophets in the midst thereof, like a roaring lion ravening the prey; they have devoured souls; they have taken the treasure and precious things; they have made her many widows in the midst thereof.
26 Her priests have violated my law, and have profaned mine holy things: they have put no difference between the holy and profane, neither have they shewed difference between the unclean and the clean, and have hid their eyes from my sabbaths, and I am profaned among them.
27 Her princes in the midst thereof are like wolves ravening the prey, to shed blood, and to destroy souls, to get dishonest gain.
28 And her prophets have daubed them with untempered morter, seeing vanity, and divining lies unto them, saying, Thus saith the Lord GOD, when the LORD hath not spoken.
29 The people of the land have used oppression, and exercised robbery, and have vexed the poor and needy: yea, they have oppressed the stranger wrongfully.
30 And I sought for a man among them, that should make up the hedge, and stand in the gap before me for the land, that I should not destroy it: but I found none.
31 Therefore have I poured out mine indignation upon them; I have consumed them with the fire of my wrath: their own way have I recompensed upon their heads, saith the Lord GOD.

Once the apostasy is complete, and the prophets are killed off or driven away, Israel becomes "the land that is not cleansed, nor rained upon." In this state, false prophets are given full reign over the people to pervert the ways of the Lord, to withhold truth, and to "destroy souls, to get dishonest gain." On the surface, the new laws and observances that are developed by these false teachers have the appearance of protecting the people, but the Lord compares these falsehoods to them being "daubed" with "untempered mortar," which concept we have seen before. They say, "Thus saith the Lord GOD, when the LORD hath not spoken." Unfortunately, the people are deceived with a great "conspiracy" that is so diabolical in nature that the pure in heart can hardly be convinced that it has really occurred. In the latter days, the Lord will finally come forth from his hiding place where he has concealed himself. He will once again restore Zion to the earth. He will then begin his marvelous work among the children of men to bring again truth and salvation to the earth. Then shall the devil and his followers be driven back by the sword of the Lord, which is his word—his word, given to his servants, the prophets.

> **Ezekiel 38:14-23**
> 14 Therefore, son of man, prophesy and say unto Gog, Thus saith the Lord GOD; In that day when my people of Israel dwelleth safely, shalt thou not know it?
> 15 And thou shalt come from thy place out of the north parts, thou, and many people with thee, all of them riding upon horses, a great company, and a mighty army:
> 16 And thou shalt come up against my people of Israel, as a cloud to cover the land; it shall be in the latter days, and I will bring thee against my land, that the heathen may know me, when I shall be sanctified in thee, O Gog, before their eyes.
> 17 Thus saith the Lord GOD; Art thou he of whom I have spoken in old time by my servants the prophets of Israel, which prophesied in those days many years that I would bring thee against them?
> 18 And it shall come to pass at the same time when Gog shall come against the land of Israel, saith the Lord GOD, that my fury shall come up in my face.
> 19 For in my jealousy and in the fire of my wrath have I spoken, Surely in that day there shall be a great shaking in the land of Israel;
> 20 So that the fishes of the sea, and the fowls of the heaven, and the beasts of the field, and all creeping things that creep upon the earth, and all the men that are upon the face of the earth, shall shake at my presence, and the mountains shall be thrown down, and the steep places shall fall, and every wall shall fall to the ground.
> 21 And I will call for a sword against him throughout all my mountains, saith the Lord GOD: every man's sword shall be against his brother.
> 22 And I will plead against him with pestilence and with blood; and I will rain upon him, and upon his bands, and upon the many people that are with him, an overflowing rain, and great hailstones, fire, and brimstone.
> 23 Thus will I magnify myself, and sanctify myself; and I will be known in the eyes of many nations, and they shall know that I am the LORD.

In the end, the Lord will again wield the sword (his word and his true doctrine). He will once again call prophets in the earth. Thus, "I will rain upon him, and upon his bands, and upon the many people that are with him, an overflowing rain." The many and diverse false doctrines that exist in the earth will be swallowed up and put down by the true Gospel that will flow forth from the presence of God, through his chosen servants, in the latter days. Satan will be no match for it.

A Remnant Shall Remain

We have seen before the idea that the Lord will allow a remnant to remain. At first it might be tempting to assume that this means that a group of people will remain on the earth with the true religion in their midst. But, this is not the case.

> **Ezekiel 6:8-10**
> 8 Yet will I leave a remnant, that ye may have some that shall escape the sword among the nations, when ye shall be scattered through the countries.

> 9 And they that escape of you shall remember me among the nations whither they shall be carried captives, because I am broken with their whorish heart, which hath departed from me, and with their eyes, which go a whoring after their idols: and they shall lothe themselves for the evils which they have committed in all their abominations.
> 10 And they shall know that I am the LORD, and that I have not said in vain that I would do this evil unto them.

We learn here that some will escape the sword and they "shall remember me among the nations whither they shall be carried captives." The Lord will allow a remnant of the House of Israel to remain visible to the eyes of the world, as a reminder to the world of her "whorish heart, which hath departed from me." This seems to occur both temporally and spiritually. He could have scattered Israel completely, leaving no trace of who is a descendant of former Israel and who is not. Instead, he left the Jews as a physical remnant and distinguishable branch of his chosen people. While they remain visible and identifiable, they are still not restored to their former glory. They nonetheless serve a great purpose as a physical reminder of the Lord's covenant with his people.

Likewise, the Lord has left the good people of the earth from all faiths, religions, and doctrines, both Jew and Gentile, as a spiritual remnant to "remember me among the nations whither they shall be carried captives." The actions and deeds of the just and the true seekers of righteousness stand as a testament of the divine nature of mankind. While they suffer persecutions and terrible trials during this dark period of history, in the end they will be recovered through the wisdom and justice of God. It is this spiritual remnant (the just people of the earth) that must ultimately lead man to the point of returning to God, and seeking again Zion in its fullness.

Ezekiel 14:22-23
> 22 Yet, behold, therein shall be left a remnant that shall be brought forth, both sons and daughters: behold, they shall come forth unto you, and ye shall see their way and their doings: and ye shall be comforted concerning the evil that I have brought upon Jerusalem, even concerning all that I have brought upon it.
> 23 And they shall comfort you, when ye see their ways and their doings: and ye shall know that I have not done without cause all that I have done in it, saith the Lord GOD.

This remnant that is left to wander among the heathen will remind the world of the abominations that their parents had done in Israel. We learn in Ezekiel 14 that this remnant will also be a comfort to Israel when "ye shall see their way and their doings." The good works and accomplishments of this "remnant" of Israel serves as a vivid reminder to the other lost tribes scattered among the nations of the world that Zion will eventually return. Historically speaking, Judah (the Jews) is the only tribe remaining intact as an identifiable branch of ancient Israel. However, the good deeds and actions of both Jews and others all testify that goodness and righteousness cannot be suppressed forever. Zion will ultimately spring forth again!

Whoredom: Playing the Harlot

As in Chapter 3 of the Book of Jeremiah, Ezekiel also refers to Israel's departure from the correct path as her having "played the harlot." In fact, Ezekiel is even more thorough in developing this type, or symbolic reference, than either Isaiah or Jeremiah. He devotes two entire chapters to this concept. Ezekiel Chapters 16 and 23 both show that Israel (or Ephraim) is the first sister to go astray and play the harlot among the other nations surrounding Zion. Then Judah, her sister to the south, follows suit and plays the harlot as well. It is also made clear that, while Judah hangs on for a while longer before falling from grace through infidelity to the Lord, when she does finally go a whoring after the nations, she is even worse than her sister Ephraim, causing her children to pass through fire and paying her suitors to come in unto her.

Ezekiel 16:1-14
1 Again the word of the LORD came unto me, saying,
2 Son of man, cause Jerusalem to know her abominations,
3 And say, Thus saith the Lord GOD unto Jerusalem; Thy birth and thy nativity is of the land of Canaan; thy father was an Amorite, and thy mother an Hittite.
4 And as for thy nativity, in the day thou wast born thy navel was not cut, neither wast thou washed in water to supple thee; thou wast not salted at all, nor swaddled at all.
5 None eye pitied thee, to do any of these unto thee, to have compassion upon thee; but thou wast cast out in the open field, to the lothing of thy person, in the day that thou wast born.
6 And when I passed by thee, and saw thee polluted in thine own blood, I said unto thee when thou wast in thy blood, Live; yea, I said unto thee when thou wast in thy blood, Live.
7 I have caused thee to multiply as the bud of the field, and thou hast increased and waxen great, and thou art come to excellent ornaments: thy breasts are fashioned, and thine hair is grown, whereas thou wast naked and bare.
8 Now when I passed by thee, and looked upon thee, behold, thy time was the time of love; and I spread my skirt over thee, and covered thy nakedness: yea, I sware unto thee, and entered into a covenant with thee, saith the Lord GOD, and thou becamest mine.
9 Then washed I thee with water; yea, I throughly washed away thy blood from thee, and I anointed thee with oil.
10 I clothed thee also with broidered work, and shod thee with badgers' skin, and I girded thee about with fine linen, and I covered thee with silk.
11 I decked thee also with ornaments, and I put bracelets upon thy hands, and a chain on thy neck.
12 And I put a jewel on thy forehead, and earrings in thine ears, and a beautiful crown upon thine head.
13 Thus wast thou decked with gold and silver; and thy raiment was of fine linen, and silk, and broidered work; thou didst eat fine flour, and honey, and oil: and thou wast exceeding beautiful, and thou didst prosper into a kingdom.
14 And thy renown went forth among the heathen for thy beauty: for it was perfect through my comeliness, which I had put upon thee, saith the Lord GOD.

This first section of Ezekiel Chapter 16 shows how God selected the children of Israel as his "chosen people," and put his seal upon them and made them his. In this way, he separated them from the heathen and set them apart, teaching them the way of happiness through the administration of the saving ordinances through the Priesthood, and by giving them his commandments for their protection and prosperity. At the peak of this period of prosperity, the united Kingdom of Israel was indeed "decked with gold and silver; and thy raiment was of fine linen, and silk, and embroidered work; thou didst eat fine flour, and honey, and oil: and thou wast exceeding beautiful, and thou didst prosper into a kingdom." At that point, Israel was an example to the nations of what the Lord's presence could do for a people. "And thy renown went forth among the heathen for thy beauty: for it was perfect through my comeliness, which I had put upon thee, saith the Lord GOD." Unfortunately, the children of Israel did not remain in this state of righteousness.

> **Ezekiel 16:15-21**
> 15 But thou didst trust in thine own beauty, and playedst the harlot because of thy renown, and pouredst out thy fornications on every one that passed by; his it was.
> 16 And of thy garments thou didst take, and deckedst thy high places with divers colours, and playedst the harlot thereupon: the like things shall not come, neither shall it be so.
> 17 Thou hast also taken thy fair jewels of my gold and of my silver, which I had given thee, and madest to thyself images of men, and didst commit whoredom with them,
> 18 And tookest thy broidered garments, and coveredst them: and thou hast set mine oil and mine incense before them.
> 19 My meat also which I gave thee, fine flour, and oil, and honey, wherewith I fed thee, thou hast even set it before them for a sweet savour: and thus it was, saith the Lord GOD.
> 20 Moreover thou hast taken thy sons and thy daughters, whom thou hast borne unto me, and these hast thou sacrificed unto them to be devoured. Is this of thy whoredoms a small matter,
> 21 That thou hast slain my children, and delivered them to cause them to pass through the fire for them?

This description above shows that Israel eventually forsook the true path and went off to play the harlot among the nations. This dual prophecy is both literal and symbolic in its meaning. In a literal sense, the Israelites did use their riches, gold, and silver to make idols and to worship false gods like the heathen. They also literally made their children to pass through fire, sacrificing them in the manner taught to them by the heathen nations round about them. Symbolically, however, Israel has taken the choice things that the Lord bestowed upon them—the scriptures, the priesthood, the miracles and the blessings of the Gospel—and have turned them into falsehood and false doctrines. Men have taken the writings found in the scriptures and manipulated them to form numerous different doctrines and creeds, none having true prophets to guide them, nor having the divine authority of the true priesthood. In this manner, the wicked inhabitants of Zion that caused this falling away to occur have, in a figurative sense, caused their descendants or children to pass through a symbolic fire, namely the hell of the great Spiritual Famine period.

> **Ezekiel 16:30-34**
> 30 How weak is thine heart, saith the Lord GOD, seeing thou doest all these things, the work of an imperious whorish woman;
> 31 In that thou buildest thine eminent place in the head of every way, and makest thine high place in every street; and hast not been as an harlot, in that thou scornest hire;
> 32 But as a wife that committeth adultery, which taketh strangers instead of her husband!
> 33 They give gifts to all whores: but thou givest thy gifts to all thy lovers, and hirest them, that they may come unto thee on every side for thy whoredom.
> 34 And the contrary is in thee from other women in thy whoredoms, whereas none followeth thee to commit whoredoms: and in that thou givest a reward, and no reward is given unto thee, therefore thou art contrary.

In this symbolic message, the Lord is the husband and the children of Israel are the "wife that committeth adultery, which taketh strangers instead of her husband!" And, where normally gifts and payments are made to whores when they provide their services to men, in the case of the children of Israel, the Lord is saying they are contrary. In other words, they even pay men to come in unto them and receive no reward themselves.

Ephraim first played the harlot with the Assyrians, and was later carried away captive by them. Then Judah followed suit, "Thou hast moreover multiplied thy fornication in the land of Canaan unto Chaldea," which is representative of Babylon. This "harlot" symbolism is completely consistent with the sword analogy where the kingdom of Satan (Assyria or Babylon) is allowed to overcome Israel first and then Judah. It also matches well with the famine concept, in that the children of Israel faint for lack of nourishment or water, and ultimately are left desolate. "Playing the harlot" is just another way of saying exactly the same thing as before: Samaria and Jerusalem, first one and then the other, lost the divine priesthood and the guidance of the true and living prophets, thus sending the entire world into a state of darkness (the Dark Ages) with respect to hearing the word of the Lord. During this period of dearth, there are no new scriptures and no new prophets, leaving the children of men to fend for themselves and derive as much hope as they can from the scriptures that are still available, namely the Old and New Testament.

Ezekiel 16:37-40

37 Behold, therefore I will gather all thy lovers, with whom thou hast taken pleasure, and all them that thou hast loved, with all them that thou hast hated; I will even gather them round about against thee, and will discover thy nakedness unto them, that they may see all thy nakedness.
38 And I will judge thee, as women that break wedlock and shed blood are judged; and I will give thee blood in fury and jealousy.
39 And I will also give thee into their hand, and they shall throw down thine eminent place, and shall break down thy high places: they shall strip thee also of thy clothes, and shall take thy fair jewels, and leave thee naked and bare.
40 They shall also bring up a company against thee, and they shall stone thee with stones, and thrust thee through with their swords.

The very nations from which the Israelites had borrowed and with which they had profaned the right ways of the Lord are the same nations that ultimately overthrow them. This is another example of dual prophecy. In a literal sense, the heathen nations overcame Israel, the Northern Kingdom, first and then the Jews also in Jerusalem. In a figurative sense, the churches that were later formed in the wake of the fall of Zion, and the withdrawal of the Lord from the earth, all use the scriptures and the traditions of the Jews and the people of Israel to develop their doctrines and ordinances. With respect to the remnant of the children of Israel that yet remains visible on the earth, namely the Jews, these churches persecute and condemn the Jews, driving them, hating them, and killing them in the name of the Lord. They thank not the Jews for the things which they have received from their hand: the scriptures, prophecies and covenants made between the Lord and his people. The false shepherds persecute not only the Jews, but also anyone that seeks for truth, and wants out of the oppression and bondage of falsehood. The righteous of both the Jews and the Gentiles are forced to endure grievous tyranny against them as the devil and his false prophets reign in terror on the earth.

> **Ezekiel 16:48-56**
> 48 As I live, saith the Lord GOD, Sodom thy sister hath not done, she nor her daughters, as thou hast done, thou and thy daughters.
> 49 Behold, this was the iniquity of thy sister Sodom, pride, fulness of bread, and abundance of idleness was in her and in her daughters, neither did she strengthen the hand of the poor and needy.
> 50 And they were haughty, and committed abomination before me: therefore I took them away as I saw good.
> 51 Neither hath Samaria committed half of thy sins; but thou hast multiplied thine abominations more than they, and hast justified thy sisters in all thine abominations which thou hast done.
> 52 Thou also, which hast judged thy sisters, bear thine own shame for thy sins that thou hast committed more abominable than they: they are more righteous than thou: yea, be thou confounded also, and bear thy shame, in that thou hast justified thy sisters.
> 53 When I shall bring again their captivity, the captivity of Sodom and her daughters, and the captivity of Samaria and her daughters, then will I bring again the captivity of thy captives in the midst of them:
> 54 That thou mayest bear thine own shame, and mayest be confounded in all that thou hast done, in that thou art a comfort unto them.
> 55 When thy sisters, Sodom and her daughters, shall return to their former estate, and Samaria and her daughters shall return to their former estate, then thou and thy daughters shall return to your former estate.
> 56 For thy sister Sodom was not mentioned by thy mouth in the day of thy pride.

Several interesting things occur in this section of Ezekiel 16. First, the Lord repeats his former statement that the sins of Sister Judah were greater than those of her sisters, Sodom and Samaria. Evidently, the Lord felt that Judah had sinned against a greater light, and did things that were even more abominable than her sisters had done. Next, we learn that there will be an order to the return of the true doctrine to the earth. In verse 53 we see, "When I shall bring again their captivity, the captivity of Sodom and her daughters, and the captivity of Samaria and her daughters, then will I bring again the captivity of thy captives in the midst of them." While Judah hung on longer than her sisters before she too played the harlot, it will be reversed in the last days. The Northern Kingdom of Israel or Ephraim, along with the heathen that is mixed within it (Sodom), will be gathered first, then will the Jews be gathered in among them as well. "When thy sisters, Sodom and her daughters, shall return to their former estate, and Samaria and her daughters shall return to their former estate, then thou and thy daughters shall return to your former estate." This not only shows the order in which the return to grace will occur, but it also shows that the former estate was indeed lost. In other words, there was in fact a fall from grace, and it encompassed the whole earth.

Another thing worthy of note in these verses above is the mention of the sister Sodom. In fact, in verse 56 above, it says, "For thy sister Sodom was not mentioned by thy mouth in the day of thy pride." In most other references in the scriptures, including within the Book of Ezekiel (Chapter 23), usually only two "harlot-playing" sisters are mentioned, Samaria (or Ephraim, representing the Northern

Ten Tribes) and Judah (or the Jews, representing the Southern Two Tribes). While it is true that the children of Israel are the chosen people of the Lord, we also know that God is not a respecter of persons. Those that call upon his name and keep his commandments are favored, and those that are wicked and hypocritical are brought under the judgment of God.

Father Abraham was promised by the Lord, "And in thy seed shall all the nations of the earth be blessed; because thou hast obeyed my voice," as recorded in Genesis 22:18. Why was Abraham given this great promise? He was given this great promise because he called upon the name of the Lord and obeyed the voice of the Lord in all things. Likewise, anyone, despite their blood lineage with respect to the Tribes of Israel, is eligible for the blessings of God to become active if they will call upon God the Father and keep and do that which they are commanded. This point is made clear in the New Testament, when John the Baptist is confronting a group of Pharisees and Sadducees:

Matthew 3:7-9
7 But when he saw many of the Pharisees and Sadducees come to his baptism, he said unto them, O generation of vipers, who hath warned you to flee from the wrath to come?
8 Bring forth therefore fruits meet for repentance:
9 And think not to say within yourselves, We have Abraham to our father: for I say unto you, that God is able of these stones to raise up children unto Abraham.

Anyone who will "bring forth fruits worthy of repentance" is eligible for the Kingdom of God. This is a very comforting thought! It demonstrates the true kindness and justice of God. Thus, the inclusion of Sister Sodom in the above passages shows great wisdom by the Lord through his prophet Ezekiel. While we see that all who repent are accepted of God, we also learn from the above scriptures that having direct family connections to the Tribes of Israel gives no guarantee of salvation without first having a broken heart and a contrite spirit.

Ezekiel 16:60-63
60 Nevertheless I will remember my covenant with thee in the days of thy youth, and I will establish unto thee an everlasting covenant.
61 Then thou shalt remember thy ways, and be ashamed, when thou shalt receive thy sisters, thine elder and thy younger: and I will give them unto thee for daughters, but not by thy covenant.
62 And I will establish my covenant with thee; and thou shalt know that I am the LORD:
63 That thou mayest remember, and be confounded, and never open thy mouth any more because of thy shame, when I am pacified toward thee for all that thou hast done, saith the Lord GOD.

The Lord is clear to demonstrate that, while the nations of the earth will be blessed through Father Abraham and his seed, all men and women who are willing to call upon the name of the Lord, and have him to be their God are eligible for full fellowship within the Church and Kingdom of God. Those who are not necessarily literal descendants of a specific tribe of Israel are adopted into the tribes of Israel upon their acceptance of the truth, and their participation in the ordinances of salvation by those having the authority to administer such blessings. Therefore, the mention of sister Sodom shows the great compassion, charity, and grace that the Lord has for all his children. Indeed he is not a respecter of persons, but invites all to participate in the blessings of salvation. While the scattering of the children of Israel among the nations of the world may seem like a curse on the surface, in reality it has allowed for the literal blood of the Twelve Tribes of Israel to be mixed with the heathen nations as well. Most of the people alive today are probably, in one way or another, descendants of former Israel. In the event that they are not literal descendants, it is still the intention of the Lord to gather them into the fold of God.

The mention of Sister Sodom is limited to Chapter 16 of Ezekiel alone. In Chapter 23 of Ezekiel, the comparison of Israel's two sisters to whorish women is again taken up, but without mention of the third sister, Sodom.

Ezekiel 23:1-4

1 The word of the LORD came again unto me, saying,
2 Son of man, there were two women, the daughters of one mother:
3 And they committed whoredoms in Egypt; they committed whoredoms in their youth: there were their breasts pressed, and there they bruised the teats of their virginity.
4 And the names of them were Aholah the elder, and Aholibah her sister: and they were mine, and they bare sons and daughters. Thus were their names; Samaria is Aholah, and Jerusalem Aholibah.

To clarify, we see that Sister Samaria is given a different name, Aholah, yet still represents the Northern Ten Tribes of Israel. Thus, whether we say:

1) Aholah, this new name given in Ezekiel 23,
2) Samaria, referring to the capital city of the Northern Ten Tribes,
3) Joseph, the birthright son of Jacob,
4) Ephraim, the son of Joseph, and general tribe name associated with the Northern Ten Tribes that divided themselves from Judah after Solomon's reign (they became the Lost Ten Tribes after 721 BC), or
5) Gentiles, those not of the Tribe of Judah.

We are, nevertheless, still referring to the same group of people—the Northern Ten Tribes of Israel and their descendants. Likewise, we see that Sister Jerusalem is given a different name, Aholibah, which represents the Two Southern Tribes of Israel—Judah and Benjamin. Whether we say, "Aholibah," this new name given in Chapter 23, or "Jerusalem," the capital city of the Southern Two Tribes, we are still referring to Judah or the Jews.

This association of Ephraim and Judah as being women caught in adultery as well as their subsequent punishment is in reality a type, symbolizing the demise of the Kingdom of God on earth, or the removal of true religion from the earth. It did in fact occur, and, it occurred in two separate phases. First, the Northern Ten Tribes were taken, scattered, and left without prophets or any other administrators of the Priesthood. Next, the Southern Two Tribes suffered a similar fate several hundred years later. While in the end both Ephraim and Judah were completely forsaken and left without guidance, Judah was never completely lost physically from the sight of the world, as occurred with the tribes from the north.

THE LATTER RAIN

Zion Will Return and Be Gathered

It has been written that "in the mouth of two or three witnesses every word may be established" (Matthew 18:16). The testimonies of Isaiah, Jeremiah, and Ezekiel are clear that a period of worldwide apostasy must occur, leaving the inhabitants of the earth without prophets and without the true religion of God. All three books foretell the return of Zion to the earth, and the ultimate gathering of Israel from the four corners of the earth where it has been scattered. According to the Book of Ezekiel, the Kingdom of God, or Zion, will once again be established on the earth in the latter days. As was done in Isaiah and Jeremiah, the coming forth of Zion in the last days is described by Ezekiel as if it were an army marching forth to avenge those who have been against Israel, and enjoyed her captivity and downfall.

Ezekiel 25:1-7

1 The word of the LORD came again unto me, saying,
2 Son of man, set thy face against the Ammonites, and prophesy against them;
3 And say unto the Ammonites, Hear the word of the Lord GOD; Thus saith the Lord GOD; Because thou saidst, Aha, against my sanctuary, when it was profaned; and against the land of Israel, when it was desolate; and against the house of Judah, when they went into captivity;
4 Behold, therefore I will deliver thee to the men of the east for a possession, and they shall set their palaces in thee, and make their dwellings in thee: they shall eat thy fruit, and they shall drink thy milk.
5 And I will make Rabbah a stable for camels, and the Ammonites a couchingplace for flocks: and ye shall know that I am the LORD.
6 For thus saith the Lord GOD; Because thou hast clapped thine hands, and stamped with the feet, and rejoiced in heart with all thy despite against the land of Israel;
7 Behold, therefore I will stretch out mine hand upon thee, and will deliver thee for a spoil to the heathen; and I will cut thee off from the people, and I will cause thee to perish out of the countries: I will destroy thee; and thou shalt know that I am the LORD.

As the armies of the Lord (his disciples), march forward against the falsehoods of the world, it will begin little by little to throw down these false doctrines and to establish once again the true doctrine of Christ. Through this process, the Lord will also begin to gather out the children of Israel from the places were they have been scattered among the heathen.

Ezekiel 28:25-26

25 Thus saith the Lord GOD; When I shall have gathered the house of Israel from the people among whom they are scattered, and shall be sanctified in them in the sight of the heathen, then shall they dwell in their land that I have given to my servant Jacob.
26 And they shall dwell safely therein, and shall build houses, and plant vineyards; yea, they shall dwell with confidence, when I have executed judgments upon all those that despise them round about them; and they shall know that I am the LORD their God.

Ezekiel 38:8-9

8 After many days thou shalt be visited: in the latter years thou shalt come into the land that is brought back from the sword, and is gathered out of many people, against the mountains of Israel, which have been always waste: but it is brought forth out of the nations, and they shall dwell safely all of them.
9 Thou shalt ascend and come like a storm, thou shalt be like a cloud to cover the land, thou, and all thy bands, and many people with thee.

The restored Gospel, once it springs forth in the last days, will be so sound and so perfect in terms of its doctrine, that it will form a safe haven for those that embrace it. "They shall dwell with confidence" as this new doctrine rolls forth through the earth.

Ezekiel 39:23-29
23 And the heathen shall know that the house of Israel went into captivity for their iniquity: because they trespassed against me, therefore hid I my face from them, and gave them into the hand of their enemies: so fell they all by the sword.
24 According to their uncleanness and according to their transgressions have I done unto them, and hid my face from them.
25 Therefore thus saith the Lord GOD; Now will I bring again the captivity of Jacob, and have mercy upon the whole house of Israel, and will be jealous for my holy name;
26 After that they have borne their shame, and all their trespasses whereby they have trespassed against me, when they dwelt safely in their land, and none made them afraid.
27 When I have brought them again from the people, and gathered them out of their enemies' lands, and am sanctified in them in the sight of many nations;
28 Then shall they know that I am the LORD their God, which caused them to be led into captivity among the heathen: but I have gathered them unto their own land, and have left none of them any more there.
29 Neither will I hide my face any more from them: for I have poured out my spirit upon the house of Israel, saith the Lord GOD.

At some point in time, the world will be enlightened to the fact that there was indeed a period of Spiritual Famine, in which God withdrew his presence and his servants from the earth—even "the heathen shall know." The inhabitants of the earth will then understand that this was done because of the wickedness of the children of Israel, for their wicked priests, whoredoms, murders and abominations before him. The world will at some point be taught that this event did indeed occur, and that for a space of time, man was left to fend for himself without the guidance and direction of the Lord through living prophets. However, verses 26 through 29 indicate that, after this period of Spiritual Famine, the Lord will again pour out his spirit upon the house of Israel, and they will begin to be gathered in from wherever they have been led away captive.

Some may argue that while Israel went astray, the Gospel of Jesus Christ remained intact through the preaching of the apostles after the death of Christ. But, it will be shown that this is not the case. While Peter did indeed receive the great revelation to extend the preaching of the Gospel to the Gentiles, and no longer limit it only to the Jews, this does not mean that the Church of Christ was no longer a part of the tribes of Israel. The Gentiles that joined the Church during that period of time were adopted into the nation and Kingdom of Israel. The point is, and will be made stronger in subsequent discussions, that the apostasy spoken of in Isaiah, Jeremiah, and Ezekiel was all-encompassing, and there was not even a thread of Priesthood authority left on the earth with which to perform the saving ordinances. This terrible event must, therefore, have occurred at some point after the resurrection of Jesus Christ. Furthermore, only through a restoration of the lost priesthood power and lost keys of authority could the Church of Christ, namely Zion, be reestablished in its entirety to the earth.

THE LATTER RAIN

While the scriptures cited thus far in our discussion of the Book of Ezekiel have done much to establish the truth concerning the famine period and the subsequent restoration, or Latter Rain, Chapters 34-37 of Ezekiel stand out as being incontrovertible in terms of their power and clarity with respect to this important subject. Therefore, I have chosen to discuss these chapters as a group. My hope is to elucidate the true intent of the prophet's words as they pertain to events that should occur prior to the Second Coming of Jesus Christ.

Reuniting Judah and Ephraim--Ezekiel 34-37

Ezekiel 34:1-6

1 And the word of the LORD came unto me, saying,
2 Son of man, prophesy against the shepherds of Israel, prophesy, and say unto them, Thus saith the Lord GOD unto the shepherds; Woe be to the shepherds of Israel that do feed themselves! should not the shepherds feed the flocks?
3 Ye eat the fat, and ye clothe you with the wool, ye kill them that are fed: but ye feed not the flock.
4 The diseased have ye not strengthened, neither have ye healed that which was sick, neither have ye bound up that which was broken, neither have ye brought again that which was driven away, neither have ye sought that which was lost; but with force and with cruelty have ye ruled them.
5 And they were scattered, because there is no shepherd: and they became meat to all the beasts of the field, when they were scattered.
6 My sheep wandered through all the mountains, and upon every high hill: yea, my flock was scattered upon all the face of the earth, and none did search or seek after them.

As we saw in Amos 8:11 concerning "the famine in the land," these first six verses of Chapter 34 of the Book of Ezekiel indicate that the shepherds, who should have guided the children of Israel in the ways of righteousness, in the end actually led them astray such that they were scattered, smitten, and lost. The true prophets of the Lord, on the other hand, are killed by these wicked men who lead in Israel. Finally, when the prophets were removed due to this gross iniquity of the leaders of Israel, the children of Israel "were scattered, because there is no shepherd" or prophet. Without living prophets to guide them correctly, they became "meat to all the beasts of the field, when they were scattered (…) and none did seek after them."

Ezekiel 34:7-10

7 Therefore, ye shepherds, hear the word of the LORD;
8 As I live, saith the Lord GOD, surely because my flock became a prey, and my flock became meat to every beast of the field, because there was no shepherd, neither did my shepherds search for my flock, but the shepherds fed themselves, and fed not my flock;
9 Therefore, O ye shepherds, hear the word of the LORD;
10 Thus saith the Lord GOD; Behold, I am against the shepherds; and I will require my flock at their hand, and cause them to cease from feeding the flock; neither shall the shepherds feed themselves any more; for I will deliver my flock from their mouth, that they may not be meat for them.

The churches of the world during this dark period of apostasy are not built up to reestablish the saving ordinances of God, but rather to get gain and the glory of men. These institutions will gradually lose power as the message of a restored Zion begins to flow throughout the earth. The Lord will begin to "deliver my flock from their mouth, that they may not be meat for them." In other words, the children of Israel that are held captive by these false churches and organizations will little by little begin to leave these churches as they recognize the true doctrine once it has been restored to the earth by God himself.

> **Ezekiel 34:11-19**
> 11 For thus saith the Lord GOD; Behold, I, even I, will both search my sheep, and seek them out.
> 12 As a shepherd seeketh out his flock in the day that he is among his sheep that are scattered; so will I seek out my sheep, and will deliver them out of all places where they have been scattered in the cloudy and dark day.
> 13 And I will bring them out from the people, and gather them from the countries, and will bring them to their own land, and feed them upon the mountains of Israel by the rivers, and in all the inhabited places of the country.
> 14 I will feed them in a good pasture, and upon the high mountains of Israel shall their fold be: there shall they lie in a good fold, and in a fat pasture shall they feed upon the mountains of Israel.
> 15 I will feed my flock, and I will cause them to lie down, saith the Lord GOD.
> 16 I will seek that which was lost, and bring again that which was driven away, and will bind up that which was broken, and will strengthen that which was sick: but I will destroy the fat and the strong; I will feed them with judgment.
> 17 And as for you, O my flock, thus saith the Lord GOD; Behold, I judge between cattle and cattle, between the rams and the he goats.
> 18 Seemeth it a small thing unto you to have eaten up the good pasture, but ye must tread down with your feet the residue of your pastures? and to have drunk of the deep waters, but ye must foul the residue with your feet?
> 19 And as for my flock, they eat that which ye have trodden with your feet; and they drink that which ye have fouled with your feet.

The Lord himself will seek out his sheep, "and will deliver them out of all places where they have been scattered in the cloudy and dark day." The cloudy and dark day is the apostasy period, a period without the rain of revelation and without prophets on the earth to guide man. As the Lord reestablishes his Kingdom once again on the earth and calls a new prophet, the Lord will then begin to feed his "people in a good pasture, and upon the high mountains of Israel." Likewise, it says that he will "seek that which was lost, and bring again that which was driven away, and will bind up that which was broken, and will strengthen that which was sick." How can the Lord "bind up that which was broken" unless indeed it was broken in the first place?

In the above passage, the Lord expresses his disdain for those that led the children of Israel into this period of apostasy. These are "supposed spiritual leaders" that killed the prophets and perverted the right ways of the Lord. They changed the doctrines and ordinances without having the priesthood or authority from God to do so. Not only do they set up false priesthoods to usurp authority over the children of men, and to get gain and glory of the world, but as the Lord says, they have "fouled the residue with your feet." Is not this similar to the symbolic image of eating bread with dung in it as we discussed before? They have

THE LATTER RAIN

taken away from the scriptures the plain and precious things that would have otherwise resolved conflicts and clarified the correct way to worship. During this apostasy period, the children of men are left to "eat that which ye have trodden with your feet, and they drink that which ye have fouled with your feet."

Ezekiel 34:20-31

20 Therefore thus saith the Lord GOD unto them; Behold, I, even I, will judge between the fat cattle and between the lean cattle.
21 Because ye have thrust with side and with shoulder, and pushed all the diseased with your horns, till ye have scattered them abroad;
22 Therefore will I save my flock, and they shall no more be a prey; and I will judge between cattle and cattle.
23 And I will set up one shepherd over them, and he shall feed them, even my servant David; he shall feed them, and he shall be their shepherd.
24 And I the Lord will be their God, and my servant David a prince among them; I the LORD have spoken it.
25 And I will make with them a covenant of peace, and will cause the evil beasts to cease out of the land: and they shall dwell safely in the wilderness, and sleep in the woods.
26 And I will make them and the places round about my hill a blessing; and I will cause the shower to come down in his season; there shall be showers of blessing.
27 And the tree of the field shall yield her fruit, and the earth shall yield her increase, and they shall be safe in their land, and shall know that I am the LORD, when I have broken the bands of their yoke, and delivered them out of the hand of those that served themselves of them.
28 And they shall no more be a prey to the heathen, neither shall the beast of the land devour them; but they shall dwell safely, and none shall make them afraid.
29 And I will raise up for them a plant of renown, and they shall be no more consumed with hunger in the land, neither bear the shame of the heathen any more.
30 Thus shall they know that I the LORD their God am with them, and that they, even the house of Israel, are my people, saith the Lord GOD.
31 And ye my flock, the flock of my pasture, are men, and I am your God, saith the Lord GOD.

In the last days, the Lord promises us through the prophet Ezekiel that he will once again establish his Church on the earth. He will "make with them a covenant of peace, and will cause the evil beasts to cease out of the land." He will also "cause the shower to come down in his season; there shall be showers of blessing." Thus, in the latter days, the Lord will give the Latter Rain. He will shower the earth with inspiration and revelation through newly-called and anointed living prophets, apostles, and teachers of the people. In this restored state, with prophets to guide her, Zion shall once again begin to flourish on the earth. For the final time, the Church of God shall "yield her fruit, and the earth shall yield her increase." Those that join the restored Church and accept its authority and doctrine "shall be safe in their land, and shall know that I am the LORD, when I have broken the bands of their yoke, and delivered them out of the hand of those that served themselves of them. And they shall no more be a prey to the heathen, neither shall the beast of the land devour them; but they shall dwell safely, and none shall make them afraid. And I will raise up for them a plant of renown, and they shall be no more consumed with hunger in the land, neither bear the shame of the heathen any more." In response to Amos 8:11-12, we learn from the above passage that the famine of hearing the words of the Lord will ultimately cease.

BOOK OF EZEKIEL

Ezekiel 35:1-10

1 Moreover the word of the LORD came unto me, saying,
2 Son of man, set thy face against mount Seir, and prophesy against it,
3 And say unto it, Thus saith the Lord GOD; Behold, O mount Seir, I am against thee, and I will stretch out mine hand against thee, and I will make thee most desolate.
4 I will lay thy cities waste, and thou shalt be desolate, and thou shalt know that I am the LORD.
5 Because thou hast had a perpetual hatred, and hast shed the blood of the children of Israel by the force of the sword in the time of their calamity, in the time that their iniquity had an end:
6 Therefore, as I live, saith the Lord GOD, I will prepare thee unto blood, and blood shall pursue thee: sith thou hast not hated blood, even blood shall pursue thee.
7 Thus will I make mount Seir most desolate, and cut off from it him that passeth out and him that returneth.
8 And I will fill his mountains with his slain men: in thy hills, and in thy valleys, and in all thy rivers, shall they fall that are slain with the sword.
9 I will make thee perpetual desolations, and thy cities shall not return: and ye shall know that I am the LORD.
10 Because thou hast said, These two nations and these two countries shall be mine, and we will possess it; whereas the LORD was there:

The term "mount Seir" represents the kingdom of the devil, his churches and institutions, which thrive during the great apostasy period. Once Zion is reestablished on the earth, however, the Lord will come against mount Seir in a manner similar to the way mount Seir was allowed to come against Israel in the day of their falling from grace. The false churches and organizations of the earth will begin to lose power as the true doctrines of God gain momentum and are preached throughout the earth. Taking a key from Isaiah, when the scripture says in verse eight, "I will fill his mountains with the slain men: in thy hills, and in thy valleys, and in all thy rivers, shall they fall that are slain with the sword," we know that the sword of the Lord is his word. The word of God therefore comes to those slain to falsehood, and they are thus converted to righteousness and restored to the Church of God or Zion. While Zion was made desolate, in the end, the kingdom of the devil will be made desolate and cease from the earth, never to be restored again.

Verse ten reiterates the fact that both Joseph and Judah were overrun by the kingdom of the devil, and by the false doctrines and religions of the heathen nations. Speaking to false shepherds, the Lord says, "Because thou has said, These two nations [Joseph and Judah] and these two countries shall be mine, and we will possess it; whereas the Lord was there." During the period of the Former Rain, the Lord was there and spoke to his people through authorized prophets. He withdrew his authority and his prophets first from the Northern Ten Tribes (or Joseph). Shortly after the death and resurrection of Jesus Christ and the deaths of his disciples, the Lord withdrew his authority and prophets from the Southern Two Tribes (or Judah) as well. From that point on, the Kingdom of God or Zion was no longer found anywhere on the earth at all. Nowhere!

Ezekiel 35:11-15

11 Therefore, as I live, saith the Lord GOD, I will even do according to thine anger, and according to thine envy which thou hast used out of thy hatred against them; and I will make myself known among them, when I have judged thee.

12 And thou shalt know that I am the LORD, and that I have heard all thy blasphemies which thou hast spoken against the mountains of Israel, saying, They are laid desolate, they are given us to consume.
13 Thus with your mouth ye have boasted against me, and have multiplied your words against me: I have heard them.
14 Thus saith the Lord GOD; When the whole earth rejoiceth, I will make thee desolate.
15 As thou didst rejoice at the inheritance of the house of Israel, because it was desolate, so will I do unto thee: thou shalt be desolate, O mount Seir, and all Idumea, even all of it: and they shall know that I am the LORD.

During the Latter Rain period following the great period of Spiritual Famine, when Zion is once again established on the earth, the Lord himself "will make myself known among them, when I have judged thee." He will appear again to living prophets and he will send messengers again from heaven to reestablish the lost keys and authority of the Kingdom of God to the earth. Over time, the Lord's doctrine will fill the earth until it ultimately subdues all false doctrines. Eventually, all false churches will cease, never again to be rebuilt. They are made desolate, just as Zion was once made desolate, with the exception that this final desolation which will befall the kingdom of the devil will be eternal and everlasting.

Ezekiel 36:1-12

1 Also, thou son of man, prophesy unto the mountains of Israel, and say, Ye mountains of Israel, hear the word of the LORD:
2 Thus saith the Lord GOD; Because the enemy hath said against you, Aha, even the ancient high places are ours in possession:
3 Therefore prophesy and say, Thus saith the Lord GOD; Because they have made you desolate, and swallowed you up on every side, that ye might be a possession unto the residue of the heathen, and ye are taken up in the lips of talkers, and are an infamy of the people:
4 Therefore, ye mountains of Israel, hear the word of the Lord GOD; Thus saith the Lord GOD to the mountains, and to the hills, to the rivers, and to the valleys, to the desolate wastes, and to the cities that are forsaken, which became a prey and derision to the residue of the heathen that are round about;
5 Therefore thus saith the Lord GOD; Surely in the fire of my jealousy have I spoken against the residue of the heathen, and against all Idumea, which have appointed my land into their possession with the joy of all their heart, with despiteful minds, to cast it out for a prey.
6 Prophesy therefore concerning the land of Israel, and say unto the mountains, and to the hills, to the rivers, and to the valleys, Thus saith the Lord GOD; Behold, I have spoken in my jealousy and in my fury, because ye have borne the shame of the heathen:
7 Therefore thus saith the Lord GOD; I have lifted up mine hand, Surely the heathen that are about you, they shall bear their shame.
8 But ye, O mountains of Israel, ye shall shoot forth your branches, and yield your fruit to my people of Israel; for they are at hand to come.
9 For, behold, I am for you, and I will turn unto you, and ye shall be tilled and sown:
10 And I will multiply men upon you, all the house of Israel, even all of it: and the cities shall be inhabited, and the wastes shall be builded:
11 And I will multiply upon you man and beast; and they shall increase and bring fruit: and I will settle you after your old estates, and will do better unto you than at your beginnings: and ye shall know that I am the LORD.
12 Yea, I will cause men to walk upon you, even my people Israel; and they shall possess thee, and thou shalt be their inheritance, and thou shalt no more henceforth bereave them of men.

The same promise made in Chapter 35 is repeated again by Ezekiel in Chapter 36. Namely, the Lord promises to swallow up the kingdom of the devil and his churches and organizations. The Lord's victory over the prevalent falsehood in the earth will occur in a manner similar to the way Zion had been overrun by falsehood in times past. Zion was overcome, and the children of Israel were scattered and driven away. The false churches of the world will become weak and unable to further contend against the true doctrine of the Lord, which will issue forth from the mouth of his living prophets, apostles and teachers called forth in the latter days. Speaking of Israel, the Lord says in verse three, "Because they have made you desolate, and swallowed you up on every side, that ye might be a possession unto the residue of the heathen." In verse five, he shows that the residue of the heathen "have appointed my land into their possession with the joy of all their heart, with despiteful minds, to cast it out for a prey." These verses describe a situation in which the heathen nations basically possess the land of the Lord, but they do so as imposters. They draw from the divine scriptures and sacred rituals of the former true faith, but they lack the authority from God to actually perform any of the saving ordinances. In fact, they willfully pervert these ordinances. They alter the scriptures and they use false priesthood in order to deceive the people, to get wealth, and to usurp power and glory of the world.

While this seems to be a hopeless situation for the scattered children of Israel, the Lord indicates his intention to come out of hiding and to begin the recovery of his people. Once the Lord himself lifts up his hand again in the defense of his people, we see in verse eight that Zion and its members will again begin to bear righteous fruit. "But ye, o mountains of Israel, ye shall shoot forth your branches, and yield your fruit to my people of Israel; for they are at hand to come." What are the fruits of the modern-day Zion? They should be fruits similar to those found in the primitive Church, namely miracles, visions, doctrine, angels, priesthood authority, scripture, revelations, prophets, apostles, and so forth. In any case, the fruits that come forth will be sufficient to convince the children of Israel, held captive by the churches of the heathen, that the restored Zion is indeed the Church of God. It follows that the children of Israel will begin to recognize the truth of it and will begin to return to Zion and possess it again.

Ezekiel 36:13-20

13 Thus saith the Lord GOD; Because they say unto you, Thou land devourest up men, and hast bereaved thy nations;
14 Therefore thou shalt devour men no more, neither bereave thy nations any more, saith the Lord GOD.
15 Neither will I cause men to hear in thee the shame of the heathen any more, neither shalt thou bear the reproach of the people any more, neither shalt thou cause thy nations to fall any more, saith the Lord GOD.
16 Moreover the word of the LORD came unto me, saying,
17 Son of man, when the house of Israel dwelt in their own land, they defiled it by their own way and by their doings: their way was before me as the uncleanness of a removed woman.
18 Wherefore I poured my fury upon them for the blood that they had shed upon the land, and for their idols wherewith they had polluted it:
19 And I scattered them among the heathen, and they were dispersed through the countries: according to their way and according to their doings I judged them.
20 And when they entered unto the heathen, whither they went, they profaned my holy name, when they said to them, These are the people of the LORD, and are gone forth out of his land.

THE LATTER RAIN

While the name of the Lord was spoken during the dark period of Spiritual Famine, it was profaned in its use. It was used without authority from God and without guidance from living prophets. Instead, men used the sacred things left over from the true Church of God, namely the scriptures and the ordinances, and used them to get gain and to usurp authority over the children of men.

Ezekiel 36:21-30
21 But I had pity for mine holy name, which the house of Israel had profaned among the heathen, whither they went.
22 Therefore say unto the house of Israel, Thus saith the Lord GOD; I do not this for your sakes, O house of Israel, but for mine holy name's sake, which ye have profaned among the heathen, whither ye went.
23 And I will sanctify my great name, which was profaned among the heathen, which ye have profaned in the midst of them; and the heathen shall know that I am the LORD, saith the Lord GOD, when I shall be sanctified in you before their eyes.
24 For I will take you from among the heathen, and gather you out of all countries, and will bring you into your own land.
25 Then will I sprinkle clean water upon you, and ye shall be clean: from all your filthiness, and from all your idols, will I cleanse you.
26 A new heart also will I give you, and a new spirit will I put within you: and I will take away the stony heart out of your flesh, and I will give you an heart of flesh.
27 And I will put my spirit within you, and cause you to walk in my statutes, and ye shall keep my judgments, and do them.
28 And ye shall dwell in the land that I gave to your fathers; and ye shall be my people, and I will be your God.
29 I will also save you from all your uncleannesses: and I will call for the corn, and will increase it, and lay no famine upon you.
30 And I will multiply the fruit of the tree, and the increase of the field, that ye shall receive no more reproach of famine among the heathen.

In the latter days, the Lord indicates that for his names' sake, he will "sanctify my great name, which was profaned among the heathen, which ye have profaned among the heathen, which ye have profaned in the midst of them, and the heathen shall know that I am the Lord, saith the Lord GOD, when I shall be sanctified in you before their eyes." Something will occur that reestablishes the Lord's presence on earth. A new prophet must be called and the keys of the priesthood restored.

At that point, the Lord begins to "take you from among the heathen, and gather you out of all countries, and will bring you into your own land. Then will I sprinkle clean water upon you, and ye shall be clean." The clean water of revelation will resume, and the long drought of no prophets on the earth will finally come to an end. A new prophet will be called, and from this prophet and subsequent prophets will come forth fruits worthy of a prophet, and works that demonstrate clearly his divine calling and authority. Ezekiel 30:36 sums up this process: "And I will multiply the fruit of the tree, and the increase of the field, that ye shall receive no more reproach of famine among the heathen." In other words, the revelations and blessings that are ultimately poured out upon the restored Church of God will be so great and so powerful in nature that it will be hard to deny that it is truly of God. No one will be deceived who really studies it out and investigates it seriously, calling upon the Lord for a confirmation of its truth. The Spirit of God will confirm in the hearts of the scattered children of Israel that this newly restored Church is indeed the true Church of God.

Ezekiel 36:31-38

31 Then shall ye remember your own evil ways, and your doings that were not good, and shall lothe yourselves in your own sight for your iniquities and for your abominations.

32 Not for your sakes do I this, saith the Lord GOD, be it known unto you: be ashamed and confounded for your own ways, O house of Israel.

33 Thus saith the Lord GOD; In the day that I shall have cleansed you from all your iniquities I will also cause you to dwell in the cities, and the wastes shall be builded.

34 And the desolate land shall be tilled, whereas it lay desolate in the sight of all that passed by.

35 And they shall say, This land that was desolate is become like the garden of Eden; and the waste and desolate and ruined cities are become fenced, and are inhabited.

36 Then the heathen that are left round about you shall know that I the LORD build the ruined places, and plant that that was desolate: I the LORD have spoken it, and I will do it.

37 Thus saith the Lord GOD; I will yet for this be enquired of by the house of Israel, to do it for them; I will increase them with men like a flock.

38 As the holy flock, as the flock of Jerusalem in her solemn feasts; so shall the waste cities be filled with flocks of men: and they shall know that I am the LORD.

As the true Church of God begins to prosper and to spread abroad on the earth, it will be amazing to see how the once forsaken and powerless Zion becomes populated again with the scattered children of Israel. "And they shall say, This land that was desolate is become like the Garden of Eden; and the waste and desolate is become fenced, and are inhabited."

Ezekiel 37:1-10

1 The hand of the LORD was upon me, and carried me out in the spirit of the LORD, and set me down in the midst of the valley which was full of bones,

2 And caused me to pass by them round about: and, behold, there were very many in the open valley; and, lo, they were very dry.

3 And he said unto me, Son of man, can these bones live? And I answered, O Lord GOD, thou knowest.

4 Again he said unto me, Prophesy upon these bones, and say unto them, O ye dry bones, hear the word of the LORD.

5 Thus saith the Lord GOD unto these bones; Behold, I will cause breath to enter into you, and ye shall live:

6 And I will lay sinews upon you, and will bring up flesh upon you, and cover you with skin, and put breath in you, and ye shall live; and ye shall know that I am the LORD.

7 So I prophesied as I was commanded: and as I prophesied, there was a noise, and behold a shaking, and the bones came together, bone to his bone.

8 And when I beheld, lo, the sinews and the flesh came up upon them, and the skin covered them above: but there was no breath in them.

9 Then said he unto me, Prophesy unto the wind, prophesy, son of man, and say to the wind, Thus saith the Lord GOD; Come from the four winds, O breath, and breathe upon these slain, that they may live.

10 So I prophesied as he commanded me, and the breath came into them, and they lived, and stood up upon their feet, an exceeding great army.

In the above verses, Ezekiel describes a scene in which he is brought to a valley filled with dry bones. The word "dry" has symbolic meaning. It means the souls of those that have died during the period of the Great Spiritual Famine. While they are descendants of the literal tribes of Israel, yet they lived life and died in their sins, never hearing the true Gospel, and never partaking in the saving ordinances which can only be performed by duly authorized holders of the Priesthood of God. Thus, these bones are not only dead, but they are also dry.

In verse four, the Lord commands Ezekiel: "Prophesy upon these bones, and say unto them, O ye dry bones, hear the word of the Lord." This suggests that the Lord God will in his infinite wisdom and mercy provide a way to administer the Gospel and its saving ordinances even to those that died in their sins during the long period of time when no priesthood holders or prophets were available at all. For God to be truly just, preaching to the spirits of the dead would have to be a necessary component of the overall plan of salvation for his children. The Lord evidently provides a means for his children to hear the Gospel who missed the opportunity in their mortal life. They hear it as spirits after their death and before their resurrection and ultimate judgment. "Thus saith the Lord GOD; come from the four winds, O breath, and breath into them, and breathe upon these slain, that they may live." If there were any doubt about who these dry bones represent, Ezekiel clarifies their identity and symbolism in the following verses:

Ezekiel 37:11-14

11 Then he said unto me, Son of man, these bones are the whole house of Israel: behold, they say, Our bones are dried, and our hope is lost: we are cut off for our parts.
12 Therefore prophesy and say unto them, Thus saith the Lord GOD; Behold, O my people, I will open your graves, and cause you to come up out of your graves, and bring you into the land of Israel.
13 And ye shall know that I am the LORD, when I have opened your graves, O my people, and brought you up out of your graves,
14 And shall put my spirit in you, and ye shall live, and I shall place you in your own land: then shall ye know that I the LORD have spoken it, and performed it, saith the LORD.

Can there be any confusion on this point? It clearly refers to those that are dead, since he says, "I will open your graves, and cause you to come up out of your graves, and bring you into the land of Israel." Finally, in verse 14, the Lord indicates that he "shall put my spirit in you, and ye shall live, and I shall place you in your own land." Not only will these dead children of Israel be made alive again, but they will have heard "the word of the Lord" such that the Spirit of the Lord or the Holy Ghost can dwell in them. They will not only be made alive physically, they will be made alive spiritually to again have the presence of the Lord's spirit among them. This concept of bringing Israel back from the dead is, therefore, symbolic of Israel being scattered among the Gentiles and considered dead. In an acceptable time of the Lord, he will show that they are yet alive.

New Scriptures

Ezekiel 37:15-17

15 The word of the LORD came again unto me, saying,
16 Moreover, thou son of man, take thee one stick, and write upon it, For Judah, and for the children of Israel his companions: then take another stick, and write upon it, For Joseph, the stick of Ephraim, and for all the house of Israel his companions:
17 And join them one to another into one stick; and they shall become one in thine hand.

What is meant by a "stick" in the above verses? First of all he says, "take thee one stick, and write upon it." This means that a "stick" must be something that can be written upon. In my mind, it refers to a scroll, which is a stick around which words written on paper are rolled up to be stored. In other words, a stick is a book. Ezekiel shows in these verses that two scrolls or books are being described. One is written for "Judah, and for the children of Israel his companions." This represents the Bible (the Old and New Testaments), since it describes for the most part the dealings of the Jews, their works, their kings, their victories and their defeats. The Jews and the literal descendants of Judah and Benjamin are taken together as one and referred to as Judah.

Ezekiel describes another book that is written, "For Joseph, the stick of Ephraim, and for all the house of Israel his companions." In the same way that the companions of Judah include Judah and Benjamin, or the Southern Two Tribes, the companions of Joseph include not only Joseph, but all the Ten Lost Tribes from the north. When we read Ephraim, Joseph, Israel, or the Ten Lost Tribes, we are still referring to the Northern Ten Tribes. According to Ezekiel, in the above verses, the Lord God in his infinite wisdom has commanded that another book be written for Joseph to explain his story.

John 10:16

16 And other sheep I have, which are not of this fold: them also I must bring, and they shall hear my voice; and there shall be one fold, and one shepherd.

In the latter days, the two separate kingdoms of Judah and Joseph will be combined into one. Each group, Judah and Ephraim (the son of Joseph), will have a book that will be written for them, to go forth unto the children of men, for convincing them of the power and authority of God and his prophets. Therefore, restored Zion will have the advantage of new knowledge and new wisdom from God. Not only will there be prophets and priesthood again on the earth, but apparently a new book will also come forth that describes God's interactions with his children from the scattered ten tribes from the north, or Joseph.

Recall that, during his mortal ministry on the earth, Jesus Christ only administered the Gospel to the Jews. While the Gospel was later sent to the Gentiles too, Jesus only taught the Jews, with perhaps the exception of his encounter with the Samaritan woman at Jacob's well near Samaria (John 4). Peter, as the head of the Church, received the revelation regarding the preaching of the word to all people only after Jesus was departed. Therefore, one should not think that the other sheep spoken of in John 10:16 refers to the Gentiles taught by the apostles. Whatever form this book takes, it will most likely contain the revelations, teachings, and ministry of the Lord's prophets, priests, and teachers living in other parts of the world, just like the Bible does for the Jews.

If we believe that God is all-powerful, and all-knowing, then why can he not command prophets from the tribe of Joseph, the father of Ephraim, to write and for it to be recorded into a book? The scriptures we have cited from Ezekiel suggest this will indeed happen. When they come together, they will help the children of Israel see the hand of the Lord again. They will understand and accept this new book, which will clarify and expound the things written in the Bible. They will ultimately carry them both together, such that they become, "one in thine hand." Finally, if I am correct about what the Lord said in John 10:16, it will probably contain an account of some sort of this amazing visit of the resurrected Lord to those scattered people.

> **Ezekiel 37:18-22**
> 18 And when the children of thy people shall speak unto thee, saying, Wilt thou not shew us what thou meanest by these?
> 19 Say unto them, Thus saith the Lord GOD; Behold, I will take the stick of Joseph, which is in the hand of Ephraim, and the tribes of Israel his fellows, and will put them with him, even with the stick of Judah, and make them one stick, and they shall be one in mine hand.
> 20 And the sticks whereon thou writest shall be in thine hand before their eyes.
> 21 And say unto them, Thus saith the Lord GOD; Behold, I will take the children of Israel from among the heathen, whither they be gone, and will gather them on every side, and bring them into their own land:
> 22 And I will make them one nation in the land upon the mountains of Israel; and one king shall be king to them all: and they shall be no more two nations, neither shall they be divided into two kingdoms any more at all:

When these two books come together, it will occur at a time when the Lord will have commenced the literal gathering of the "children of Israel from among the heathen, where they be gone, and will gather them on every side, and bring them into their own land." When Zion is once again established, and the Bible and this other book of Ephraim run together, "I will make them one nation in the land upon the mountain of Israel; and one king shall be king to them all: and they shall be no more two nations (Judah and Ephraim), neither shall they be divided into two kingdoms any more at all."

In verse 19 above, we see that the stick of Joseph will be added to the stick of Judah, and then the two of them together will be presented to the children of Israel that are scattered among the nations of the earth and mingled with the heathen. The Bible or stick of Judah comes first, and then the Book of Ephraim is added to it. When the sons and daughters of Israel examine and call upon the Father to know what these things mean, they will be touched by the Holy Spirit, and thus know that they are both the word of God. In this manner, God in his infinite wisdom and mercy will be able to draw the true seekers of truth from among the false churches and doctrines that hold the children of Israel captive. This new book from Ephraim, when combined with the Bible, should become an important tool of modern Zion. It will be something new. It will be something unexpected. It will serve as a strong tool for convincing others of the truth. If the sword of the Lord is his word, as we learned in Isaiah, then this new Book of Ephraim (Joseph and his companions), will contain the word of God and confound the conventional wisdom of the world. It will no doubt come through the work of some modern-day prophet, since God does nothing without prophets (Amos 3:7).

The Temple of the Lord

> **Ezekiel 37:23-28**
> 23 Neither shall they defile themselves any more with their idols, nor with their detestable things, nor with any of their transgressions: but I will save them out of all their dwellingplaces,

wherein they have sinned, and will cleanse them: so shall they be my people, and I will be their God.
24 And David my servant shall be king over them; and they all shall have one shepherd: they shall also walk in my judgments, and observe my statutes, and do them.
25 And they shall dwell in the land that I have given unto Jacob my servant, wherein your fathers have dwelt; and they shall dwell therein, even they, and their children, and their children's children for ever: and my servant David shall be their prince for ever.
26 Moreover I will make a covenant of peace with them; it shall be an everlasting covenant with them: and I will place them, and multiply them, and will set my sanctuary in the midst of them for evermore.
27 My tabernacle also shall be with them: yea, I will be their God, and they shall be my people.
28 And the heathen shall know that I the LORD do sanctify Israel, when my sanctuary shall be in the midst of them for evermore.

A major doctrinal issue that seems to have been lost to the world during the Dark Ages is the understanding of the workings and function of the temple. The temple was no doubt part of the Church of Jesus Christ, since the Lord was often there and often referred to it in his teachings. The tabernacle was the traveling temple of the Lord in the time of Moses, Joshua, and so forth, up until the time that the Lord permitted Solomon to construct a building in Jerusalem which was dedicated and set apart as a Temple of the Lord. Although it was ultimately destroyed and laid waste, both Christians and Jews alike still revere the Temple of Solomon as a holy place. Many people of various faiths worship at the Western Wall in Jerusalem. While this structure may not be part of the actual Temple of Solomon, it is still representative of that structure to many people that visit it. The ultimate point is that an understanding of the true doctrine associated with temples has been lost during the long period of apostasy that has covered the earth.

The scriptures indicate that the tabernacle and the temple in Jerusalem were not the same as chapels or synagogues. According to verses 27 and 28 above from Ezekiel Chapter 37, we see that when the Lord reestablishes Zion to the earth, "My tabernacle also shall be with them: yea, I will be their God, and they shall be my people. And the heathen shall know that I the LORD do sanctify Israel, when my sanctuary shall be in the midst of them for evermore." A true sign of the restored Gospel is the construction, dedication, and use of the temple. Whether there will be one temple or many is not clear. What is clear is that the Lord's people will have access to the ordinances or rituals that were performed in the temple in ancient times. The true function and purpose of the temple will be restored, and members of Zion will go to the temple to be instructed of the Lord in the ways of holiness.

So important is the temple to the Lord's plan of salvation for his children that Ezekiel dedicates his final nine chapters (Chapters 40-48) to a detailed description of the future temple to be rebuilt in Jerusalem. Many predictions are given in these chapters of events that precede the Second Coming of the Lord Jesus Christ in his glory. One of the most symbolic images portrayed in these predictions is the one concerning the relationship between the Temple and the Dead Sea.

THE LATTER RAIN

Ezekiel 47:1

1 Afterward he brought me again unto the door of the house; and, behold, waters issued out from under the threshold of the house eastward: for the forefront of the house stood toward the east, and the waters came down from under from the right side of the house, at the south side of the altar.

The establishment of the temple again in the last days will lead to a flooding of the dead portions of the earth. Applying the symbolic keys derived from our study of Isaiah, we can again associate water with revelation or inspiration given not only to the prophet, but to all members of the Church of God who worship in His Temple. The temple of the Lord will be a place of inspiration, a place of learning, and from the temples will come forth many mighty fruits for the benefit and blessing of mankind. The revelation flowing from the temple of God will flood the dead doctrines of the earth and bring them back to life. The result will be new doctrine and new knowledge directly from God through his modern prophets. The knowledge of the Lord will fill the earth, healing the waters of the Dead Sea.

Ezekiel 47:6-9

6 And he said unto me, Son of man, hast thou seen this? Then he brought me, and caused me to return to the brink of the river.
7 Now when I had returned, behold, at the bank of the river were very many trees on the one side and on the other.
8 Then said he unto me, These waters issue out toward the east country, and go down into the desert, and go into the sea: which being brought forth into the sea, the waters shall be healed.
9 And it shall come to pass, that every thing that liveth, which moveth, whithersoever the rivers shall come, shall live: and there shall be a very great multitude of fish, because these waters shall come thither: for they shall be healed; and every thing shall live whither the river cometh.

While there may also be a literal outpouring of water from the temple to be built in Jerusalem at some later day, the symbolism of the event as predicted in Ezekiel should not be ignored. Any church claiming authority and divinity from God Almighty should therefore know how to construct a temple. Such a church should also claim to have received revelations and instructions from God, describing the precise function and purpose of the Holy Temple. The Temple, a building with a function totally different from a chapel or synagogue, is therefore an essential indicator for the scattered children of Israel to recognize the true Church of God as it becomes reestablished on the earth.

Testimony of Ezekiel

The powerful words of Ezekiel not only concur with those of Isaiah and Jeremiah, but they seem to expound even further on two points. We learn from Ezekiel that not only will Zion be reestablished in the last days, but that a new book will come forth as well. This new book from Ephraim should therefore describe the dealings of the Lord with descendants of Joseph and his companions, the Lost Ten Tribes of Israel. We have also seen that the reestablishment of the temple will occur during this Latter Rain period. As we now turn our attention to the Book of Daniel, let us keep these issues in mind and look for corroborative information within the other books of the Bible.

CHAPTER SEVEN

The Book of Daniel

When we think of the Book of Daniel, two great stories come almost instantly to mind. First, in Daniel Chapter 3, Shadrach, Meshach, and Abednego refuse to worship an idol erected by the king, Nebuchadnezzar, and are thus cast into a fiery furnace to die. Miraculously, however, they come forth from the furnace unharmed. Second, in Daniel Chapter 6, Daniel worships the Lord in defiance of a decree by King Darius. He is turned in by his political enemies, and Darius is forced by his own law to cast Daniel into a den of lions. Daniel is protected by the Lord during the night and comes forth unharmed in the morning. King Darius is so amazed and relieved by this divine intervention that he exalts Daniel in his kingdom, and casts his foes into the lions' den in his stead. They are devoured.

Truly these are great stories of faith and devotion. In a sense, they are both the same story retold in different fashions. Plus, both stories can be applied to our topic of discussion, namely the Former Rain/Famine/Latter Rain concept. In both cases, the servant of the Lord has a period of moderate success at the beginning. Next, a significant trial of faith comes. Finally, the servant is freed from the danger and exhaulted to a high position. While we see the obvious meaning of these stories for the individuals that experienced the events (Shadrach, Meshach, Abednego, and Daniel), a broader scope of these two stories can be applied to the children of Israel as a whole. The children of Israel prospered when they followed the Lord's commandments during the Former Rain period. Eventually, however, the good servants of the Lord are forced into a trap because of the evil leaders of the people (the famine period). It appears from all observations that this period of Spiritual Famine will surely "do them in," only to find that they are not done in, but survive and thrive in the end.

The disciples of God living during the famine period were often tortured for refusing to worship falsehood. The good people living on the earth during this dark time tried their best to live righteously and to teach good principles to their children. Little by little, the righteous began to fight back until we have now arrived at a time when we are able to worship openly and without censure. Religious freedom has been restored in many parts of the world, and a respect for true faith ultimately prevails. However, the Book of Daniel contains other verses that are even more relevant to our present discussion.

> **Daniel 9:24-27**
> 24 Seventy weeks are determined upon thy people and upon thy holy city, to finish the transgression, and to make an end of sins, and to make reconciliation for iniquity, and to bring in everlasting righteousness, and to seal up the vision and prophecy, and to anoint the most Holy.
> 25 Know therefore and understand, that from the going forth of the commandment to restore and to build Jerusalem unto the Messiah the Prince shall be seven weeks, and threescore and two weeks: the street shall be built again, and the wall, even in troublous times.
> 26 And after threescore and two weeks shall Messiah be cut off, but not for himself: and the people of the prince that shall come shall destroy the city and the sanctuary; and the end thereof shall be with a flood, and unto the end of the war desolations are determined.
> 27 And he shall confirm the covenant with many for one week: and in the midst of the week he shall cause the sacrifice and the oblation to cease, and for the overspreading of abominations he shall make it desolate, even until the consummation, and that determined shall be poured upon the desolate.

The first thing that stands out in these verses is the statement, "After threescore and two weeks shall Messiah be cut off, but not for himself." In the eyes of Herod, Pilate, and the leaders of the Jews, the Messiah's crucifixion and subsequent death put an end to Jesus Christ and his threat to their sovereignty and rule over the people. His disciples that remained were martyred one by one for the cause of the Lord's Gospel. By the time that Jerusalem was sieged in 70 AD and the temple destroyed, one could say that for all intents and purposes the true Church of Christ had been destroyed as well.

"For himself" the Lord was not cut off. We know from the Gospels in the New Testament that Christ was resurrected. He appeared to his disciples, and his Church and Gospel continued to be administered on the earth through his Apostles, with Peter being the prophet and leader of this divine organization. Thus, he confirmed the covenant and allowed the saving ordinances of the Gospel to continue for a short time, figuratively "for one week." Despite this brief period of continuance of Zion and its extension to the Gentiles, "the people of the prince" (Satan's agents and followers) were allowed to overcome the saints, "and for the overspreading of abominations he shall make it desolate, even until the consummation, and that determined shall be poured upon the desolate." Hence, a time is given in which, due to the iniquity of the children of Israel, the true priesthood of God and the true prophets of the Lord are completely removed from the earth—wiped out! From that time forth, Israel is left to fend for itself without the guidance of duly-called and ordained prophets. They thereby become desolate: "and that determined shall be poured upon the desolate."

At that point, the world entered the period and era of the Great Spiritual Famine, the "Dark Ages," during which time man was held captive by falsehood and subdued by the dominion and power of Satan through his organizations and false priesthoods. As we already noted from Amos 8:11-12, "Behold, the days come, saith the Lord GOD, that I will send a famine in the land, not a famine of bread, nor a thirst for water, but of hearing the words of the LORD: And they shall wander from sea to sea, and from the north even to the east, they shall run to and fro to seek the word of the LORD, and shall not find it." In his prophecies, Daniel is seeing the same event—the time when the Messiah is "cut off, but not for himself" and the time when "that determined shall be poured upon the desolate."

Daniel 2:1-12

1 And in the second year of the reign of Nebuchadnezzar Nebuchadnezzar dreamed dreams, wherewith his spirit was troubled, and his sleep brake from him.
2 Then the king commanded to call the magicians, and the astrologers, and the sorcerers, and the Chaldeans, for to shew the king his dreams. So they came and stood before the king.
3 And the king said unto them, I have dreamed a dream, and my spirit was troubled to know the dream.
4 Then spake the Chaldeans to the king in Syriack, O king, live for ever: tell thy servants the dream, and we will shew the interpretation,
5 The king answered and said to the Chaldeans, The thing is gone from me: if ye will not make known unto me the dream, with the interpretation thereof, ye shall be cut in pieces, and your houses shall be made a dunghill.
6 But if ye shew the dream, and the interpretation thereof, ye shall receive of me gifts and rewards and great honour: therefore shew me the dream, and the interpretation thereof.
7 They answered again and said, Let the king tell his servants the dream, and we will shew the interpretation of it.
8 The king answered and said, I know of certainty that ye would gain the time, because ye see the thing is gone from me.
9 But if ye will not make known unto me the dream, there is but one decree for you: for ye have prepared lying and corrupt words to speak before me, till the time be changed: therefore tell me the dream, and I shall know that ye can shew me the interpretation thereof.
10 The Chaldeans answered before the king, and said, There is not a man upon the earth that can shew the king's matter: therefore there is no king, lord, nor ruler, that asked such things at any magician, or astrologer, or Chaldean.
11 And it is a rare thing that the king requireth, and there is none other that can shew it before the king, except the gods, whose dwelling is not with flesh.
12 For this cause the king was angry and very furious, and commanded to destroy all the wise men of Babylon.

In the above chapter of Daniel, a dramatic situation develops in which, Nebuchadnezzar, king of Babylon, dreams a dream and desires not only to know the interpretation thereof, but also the dream itself. Nebuchadnezzar cannot remember his own dream, but has the strong impression that it is something very important. Thus, he makes the preposterous demand on his counselors to first tell him what he dreamed, and then to tell him what it means. When he is told that no one can interpret his dream, he becomes so angry that he orders all the wise men in Babylon to be destroyed. This would have also included Daniel and his brethren, as we see in the next verse.

Daniel 2:13-23

13 And the decree went forth that the wise men should be slain; and they sought Daniel and his fellows to be slain.

14 Then Daniel answered with counsel and wisdom to Arioch the captain of the king's guard, which was gone forth to slay the wise men of Babylon:
15 He answered and said to Arioch the king's captain, Why is the decree so hasty from the king? Then Arioch made the thing known to Daniel.
16 Then Daniel went in, and desired of the king that he would give him time, and that he would shew the king the interpretation.
17 Then Daniel went to his house, and made the thing known to Hananiah, Mishael, and Azariah, his companions:
18 That they would desire mercies of the God of heaven concerning this secret; that Daniel and his fellows should not perish with the rest of the wise men of Babylon.
19 Then was the secret revealed unto Daniel in a night vision. Then Daniel blessed the God of heaven.
20 Daniel answered and said, Blessed be the name of God for ever and ever: for wisdom and might are his:
21 And he changeth the times and the seasons: he removeth kings, and setteth up kings: he giveth wisdom unto the wise, and knowledge to them that know understanding:
22 He revealeth the deep and secret things: he knoweth what is in the darkness, and the light dwelleth with him.
23 I thank thee, and praise thee, O thou God of my fathers, who hast given me wisdom and might, and hast made known unto me now what we desired of thee: for thou hast now made known unto us the king's matter.

When Daniel finds out about the king's decree, he does two important things. First, he goes to the king to get time to solve the king's dilemma, and second he goes to his friends and asks them to "desire mercies of the God of heaven concerning this secret." This is an important and crucial point to be made with respect to our dealings with God. Any time we face a challenge or have a question to be resolved, if we are wise we will stop and seek help from the God of heaven concerning the issue. Just as in the case of Daniel, the Lord God of Israel will answer our prayers if we truly seek to know the truth. In contrast, if we seek counsel only of men rather than God, we are then left to ourselves. God is not a God of confusion. He will answer our prayers, just as he did in the case of Daniel. When he does, we should all remember to thank him for his mercy and kindness.

Daniel 2:24-28

24 Therefore Daniel went in unto Arioch, whom the king had ordained to destroy the wise men of Babylon: he went and said thus unto him; Destroy not the wise men of Babylon: bring me in before the king, and I will shew unto the king the interpretation.
25 Then Arioch brought in Daniel before the king in haste, and said thus unto him, I have found a man of the captives of Judah, that will make known unto the king the interpretation.
26 The king answered and said to Daniel, whose name was Belteshazzar, Art thou able to make known unto me the dream which I have seen, and the interpretation thereof?
27 Daniel answered in the presence of the king, and said, The secret which the king hath demanded cannot the wise men, the astrologers, the magicians, the soothsayers, shew unto the king;
28 But there is a God in heaven that revealeth secrets, and maketh known to the king Nebuchadnezzar what shall be in the latter days. Thy dream, and the visions of thy head upon thy bed, are these;

The king's dream pertains to actions and events that will occur in the latter days. Therefore, we can look for the importance of Daniel's interpretation for our day and our times.

Daniel 2:29-30

29 As for thee, O king, thy thoughts came into thy mind upon thy bed, what should come to pass hereafter: and he that revealeth secrets maketh known to thee what shall come to pass. 30 But as for me, this secret is not revealed to me for any wisdom that I have more than any living, but for their sakes that shall make known the interpretation to the king, and that thou mightest know the thoughts of thy heart.

When Daniel tells Arioch, the captain of the Guard, "Destroy not the wise men of Babylon: bring me in before the king, and I will shew unto the king the interpretation," Arioch immediately brings Daniel to the king in haste! We should note that along with Daniel's wisdom in obtaining the interpretation of the dream from the Lord, he is careful to not take credit for the revelation, but gives all glory to God. Daniel states clearly to the king in verse 28, "there is a God in heaven that revealeth secrets, and maketh known to the King Nebuchadnezzar what shall be in the latter days." This not only shows Daniel's humility, but it also states clearly that the king's dream pertains to events that will occur in the latter days. In verse 30, Daniel again gives credit to God by saying, "But as for me, this secret is not revealed to me for any wisdom that I have more than any living, but for their sakes that shall make known the interpretation to the king, and that thou mightest know the thoughts of thy heart." Daniel is completely humble in this respect, and we can all learn from his actions how we should handle that which we receive from God—namely, with gratitude and humility. Daniel also demonstrates to us living today that what he did to obtain knowledge from the Lord could be done by anyone. When we lack knowledge we should feel confident that God himself can respond to our pleas if we ask with sincerity of heart, having faith, and wanting to know the truth of the matter.

Daniel 2:31-36

31 Thou, O king, sawest, and behold a great image. This great image, whose brightness was excellent, stood before thee; and the form thereof was terrible.
32 This image's head was of fine gold, his breast and his arms of silver, his belly and his thighs of brass,
33 His legs of iron, his feet part of iron and part of clay.
34 Thou sawest till that a stone was cut out without hands, which smote the image upon his feet that were of iron and clay, and brake them to pieces.
35 Then was the iron, the clay, the brass, the silver, and the gold, broken to pieces together, and became like the chaff of the summer threshingfloors; and the wind carried them away, that no place was found for them: and the stone that smote the image became a great mountain, and filled the whole earth.
36 This is the dream; and we will tell the interpretation thereof before the king.

Daniel first tells the king the dream. Recall that King Nebuchadnezzar had totally forgotten his own dream. He could not even tell his wise men what he had dreamed, yet he felt so impressed of its importance, that he wanted his counselors to not only interpret the dream, but to also recall it for him in the first place. This, Daniel was able to do even before giving the interpretation thereof.

Daniel 2:37-45

37 Thou, O king, art a king of kings: for the God of heaven hath given thee a kingdom, power, and strength, and glory.

> 38 And wheresoever the children of men dwell, the beasts of the field and the fowls of the heaven hath he given into thine hand, and hath made thee ruler over them all. Thou art this head of gold.
> 39 And after thee shall arise another kingdom inferior to thee, and another third kingdom of brass, which shall bear rule over all the earth.
> 40 And the fourth kingdom shall be strong as iron: forasmuch as iron breaketh in pieces and subdueth all things: and as iron that breaketh all these, shall it break in pieces and bruise.
> 41 And whereas thou sawest the feet and toes, part of potters' clay, and part of iron, the kingdom shall be divided; but there shall be in it of the strength of the iron, forasmuch as thou sawest the iron mixed with miry clay.
> 42 And as the toes of the feet were part of iron, and part of clay, so the kingdom shall be partly strong, and partly broken.
> 43 And whereas thou sawest iron mixed with miry clay, they shall mingle themselves with the seed of men: but they shall not cleave one to another, even as iron is not mixed with clay.
> 44 And in the days of these kings shall the God of heaven set up a kingdom, which shall never be destroyed: and the kingdom shall not be left to other people, but it shall break in pieces and consume all these kingdoms, and it shall stand for ever.
> 45 Forasmuch as thou sawest that the stone was cut out of the mountain without hands, and that it brake in pieces the iron, the brass, the clay, the silver, and the gold; the great God hath made known to the king what shall come to pass hereafter: and the dream is certain, and the interpretation thereof sure.

In verse 39, we see that Daniel tells the king that, eventually, there will be a kingdom that "shall bear rule over all the earth." As was pointed out during the discussion of Isaiah, there never has been, nor is there ever likely to be an earthly government that could conquer and rule over the entire earth. We should again look not for an earthly kingdom, but for a spiritual government. This dream of Nebuchadnezzar is showing the development and establishment of the churches of the apostasy, or the kingdom and dominion of the devil, which are allowed to overcome the whole earth as the prophets and priesthood of God are withdrawn according to prophecy. During the Dark Ages, one kingdom after another is established, but in a sense they are still the same kingdom. At first, the kingdom is unified to some degree, but eventually it becomes many different and dissenting churches. They all have the same result—the spread of falsehood and confusion, hindering the children of men in their search for true doctrine and salvation. While the good people of the earth may be among these organizations, and even bring forth good works in the name of God, the organizations themselves are not able to provide the children of men with the saving ordinances of God. They are like iron held together by clay.

We have already learned from previously-cited scriptures that the Lord will ultimately have mercy upon his children, and will come forth to save them, reestablishing his kingdom, Zion, once again upon the earth. In Nebuchadnezzar's dream, Zion is represented by the stone that was "cut out of the mountain without hands." In verse 44 we read, "And in the days of these kings shall the God of heaven set up a kingdom, which shall never be destroyed: and the kingdom shall not be left to other people, but it shall break in pieces and consume all these kingdoms, and it shall stand for ever." This is entirely consistent with Isaiah, Jeremiah, and Ezekiel on this matter. Zion as it rolls forth will start out small. With time, it will gain momentum and strength.

THE BOOK OF DANIEL

As in Isaiah, where the king of Assyria conquers the entire earth, here King Nebuchadnezzar is told that God "hath made thee ruler over them all. Thou art this head of Gold." Nebuchadnezzar represents Satan in his role as the king of Babylon as we already saw in Jeremiah and Ezekiel. Hence, the head of Gold is the church of the devil, and the other kingdoms are man-made versions of the same. In the end, none of them will survive.

Daniel explained to the king, "Thou sawest till that a stone was cut out without hands, which smote the image upon his feet that were of iron and clay, and brake them to pieces. Then was the iron, the clay, the brass, the silver, and the gold, broken to pieces together, and became like the chaff of the summer threshingfloors; and the wind carried them away, that no place was found for them: and the stone that smote the image became a great mountain, and filled the whole earth." Zion will do likewise, it will start out small, but will eventually draw the captive sons and daughters of Israel out from among the falsehood of the world, until Zion and the truth of God consume the entire earth. While there may be physical battles yet to be waged in the cause of religious freedom, the events described here in Daniel, like those described in Isaiah, are mainly spiritual conflicts. Daniel, like Isaiah, is describing a battle for the souls of men and for the establishment of the Kingdom of God on earth.

Daniel 2:46-49
46 Then the king Nebuchadnezzar fell upon his face, and worshipped Daniel, and commanded that they should offer an oblation and sweet odours unto him.
47 The king answered unto Daniel, and said, Of a truth it is, that your God is a God of gods, and a Lord of kings, and a revealer of secrets, seeing thou couldest reveal this secret.
48 Then the king made Daniel a great man, and gave him many great gifts, and made him ruler over the whole province of Babylon, and chief of the governors over all the wise men of Babylon.
49 Then Daniel requested of the king, and he set Shadrach, Meshach, and Abed-nego, over the affairs of the province of Babylon: but Daniel sat in the gate of the king.

We learn from the stories contained in Daniel that the concepts of a Former Rain period, Spiritual Famine period and Latter Rain period are not isolated in Isaiah alone, but are found throughout the Old Testament. In the last days, Zion will roll forth as a stone "cut out of the mountain without hands, and that it brake in pieces the iron, the brass, the clay, the silver, and the gold; the great God hath made known to the king what shall come to pass hereafter: and the dream is certain, and the interpretation thereof sure." The true doctrine coming forth from modern Zion and its living prophets will consume the false doctrines of the earth. This is indeed the interpretation of this section of Daniel. It follows that this same interpretation should also be found in other books of scripture as well. Let us now break from our sequential analysis of the books of the Bible, and see how this concept is taken up by the Psalmist in the Book of Psalms.

CHAPTER EIGHT

The Book of Psalms

David, the great King of Israel, was known to have musical talent, as seen from his harp-playing before King Saul in 1 Samuel 16:23. In first and second Chronicles, David is shown to have composed Psalms, which are lyrical expressions of thanksgiving, lamentation, or praise for the Lord, and probably set to music. Many of the 150 psalms contained in the Book of Psalms are ascribed to King David. Collectively, the Book of Psalms is generally viewed as an expression of King David, although he was most likely not the author of them all.

Another characteristic of the Book of Psalms is its fairly Christian attributes. Over a hundred psalms are quoted in the New Testament, many of which are used as evidence of the fulfillment of prophecy concerning the promised Messiah as seen in the life of Jesus Christ. For example, Psalm 22:18, which reads, "They part my garments among them, and cast lots upon my vesture," is shown to be fulfilled in Matthew 27:35, Mark 15:24, Luke 23:34, and John 19:24. In this manner, the Book of Psalms is a book of prophecy and we should, therefore, examine how this book of scripture supports our discussion concerning God's dealings with the inhabitants of the earth.

Psalm 2:1-12
1 Why do the heathen rage, and the people imagine a vain thing?
2 The kings of the earth set themselves, and the rulers take counsel together, against the LORD, and against his anointed, saying,
3 Let us break their bands asunder, and cast away their cords from us.
4 He that sitteth in the heavens shall laugh: the Lord shall have them in derision.
5 Then shall he speak unto them in his wrath, and vex them in his sore displeasure.
6 Yet have I set my king upon my holy hill of Zion.
7 I will declare the decree: the LORD hath said unto me, Thou art my Son; this day have I begotten thee.
8 Ask of me, and I shall give thee the heathen for thine inheritance, and the uttermost parts of the earth for thy possession.
9 Thou shalt break them with a rod of iron; thou shalt dash them in pieces like a potter's vessel.

THE BOOK OF PSALMS

10 Be wise now therefore, O ye kings: be instructed, ye judges of the earth.
11 Serve the LORD with fear, and rejoice with trembling.
12 Kiss the Son, lest he be angry, and ye perish from the way, when his wrath is kindled but a little. Blessed are all they that put their trust in him.

This Psalm fits well into the framework described in Daniel. Daniel told king Nebuchadnezzar that his dream represented the setting up of kingdoms on the earth. The second verse of Psalm 2 describes the same thing, "The kings of the earth set themselves, and the rulers take counsel together, against the LORD, and against his anointed." The kings of the earth in this sense are the leaders of false churches, and the Lord's anointed are his true prophets and other administrators in the Lord's Kingdom.

Daniel 2 and Psalm 2 both describe the idea that eventually the Lord "shall give thee the heathen for thine inheritance, and the uttermost parts of the earth for thy possession." From our Isaiah analysis, we can infer that these kingdoms are not actual nation states, but rather false religions that claim divine authority without truly possessing it. Their meaning is symbolic. When the Lord reestablishes Zion, it will overcome these false institutions through the preaching of the truth. This is completely consistent with Nebuchadnezzar's dream, where the stone cut out of the mountain without hands rolls forth and breaks down the kingdoms of the earth and becomes a mountain itself, consuming the whole earth. "And," as we saw in Daniel 2:44, "in the days of these kings shall the God of heaven set up a kingdom, which shall never be destroyed: and the kingdom shall not be left to other people, but it shall break in pieces and consume all these kingdoms, and it shall stand for ever." Daniel 2 and Psalm 2 are describing the same event: the temporary triumph of the kingdom of the devil when the Lord withdraws his prophets and priesthood from the earth, followed by the eventual restoration of Zion and its ultimate consummation of all falsehood from off the earth.

Psalm 10:1-11

1 Why standest thou afar off, O LORD? why hidest thou thyself in times of trouble?
2 The wicked in his pride doth persecute the poor: let them be taken in the devices that they have imagined.
3 For the wicked boasteth of his heart's desire, and blesseth the covetous, whom the LORD abhorreth.
4 The wicked, through the pride of his countenance, will not seek after God: God is not in all his thoughts.
5 His ways are always grievous; thy judgments are far above out of his sight: as for all his enemies, he puffeth at them.
6 He hath said in his heart, I shall not be moved: for I shall never be in adversity.
7 His mouth is full of cursing and deceit and fraud: under his tongue is mischief and vanity.
8 He sitteth in the lurking places of the villages: in the secret places doth he murder the innocent: his eyes are privily set against the poor.
9 He lieth in wait secretly as a lion in his den: he lieth in wait to catch the poor: he doth catch the poor, when he draweth him into his net.
10 He croucheth, and humbleth himself, that the poor may fall by his strong ones.
11 He hath said in his heart, God hath forgotten: he hideth his face; he will never see it.

During the period of the Great Spiritual Famine, the Lord appears to be standing "afar off." The humble seekers of truth who are alive during this era are forced to endure the tyranny of a false ruler, who "draws them into his net"—the net of false doctrine and unauthorized priesthood ordinances. If they resist, they are persecuted for their attempts to become righteous and seek for truth. The faithful do the best they can with what they remember from the Bible stories they have heard, or what they feel in their hearts. This evil tyrant is able to deceive, and continues to do so freely because to him and his followers: "God hath forgotten: he hideth his face; he will never see it."

Psalm 10:12-18

12 Arise, O LORD; O God, lift up thine hand: forget not the humble.
13 Wherefore doth the wicked contemn God? he hath said in his heart, Thou wilt not require it.
14 Thou hast seen it; for thou beholdest mischief and spite, to requite it with thy hand: the poor committeth himself unto thee; thou art the helper of the fatherless.
15 Break thou the arm of the wicked and the evil man: seek out his wickedness till thou find none.
16 The LORD is King for ever and ever: the heathen are perished out of his land.
17 LORD, thou hast heard the desire of the humble: thou wilt prepare their heart, thou wilt cause thine ear to hear:
18 To judge the fatherless and the oppressed, that the man of the earth may no more oppress.

In response to this terrible scene of oppression described in the narrative of Psalm 10, the Psalmist makes a desperate plea for help: "Arise, O LORD; O God, lift up thine hand: forget not the humble." In verses 15 through 18, we see an image similar to that observed in Daniel 2 and Psalm 2, "Break thou the arm of the wicked and the evil man: seek out his wickedness till thou find none. The Lord is King for ever and ever: the heathen are perished out of his land... that the man of the earth may no more oppress." The man of the earth spoken of here is actually Lucifer, who was cast down to earth for rebellion.

Psalm 11:3

3 If the foundations be destroyed, what can the righteous do?

What a powerful verse of scripture, especially as it pertains to our subject of revelation and Spiritual Famine. Without the foundation of revelation and direction from living prophets, the righteous are left to fend for themselves among the heathen churches and false doctrines of the world.

Psalm 12:1-8

1 Help, Lord; for the godly man ceaseth; for the faithful fail from among the children of men.
2 They speak vanity every one with his neighbour: with flattering lips and with a double heart do they speak.
3 The LORD shall cut off all flattering lips, and the tongue that speaketh proud things:
4 Who have said, With our tongue will we prevail; our lips are our own: who is lord over us?
5 For the oppression of the poor, for the sighing of the needy, now will I arise, saith the LORD; I will set him in safety from him that puffeth at him.
6 The words of the LORD are pure words: as silver tried in a furnace of earth, purified seven times.
7 Thou shalt keep them, O LORD, thou shalt preserve them from this generation for ever.
8 The wicked walk on every side, when the vilest men are exalted.

Can it be any clearer than in verse one above? The Lord's prophets, or godly men, cease from the earth. In place thereof, the imposters (leaders of the churches of men and devils) arise, who teach vanity and use flattery to prevail over the children of men. The words of false teachers are like gall, full of flattery and proud things. In contrast, the words of the Lord are pure as silver, like the heavenly dew that distills upon the minds of the Lord's prophets (Deuteronomy 32:1-3).

Psalm 14:1-7
1 The fool hath said in his heart, There is no God. They are corrupt, they have done abominable works, there is none that doeth good.
2 The LORD looked down from heaven upon the children of men, to see if there were any that did understand, and seek God.
3 They are all gone aside, they are all together become filthy: there is none that doeth good, no, not one.
4 Have all the workers of iniquity no knowledge? who eat up my people as they eat bread, and call not upon the LORD.
5 There were they in great fear: for God is in the generation of the righteous.
6 Ye have ashamed the counsel of the poor, because the LORD is his refuge.
7 Oh that the salvation of Israel were come out of Zion! when the LORD bringeth back the captivity of his people, Jacob shall rejoice, and Israel shall be glad.

Some today even say, "There is no God," not because they are wicked, but because they are confused. Considering the chaos that has prevailed on the earth concerning religion since the apostles were taken away, there is no wonder some feel that "there is no God." Only with knowledge of the predicted famine of hearing the words of the Lord do we understand the meaning of this chaos period. In verse two, we see that the Lord has been looking "down from heaven upon the children of men, to see if there were any that did understand and seek God." What does he find out as he looks down from heaven during the dark ages of apostasy? "They are all gone aside, they are all together become filthy: there is none that doeth good, no, not one. Have all the workers of iniquity no knowledge? who eat up my people as they eat bread, and call not upon the LORD." In the place of true prophets, the leaders and teachers of the false churches confuse the people and lead them astray into falsehood. The righteous and humble people living during this time "call not upon the LORD," because they are not taught to do so. Even the good people of the earth are led away into mistakes and misjudgments. They stumble, so to speak, because they are deceived by falsehood and incorrect doctrine. In Psalm 14, we see that the Lord is waiting for someone among all the children of men to "call upon the Lord" and to seek counsel from God directly. When that finally occurs, then the salvation of Israel will again come out of Zion! "When the LORD bringeth back the captivity of his people, Jacob shall rejoice, and Israel shall be glad."

Psalm 17:8-15
8 Keep me as the apple of the eye, hide me under the shadow of thy wings,
9 From the wicked that oppress me, from my deadly enemies, who compass me about.
10 They are inclosed in their own fat: with their mouth they speak proudly.
11 They have now compassed us in our steps: they have set their eyes bowing down to the earth;

12 Like as a lion that is greedy of his prey, and as it were a young lion lurking in secret places.
13 Arise, O LORD, disappoint him, cast him down: deliver my soul from the wicked, which is thy sword:
14 From men which are thy hand, O LORD, from men of the world, which have their portion in this life, and whose belly thou fillest with thy hid treasure: they are full of children, and leave the rest of their substance to their babes.
15 As for me, I will behold thy face in righteousness: I shall be satisfied, when I awake, with thy likeness.

In Isaiah, we learned that the king of Assyria was indeed Satan, and that the Lord would use the king of Assyria as his sword, and as his weapon or arm against the wickedness of Israel. The Lord sought to gather Israel, but they rejected his leadership and crucified him. In our day, we may disregard the dual aspect of this prophecy, and concentrate on the symbolic meaning associated with this type. Thus, as the Lord had warned them through his many prophets and servants, he sent the famine, the sword, and the pestilence, until Zion was found no more on the earth, and Israel lay desolate with no prophets to guide her. In Psalm 17, we see the same imagery presented. Israel finally feels the oppression and recognizes its lost and fallen state. They begin to call out to the Lord for help. Look how closely this compares with a similar verse found in Isaiah:

Isaiah 10:5-6

5 O Assyrian, the rod of mine anger, and the staff in their hand is mine indignation.
6 I will send him against an hypocritical nation, and against the people of my wrath will I give him a charge, to take the spoil, and to take the prey, and to tread them down like the mire of the streets.

The Lord uses the Assyrian, who is Satan, to beat down Israel and to punish them for their wickedness. In Psalm 17, we see that the children of Israel finally realize their predicament and begin to ask the Lord to deliver them. Psalm 22, which is a Messianic psalm, continues this same lament.

Psalm 22:1-8

1 My God, my God, why hast thou forsaken me? why art thou so far from helping me, and from the words of my roaring?
2 O my God, I cry in the daytime, but thou hearest not; and in the night season, and am not silent.
3 But thou art holy, O thou that inhabitest the praises of Israel.
4 Our fathers trusted in thee: they trusted, and thou didst deliver them.
5 They cried unto thee, and were delivered: they trusted in thee, and were not confounded.
6 But I am a worm, and no man; a reproach of men, and despised of the people.
7 All they that see me laugh me to scorn: they shoot out the lip, they shake the head, saying,
8 He trusted on the LORD that he would deliver him: let him deliver him, seeing he delighted in him.

In Matthew 27:46, and again in Mark 15:34, we read the account of the crucifixion of Jesus Christ when he says the same words found in Psalm 22:1, "And about the ninth hour Jesus cried with a loud voice, saying, Eli, Eli, lama sabachthani? that is to say, My God, my God, why has thou forsaken me?" It may be that in order to fulfill the demands of the Great Atonement for the sins of the world, God the Father may have actually withdrawn his spirit from his son at this final moment.

THE BOOK OF PSALMS

While some may see this as a possible sign of weakness, in reality it demonstrates the divine wisdom of the Lord. The Savior at this final moment on the cross is not only expressing his feelings of being alone, but he is also referring us to the 22nd Psalm.

As the Psalmist laments the fact that his God has apparently forsaken him, so too the Savior is announcing at his death the forthcoming of that great event, foretold by the prophets—the period of the Great Spiritual Famine. Israel during the "Former Rain" period, when it had prophets and spiritual guidance, is in stark contrast with Israel during the Dark Ages of apostasy as seen in verses 4-6: "Our fathers trusted in thee: they trusted, and thou didst deliver them. They cried unto thee, and were delivered: they trusted in thee, and were not confounded. But I am a worm, and no man; a reproach of men, and despised of the people." Once the Lord withdraws his prophets from them, the children of Israel become oppressed and feed upon falsehood during the great period of desolation. The Lord's final words on the cross are letting us know that the prophecies contained in the 22nd Psalm are about to be fulfilled.

Another messianic message pertaining to Jesus Christ's mortal ministry is also found in Psalm 22:15-16: "My strength is dried up like a potsherd; and my tongue cleaveth to my jaws; and thou hast brought me into the dust of death. For dogs have compassed me: the assembly of the wicked have inclosed me: they pierced my hands and my feet." While the image of the piecing of his hands and his feet is a clear reference to Christ's death by crucifixion, the symbolic description of his being in a state of severe thirst is also worthy of note. We have already made the association between references to water, dew or rain and the word of God as given to his prophets, as in Deuteronomy 32:1-3. Here the Psalmist describes a state of thirst, while at the same time being compassed by dogs, "the assembly of the wicked have inclosed me." These symbolic images fit well into the constructs derived from the Book of Isaiah, and are thus references to the onset of the period of Spiritual Famine.

Psalm 22:19-28

19 But be not thou far from me, O LORD: O my strength, haste thee to help me.
20 Deliver my soul from the sword; my darling from the power of the dog.
21 Save me from the lion's mouth: for thou hast heard me from the horns of the unicorns.
22 I will declare thy name unto my brethren: in the midst of the congregation will I praise thee.
23 Ye that fear the LORD, praise him; all ye the seed of Jacob, glorify him; and fear him, all ye the seed of Israel.
24 For he hath not despised nor abhorred the affliction of the afflicted; neither hath he hid his face from him; but when he cried unto him, he heard.
25 My praise shall be of thee in the great congregation: I will pay my vows before them that fear him.
26 The meek shall eat and be satisfied: they shall praise the LORD that seek him: your heart shall live for ever.
27 All the ends of the world shall remember and turn unto the LORD: and all the kindreds of the nations shall worship before thee.
28 For the kingdom is the LORD's: and he is the governor among the nations.

Reference is made to former prosperity, the current state of desolation, and then finally the wonderful period of restoration is either hoped for, announced or predicted. In the above verses, Israel is asking the Lord for deliverance from the sword, and from "the power of the dog." In verse 21, he asks the Lord to save him from the lion's mouth, which makes me wonder if the story of Daniel being cast in the lion's den is not even more applicable to this subject than I had previously noted. It does convey the same pattern of action on the part of the Lord: his servant enjoys a period of early prosperity and recognition, then comes a dark period when Daniel spends the whole night in the den of lions. This dark phase is finally ended when Daniel is brought forth from the den unharmed. He is exalted by the king, and made ruler over the province. The true Church and Kingdom of God, or Zion, had its period of early prosperity, its dark period of being forsaken of the Lord, and will now, in the latter days, see its former glory restored. Prophets, priesthood power, and the saving ordinances of the Kingdom of God must once again be made available to God's children. "All the ends of the world shall remember and turn unto the LORD: and all the kindreds of the nations shall worship before thee. For the kingdom is the LORD's: and he is the governor among the nations."

These verses are significant because: (1) they show that all the ends of the world will be turned unto the Lord, and (2) at some point, all the people on the earth were in a situation where they needed to be turned back to the truth. This is a fundamental realization.

Psalm 23:1-6
1 The Lord is my shepherd; I shall not want.
2 He maketh me to lie down in green pastures: he leadeth me beside the still waters.
3 He restoreth my soul: he leadeth me in the paths of righteousness for his name's sake.
4 Yea, though I walk through the valley of the shadow of death, I will fear no evil: for thou art with me; thy rod and thy staff they comfort me.
5 Thou preparest a table before me in the presence of mine enemies: thou anointest my head with oil; my cup runneth over.
6 Surely goodness and mercy shall follow me all the days of my life: and I will dwell in the house of the LORD for ever.

Could a discussion of the Psalms be complete without mentioning the 23rd Psalm? Psalm 23 is probably the most famous and oft quoted of all the psalms. It is a favorite, especially at funeral services. Some years ago, I attended the funeral of a former high school teacher, and indeed the 23rd Psalm was read at the service. Over the course of the week following the funeral services, I could not help but wonder what it was about this passage of scripture that so appealed to people. I asked myself again and again, "Why is it always read at funerals?" As I pondered and later prayed about the passage, I finally realized two things. First, I felt that most Christians love this passage of scripture because it soothes them at the time of departure from mortality. Many people view the message of the 23rd Psalm as follows:

1. Since I have accepted Jesus Christ as my Savior and Redeemer, then I will be okay.
2. Even though I die, and "walk through the valley of the shadow of death," leaving mortality as a sinner, I will still be okay because Jesus Christ has taken my sins upon him and I can die in peace, knowing all is well.

3. Therefore, in the end, I will "dwell in the house of the Lord forever" even though I am a sinner and would normally fear death.

This realization explained why it is such a favorite at funerals, when people are facing the transition from mortality to the afterlife. Family members want to feel comforted at such a time. They want to feel that even though their deceased loved one had many faults, perhaps it will still be okay. I do not necessarily disagree with this view of the verse. As I stated earlier, scripture study is a personal matter, and a verse of scripture can have various interpretations depending on the context that exists for the reader at the time. At the death of a loved one, I would agree that Psalm 23 is a very comforting passage, and gives hope to those left behind.

The second realization about this scripture was even more meaningful. After a great deal of thought and prayer on the issue, I came to an entirely different view of the 23rd Psalm. While the passage may comfort us at the passing of a loved one, it is really not meant to be associated with death. The 23rd Psalm is a message of hope, true, but it speaks more to the living than the dead. My alternate interpretation of this passage is as follows:

1. If I hold fast to the rod and staff of the Lord (read the scriptures, pray when making decisions, and try with all my heart to keep the commandments of God), then the Lord will help me in my life.
2. He will lead me and nourish me in green pastures and beside still waters, meaning he will give me knowledge through personal revelations from him that pertain specifically to me and to the decisions that I face in life.
3. Even though I may face grave dangers because of my enemies, or he may have me do things that seemingly place my life in jeopardy, I will not fear these situations. The Holy Ghost will comfort my heart, and speak peace to my soul. The Spirit of God will confirm to me that I am doing the right thing, no matter who else is against me with respect to this crucial decision.

Psalm 23 is speaking to the living, not the dead. It is a concise description of the way our Heavenly Father deals with his children that desire his guidance and help in the land of the living, not just at death. Those that seek him out, and pray sincerely, will have goodness and mercy all the days of their lives. Through obedience and instruction, they can one day abide in his presence and "dwell in the house of the Lord for ever." This interpretation is on a personal level, applying to each of God's children individually.

Taking this second interpretation one step further has led me to see yet another application of the passage. When looking for meaning in the scriptures, I have often found it helpful to consider who has written the message being considered, and then to ask these simple questions: Who is this specific author addressing? What does he desire the reader to gain from this message? In the context of our subject at hand, this was a useful exercise. While some controversy is associated with which Psalms were actually written by King David, the son of Jesse, and which ones were written by other persons on his behalf, it is nonetheless understood by most that David is the one speaking in the Psalms. Accepting this concept is helpful in understanding the meaning of the Psalms. David was King in Israel, and under his throne, all the tribes were united and brought together as one nation. The Lord also covenanted with David that, through his lineage, the rule of Israel would remain. Despite the wickedness of subsequent kings in his lineage, David was told that the Messiah would be born from his seed, and that ultimately the Lord himself would rule on the throne of David forever. In fact, during his mortal ministry, Jesus Christ is frequently referred to as the "Son of David."

Now we apply the simple questions I suggested above: Who is David, the King of Israel, addressing? And, what does he desire the reader to gain from his message? David is addressing the children of Israel, his subjects—the literal descendants of Abraham, Isaac and Jacob. He desires that the children of Israel and Judah take this type or symbolic message to heart. Even though the children of Israel will be made to pass through the valley of the shadow of death, or the great era of no living prophets, the Lord will eventually restore their souls. His rod and his staff (the scriptures in the Bible) will comfort them as he leads them out of oppression and into Zion once more. The 23rd Psalm is a type of the literal gathering of Israel in the latter days. Through personal revelation, and new knowledge and understanding that ultimately come forth, the Lord will convince his captive children to come out from the heathen churches that have no power to save. Doing so, they will feel the confirming spirit of the Holy Ghost in their hearts, and realize finally that the Lord is merciful in bringing Zion again.

The term "Valley of the Shadow of Death," therefore, is a term that means "the period of Spiritual Famine." To emphasize and clarify the association between the period of the Great Spiritual Famine and the Valley of the Shadow of Death spoken of in Psalm 23, let us look at Psalm 44, where similar language is used:

> **Psalm 44:1-4**
>
> 1 We have heard with our ears, O God, our fathers have told us, what work thou didst in their days, in the times of old.
> 2 How thou didst drive out the heathen with thy hand, and plantedst them; how thou didst afflict the people, and cast them out.
> 3 For they got not the land in possession by their own sword, neither did their own arm save them: but thy right hand, and thine arm, and the light of thy countenance, because thou hadst a favour unto them.
> 4 Thou art my King, O God: command deliverances for Jacob.

In the above verses, the Psalmist is describing the state of the children of Israel during the Great Spiritual Famine. They hear stories about what great things the Lord did for their fathers, how he drove out their enemies from before them. However, in the setting described above, Israel is not enjoying such favor as before. Therefore, the Psalmist proclaims in desperation: "Thou art my King, O God: command deliverances for Jacob." How can Jacob be delivered unless he has first been taken captive?

> **Psalm 44:5-14**
>
> 5 Through thee will we push down our enemies: through thy name will we tread them under that rise up against us.

6 For I will not trust in my bow, neither shall my sword save me.
7 But thou hast saved us from our enemies, and hast put them to shame that hated us.
8 In God we boast all the day long, and praise thy name for ever. Selah.
9 But thou hast cast off, and put us to shame; and goest not forth with our armies.
10 Thou makest us to turn back from the enemy: and they which hate us spoil for themselves.
11 Thou hast given us like sheep appointed for meat; and hast scattered us among the heathen.
12 Thou sellest thy people for nought, and dost not increase thy wealth by their price.
13 Thou makest us a reproach to our neighbours, a scorn and a derision to them that are round about us.
14 Thou makest us a byword among the heathen, a shaking of the head among the people.

Now we see the reason for Jacob's lament. "But thou hast cast off, and put us to shame; and goest not forth with our armies." "Thou hast given us like sheep appointed for meat; and scattered us among the heathen," or, based on our previous analysis, we might say among the heathen churches. The children of Israel are scattered among all the people of the world, and when they try to seek their God, they are unable to find him anywhere. He has "cast off" and left Israel with no guidance through his prophets, for they are not found on the earth. The good people of the earth may still seek to do good works, and they may call upon the Lord, but they are unable to receive the saving ordinances that can only come through the true Priesthood of God. They are often held captive in organizations professing to be of God, but lacking in authority. They are entrapped by falsehood and vanity, they have inherited lies, leaving them dazed and confused.

Psalm 44:15-19

15 My confusion is continually before me, and the shame of my face hath covered me,
16 For the voice of him that reproacheth and blasphemeth; by reason of the enemy and avenger.
17 All this is come upon us; yet have we not forgotten thee, neither have we dealt falsely in thy covenant.
18 Our heart is not turned back, neither have our steps declined from thy way;
19 Though thou hast sore broken us in the place of dragons, and covered us with the shadow of death.

Here again, the Psalmist uses the term "shadow of death." But from the context of this Psalm, Psalm 44, it is even clearer than before what is meant by the shadow of death. The shadow of death is the great period of apostasy—the Spiritual Famine or dearth that was pronounced upon the children of Israel for the disobedience of their fathers. While they were warned repeatedly by the prophets of God to repent and to return unto their God, they would not. Instead, they stoned the prophets and killed them, and cast them out from among them. Ultimately, our Heavenly Father sent his Only Begotten Son, Jesus Christ, into the world to call them to the wedding supper, yet they rejected him as well. He was delivered up unto the crucifixion by his own people, and he suffered it without retaliation. He could have saved himself with legions of angels at his command, but he chose not to do so. Instead, he allowed Israel to have that which they were requesting at the time. Within a few hundred years, all his prophets, seers, and authorized priesthood leaders had been removed from the earth, leaving the children of Israel in a lost and fallen state, and subject to the dominion of Satan with his false institutions and organizations of oppression.

> **Psalm 44:20-26**
> 20 If we have forgotten the name of our God, or stretched out our hands to a strange god;
> 21 Shall not God search this out? for he knoweth the secrets of the heart.
> 22 Yea, for thy sake are we killed all the day long; we are counted as sheep for the slaughter.
> 23 Awake, why sleepest thou, O Lord? arise, cast us not off for ever.
> 24 Wherefore hidest thou thy face, and forgettest our affliction and our oppression?
> 25 For our soul is bowed down to the dust: our belly cleaveth unto the earth.
> 26 Arise for our help, and redeem us for thy mercies' sake.

Here, the children of Israel recognize that they are "cast off" and that the Lord has hidden his face from them. They ask him to "Arise for our help, and redeem us for thy mercies' sake." Redeem them from what? Verse 24 indicates that it is from "affliction and oppression." If not during the Dark Ages, which history itself attests to being a period of "affliction, tyranny, and oppression," then when did this dearth occur in the past, or when will it occur in the future? Zion, or the Kingdom of God, was taken completely off the earth within a few generations after the death and resurrection of Jesus Christ. It was overrun by the followers of Satan, who persecuted and destroyed the saints of God until no one having the true priesthood of God remained. The Psalmist is referring to this great period of apostasy when he uses the term, "Shadow of Death." When the 23rd Psalm says, "Yea, though I walk through the valley of the shadow of death, I will fear no evil: for thou art with me; thy rod and thy staff they comfort me," it means that the good people of the earth will not be harmed by this event. Those that are tortured and persecuted during the Dark Ages of oppression will rise in the resurrection of the just. Those that were wicked and served the adversary will rise in the resurrection, but will be brought to judgment for their evil actions. The righteous have no need to fear the Shadow of Death, since the Lord will provide a means for their salvation and redemption.

The term "Shadow of Death" is quite applicable to this great period of Spiritual Famine on the earth (the period between the Former Rain and the Latter Rain). Without the promised restoration, when the Lord restores Zion again to the earth and calls prophets to guide his children, then this would be "death" indeed. Since the famine period is only temporary, and the Lord has promised to redeem and gather his lost sheep in the end, we see that this terrible period of trial and tribulation is only a "shadow of death." It is a taste of what it is like to be without God to guide and direct the affairs of his children. It is a period when it would appear to a third party looking onto the world scene that Satan had indeed been victorious and conquered Zion, the Lord's Kingdom, on earth. If this situation were allowed to stand without a restoration, this would mean the death of the Saints of God, both physically and spiritually speaking.

Through his resurrection and atoning sacrifice for sin, the Lord God has all control over death and hell. We must remember that the Lord allowed the king of Assyria, or Satan, to overrun the whole earth as a punishment to his wicked and idolatrous people. It was a voluntary act on his part, and not actually a defeat at all. When he was rejected by the children of Israel after years and years of warning, he finally gave them that which they desired—to be like the heathen and to walk after their ways. The righteous that were caught up in this period need not fear. Although they had to suffer much at the hands of the wicked, the Lord is able to reach back through the ages to redeem the good people of the earth who have died without receiving the saving ordinances during their mortal existence. This period does not hurt the righteous martyrs, yet serves to identify the wicked and those that served up the affliction and oppression of this horrific era. To stress the point even further, let us look at other places in the scriptures where the term "Shadow of Death" is used by the Lord as he talks to his children through his prophets.

Isaiah 9:2
2 The people that walked in darkness have seen a great light: they that dwell in the land of the shadow of death, upon them hath the light shined.

This verse in Isaiah describes a people walking in darkness—they that dwell in the shadow of death. Yet, upon this people springs forth a light. After years of being lost and forsaken, they are finally given a prophet to guide them again. Zion is once again established and the Lord returns with a strong arm to redeem his lost sheep. His lost people are delivered from the Shadow of Death.

Jeremiah 13:15-17
15 Hear ye, and give ear; be not proud: for the LORD hath spoken.
16 Give glory to the LORD your God, before he cause darkness, and before your feet stumble upon the dark mountains, and, while ye look for light, he turn it into the shadow of death, and make it gross darkness.
17 But if ye will not hear it, my soul shall weep in secret places for your pride; and mine eye shall weep sore, and run down with tears, because the LORD's flock is carried away captive.

In these verses from Jeremiah, the Lord is giving his children a strict warning. He is basically saying that if they do not give heed to his counsels and to his word, he will turn the light into the shadow of death, and make it gross darkness. He will cover the prophets and the seers, and withdraw his priesthood, leaving the children of Israel to stumble upon the dark mountains of idolatry, falsehood, and vanity. "But if ye will not hear it, my soul shall weep in secret places for your pride; and mine eye shall weep sore, and run down with tears, because the LORD's flock is carried away captive." It was not the Lord's desire for his children to reject him and his message of salvation, but he was constrained to suffer them to pass through pain that they might learn the true consequence of their actions.

Now, if that is not enough to convince one of the symbolic meaning of this term, "Shadow of Death," let us now read Psalm 107. It is a clear description of the entire spectrum of events: First, the wickedness and rebellion of ancient Israel; second, the Shadow of Death period when they are bound in affliction and iron; and finally, the period of mercy and restoration when prophets are again called. This starts the period of the Latter Rain.

THE LATTER RAIN

Psalm 107:1-10

1 O give thanks unto the LORD, for he is good: for his mercy endureth for ever.
2 Let the redeemed of the LORD say so, whom he hath redeemed from the hand of the enemy;
3 And gathered them out of the lands, from the east, and from the west, from the north, and from the south.
4 They wandered in the wilderness in a solitary way; they found no city to dwell in.
5 Hungry and thirsty, their soul fainted in them.
6 Then they cried unto the LORD in their trouble, and he delivered them out of their distresses.
7 And he led them forth by the right way, that they might go to a city of habitation.
8 Oh that men would praise the LORD for his goodness, and for his wonderful works to the children of men!
9 For he satisfieth the longing soul, and filleth the hungry soul with goodness.
10 Such as sit in darkness and in the shadow of death, being bound in affliction and iron;

We again see references to darkness and the shadow of death. These symbols should be clear by now. They are referring to those without the guidance of authorized prophets of God. But, in his goodness, the Lord is finally coming to their rescue and leading "them forth by the right way." Why are they in this state of captivity and in need of rescue?

Psalm 107:11-16

11 Because they rebelled against the words of God, and contemned the counsel of the most High:
12 Therefore he brought down their heart with labour; they fell down, and there was none to help.
13 Then they cried unto the LORD in their trouble, and he saved them out of their distresses.
14 He brought them out of darkness and the shadow of death, and brake their bands in sunder.
15 Oh that men would praise the LORD for his goodness, and for his wonderful works to the children of men!
16 For he hath broken the gates of brass, and cut the bars of iron in sunder.

Recall our discussion about Daniel's interpretation of Nebuchadnezzar's dream. The stone cut out of the mountain without hands rolls forth and breaks the symbolic statue made of brass, iron, clay, and other materials into pieces. Ultimately, this stone becomes a huge mountain, filling the whole earth.

Psalm 107:17-29

17 Fools because of their transgression, and because of their iniquities, are afflicted.
18 Their soul abhorreth all manner of meat; and they draw near unto the gates of death.
19 Then they cry unto the LORD in their trouble, and he saveth them out of their distresses.
20 He sent his word, and healed them, and delivered them from their destructions.
21 Oh that men would praise the LORD for his goodness, and for his wonderful works to the children of men!
22 And let them sacrifice the sacrifices of thanksgiving, and declare his works with rejoicing.
23 They that go down to the sea in ships, that do business in great waters;
24 These see the works of the LORD, and his wonders in the deep.
25 For he commandeth, and raiseth the stormy wind, which lifteth up the waves thereof.
26 They mount up to the heaven, they go down again to the depths: their soul is melted because of trouble.
27 They reel to and fro, and stagger like a drunken man, and are at their wits' end.

> 28 Then they cry unto the LORD in their trouble, and he bringeth them out of their distresses.
> 29 He maketh the storm a calm, so that the waves thereof are still.

This last verse is a clear reference to Jesus Christ, the Savior and Redeemer, who was shown during his mortal life to have the power to calm the raging storm. In the last days, he will calm the raging storm of religious confusion. He will bring the dispersed of Israel "out of their distress" and lead them to Zion, once he has restored it again to the earth in the last days.

Psalm 107:30-34

> 30 Then are they glad because they be quiet; so he bringeth them unto their desired haven.
> 31 Oh that men would praise the LORD for his goodness, and for his wonderful works to the children of men!
> 32 Let them exalt him also in the congregation of the people, and praise him in the assembly of the elders.
> 33 He turneth rivers into a wilderness, and the watersprings into dry ground;
> 34 A fruitful land into barrenness, for the wickedness of them that dwell therein.

Here we see the prophecy of his great withdrawal from the chosen people of the earth. "He turneth rivers into a wilderness, and the waterspings into dry ground." The Lord withdraws his presence from his once-chosen people because of their wickedness. He turns off the river of revelation and the waterspings of prophecy. In the last days, however, the situation will ultimately be reversed.

Psalm 107:35-38

> 35 He turneth the wilderness into a standing water, and dry ground into watersprings.
> 36 And there he maketh the hungry to dwell, that they may prepare a city for habitation;
> 37 And sow the fields, and plant vineyards, which may yield fruits of increase.
> 38 He blesseth them also, so that they are multiplied greatly; and suffereth not their cattle to decrease.

Now we see the opposite phenomenon, that of turning "the wilderness into a standing water, and dry ground into waterspings." Just as he had the power to overcome death through the resurrection and overcome hell through his atonement for sins, the Lord also has the power to withdraw his presence from the children of men, and the power to return and visit them again. There is nothing on this earth that can stop the Lord God of Israel from calling a new prophet to guide his people back to safety in these latter times.

Psalm 107:39-43

> 39 Again, they are minished and brought low through oppression, affliction, and sorrow.
> 40 He poureth contempt upon princes, and causeth them to wander in the wilderness, where there is no way.
> 41 Yet setteth he the poor on high from affliction, and maketh him families like a flock.
> 42 The righteous shall see it, and rejoice: and all iniquity shall stop her mouth.
> 43 Whoso is wise, and will observe these things, even they shall understand the lovingkindness of the LORD.

Through the symbolic framework derived from the Book of Isaiah, we now see new meaning in Psalm 107. We see many of the symbolic types that we have already discussed. We see how the Lord can bring light to those in darkness. We see how he can turn rivers into wilderness and dry ground into waterspings. In

THE LATTER RAIN

Psalm 107, the Lord wants us to know that all these things that have transpired are according to his plan. They are wonderful events that demonstrate his wisdom, power, and mercy toward the children of men. He assures us that he sets "the poor on high from affliction, and maketh him families like a flock. The righteous shall see it, and rejoice: and all iniquity shall stop her mouth."

Psalm 81:11-12

11 But my people would not hearken to my voice; and Israel would none of me.
12 So I gave them up unto their own hearts' lust: and they walked in their own counsels.

The dark times of the apostasy period were predicted and foreseen by the Lord God of Hosts, and while they cause stress and affliction to the righteous who must endure them, in the end they are rescued from this cruel era, and ultimately see the wisdom and mercy of the Lord. In contrast, those that took advantage of God's absence from the affairs of men during the great age of Spiritual Famine will reap the condemnation for their actions through the judgments of God upon them. Some may marvel and wonder how a just God could allow such harsh wickedness and oppression to prevail during this period of time, and for it to occur at the hands of those claiming to be priests and leaders of the Lord's Church. In the end, the just are separated from the unjust, and the righteous from the wicked.

Anything that is good comes from God, and that which is evil comes from the devil. While God withdrew his protection from the just of the earth, it was done with great remorse of spirit on his part. The Lord allows us to exercise our agency even to the point of detriment in order to teach us the hard lessons of life. He will never force us to do what is right. His atonement and sacrifice allows us to repent, and to be cleansed of all our unrighteousness. He saves many from spiritual death and suffering if they accept his Gospel and enter into the fold of God. The falling-away period does not hurt the just, for the Lord is mindful of them and will provide a means for their return to his flock. It gives the wicked the opportunity to exercise their agency to do evil, and bring upon them the righteous judgment of the Lord in the great and final day.

Many other verses from the Psalms shed light on this subject. Notice the wording used by the Psalmist in the following citations, and ask yourself if this applies to King David as an individual, or to Israel as a nation.

Psalm 42:1-2, 9-11

1 As the hart panteth after the water brooks, so panteth my soul after thee, O God.
2 My soul thirsteth for God, for the living God: when shall I come and appear before God?
9 I will say unto God my rock, Why hast thou forgotten me? why go I mourning because of the oppression of the enemy?
10 As with a sword in my bones, mine enemies reproach me; while they say daily unto me, Where is thy God?
11 Why art thou cast down, O my soul? and why art thou disquieted within me? hope thou in God: for I shall yet praise him, who is the health of my countenance, and my God.

Psalm 43:1-4

1 Judge me, O God, and plead my cause against an ungodly nation: O deliver me from the deceitful and unjust man.

2 For thou art the God of my strength: why dost thou cast me off? why go I mourning because of the oppression of the enemy?
3 O send out thy light and thy truth: let them lead me; let them bring me unto thy holy hill, and to thy tabernacles.
4 Then will I go unto the altar of God, unto God my exceeding joy: yea, upon the harp will I praise thee, O God my God.

Psalm 72:4-7

4 He shall judge the poor of the people, he shall save the children of the needy, and shall break in pieces the oppressor. [Recall Nebuchadnezzar's dream]
5 They shall fear thee as long as the sun and moon endure, throughout all generations.
6 He shall come down like rain upon the mown grass: as showers that water the earth.
7 In his days shall the righteous flourish; and abundance of peace so long as the moon endureth.

When Zion is restored, the revelation from God will "come down like rain upon the mown grass: as showers that water the earth." The leaders of other religions will view Zion's development and marvel. They will be troubled and flee away. It will be so different from their traditions that many will resist the new doctrine. Many will cling to their folly and view the restored Zion as a threat to their established religion, their livelihood, and their glory before men. The Kingdom of God will roll forth as we saw in Daniel, like a stone cut from the mountain without hands, and will consume all the false doctrines and false teachings that exist in the earth. It "shall break in pieces the oppressor" as in Psalm 72:4. The sword of the Lord will be his word, not a physical sword. The siege will be a siege of doctrine and authority, not of bloodshed and carnage.

Psalm 50:16-17

16 But unto the wicked God saith, What hast thou to do to declare my statutes, or that thou shouldest take my covenant in thy mouth?
17 Seeing thou hatest instruction, and castest my words behind thee.

In these verses, God not only admonishes us to call upon him directly for discernment, but he also asks the wicked how they can "declare his statutes," or "take his covenant in their mouths." This infers that many will profess to be genuine servants of the Lord while having no authority at all. These are the ones that fear Zion when it sprouts forth and begins to grow. These are they that fight against the true doctrines of God in the latter days. Yet, they do so in vain, for Zion will ultimately fill the whole earth. By conversion are the sinners destroyed out of the land.

Psalm 51:12-13

12 Restore unto me the joy of thy salvation; and uphold me with thy free spirit.
13 Then will I teach transgressors thy ways; and sinners shall be converted unto thee.

As the Psalmist prays for relief from confusion and freedom from falsehood, he describes the terrible scene of carnage that occurred as the dark ages of Spiritual Famine were being ushered in.

Psalm 79:1-3

1 O God, the heathen are come into thine inheritance; thy holy temple have they defiled; they have laid Jerusalem on heaps.
2 The dead bodies of thy servants have they given to be meat unto the fowls of the heaven, the flesh of thy saints unto the beasts of the earth.

THE LATTER RAIN

3 Their blood have they shed like water round about Jerusalem; and there was none to bury them.

Psalm 79 shows the killing off of the prophets, apostles and disciples of the Lord Jesus Christ not many years after his resurrection and ascension into Heaven. The Lord allowed these saints to be overcome, thus leaving the wicked to enter into the sanctuaries and feign divine authority. They took it by force, and they took it with violence and bloodshed. The righteous children of Israel and good people of the earth are left to wander to and fro without guidance from God, and are in bondage to evil ministers of falsehood. The evil tyrant leaders of these false churches continue to persecute the righteous and the humble.

Psalm 79:5-11

5 How long, LORD? wilt thou be angry for ever? shall thy jealousy burn like fire?
6 Pour out thy wrath upon the heathen that have not known thee, and upon the kingdoms that have not called upon thy name.
7 For they have devoured Jacob, and laid waste his dwelling place.
8 O remember not against us former iniquities: let thy tender mercies speedily prevent us: for we are brought very low.
9 Help us, O God of our salvation, for the glory of thy name: and deliver us, and purge away our sins, for thy name's sake.
10 Wherefore should the heathen say, Where is their God? let him be known among the heathen in our sight by the revenging of the blood of thy servants which is shed.
11 Let the sighing of the prisoner come before thee; according to the greatness of thy power preserve thou those that are appointed to die;

The Psalmist again laments the slaughter of the prophets and the killing of the authorized servants of the Lord. The Lord's temple and sanctuaries are overrun by unauthorized ministers pretending to be sent from the Lord. Finally, the children of Israel, as prisoners to this oppression, plead for the Lord to intervene on their behalf. Again, were these Psalms applicable just to David, or to all of Israel?

Psalm 78:58-62

58 For they provoked him to anger with their high places, and moved him to jealousy with their graven images.
59 When God heard this, he was wroth, and greatly abhorred Israel:
60 So that he forsook the tabernacle of Shiloh, the tent which he placed among men;
61 And delivered his strength into captivity, and his glory into the enemy's hand.
62 He gave his people over also unto the sword; and was wroth with his inheritance.

In verse 60, we see that the Lord allowed his Holy Temple to cease from the earth. The knowledge and understanding of this important structure was taken as well, and thus the false churches of the Great Famine period had no idea or concept of what to do with such doctrine. They did their best to imitate the known ordinances and mimicked the priesthood structure in order to get gain and to usurp power and dominion over the innocent and the meek.

Psalm 83:3-4, 12

3 They have taken crafty counsel against thy people, and consulted against thy hidden ones.
4 They have said, Come, and let us cut them off from being a nation; that the name of Israel may be no more in remembrance.
12 Who said, Let us take to ourselves the houses of God in possession.

Let us summarize by saying that the Book of Psalms is filled with language that is entirely consistent with the Former Rain/Famine/Latter Rain concept. With the aid of our analysis of Isaiah's symbolic types, we can now see significant meaning in verses that were once obscured in symbolism. While we could cite many other Psalms here, instead, let us make a transition to another section of the Bible using the following verses in Psalm 105.

Psalm 105:12-22

12 When they were but a few men in number; yea, very few, and strangers in it.
13 When they went from one nation to another, from one kingdom to another people;
14 He suffered no man to do them wrong: yea, he reproved kings for their sakes;
15 Saying, Touch not mine anointed, and do my prophets no harm.
16 Moreover he called for a famine upon the land: he brake the whole staff of bread.
17 He sent a man before them, even Joseph, who was sold for a servant:
18 Whose feet they hurt with fetters: he was laid in iron:
19 Until the time that his word came: the word of the LORD tried him.
20 The king sent and loosed him; even the ruler of the people, and let him go free.
21 He made him lord of his house, and ruler of all his substance:
22 To bind his princes at his pleasure; and teach his senators wisdom.

Once again we see the idea of the Lord sending a famine in the land, "he brake the whole staff of bread," as we have seen before in other scriptures. What I want to focus on now is the idea presented in verse 17 above, "He sent a man before them, even Joseph, who was sold for a servant." Let us now turn to the story of Joseph, who was sold into Egypt, and see what meaning we can derive from his story, contained in the Book of Genesis.

CHAPTER NINE

Joseph in Egypt

The story of Joseph with his coat of many colors is a well-known story and well-loved by both Jews and Christians. It is contained in the Old Testament of the Holy Bible, beginning in Genesis 37. Joseph's life story is so captivating that it has been the subject of musicals, movies, and other theatrical productions in modern times. For the purposes of our discussion, however, I wish to make the following points about the story of Joseph, who was sold into Egypt:

1. Joseph is a symbolic type representing Jesus Christ.
2. Joseph was separated from his brothers and forgotten. He was presumed dead, just as Christ was presumed dead by his enemies. Joseph's descendants are considered lost to the people of the world.
3. In the literal story contained in the Bible, Joseph plays a key roll in bringing salvation to the children of Israel by saving them from a severe famine. In the latter days, the seed of Joseph (the tribe of Ephraim or Ten Lost Tribes from the north) will play a major role in the restoration of Zion to the earth.
4. The help received by the good Pharaoh of Egypt who exalts Joseph to Governor over all the land is also a type that can be identified with the help of the Isaiah framework.
5. The ultimate deterioration in the relationship between the children of Israel and the Egyptian Pharaohs after the death of Joseph is also significant, and will lead us into our discussion of Moses.

Genesis 35:22-26
22 And it came to pass, when Israel dwelt in that land, that Reuben went and lay with Bilhah his father's concubine: and Israel heard it. Now the sons of Jacob were twelve:
23 The sons of Leah; Reuben, Jacob's firstborn, and Simeon, and Levi, and Judah, and Issachar, and Zebulun:
24 The sons of Rachel; Joseph, and Benjamin:
25 And the sons of Bilhah, Rachel's handmaid; Dan, and Naphtali:
26 And the sons of Zilpah, Leah's handmaid; Gad, and Asher: these are the sons of Jacob, which were born to him in Padan-aram.

JOSEPH IN EGYPT

The complete story of Joseph, the eleventh son of Jacob, and first-born of Rachael, runs from Chapter 37 to Chapter 50 of Genesis, with a brief departure in Chapter 38. Joseph's eldest brother, Reuben, should have been the birthright son of Jacob since he was the first-born son. Due to Reuben's infidelity, the birthright was passed to Joseph.

1 Chronicles 5:1-2

1 NOW the sons of Reuben the firstborn of Israel, (for he was the firstborn; but, forasmuch as he defiled his father's bed, his birthright was given unto the sons of Joseph the son of Israel: and the genealogy is not to be reckoned after the birthright.
2 For Judah prevailed above his brethren, and of him came the chief ruler; but the birthright was Joseph's:)

Both Judah and Joseph have special roles. Judah's posterity would give rise to the Savior's birth, while Joseph's genealogy is to be reckoned after the birthright. While the role of Judah is fairly well recognized by both Jews and Christians, the role of Joseph is often overlooked. Reuben was born to Leah, while Joseph was born to Rachael. When Reuben lost his birthright by sleeping with his father's concubine, Bilhah, the birthright actually went to Joseph as the first-born son of Rachael, rather than to Simeon, the second born son of Leah. This is a significant issue. It follows that Joseph and his lineage should receive blessings according to that of a birthright son, which is consistent with what we find in the blessings Joseph received by the hand of his father Jacob in Chapters 48 and 49 of Genesis.

Genesis 49:1-2

1 And Jacob called unto his sons, and said, Gather yourselves together, that I may tell you that which shall befall you in the last days.
2 Gather yourselves together, and hear, ye sons of Jacob; and hearken unto Israel your father.

These verses indicate that the blessings about to be pronounced on the sons of Jacob concern "that which shall befall you in the last days." Such phrases in the scriptures should cause us to pay particular attention as to how they apply to us living in the latter times. Of all the blessings given by Jacob to his twelve sons, only two stand out as was alluded to in 1 Chronicles 5 above—that of Judah and that of Joseph.

Genesis 49:8-12

8 Judah, thou art he whom thy brethren shall praise: thy hand shall be in the neck of thine enemies; thy father's children shall bow down before thee.
9 Judah is a lion's whelp: from the prey, my son, thou art gone up: he stooped down, he couched as a lion, and as an old lion; who shall rouse him up?
10 The sceptre shall not depart from Judah, nor a lawgiver from between his feet, until Shiloh come; and unto him shall the gathering of the people be.
11 Binding his foal unto the vine, and his ass's colt unto the choice vine; he washed his garments in wine, and his clothes in the blood of grapes:
12 His eyes shall be red with wine, and his teeth white with milk.

Judah is promised that "the sceptre shall not depart from Judah, nor a lawgiver from between his feet, until Shiloh come; and unto him shall the gathering of the people be." This indicates that Christ will come through the lineage of Judah and David the king. The royal lineage of the kings of Israel will continue through

Judah and his descendants until Jesus Christ finally assumes the throne at his second coming in the last days. Even this great blessing given to Judah is not nearly as significant as that given to Joseph.

> **Genesis 49:22-26**
>
> 22 Joseph is a fruitful bough, even a fruitful bough by a well; whose branches run over the wall:
> 23 The archers have sorely grieved him, and shot at him, and hated him:
> 24 But his bow abode in strength, and the arms of his hands were made strong by the hands of the mighty God of Jacob; (from thence is the shepherd, the stone of Israel:)
> 25 Even by the God of thy father, who shall help thee; and by the Almighty, who shall bless thee with blessings of heaven above, blessings of the deep that lieth under, blessings of the breasts, and of the womb:
> 26 The blessings of thy father have prevailed above the blessings of my progenitors unto the utmost bound of the everlasting hills: they shall be on the head of Joseph, and on the crown of the head of him that was separate from his brethren.

"The blessings of thy father have prevailed above the blessings of my progenitors unto the utmost bound of the everlasting hills: they shall be on the head of Joseph, and on the crown of the head of him that was separate from his brethren." Mention of "the crown of the head" indicates a sense of royalty being applicable to Joseph as well as to Judah. From this verse, it seems that Joseph's blessings are the greatest of all his brothers, exceeding even that given to Judah. If this is indeed the case, then where is the fulfillment of these blessings? How do they apply to us living in the latter days? The blessings of Joseph should become apparent in the last days of the earth, prior to the Second Coming of Jesus Christ in his glory. They should, therefore, play a significant role in the Latter Rain era of the world, when living prophets and the true priesthood of God are again restored to the earth.

Joseph also received another blessing from Jacob as recorded in Genesis 48. This other blessing occurred when Joseph went to Jacob with his two sons, Manasseh and Ephraim, to have them blessed by their grandfather prior to his death. Jacob not only blessed Joseph's sons, but also gave them a place among the tribes of Israel as if they were his literal sons, rather than his grandsons. Interestingly, the younger son, Ephraim, received the greater blessing. Because of this favored status of Ephraim, the Ten Tribes of Israel to the north are often referred to as Ephraim instead of Joseph. This is important to understand while studying these issues. The terms Israel, Joseph, Ephraim, the Ten Lost Tribes, or Gentiles (in many contexts)—all refer to the descendants of Joseph, with Samaria as their capital. They would be applicable to Joseph in the latter days as well. References to Judah, Jesse (the father of David), David (the king who slew Goliath), or the term "Jews" all refer to the Tribe of Judah, with Jerusalem as its capital. With these designations in mind, let us now examine the blessings given to the sons of Joseph at the hands of their grandfather, Jacob.

> **Genesis 48:5-7**
>
> 5 And now thy two sons, Ephraim and Manasseh, which were born unto thee in the land of Egypt before I came unto thee into Egypt, are mine; as Reuben and Simeon, they shall be mine.

6 And thy issue, which thou begettest after them, shall be thine, and shall be called after the name of their brethren in their inheritance.
7 And as for me, when I came from Padan, Rachel died by me in the land of Canaan in the way, when yet there was but a little way to come unto Ephrath: and I buried her there in the way of Ephrath; the same is Beth-lehem.

Notice that Rachael died and was buried in Bethlehem. This is significant, seeing that the place that Rachael died is the same place that the Savior Jesus Christ was born. This was also the place of residence of Jesse, and then David as well. The Lord Jesus Christ is shown in Matthew 1 to be a descendant of Judah, which is consistent with the blessing Judah received from Jacob. Still, the relationship between Judah and Joseph must ultimately be resolved, and healed, such that in the end these two great families are reunited into one kingdom, with Jesus as their head. This story of Rachael being buried in Bethlehem speaks to that issue and should therefore be noted. We note that Ephraim, the younger son, received the favored position of having his grandfather's right hand placed on his head, rather than on the head of his older brother Manasseh.

Genesis 48:15-22
15 And he blessed Joseph, and said, God, before whom my fathers Abraham and Isaac did walk, the God which fed me all my life long unto this day.
16 The Angel which redeemed me from all evil, bless the lads; and let my name be named on them, and the name of my fathers Abraham and Isaac; and let them grow into a multitude in the midst of the earth.
17 And when Joseph saw that his father laid his right hand upon the head of Ephraim, it displeased him: and he held up his father's hand, to remove it from Ephraim's head unto Manasseh's head.
18 And Joseph said unto his father, Not so, my father: for this is the firstborn; put thy right hand upon his head.
19 And his father refused, and said, I know it, my son, I know it: he also shall become a people, and he also shall be great: but truly his younger brother shall be greater than he, and his seed shall become a multitude of nations.
20 And he blessed them that day, saying, In thee shall Israel bless, saying, God make thee as Ephraim and as Manasseh: and he set Ephraim before Manasseh.
21 And Israel said unto Joseph, Behold, I die: but God shall be with you, and bring you again unto the land of your fathers.
22 Moreover I have given to thee one portion above thy brethren, which I took out of the hand of the Amorite with my sword and with my bow.

Verse 22 shows that Joseph's blessing is a double blessing, and that he is highly favored of the Lord in that Jacob gave him "one portion above thy brethren." The blessings given to Ephraim and Manasseh are in reality blessings upon the head of Joseph, since they are his direct offspring. It is repeated twice in the above verses that the offspring of Joseph will "grow into a multitude in the midst of the earth," as in verse 16. Jacob blesses Ephraim specifically saying, "his seed shall become a multitude of nations." In verse 20, Jacob clarifies again by saying, "In thee shall Israel bless, saying, God make thee as Ephraim and as Manasseh: and he set Ephraim before Manasseh." Through the seed of Joseph, Israel shall bless the world and help it in some manner. Let us keep the following concepts in mind as we continue our analysis of the life story of Joseph, the eleventh son of Jacob.

THE LATTER RAIN

The blessing of Joseph and his life story have significance to us living in these latter times. Joseph evidently plays a critical role in the salvation of the children of Israel who are caught in a state of famine.

> **Genesis 37:1-4**
>
> 1 And Jacob dwelt in the land wherein his father was a stranger, in the land of Canaan.
> 2 These are the generations of Jacob. Joseph, being seventeen years old, was feeding the flock with his brethren; and the lad was with the sons of Bilhah, and with the sons of Zilpah, his father's wives: and Joseph brought unto his father their evil report.
> 3 Now Israel loved Joseph more than all his children, because he was the son of his old age: and he made him a coat of many colours.
> 4 And when his brethren saw that their father loved him more than all his brethren, they hated him, and could not speak peaceably unto him.

Joseph's Dreams

Jacob seemed to favor Joseph over his brethren. Perhaps it was due to the fact that he was the first-born of Rachael, who had been barren for many years prior to his birth. This favoritism led Joseph's elder brethren to dislike him and to become jealous towards him, even before he had his most interesting dreams.

> **Genesis 37:5-8**
>
> 5 And Joseph dreamed a dream, and he told it his brethren: and they hated him yet the more.
> 6 And he said unto them, Hear, I pray you, this dream which I have dreamed:
> 7 For, behold, we were binding sheaves in the field, and, lo, my sheaf arose, and also stood upright; and, behold, your sheaves stood round about, and made obeisance to my sheaf.
> 8 And his brethren said to him, Shalt thou indeed reign over us? or shalt thou indeed have dominion over us? And they hated him yet the more for his dreams, and for his words.

The hatred for Joseph was multiplied several-fold by the dream which he related to his brethren. Joseph was naïve when he told his brothers about the dream, with no intention to anger them. When his elder brethren heard that in Joseph's first dream they would one day bow down to him, they envied him all the more.

> **Genesis 37:9-11**
>
> 9 And he dreamed yet another dream, and told it his brethren, and said, Behold, I have dreamed a dream more; and, behold, the sun and the moon and the eleven stars made obeisance to me.
> 10 And he told it to his father, and to his brethren: and his father rebuked him, and said unto him, What is this dream that thou hast dreamed? Shall I and thy mother and thy brethren indeed come to bow down ourselves to thee to the earth?
> 11 And his brethren envied him; but his father observed the saying.

Joseph's second dream created even more indignation between him and his brethren. It not only includes his brothers, but this time it extended to his father and mother too, as symbolized by the sun and the moon. Jacob quickly picks up on this symbolic message being professed by his son, and rebukes Joseph accordingly: "Shall I and thy mother and thy brethren indeed come to bow down ourselves to thee to the earth?" While the first dream may not have bothered Jacob, this second dream was more personal and not to be taken lightly. Note the difference between the reaction of Joseph's father, Jacob, and that of Joseph's brothers. "And his brethren envied him; but his father observed the saying." While the dream bothered Jacob to some degree, he still held off final judgment until he was able to ponder it thoroughly or take the issue to the Lord for clarification.

Often we may hear things from others that at first seem harmful or offensive. If we are sensitive to the spirit and "observe the saying" with an open mind, praying about it before making a rash judgment, we may be able to make sense of things that would otherwise be misinterpreted on our part. We may avoid the temptation to become angry, as his brothers did. Therefore, I make special note of Jacob's reaction: he tested his son's vision by questioning him forcefully, but then left room in his heart for the Lord to help him better understand the meaning of it all. In contrast, his brothers become angry to the point of violence.

Genesis 37:18-22
18 And when they saw him afar off, even before he came near unto them, they conspired against him to slay him.
19 And they said one to another, Behold, this dreamer cometh.
20 Come now therefore, and let us slay him, and cast him into some pit, and we will say, Some evil beast hath devoured him: and we shall see what will become of his dreams.
21 And Reuben heard it, and he delivered him out of their hands; and said, Let us not kill him.
22 And Reuben said unto them, Shed no blood, but cast him into this pit that is in the wilderness, and lay no hand upon him; that he might rid him out of their hands, to deliver him to his father again.

Reuben was Joseph's ally in the above scene. Of all his elder brethren, Reuben had the greatest reason to envy his younger brother Joseph, especially in light of the birthright issue. Yet, instead of becoming part of the plot to kill Joseph, he intervened and calmed their passion to kill him by recommending an alternative plan—throwing him in a pit instead. Somehow Reuben is drawn away from the situation for a while, and Judah comes up with the plan that will rid them of Joseph without having to kill him.

Genesis 37:23-28
23 And it came to pass, when Joseph was come unto his brethren, that they stript Joseph out of his coat, his coat of many colours that was on him;
24 And they took him, and cast him into a pit: and the pit was empty, there was no water in it.
25 And they sat down to eat bread: and they lifted up their eyes and looked, and, behold, a company of Ishmeelites came from Gilead with their camels bearing spicery and balm and myrrh, going to carry it down to Egypt.
26 And Judah said unto his brethren, What profit is it if we slay our brother, and conceal his blood?
27 Come, and let us sell him to the Ishmeelites, and let not our hand be upon him; for he is our brother and our flesh. And his brethren were content.
28 Then there passed by Midianites merchantmen; and they drew and lifted up Joseph out of the pit, and sold Joseph to the Ishmeelites for twenty pieces of silver: and they brought Joseph into Egypt.

In this way, his brethren felt they had the perfect plan. By selling him to the merchants heading to Egypt, they were rid of their despised younger brother, and yet were relieved of the burden of shedding innocent blood. The Ishmeelites also paid them twenty pieces of silver. The symbolism with this action and the betrayal of Jesus Christ by Judas Iscariot should also be noted. In Matthew 26:15, Judas asks the leaders of the Jews: "What will ye give me, and I will deliver him unto you? And they covenanted with him for thirty pieces of silver." While the amounts are not exactly the same, the symbolism of the two betrayals cannot be overlooked, and becomes even more evident in the following verses.

> **Genesis 37:29-36**
>
> 29 And Reuben returned unto the pit; and, behold, Joseph was not in the pit; and he rent his clothes.
> 30 And he returned unto his brethren, and said, The child is not; and I, whither shall I go?
> 31 And they took Joseph's coat, and killed a kid of the goats, and dipped the coat in the blood;
> 32 And they sent the coat of many colours, and they brought it to their father; and said, This have we found: know now whether it be thy son's coat or no.
> 33 And he knew it, and said, It is my son's coat; an evil beast hath devoured him; Joseph is without doubt rent in pieces.
> 34 And Jacob rent his clothes, and put sackcloth upon his loins, and mourned for his son many days.
> 35 And all his sons and all his daughters rose up to comfort him; but he refused to be comforted; and he said, For I will go down into the grave unto my son mourning. Thus his father wept for him.
> 36 And the Midianites sold him into Egypt unto Potiphar, an officer of Pharaoh's, and captain of the guard.

Why Reuben was away during all this action is not clear. Upon his return, he is horrified about what his brothers have done. Despite his concern and dismay, he too joins in the conspiracy to feign Joseph's death before his father Jacob. Just as Joseph was presumed dead to his father and mother, so too Jesus Christ was presumed dead by the leaders of the Jews and Romans who were responsible for his crucifixion. Likewise, the Gospel of Jesus Christ might seem to be "dead" to many. Without living prophets or priesthood authority to perform the saving ordinances, this symbolic image of Joseph's coat being dipped in blood finds meaning in the life and mission of the Savior as well.

> **Genesis 39:1-6**
>
> 1 And Joseph was brought down to Egypt; and Potiphar, an officer of Pharaoh, captain of the guard, an Egyptian, bought him of the hands of the Ishmeelites, which had brought him down thither.
> 2 And the Lord was with Joseph, and he was a prosperous man; and he was in the house of his master the Egyptian.
> 3 And his master saw that the LORD was with him, and that the LORD made all that he did to prosper in his hand.
> 4 And Joseph found grace in his sight, and he served him: and he made him overseer over his house, and all that he had he put into his hand.
> 5 And it came to pass from the time that he had made him overseer in his house, and over all that he had, that the LORD blessed the Egyptian's house for Joseph's sake; and the blessing of the LORD was upon all that he had in the house, and in the field.
> 6 And he left all that he had in Joseph's hand; and he knew not ought he had, save the bread which he did eat. And Joseph was a goodly person, and well favoured.

Not only does Joseph find favor in Potiphar's house, but the Lord blesses his master for Joseph's sake. Just as the Ark of the Covenant blessed the house of

JOSEPH IN EGYPT

Obed-edom when it was allowed to dwell among him (2 Samuel 6:10-12), Joseph's presence blessed the house of Potiphar, and all that he had. Despite this outpouring of blessings upon the house of Potiphar, this was not to be Joseph's means to success. Potiphar's wife lusted after Joseph, which ultimately led to Joseph's arrest on false charges of attempted adultery, and his being placed in prison.

> **Genesis 39:17-20**
>
> 17 And she spake unto him according to these words, saying, The Hebrew servant, which thou hast brought unto us, came in unto me to mock me:
> 18 And it came to pass, as I lifted up my voice and cried, that he left his garment with me, and fled out.
> 19 And it came to pass, when his master heard the words of his wife, which she spake unto him, saying, After this manner did thy servant to me; that his wrath was kindled.
> 20 And Joseph's master took him, and put him into the prison, a place where the king's prisoners were bound: and he was there in the prison.

The false testimony of Potipher's wife causes Joseph to go from a favored status in the home of Potipher to being a prisoner again. This seems like a harsh situation at first, but we must remember that sometimes the Lord has us pass through trials in order to put us into position for greater blessings in the future. As was the case with Potipher, the keeper of the prison is also now favored by Joseph's presence. It is obvious that Joseph's entry into the prison is not a punishment from God for any act on Joseph's part, but rather a stepping stone for him. In this way the Lord makes "crooked things straight."

> **Isaiah 42:16**
>
> 16 And I will bring the blind by a way that they knew not; I will lead them in paths that they have not known: I will make darkness light before them, and crooked things straight. These things will I do unto them, and not forsake them.

I have often relied on the above verse to comfort me when facing hard challenges or going through tough times. It has helped me to realize that the Lord is able to do things for us only when we allow him to lead us. When he is leading us, we may be required to take paths that are not orthodox, and may seem strange, dangerous, or even terrifying at first. When we look back on the situation later, we see the wisdom in his direction. This same phenomenon was occurring with Joseph, and we can see that even in his suffering, the Lord was with him and blessed him.

> **Genesis 39:21-23**
>
> 21 But the Lord was with Joseph, and shewed him mercy, and gave him favour in the sight of the keeper of the prison.
> 22 And the keeper of the prison committed to Joseph's hand all the prisoners that were in the prison; and whatsoever they did there, he was the doer of it.
> 23 The keeper of the prison looked not to any thing that was under his hand; because the LORD was with him, and that which he did, the LORD made it to prosper.

Not only did the Lord prosper Joseph and his masters, but each of these situations gave Joseph experience in management and administration. He learned to handle the material assets and resources of Potipher while in charge of his affairs. Likewise, while in the prison, Joseph is given command over "all the prisoners that were in the prison." While Joseph was in the lowly place (prison), he was nonetheless gaining experience and knowledge that would later serve him well. While Joseph may have had some idea of his destiny, he still had questions as to how it would play out. Let us keep this idea in mind as we look at the next section of his story: his encounter with the chief butler and the chief baker of Pharaoh, king of Egypt.

> **Genesis 40:1-8**
>
> 1 And it came to pass after these things, that the butler of the king of Egypt and his baker had offended their lord the king of Egypt.
> 2 And Pharaoh was wroth against two of his officers, against the chief of the butlers, and against the chief of the bakers.
> 3 And he put them in ward in the house of the captain of the guard, into the prison, the place where Joseph was bound.
> 4 And the captain of the guard charged Joseph with them, and he served them: and they continued a season in ward.
> 5 And they dreamed a dream both of them, each man his dream in one night, each man according to the interpretation of his dream, the butler and the baker of the king of Egypt, which were bound in the prison.
> 6 And Joseph came in unto them in the morning, and looked upon them, and, behold, they were sad.
> 7 And he asked Pharaoh's officers that were with him in the ward of his lord's house, saying, Wherefore look ye so sadly to day?
> 8 And they said unto him, We have dreamed a dream, and there is no interpreter of it. And Joseph said unto them, Do not interpretations belong to God? tell me them, I pray you.

After serving in the prison for a time, he is now given the assignment to care for the chief butler and the chief baker of not just Potiphar, but of Pharaoh himself, the king of the entire land. Joseph's confidence must have been high that the Lord would indeed help him in some way due to this curious set of circumstances.

> **Genesis 40:9-23**
>
> 9 And the chief butler told his dream to Joseph, and said to him, In my dream, behold, a vine was before me;
> 10 And in the vine were three branches: and it was as though it budded, and her blossoms shot forth; and the clusters thereof brought forth ripe grapes:
> 11 And Pharaoh's cup was in my hand: and I took the grapes, and pressed them into Pharaoh's cup, and I gave the cup into Pharaoh's hand.
> 12 And Joseph said unto him, This is the interpretation of it: The three branches are three days:
> 13 Yet within three days shall Pharaoh lift up thine head, and restore thee unto thy place: and thou shalt deliver Pharaoh's cup into his hand, after the former manner when thou wast his butler.
> 14 But think on me when it shall be well with thee, and shew kindness, I pray thee, unto me, and make mention of me unto Pharaoh, and bring me out of this house:
> 15 For indeed I was stolen away out of the land of the Hebrews: and here also have I done nothing that they should put me into the dungeon.
> 16 When the chief baker saw that the interpretation was good, he said unto Joseph, I also was in my dream, and, behold, I had three white baskets on my head:
> 17 And in the uppermost basket there was of all manner of bakemeats for Pharaoh; and the birds did eat them out of the basket upon my head.
> 18 And Joseph answered and said, This is the interpretation thereof: The three baskets are three days:
> 19 Yet within three days shall Pharaoh lift up thy head from off thee, and shall hang thee on a tree; and the birds shall eat thy flesh from off thee.

JOSEPH IN EGYPT

20 And it came to pass the third day, which was Pharaoh's birthday, that he made a feast unto all his servants: and he lifted up the head of the chief butler and of the chief baker among his servants.
21 And he restored the chief butler unto his butlership again; and he gave the cup into Pharaoh's hand:
22 But he hanged the chief baker: as Joseph had interpreted to them.
23 Yet did not the chief butler remember Joseph, but forgat him.

As the weeks turned to months and he remained in the prison, Joseph must have been disappointed that Pharaoh's butler forgot him. The timing of the Lord is often different than what we might prefer. We know that the butler eventually did remember Joseph. Still, Joseph was forced to wait two years from the time he interpreted the dreams of the butler and the baker before he was finally released from prison.

Genesis 41:1-16

1 And it came to pass at the end of two full years, that Pharaoh dreamed: and, behold, he stood by the river.
2 And, behold, there came up out of the river seven well favoured kine and fatfleshed; and they fed in a meadow.
3 And, behold, seven other kine came up after them out of the river, ill favoured and leanfleshed; and stood by the other kine upon the brink of the river.
4 And the ill favoured and leanfleshed kine did eat up the seven well favoured and fat kine. So Pharaoh awoke.
5 And he slept and dreamed the second time: and, behold, seven ears of corn came up upon one stalk, rank and good.
6 And, behold, seven thin ears and blasted with the east wind sprung up after them.
7 And the seven thin ears devoured the seven rank and full ears. And Pharaoh awoke, and, behold, it was a dream.
8 And it came to pass in the morning that his spirit was troubled; and he sent and called for all the magicians of Egypt, and all the wise men thereof: and Pharaoh told them his dream; but there was none that could interpret them unto Pharaoh.
9 Then spake the chief butler unto Pharaoh, saying, I do remember my faults this day:
10 Pharaoh was wroth with his servants, and put me in ward in the captain of the guard's house, both me and the chief baker:
11 And we dreamed a dream in one night, I and he; we dreamed each man according to the interpretation of his dream.
12 And there was there with us a young man, an Hebrew, servant to the captain of the guard; and we told him, and he interpreted to us our dreams; to each man according to his dream he did interpret.
13 And it came to pass, as he interpreted to us, so it was; me he restored unto mine office, and him he hanged.
14 Then Pharaoh sent and called Joseph, and they brought him hastily out of the dungeon: and he shaved himself, and changed his raiment, and came in unto Pharaoh.
15 And Pharaoh said unto Joseph, I have dreamed a dream, and there is none that can interpret it: and I have heard say of thee, that thou canst understand a dream to interpret it.
16 And Joseph answered Pharaoh, saying, It is not in me: God shall give Pharaoh an answer of peace.

Note Joseph's humility in this situation. He does not take credit for understanding and interpreting Pharaoh's dream. Instead, he gives credit to God for his gift of interpretation just as he did when he interpreted the dream of the butler and the baker.

THE LATTER RAIN

Genesis 41:17-32

17 And Pharaoh said unto Joseph, In my dream, behold, I stood upon the bank of the river:
18 And, behold, there came up out of the river seven kine, fatfleshed and well favoured; and they fed in a meadow:
19 And, behold, seven other kine came up after them, poor and very ill favoured and leanfleshed, such as I never saw in all the land of Egypt for badness:
20 And the lean and the ill favoured kine did eat up the first seven fat kine:
21 And when they had eaten them up, it could not be known that they had eaten them; but they were still ill favoured, as at the beginning. So I awoke.
22 And I saw in my dream, and, behold, seven ears came up in one stalk, full and good:
23 And, behold, seven ears, withered, thin, and blasted with the east wind, sprung up after them:
24 And the thin ears devoured the seven good ears: and I told this unto the magicians; but there was none that could declare it to me.
25 And Joseph said unto Pharaoh, The dream of Pharaoh is one: God hath shewed Pharaoh what he is about to do.
26 The seven good kine are seven years; and the seven good ears are seven years: the dream is one.
27 And the seven thin and ill favoured kine that came up after them are seven years; and the seven empty ears blasted with the east wind shall be seven years of famine.
28 This is the thing which I have spoken unto Pharaoh: What God is about to do he sheweth unto Pharaoh.
29 Behold, there come seven years of great plenty throughout all the land of Egypt:
30 And there shall arise after them seven years of famine; and all the plenty shall be forgotten in the land of Egypt; and the famine shall consume the land;
31 And the plenty shall not be known in the land by reason of that famine following; for it shall be very grievous.
32 And for that the dream was doubled unto Pharaoh twice; it is because the thing is established by God, and God will shortly bring it to pass.

Recall here that Joseph's earlier dreams were also doubled, and should also be attributed to God. As in the case of Pharaoh's dream, Joseph's dream was repeated twice with a slight variation in the presentation. We will see that both Joseph's dream and Pharaoh's dream have a dual prophecy attached to them. Both are types of things to occur in the Lord's overall plan for the children of Israel. With this in mind, let us now continue to examine Joseph's ultimate rise to honor and stature after being in bondage for 13 years of his life.

Genesis 41:33-45

33 Now therefore let Pharaoh look out a man discreet and wise, and set him over the land of Egypt.
34 Let Pharaoh do this, and let him appoint officers over the land, and take up the fifth part of the land of Egypt in the seven plenteous years.
35 And let them gather all the food of those good years that come, and lay up corn under the hand of Pharaoh, and let them keep food in the cities.
36 And that food shall be for store to the land against the seven years of famine, which shall be in the land of Egypt; that the land perish not through the famine.
37 And the thing was good in the eyes of Pharaoh, and in the eyes of all his servants.
38 And Pharaoh said unto his servants, Can we find such a one as this is, a man in whom the Spirit of God is?
39 And Pharaoh said unto Joseph, Forasmuch as God hath shewed thee all this, there is none so discreet and wise as thou art:

40 Thou shalt be over my house, and according unto thy word shall all my people be ruled: only in the throne will I be greater than thou.
41 And Pharaoh said unto Joseph, See, I have set thee over all the land of Egypt.
42 And Pharaoh took off his ring from his hand, and put it upon Joseph's hand, and arrayed him in vestures of fine linen, and put a gold chain about his neck;
43 And he made him to ride in the second chariot which he had; and they cried before him, Bow the knee: and he made him ruler over all the land of Egypt.
44 And Pharaoh said unto Joseph, I am Pharaoh, and without thee shall no man lift up his hand or foot in all the land of Egypt.
45 And Pharaoh called Joseph's name Zaphnath-paaneah; and he gave him to wife Asenath the daughter of Potipherah priest of On. And Joseph went out over all the land of Egypt.

Joseph's humility is demonstrated again at this time. Instead of asking Pharaoh to pick him to execute the plan, he merely suggests that Pharaoh seek out a wise person to head up the program. How many of us could be so patient at a time like that? Often the best leaders in life are not those that usurp authority or aspire to it, but are those that have greatness thrust upon them out of necessity, or out of a recognition of their absolute suitability for leading people through the challenges ahead. This was definitely the case in Pharaoh's choice of Joseph for this important job. From a worldly perspective, he was the last person that should have been chosen. Not only was he a prisoner, but he was also a Hebrew, who were despised by the Egyptians. For Pharaoh to overlook both of these detracting attributes, and select Joseph as his chief administrator in all his affairs, this Pharaoh must have had a strong feeling from the Lord that this was indeed the man for the job.

Genesis 41:46-57
46 And Joseph was thirty years old when he stood before Pharaoh king of Egypt. And Joseph went out from the presence of Pharaoh, and went throughout all the land of Egypt.
47 And in the seven plenteous years the earth brought forth by handfuls.
48 And he gathered up all the food of the seven years, which were in the land of Egypt, and laid up the food in the cities: the food of the field, which was round about every city, laid he up in the same.
49 And Joseph gathered corn as the sand of the sea, very much, until he left numbering; for it was without number.
50 And unto Joseph were born two sons before the years of famine came, which Asenath the daughter of Potipherah priest of On bare unto him.
51 And Joseph called the name of the firstborn Manasseh: For God, said he, hath made me forget all my toil, and all my father's house.
52 And the name of the second called he Ephraim: For God hath caused me to be fruitful in the land of my affliction.
53 And the seven years of plenteousness, that was in the land of Egypt, were ended.
54 And the seven years of dearth began to come, according as Joseph had said: and the dearth was in all lands; but in all the land of Egypt there was bread.
55 And when all the land of Egypt was famished, the people cried to Pharaoh for bread: and Pharaoh said unto all the Egyptians, Go unto Joseph; what he saith to you, do.
56 And the famine was over all the face of the earth: And Joseph opened all the storehouses, and sold unto the Egyptians; and the famine waxed sore in the land of Egypt.
57 And all countries came into Egypt to Joseph for to buy corn; because that the famine was so sore in all lands.

Joseph's time in prison was a divine event that put him in a position to meet the officers of the king that had been placed in ward and under Joseph's supervision. It is not wise to judge an event in one's life as being a good thing or a bad thing until we are able to look back and see the hand of the Lord in our lives. A seemingly negative event might make it possible for us to realize our true potential in other ways. Joseph's life story teaches us that even the most negative or challenging situations can lead us to our true divine destiny. Let us now examine how Joseph's dreams are fulfilled, including how his brethren come to bow down to him.

> **Genesis 42:1-6**
>
> 1 Now when Jacob saw that there was corn in Egypt, Jacob said unto his sons, Why do ye look one upon another?
> 2 And he said, Behold, I have heard that there is corn in Egypt: get you down thither, and buy for us from thence; that we may live, and not die.
> 3 And Joseph's ten brethren went down to buy acorn in Egypt.
> 4 But Benjamin, Joseph's brother, Jacob sent not with his brethren; for he said, Lest peradventure mischief befall him.
> 5 And the sons of Israel came to buy corn among those that came: for the famine was in the land of Canaan.
> 6 And Joseph was the governor over the land, and he it was that sold to all the people of the land: and Joseph's brethren came, and bowed down themselves before him with their faces to the earth.

In verse six above, we see the first fulfillment of Joseph's dreams. His brethren "bowed down themselves before him with their faces to the earth." Joseph's intentions were not to seek revenge against his brethren, but rather to help them come to terms with the wicked act they had performed in the past, and to ultimately be relieved of the guilt therefrom.

> **Genesis 42:7-20**
>
> 7 And Joseph saw his brethren, and he knew them, but made himself strange unto them, and spake roughly unto them; and he said unto them, Whence come ye? And they said, From the land of Canaan to buy food.
> 8 And Joseph knew his brethren, but they knew not him.
> 9 And Joseph remembered the dreams which he dreamed of them, and said unto them, Ye are spies; to see the nakedness of the land ye are come.
> 10 And they said unto him, Nay, my lord, but to buy food are thy servants come.
> 11 We are all one man's sons; we are true men, thy servants are no spies.
> 12 And he said unto them, Nay, but to see the nakedness of the land ye are come.
> 13 And they said, Thy servants are twelve brethren, the sons of one man in the land of Canaan; and, behold, the youngest is this day with our father, and one is not.
> 14 And Joseph said unto them, That is it that I spake unto you, saying, Ye are spies:
> 15 Hereby ye shall be proved: By the life of Pharaoh ye shall not go forth hence, except your youngest brother come hither.
> 16 Send one of you, and let him fetch your brother, and ye shall be kept in prison, that your words may be proved, whether there be any truth in you: or else by the life of Pharaoh surely ye are spies.
> 17 And he put them all together into ward three days.
> 18 And Joseph said unto them the third day, This do, and live; for I fear God:
> 19 If ye be true men, let one of your brethren be bound in the house of your prison: go ye, carry corn for the famine of your houses:
> 20 But bring your youngest brother unto me; so shall your words be verified, and ye shall not die. And they did so.

During those three days of hell, surely Joseph's brethren suffered greatly in spirit. Not only did they fear for their own safety, but they also knew that to even hope for their release, they must also jeopardize the life of their youngest brother Benjamin. And, in so doing, they would without doubt bring their father Jacob down into the depths of worry and sorrow. According to Joseph's first words, only one of the ten brothers would be allowed to return with food. Thus, the amount of food that could be carried would be minimal. All these things must have weighed heavily on their minds as they considered their terrible circumstance and the challenge that it presented them. As we will see shortly, while they did not recognize Joseph as their long-lost brother, the situation did harrow up their minds with guilt for having been the agents of his demise as he was sold into slavery. They viewed these events as a form of punishment from God for their wicked and selfish actions of the past. Upon their release, they learned that only one brother would be required to remain behind in ward. Thus, more food could be carried back to the land of Canaan for Jacob and his people. The key stipulation remained. Benjamin would have to be brought to Egypt if they were to receive further provisions from Joseph and to prove that they were not spies, thus securing the release of their brother remaining in prison.

Genesis 42:21-28

21 And they said one to another, We are verily guilty concerning our brother, in that we saw the anguish of his soul, when he besought us, and we would not hear; therefore is this distress come upon us.
22 And Reuben answered them, saying, Spake I not unto you, saying, Do not sin against the child; and ye would not hear? therefore, behold, also his blood is required.
23 And they knew not that Joseph understood them; for he spake unto them by an interpreter.
24 And he turned himself about from them, and wept; and returned to them again, and communed with them, and took from them Simeon, and bound him before their eyes.
25 Then Joseph commanded to fill their sacks with corn, and to restore every man's money into his sack, and to give them provision for the way: and thus did he unto them.
26 And they laded their asses with the corn, and departed thence.
27 And as one of them opened his sack to give his ass provender in the inn, he espied his money; for, behold, it was in his sack's mouth.
28 And he said unto his brethren, My money is restored; and, lo, it is even in my sack: and their heart failed them, and they were afraid, saying one to another, What is this that God hath done unto us?

Joseph's action of returning their money and placing it in each of their sacks has the effect of making them feel that they are indeed being punished by God for their wicked sin against Joseph in the past. This act had been weighing heavily on their minds for years, and now they feel certain that the Lord is finally bringing forth his wrath against them. They say one to another, "What is this that God hath done unto us?" Indeed, it was the Lord that was inspiring Joseph as to how to deal with his brethren, all the while working repentance among them as they confess among themselves how their action was wrong. Only Reuben, the eldest brother, could really say, "Spake I not unto you, saying, Do not sin against the child; and ye would not hear? therefore, behold, also his blood is required." Reuben was nonetheless guilty of maintaining the conspiracy of his brethren and of not telling his father, Jacob, the truth about the matter. Had the truth been made known in a timely manner, perhaps Jacob and his sons could have intercepted the merchants on the road to Egypt, and either paid for Joseph's release or taken him by force. Reuben's inaction sealed Joseph's fate, and led to his period of suffering and bondage in Egypt. His brethren not only suffered guilt and anguish themselves, but now had to relate the affair to their elderly father and weigh him down with it as well.

Genesis 42:29-38

29 And they came unto Jacob their father unto the land of Canaan, and told him all that befell unto them; saying,
30 The man, who is the lord of the land, spake roughly to us, and took us for spies of the country.
31 And we said unto him, We are true men; we are no spies:
32 We be twelve brethren, sons of our father; one is not, and the youngest is this day with our father in the land of Canaan.
33 And the man, the lord of the country, said unto us, Hereby shall I know that ye are true men; leave one of your brethren here with me, and take food for the famine of your households, and be gone:
34 And bring your youngest brother unto me: then shall I know that ye are no spies, but that ye are true men: so will I deliver you your brother, and ye shall traffick in the land.
35 And it came to pass as they emptied their sacks, that, behold, every man's bundle of money was in his sack: and when both they and their father saw the bundles of money, they were afraid.
36 And Jacob their father said unto them, Me have ye bereaved of my children: Joseph is not, and Simeon is not, and ye will take Benjamin away: all these things are against me.
37 And Reuben spake unto his father, saying, Slay my two sons, if I bring him not to thee: deliver him into my hand, and I will bring him to thee again.
38 And he said, My son shall not go down with you; for his brother is dead, and he is left alone: if mischief befall him by the way in the which ye go, then shall ye bring down my gray hairs with sorrow to the grave.

To avoid the risk of harm to Benjamin, Jacob refused to let Reuben and his brethren take the young man with them back to Egypt. Whatever fate had come to Simeon, he must have felt it was too great a risk for his living and breathing sons to return to Egypt at that time. In his mind, he had already lost Joseph for sure. Losing Benjamin as well would mean the end of his seed through his beloved wife Rachael. As the famine worsened and their supplies again began to dwindle, Jacob finally saw that unless his sons returned to Egypt for food, his son Benjamin and his household would ultimately perish from the dearth. Even with this threat upon him, he was still reluctant to send Benjamin along.

Genesis 43:1-14

1 And the famine was sore in the land.
2 And it came to pass, when they had eaten up the corn which they had brought out of Egypt, their father said unto them, Go again, buy us a little food.
3 And Judah spake unto him, saying, The man did solemnly protest unto us, saying, Ye shall not see my face, except your brother be with you.
4 If thou wilt send our brother with us, we will go down and buy thee food:
5 But if thou wilt not send him, we will not go down: for the man said unto us, Ye shall not see my face, except your brother be with you.

JOSEPH IN EGYPT

> 6 And Israel said, Wherefore dealt ye so ill with me, as to tell the man whether ye had yet a brother?
> 7 And they said, The man asked us straitly of our state, and of our kindred, saying, Is your father yet alive? have ye another brother? and we told him according to the tenor of these words: could we certainly know that he would say, Bring your brother down?
> 8 And Judah said unto Israel his father, Send the lad with me, and we will arise and go; that we may live, and not die, both we, and thou, and also our little ones.
> 9 I will be surety for him; of my hand shalt thou require him: if I bring him not unto thee, and set him before thee, then let me bear the blame for ever:
> 10 For except we had lingered, surely now we had returned this second time.
> 11 And their father Israel said unto them, If it must be so now, do this; take of the best fruits of the land in your vessels, and carry down the man a present, a little balm, and a little honey, spices, and myrrh, nuts, and almonds:
> 12 And take double money in your hand; and the money that was brought again in the mouth of your sacks, carry it again in your hand; peradventure it was an oversight:
> 13 Take also your brother, and arise, go again unto the man:
> 14 And God Almighty give you mercy before the man, that he may send away your other brother, and Benjamin. If I be bereaved of my children, I am bereaved.

It is significant to note the air of distrust that pervades the family as they decide to risk a return to Egypt. They feared the anger of the man who has their brother Simeon in ward. While Jacob had been abundantly blessed of the Lord throughout his entire life, he now faced the chance of losing his sons and his posterity—either to the famine or to the whims of this unknown ruler in Egypt.

> **Genesis 43:15-26**
> 15 And the men took that present, and they took double money in their hand, and Benjamin; and rose up, and went down to Egypt, and stood before Joseph.
> 16 And when Joseph saw Benjamin with them, he said to the ruler of his house, Bring these men home, and slay, and make ready; for these men shall dine with me at noon.
> 17 And the man did as Joseph bade; and the man brought the men into Joseph's house.
> 18 And the men were afraid, because they were brought into Joseph's house; and they said, Because of the money that was returned in our sacks at the first time are we brought in; that he may seek occasion against us, and fall upon us, and take us for bondmen, and our asses.
> 19 And they came near to the steward of Joseph's house, and they communed with him at the door of the house,
> 20 And said, O sir, we came indeed down at the first time to buy food:
> 21 And it came to pass, when we came to the inn, that we opened our sacks, and, behold, every man's money was in the mouth of his sack, our money in full weight: and we have brought it again in our hand.
> 22 And other money have we brought down in our hands to buy food: we cannot tell who put our money in our sacks.
> 23 And he said, Peace be to you, fear not: your God, and the God of your father, hath given you treasure in your sacks: I had your money. And he brought Simeon out unto them.
> 24 And the man brought the men into Joseph's house, and gave them water, and they washed their feet; and he gave their asses provender.
> 25 And they made ready the present against Joseph came at noon: for they heard that they should eat bread there.
> 26 And when Joseph came home, they brought him the present which was in their hand into the house, and bowed themselves to him to the earth.

We see in verse 26 the fulfillment of Joseph's dream, albeit some twenty years after Joseph had related his dream to his brethren and was hated for it. We should all learn from this situation. In life, we are often presented with information that is hard to understand unless we ask God for clarification. In fact, some things might even make us angry when we first hear them; but, unless we ask God for assistance in understanding the meaning thereof, we risk missing an opportunity to be taught of the Lord. The thing that had made Joseph's brothers so angry, and had seemed so preposterous, was now being fulfilled right before their eyes.

> Genesis 43:27-34
>
> 27 And he asked them of their welfare, and said, Is your father well, the old man of whom ye spake? Is he yet alive?
> 28 And they answered, Thy servant our father is in good health, he is yet alive. And they bowed down their heads, and made obeisance.
> 29 And he lifted up his eyes, and saw his brother Benjamin, his mother's son, and said, Is this your younger brother, of whom ye spake unto me? And he said, God be gracious unto thee, my son.
> 30 And Joseph made haste; for his bowels did yearn upon his brother: and he sought where to weep; and he entered into his chamber, and wept there.
> 31 And he washed his face, and went out, and refrained himself, and said, Set on bread.
> 32 And they set on for him by himself, and for them by themselves, and for the Egyptians, which did eat with him, by themselves: because the Egyptians might not eat bread with the Hebrews; for that is an abomination unto the Egyptians.
> 33 And they sat before him, the firstborn according to his birthright, and the youngest according to his youth: and the men marvelled one at another.
> 34 And he took and sent messes unto them from before him: but Benjamin's mess was five times so much as any of theirs. And they drank, and were merry with him.

Now you would think that at this point Joseph would reveal himself unto his brethren, but not so.

> Genesis 44:1-17
>
> 1 And he commanded the steward of his house, saying, Fill the men's sacks with food, as much as they can carry, and put every man's money in his sack's mouth.
> 2 And put my cup, the silver cup, in the sack's mouth of the youngest, and his corn money. And he did according to the word that Joseph had spoken.
> 3 As soon as the morning was light, the men were sent away, they and their asses.
> 4 And when they were gone out of the city, and not yet far off, Joseph said unto his steward, Up, follow after the men; and when thou dost overtake them, say unto them, Wherefore have ye rewarded evil for good?
> 5 Is not this it in which my lord drinketh, and whereby indeed he divineth? ye have done evil in so doing.
> 6 And he overtook them, and he spake unto them these same words.
> 7 And they said unto him, Wherefore saith my lord these words? God forbid that thy servants should do according to this thing:
> 8 Behold, the money, which we found in our sacks' mouths, we brought again unto thee out of the land of Canaan: how then should we steal out of thy lord's house silver or gold?
> 9 With whomsoever of thy servants it be found, both let him die, and we also will be my lord's bondmen.
> 10 And he said, Now also let it be according unto your words: he with whom it is found shall be my servant; and ye shall be blameless.
> 11 Then they speedily took down every man his sack to the ground, and opened every man his sack.
> 12 And he searched, and began at the eldest, and left at the youngest: and the cup was found in Benjamin's sack.

13 Then they rent their clothes, and laded every man his ass, and returned to the city.
14 And Judah and his brethren came to Joseph's house; for he was yet there: and they fell before him on the ground.
15 And Joseph said unto them, What deed is this that ye have done? wot ye not that such a man as I can certainly divine?
16 And Judah said, What shall we say unto my lord? what shall we speak? or how shall we clear ourselves? God hath found out the iniquity of thy servants: behold, we are my lord's servants, both we, and he also with whom the cup is found.
17 And he said, God forbid that I should do so: but the man in whose hand the cup is found, he shall be my servant; and as for you, get you up in peace unto your father.

One can only imagine the pain and anguish of soul that must have been in the hearts of Joseph's brothers. This pain and guilt was greatest perhaps in the heart of Judah, especially after he had promised his father that Benjamin would return home safely.

Genesis 44:18-34

18 Then Judah came near unto him, and said, Oh my lord, let thy servant, I pray thee, speak a word in my lord's ears, and let not thine anger burn against thy servant: for thou art even as Pharaoh.
19 My lord asked his servants, saying, Have ye a father, or a brother?
20 And we said unto my lord, We have a father, an old man, and a child of his old age, a little one; and his brother is dead, and he alone is left of his mother, and his father loveth him.
21 And thou saidst unto thy servants, Bring him down unto me, that I may set mine eyes upon him.
22 And we said unto my lord, The lad cannot leave his father: for if he should leave his father, his father would die.
23 And thou saidst unto thy servants, Except your youngest brother come down with you, ye shall see my face no more.
24 And it came to pass when we came up unto thy servant my father, we told him the words of my lord.
25 And our father said, Go again, and buy us a little food.
26 And we said, We cannot go down: if our youngest brother be with us, then will we go down: for we may not see the man's face, except our youngest brother be with us.
27 And thy servant my father said unto us, Ye know that my wife bare me two sons:
28 And the one went out from me, and I said, Surely he is torn in pieces; and I saw him not since:
29 And if ye take this also from me, and mischief befall him, ye shall bring down my gray hairs with sorrow to the grave.
30 Now therefore when I come to thy servant my father, and the lad be not with us; seeing that his life is bound up in the lad's life;
31 It shall come to pass, when he seeth that the lad is not with us, that he will die: and thy servants shall bring down the gray hairs of thy servant our father with sorrow to the grave.
32 For thy servant became surety for the lad unto my father, saying, If I bring him not unto thee, then I shall bear the blame to my father for ever.
33 Now therefore, I pray thee, let thy servant abide instead of the lad a bondman to my lord; and let the lad go up with his brethren.
34 For how shall I go up to my father, and the lad be not with me? lest peradventure I see the evil that shall come on my father.

The tension at this point of the story is so great that Joseph can no longer restrain and he weeps openly before them. Before we continue, please note the fact that it is Judah who is humbling himself before Joseph. It is Judah who is offering to step in for Joseph's brother Benjamin, that his father Jacob might be spared the grief of losing the only remaining son of his wife Rachael. This is a curious fact considering that the Tribes of Judah and Benjamin ultimately unite to form the Southern Kingdom of Israel after the reign of King Solomon, as the other ten tribes separate themselves to the north. While they are actually a mix of Judah and Benjamin, they become known collectively as Judah, or the Jews, with Jerusalem as their capital city. It is clear at this point that both Judah and his brethren are sufficiently humbled under the weight of their guilt, and due to the peculiar situation they face; Joseph can no longer hold back his emotions. He reveals to them his true identity.

Genesis 45:1-9, 25-28

1 Then Joseph could not refrain himself before all them that stood by him; and he cried, Cause every man to go out from me. And there stood no man with him, while Joseph made himself known unto his brethren.
2 And he wept aloud: and the Egyptians and the house of Pharaoh heard.
3 And Joseph said unto his brethren, I am Joseph; doth my father yet live? And his brethren could not answer him; for they were troubled at his presence.
4 And Joseph said unto his brethren, Come near to me, I pray you. And they came near. And he said, I am Joseph your brother, whom ye sold into Egypt.
5 Now therefore be not grieved, nor angry with yourselves, that ye sold me hither: for God did send me before you to preserve life.
6 For these two years hath the famine been in the land: and yet there are five years, in the which there shall neither be earing nor harvest.
7 And God sent me before you to preserve you a posterity in the earth, and to save your lives by a great deliverance.
8 So now it was not you that sent me hither, but God: and he hath made me a father to Pharaoh, and lord of all his house, and a ruler throughout all the land of Egypt.
9 Haste ye, and go up to my father, and say unto him, Thus saith thy son Joseph, God hath made me lord of all Egypt: come down unto me, tarry not:
25 And they went up out of Egypt, and came into the land of Canaan unto Jacob their father,
26 And told him, saying, Joseph is yet alive, and he is governor over all the land of Egypt. And Jacob's heart fainted, for he believed them not.
27 And they told him all the words of Joseph, which he had said unto them: and when he saw the wagons which Joseph had sent to carry him, the spirit of Jacob their father revived:
28 And Israel said, It is enough; Joseph my son is yet alive: I will go and see him before I die.

One can only imagine the joy that Jacob must have felt to learn that not only his son Benjamin was safe, but that his son Joseph was also alive. He was alive, and he was now governor over all of Egypt. This is truly a great story. It is one of the great stories of the Bible. It stands as one of the choice stories that touches the hearts of men and women everywhere. The story of Joseph's sojourn in Egypt, with the years of plenty followed by the years of famine, is also a symbolic representation of God's overall plan of salvation for the children of the earth. With the Isaiah framework already firmly established in our minds, this story should already begin to suggest a broader, more far-reaching meaning.

Jacob, the great patriarch of the Tribes of Israel, could feel the grandeur of the moment, yet he still does one thing that is more important than anything else that we can do in life. He inquired of the Lord! The Lord tells him not to fear, but that the Lord will go down with Jacob into Egypt. He also promises that after his seed becomes a great nation, the Lord will bring them back up out of Egypt again. These promises are significant and should be noted for their symbolism and importance with respect to both the time they were given and to the events that will occur in these, the latter days.

> **Genesis 46:1-4**
> 1 And Israel took his journey with all that he had, and came to Beer-sheba, and offered sacrifices unto the God of his father Isaac.
> 2 And God spake unto Israel in the visions of the night, and said, Jacob, Jacob. And he said, Here am I.
> 3 And he said, I am God, the God of thy father: fear not to go down into Egypt; for I will there make of thee a great nation:
> 4 I will go down with thee into Egypt; and I will also surely bring thee up again: and Joseph shall put his hand upon thine eyes.

We learn that Jacob dwelt in Egypt for a time and then died. He was then carried back to the land of Canaan to be buried. But the children of Israel remained in the land of Egypt, having survived the famine of seven years. This they did due to the blessing of Joseph, "who was separated from his brethren." Finally Joseph too dies and is embalmed.

> **Genesis 50:24-26**
> 24 And Joseph said unto his brethren, I die: and God will surely visit you, and bring you out of this land unto the land which he sware to Abraham, to Isaac, and to Jacob.
> 25 And Joseph took an oath of the children of Israel, saying, God will surely visit you, and ye shall carry up my bones from hence.
> 26 So Joseph died, being an hundred and ten years old: and they embalmed him, and he was put in a coffin in Egypt.

Using Isaiah to Understand the Story of Joseph

I will now show how this great story of the patriarch Joseph fits into the Former Rain/Latter Rain paradigm. If we recall from our discussion of Isaiah, God is able in his infinite wisdom to use actual historical events to foretell other events that will occur in the future. For example, it is true that, historically, Assyria conquered the Northern Ten Tribes of Israel in approximately 721 BC and carried them away captive. Yet, we showed that this historical event was also a symbolic prophesy of things to occur later in the overall narrative of mankind. In Isaiah's description of Assyria's conquest of Zion, he showed that the king of Assyria was given dominion over the entire world, not just Northern Israel. In the Book of Isaiah, the king of Assyria was a type of something or someone else, namely Satan, or the devil.

The story of Joseph being sold into Egypt is filled with the symbols and types we identified during our analysis of the Book of Isaiah. We have a period of prosperity followed by a long period of famine. Furthermore, we have a poignant interaction between Judah and Joseph, the two prominent tribes or families of Israel. We have the nation of Egypt playing a significant role in the story, a role of saving Israel and preparing the way for their escape from the famine. Finally, recall that just before Jacob blesses his sons prior to his death, he says to them in Genesis 49:1: "Gather yourselves together, that I may tell you that which shall befall you in the last days." He is telling us that the blessings he pronounced on his sons are actually an indication of how their descendants will fair in the latter days. The events that occurred in the life of Joseph, the eleventh son of Jacob and firstborn of Rachael, are indeed symbolic teachings directly from the Lord to us in our time. To conclude this section, let me summarize the meaning of these teachings and their application to modern times.

Former Rain, Famine, Latter Rain

Early on in this book, I established the concept that in the scriptures the mention of water, rain, or dew was often symbolic of revelation, prophets, and priesthood power being bestowed upon the children of men. This imagery applies to revelations received through prophets for Zion as a whole, and to personal revelation received on an individual level. We saw that the types famine, dearth, desolation, desert, wilderness and so forth, are symbolic of periods of time when revelation, prophets, and priesthood power are not found on the earth. I used the scripture found in Amos 8:11 to make this symbolic link, as it defines the association between famine and apostasy. "Behold, the days come, saith the Lord GOD, that I will send a famine in the land, not a famine of bread, nor a thirst for water, but of hearing the words of the LORD." Applying these concepts to our current discussion, certain aspects of the story of Joseph become fairly obvious.

Pharaoh's dream (the seven healthy kine and the seven healthy ears of corn being eaten up by the seven skinny kine and the seven ill-favored ears of corn, respectively) was interpreted by Joseph to be a prediction of what would shortly occur in Egypt and the surrounding countries—the known world. Seven years of prosperity would be followed by seven years of famine, and indeed that is what occurred. We also learned from the story that due to the wisdom of Joseph, he being inspired of God to store away a portion of the harvest during the years of prosperity, Joseph was able to create a great work of salvation for not only Egypt, but also for his brethren, the tribes of Israel. This story fits into the "Former Rain, Famine, Latter Rain" framework that we have seen repeated throughout the scriptures.

Hosea 6:3

3 Then shall we know, if we follow on to know the LORD: his going forth is prepared as the morning; and he shall come unto us as the rain, as the latter and former rain unto the earth.

The famine period during Joseph's sojourn in Egypt is another scriptural type of the Great Spiritual Famine that we have shown to be predicted by all the Old Testament prophets we have analyzed thus far. The period of prosperity would be the period of time from Adam down to the time shortly after the Lord's earthly ministry, his death and resurrection. While the apostles that remained on the earth after the Lord's departure did in fact work to build up the Kingdom of God on the earth, we will show in our subsequent analysis of the New Testament that, ultimately, Satan was given complete dominion over the entire earth. The Lord's Church, or Zion, was no longer found on the earth. If we accept this view of things, then we should look forward to a period in the latter days when something will occur to restore Zion again to the earth. This restoration will occur in large part due to something that is done by Joseph, "who was separated from his brethren."

Recalling what was written in Joseph's blessing from Jacob in Genesis 49:22, we see that "Joseph is a fruitful bough, even a fruitful bough by a well; who's branches run over the wall." Whatever it is that the descendants of Joseph have done for us living in these latter times, it was done without the knowledge of the world. It was hidden in the wisdom of God from the historical records of civilization. The Ten Lost Tribes of Israel (Ephraim to the north) still had prophets among them, and they were "planted by a well" and received revelation from God to do things that would help us in our day. The branches of Joseph that "run over the wall" would mean that the prophets and people of Joseph were scattered to other parts of the world, outside of the known world at the time. This could mean the Far East or the Western Hemisphere. To the world, however, it would appear that Joseph is dead.

Joseph Thought to Be Dead

In the story of Joseph that we have just read, Jacob was lead to believe that his son Joseph was dead. After Joseph was sold into slavery, his brothers took his coat of many colors and dipped it into the blood of a goat, and showed it to Jacob who exclaimed: "It is my son's coat; an evil beast hath devoured him; Joseph is without doubt rent in pieces" (Genesis 37:33). The brothers of Joseph allowed their father to believe that Joseph was dead. While the brothers themselves knew that he was not actually killed, they nonetheless felt that they were rid of him and his dreams. Over time, even they must have forgotten about him and considered him dead.

This concept has application in today's world as well. While the Northern Ten Tribes, which are synonymous with Joseph or Ephraim his son, were carried away captive by Assyria and lost to the view of the nations, we cannot assume that they are dead. In fact, we are told repeatedly throughout the scriptures that in the latter days they will be gathered in from their dispersion. Nor can we be certain that the Lord is not able to work a work through Joseph's seed that will somehow be significant in restoring his brethren to the truth during the last days (the period of the Latter Rain). Just as occurred in the story of Joseph who was sold into Egypt, so too will the Tribe of Joseph work a work in the latter days that will prove to be a form of salvation for all of Israel. Something done by Joseph's posterity will be done in secret, without the knowledge of the world as a whole. Their works and deeds will be stored up, and will ultimately come to light in the latter times, reuniting Israel into one nation, namely Zion. It will save Joseph's brethren, the tribes of Israel, from the Great Spiritual Famine, ushering in the period of the Latter Rain.

THE LATTER RAIN

Joseph as a Symbol of Jesus Christ

Many similarities exist between Joseph and Jesus Christ. Both were betrayed and sold into bondage for a few pieces of silver. Both were betrayed by those who should have been their friends and brethren. We have already established that Joseph was in fact the birthright son, and the coat of many colors was in a way symbolic of his royal station. When he is betrayed and sold into slavery by his brethren, they took his coat of many colors and dipped it into the blood of a goat. This event is symbolic of the blood of Christ being spilt for the transgressions of the world. Just as the Lord Jesus Christ had to go through suffering and shame to save the world from its sins and transgressions, so too Joseph played a similar role. He too was caused to pass through suffering and hardship in order to work a work of salvation for Israel in his time.

Once we make the link between the events of Joseph's life with the mission of Jesus Christ, we then see other types that must be considered by genuine seekers of truth. Following his death and resurrection, Jesus Christ appeared in the flesh to many of his disciples. However, he did not appear to everyone. He did not appear to Pilate or the leaders of the Sanhedrin. Yet, there were those that knew he was alive and that he had been resurrected. After he finally departed and ascended into heaven to be with his Father, we have little or no record of what he has done since. I mean that we have no other generally accepted record showing his appearance to the earth other than that recorded in the New Testament.

My purpose in making this point is to show that like Joseph, Jesus Christ has been "away" in a sense. He has been out of the sight of the world. Some assume him to be dead; others may believe he is alive, but do not know what he has been doing. When the famine truly waxes sore in the land, it is my sincere belief that the children of Israel that are scattered throughout the earth will once again seek after their God. When that occurs, they will be surprised to learn that Jesus Christ, through his servants from the house of Joseph, has indeed stored up wisdom and doctrine that will come forth in the latter days, to the convincing of both Jew and Gentile that Jesus is the Christ and that his Church, or Zion, must indeed be restored to the earth. The great period of the apostasy will have come to an end!

Another important scripture which we already found in Amos 3:7 contains a message from the Lord that is relevant to the present discussion: "Surely the Lord GOD will do nothing, but he revealeth his secret unto his servants the prophets." When the Lord is active in the lives of his children on the earth, he will communicate his will through prophets. The corollary is that when no prophets are found on the face of the earth, as during the period of the Great Famine, "the Lord GOD will do nothing." This is entirely consistent with the observations seen in the history of the world since the writing of the New Testament. After Peter was the head of the Ancient Church of Jesus Christ, no clear record exists in terms of the leadership of the Church as to who was put in place of Peter after his death, and so on. The reason such records are not had is because the succession of the priesthood leadership of the Church of Jesus Christ came to an end. All of the apostles were either killed by the enemies of the Church or taken

JOSEPH IN EGYPT

by the Lord in some other fashion (translation). No one was left to administer the affairs of the Lord's Church and Kingdom on the earth.

Likewise, no additional scriptures have been added to the canon of scripture after the New Testament. With no indication of succession, and no additional writings from prophets to be added to the scriptures, we may indeed say that during the dark ages of the Apostasy Period, the Lord GOD did nothing. He did not call prophets and he did not make appearances to the earth, which would have certainly been recorded by prophets in scripture form. This observation is entirely consistent with the state of apostasy that is predicted by all the Books of the Old Testament we have studied thus far. It denotes the condition of "famine" spoken of in Amos 8:11-12, "not a famine of bread, nor a thirst for water, but of hearing the words of the LORD: And they shall wander from sea to sea, and from the north even to the east, they shall run to and fro to seek the word of the LORD, and shall not find it."

The seven years of famine spoken of in the story of Joseph in the Book of Genesis also denotes a period of time during which the Lord was hidden from view. It represents a time during which he is separated or withdrawn from the children of Israel and from the entire world. This is not to say that in individual cases he would not answer prayers or bless those that loved him or sought after him. It simply means that the Lord's Church or Zion ceased to exist as predicted by prophecy, and that during this era of history, it was similar to the case of Joseph: the Lord was no where to be found!

Joseph is Alive!

Just as the brothers of Joseph were astonished when they finally learned that Joseph was alive and stood before them, and that he was governor of the land of Egypt, so too will the children of Israel be astonished in the latter days when they finally recognize the works performed by the descendants of Joseph. In Genesis 45:3, it reads: "And Joseph said unto his brethren, I am Joseph; doth my father yet live? And his brethren could not answer him; for they were troubled at his presence." The works and deeds of the scattered posterity of Joseph will have a similar effect on those that encounter a restored Zion in the latter times. It will be something new; something surprising and unexpected. The hidden works of Joseph's offspring will come forth to show the world where truth can be found. It will indeed be "a marvelous work and a wonder," as spoken of in Isaiah. Despite the peculiar nature of this marvelous work, it will nonetheless be true and of God. The works that are manifest during this restoration period will be like grain, water, and nourishment to a famished Israel. Having travailed through the period of apostasy and wandered in the wilderness of confusion and doubt, the works and deeds of Joseph will come forth to the children of Israel like a saving balm that will heal their wounds and give them succor.

To summarize our discussion about Joseph, who was sold into Egypt, let us reiterate the symbols and types that are present in this great story, and made clear through our analysis of Isaiah. We have seen that Joseph and his descendants play an important role in the latter days. While the tribes of Israel were divided into two great families, Joseph to the north and Judah to the south, they both fell into a state of darkness or famine. From the story of Joseph in Egypt, we see that the Lost Tribes of Ephraim will have done something special that is stored up and reserved specifically by the Lord to come forth in the last days. It will be a new thing, and it will spring forth to the confounding of falsehood and vanity.

We also saw that Joseph was a symbolic type representing the Savior Jesus Christ. The betrayal of Joseph, and his being sold to the merchants heading to Egypt are types of the betrayal of Jesus Christ by his brethren in his day. In both cases, those who should have embraced them and upheld them ultimately sealed their fate temporally. The symbolic gestures of ripping Joseph's coat of many colors and dipping it in blood are symbolic of the crucifixion of Jesus Christ, the spilling of his blood and the dividing of his raiment by the Roman soldiers. This is clearly a link between the two events. Joseph's banishment is a symbolic prediction of Jesus Christ's departure from the world stage during the Dark Ages. The Lord Jesus Christ was literally nowhere to be found.

The symbolism of Pharaoh's dream of seven plentiful years being followed by seven years of famine is clear and direct. A link exists between the symbolic types of water, rain, or nourishment, and the concept of receiving revelation directly from God through his authorized servants, the prophets. It is also curious the similarity between Daniel's interpretation of the dream of Nebuchadnezzar and Joseph's interpretation of the dream of Pharaoh. In both cases, the interpreter of the dream gave credit to God for being able to decipher the meaning of it. In both cases, the dreams are prophetic messages concerning the unfolding of the Lord's dealings with man on earth, and specifically his coming forth again in the Last Days. Something done by the children of Ephraim during their days of being scattered and hidden from the view of the world will come forth in these latter times and mark the end of the great Famine Period, and the beginning of the period of the Latter Rain, when prophets are again called and Zion is restored.

Finally, the fact that Joseph is sold into Egypt is significant. The idea of sojourning in Egypt for a period of time brings to mind the instance when Joseph, the earthly father of Jesus, was warned in a dream to flee into Egypt to protect his son from being killed by Herod. The fact that Mary's husband is named Joseph is not by chance. It is another situation that links the life of Joseph to that of the Lord Jesus Christ.

Matthew 2:12-15

12 And being warned of God in a dream that they should not return to Herod, they departed into their own country another way.
13 And when they were departed, behold, the angel of the Lord appeareth to Joseph in a dream, saying, Arise, and take the young child and his mother, and flee into Egypt, and be thou there until I bring thee word: for Herod will seek the young child to destroy him.
14 When he arose, he took the young child and his mother by night, and departed into Egypt:
15 And was there until the death of Herod: that it might be fulfilled which was spoken of the Lord by the prophet, saying, Out of Egypt have I called my son.

From our analysis of the Book of Isaiah, we showed that references to Egypt mean references to the man-made churches of the earth. While these churches may have been started with the best of intentions and based on the things written in the Bible, they nonetheless lack the priesthood authority and divine sanction from the Lord GOD directly. While they preserve and propagate the knowledge of the Lord Jesus Christ throughout the world, they have not the power to save. It is critical to note the significant part these man-made institutions play in preparing God's children for the time of the "restitution of all things." Like the good Pharaoh who exalted Joseph to governor over all of Egypt, nations who have trusted in God and espoused religious freedom, have in a sense preserved the children of Israel, and helped them prepare for the day when Zion will be restored and the Lord can again call his sons and daughters out of Egypt, or out of the churches of the world where they are held captive.

If we apply this theory to the story of Joseph, then we might expect that the actions and deeds of prophets from the loins of Joseph will some day come to our view, although they are as of now hidden and unseen. Just as Joseph goes away and is basically forgotten by his brethren, so too the Lord Jesus Christ has been away but will return in the last days, and call modern prophets to restore his fallen people and to guide them safely to Zion. The stored provisions that Joseph prepared during the seven years of plenty are symbolic of the information about the dispersed tribe of Ephraim that will have done many works prior to the dark period of Spiritual Famine, and which will be stored away to come forth in the latter times.

Let us keep these matters in mind as we conclude our analysis of the Old Testament prophesies concerning the Latter Rain by studying the life and deeds of Moses, the great prophet whose story begins in the Book of Exodus. My objective in looking at the life of Moses is to show that Moses' life is also a type with meaning for the latter times. We will see if and how the story of Moses supports the Latter Rain hypothesis presented in this book thus far. The story of Moses will serve as a natural transition from our study of the Old Testament scriptures to the final subject of analysis, namely the scriptures contained in the New Testament.

CHAPTER TEN

Moses and the Exodus

The story of Moses and the Exodus from Egypt is full of symbolism. Moses' story begins in the Book of Exodus, and continues through Leviticus, Numbers, and Deuteronomy. The meaning of Moses' life can now be clarified through the framework of interpretation we derived from Isaiah. The most important symbols are:

1. **Moses** = Jesus Christ. Moses is a symbolic type of the Lord Jesus Christ, as was Joseph in the previous story.
2. **Egypt** = Arm of Flesh. In this story, Egypt again represents the man-made teachings and doctrines of the world that hold the modern-day children of Israel captive.
3. **The New Pharaoh** = Satan. Pharaoh has dominion and power over the children of Israel. He refuses to release them from bondage despite mighty miracles wrote by the Lord's servants. The character of Pharaoh is analogous to the king of Assyria in the Book of Isaiah, and represents Satan.
4. **Miracles** = True Doctrine of the Restored Zion. The miracles and wonders performed by the Lord to free the children of Israel from bondage are representative of the strong doctrines and truths of Zion in the last days. The works performed by modern Zion will convince the children of Israel of the power of God and the authority of his modern-day prophets.
5. **Idols** = Doctrines of Men. The worship of false gods and man-made idols by the children of Israel in the story of Moses and the Exodus are representations of the worship of man-made traditions and the vain philosophies of men that lack authority from God and have no power to save.
6. **Wilderness** = Great Famine Period. The 40-year wilderness period in the second phase of the story of Moses, like in Isaiah, represents a period of time when the Kingdom of God is nowhere to be found. The Lord allows his children to wander until they exercise enough faith to finally come into the Promised Land. The younger generation must endure the

hardships of the wilderness, even though they were not guilty of the sins of their fathers.
7. **Promised Land** = Kingdom of God on the Earth or Zion. Those that make it through the wilderness of the Famine Period are those that are able to recognize God's power and his true doctrine as contained in the restored Church of God or Zion. They are not afraid to possess the land, relying on God's protection and guidance.
8. **Manna** = Word of God. Manna, which is the bread that was prepared of the Lord to sustain the children of Israel in the wilderness, represents the word of God contained in the Holy Bible, which sustains a belief in God, but keeps them wanting more.
9. **Water** = Revelation. As in Isaiah and elsewhere in the Bible, references to water in the story of Moses are symbolic of revelation from God, and man's dependence thereon for guidance and direction.

The story of Moses can be divided into two great phases. Both phases have the same symbolic meaning, but are set in different situations and scenarios. The net result is that the Lord uses past historical occurrences to symbolize the three great divisions or eras of his dealings with his children on the earth—the Former Rain period, the wilderness or famine period, and the great period of the Latter Rain. The story of Moses relates these concepts in two different phases of Moses' life story.

1. **The Exodus.** Moses' birth and adoption into the royal Egyptian family, his departure into the wilderness, and then his return to lead the Israelites out of suffering and bondage. Moses petitions the wicked Pharaoh to release the children of Israel, but Pharaoh refuses, despite all the miracles seen from God. Finally, Pharaoh relents, but then reneges on his agreement and sends his armies to recapture the Israelites that are camped at the borders of the Red Sea. The Lord parts the waters of the Red Sea at Moses' command and the children of Israel are miraculously saved from destruction.
2. **The Journey to the Promised Land.** During this phase, the children of Israel are led through the wilderness between the Red Sea and the Promised Land of Canaan. They are brought nigh unto the borders of the Promised Land, and men are sent to spy out the inhabitants of the land. The people reject the idea of invading the land because they fear men more than God. Those of that generation are made to wander in the wilderness for the space of 40 years, being fed by the Lord with manna from heaven. When the unbelieving generation dies off, the Israelites are again brought to the borders of the Promised Land. This time they have faith in the Lord and go in and possess the land without fearing man.

Joseph's last messages to his family before his death indicated that the Lord would send a deliverer for them. This deliverer would lead them forth from Egypt and bring them to the land of Canaan, which is the land promised to Abraham, Isaac, and Jacob.

THE LATTER RAIN

Genesis 50:24-25

24 And Joseph said unto his brethren, I die: and God will surely visit you, and bring you out of this land unto the land which he sware to Abraham, to Isaac, and to Jacob.
25 And Joseph took an oath of the children of Israel, saying, God will surely visit you, and ye shall carry up my bones from hence.

While the children of Israel enjoyed their sojourn in Egypt for a while and were prospered of the Lord at the beginning, eventually that which was good about escaping to Egypt finally turned sour. The children of Israel suddenly become the targets of oppression and tyranny. This occurs because they are not in the Land of Promise, nor living to attain it, and must be brought back to it by the hand of the Lord. Their sojourn in Egypt is symbolic of the children of Israel who are now wandering to and fro in the earth seeking the word of the Lord, but not finding it. They are held down by the false traditions and incorrect doctrines that have been forced upon them by the great tyrannical leader. Even those that have tried to escape falsehood are eventually caught up in the philosophies of men. As the persecution and suffering begin to mount, Israel finally decides to call upon the Lord for help and relief, and for the fulfillment of Joseph's promise of deliverance. This promise applies literally to the children of Israel held captive in Egypt anciently, and it applies symbolically to the children of Israel alive today. In fact, in the 23rd Chapter of Jeremiah, we learn that the freeing of the children of Israel from their latter-day captivity will overshadow the great events that occurred when Moses came to lead the children of Israel out of Egypt.

Jeremiah 23:7-8

7 Therefore, behold, the days come, saith the LORD, that they shall no more say, The LORD liveth, which brought up the children of Israel out of the land of Egypt;
8 But, The LORD liveth, which brought up and which led the seed of the house of Israel out of the north country, and from all countries whither I had driven them; and they shall dwell in their own land.

This scripture not only demonstrates the symbolic connection between the two events, but it also indicates that the latter-day gathering of Israel is in fact of greater importance in terms of its significance for the inhabitants of the earth. Keep this thought in mind, as we now look more closely at the story of Moses.

The Exodus

After the death of Joseph, about 400 years went by and the Hebrews multiplied and prospered in Egypt.

Exodus 1:7-14

7 And the children of Israel were fruitful, and increased abundantly, and multiplied, and waxed exceeding mighty; and the land was filled with them.
8 Now there arose up a new king over Egypt, which knew not Joseph.
9 And he said unto his people, Behold, the people of the children of Israel are more and mightier than we:
10 Come on, let us deal wisely with them; lest they multiply, and it come to pass, that, when there falleth out any war, they join also unto our enemies, and fight against us, and so get them up out of the land.

MOSES AND THE EXODUS

11 Therefore they did set over them taskmasters to afflict them with their burdens. And they built for Pharaoh treasure cities, Pithom and Raamses.
12 But the more they afflicted them, the more they multiplied and grew. And they were grieved because of the children of Israel.
13 And the Egyptians made the children of Israel to serve with rigour:
14 And they made their lives bitter with hard bondage, in morter, and in brick, and in all manner of service in the field: all their service, wherein they made them serve, was with rigour.

Recall from Isaiah that Egypt was a symbol that represented the arm of flesh or, in other words, the development of man-made institutions and organizations that gave some refuge from the famine initially, but were eventually overrun by the king of Assyria as well. We see this same thing occurring in the Book of Exodus 1:8, "Now there arose up a new king over Egypt, which knew not Joseph." This new Pharaoh is symbolic of Satan's ability to conquer Israel and subject it, even after it has sought refuge from the famine in Egypt. This new Pharaoh is a symbol of Satan, just like the king of Assyria was in the Book of Isaiah. It is the same story, but using a different cast of characters.

The fact that this evil Pharaoh comes to power does not negate the great salvation wrought by the Lord in sending Joseph into Egypt. He became a great instrument of salvation unto the House of Israel. He was sent to Egypt before the onset of the great famine and was able to store up great sources of nourishment for his brethren. And he did so without it being known by his brethren or his father Jacob. The story of Joseph in Egypt and the story of Moses are really the same message from the Lord, reiterated in different ways. In fact, the story of Moses repeats this message twice, using the two distinct phases of the Exodus to make the point clear. Let us now analyze the first phase of the story of Moses, which starts in Exodus 1.

Exodus 1:15-22
15 And the king of Egypt spake to the Hebrew midwives, of which the name of the one was Shiphrah, and the name of the other Puah:
16 And he said, When ye do the office of a midwife to the Hebrew women, and see them upon the stools; if it be a son, then ye shall kill him: but if it be a daughter, then she shall live.
17 But the midwives feared God, and did not as the king of Egypt commanded them, but saved the men children alive.
18 And the king of Egypt called for the midwives, and said unto them, Why have ye done this thing, and have saved the men children alive?
19 And the midwives said unto Pharaoh, Because the Hebrew women are not as the Egyptian women; for they are lively, and are delivered ere the midwives come in unto them.
20 Therefore God dealt well with the midwives: and the people multiplied, and waxed very mighty.
21 And it came to pass, because the midwives feared God, that he made them houses.
22 And Pharaoh charged all his people, saying, Every son that is born ye shall cast into the river, and every daughter ye shall save alive.

It was into this environment that Moses came into the world. Not only are the Hebrews in bondage to the Egyptians, but Moses' life is in danger. This is the first indication that Moses is a type of Jesus Christ, in that both are born at time when their lives are threatened. Compare the situation faced by Jesus Christ at the time of his birth.

THE LATTER RAIN

Matthew 2:13-15, 19-20

13 And when they were departed, behold, the angel of the Lord appeareth to Joseph in a dream, saying, Arise, and take the young child and his mother, and flee into Egypt, and be thou there until I bring thee word: for Herod will seek the young child to destroy him.
14 When he arose, he took the young child and his mother by night, and departed into Egypt:
15 And was there until the death of Herod: that it might be fulfilled which was spoken of the Lord by the prophet, saying, Out of Egypt have I called my son.
19 But when Herod was dead, behold, an angel of the Lord appeareth in a dream to Joseph in Egypt,
20 Saying, Arise, and take the young child and his mother, and go into the land of Israel: for they are dead which sought the young child's life.

Notice that Joseph, the earthly father of Jesus and husband of Mary, also receives inspiration and direction through dreams, like the original Joseph who was sold into Egypt. He is warned in a dream to flee Bethlehem, and then he is warned in a second dream to return to Israel when it was finally safe to do so. When it says "Joseph in Egypt" in verse 19 above, it makes a link between the two stories. Both Moses and Jesus Christ are threatened with death at the hand of a tyrant when they are born. Both are adopted into a royal family—Joseph being a royal descendant of King David as indicated in Matthew Chapter 1. Ironically, Moses ends up being adopted into the family of the very tyrant who made the decree to have him killed.

Exodus 2:1-10

1 AND there went a man of the house of Levi, and took to wife a daughter of Levi.
2 And the woman conceived, and bare a son: and when she saw him that he was a goodly child, she hid him three months.
3 And when she could not longer hide him, she took for him an ark of bulrushes, and daubed it with slime and with pitch, and put the child therein; and she laid it in the flags by the river's brink.
4 And his sister stood afar off, to wit what would be done to him.
5 And the daughter of Pharaoh came down to wash herself at the river; and her maidens walked along by the river's side; and when she saw the ark among the flags, she sent her maid to fetch it.
6 And when she had opened it, she saw the child: and, behold, the babe wept. And she had compassion on him, and said, This is one of the Hebrews' children.
7 Then said his sister to Pharaoh's daughter, Shall I go and call to thee a nurse of the Hebrew women, that she may nurse the child for thee?
8 And Pharaoh's daughter said to her, Go. And the maid went and called the child's mother.
9 And Pharaoh's daughter said unto her, Take this child away, and nurse it for me, and I will give thee thy wages. And the woman took the child, and nursed it.
10 And the child grew, and she brought him unto Pharaoh's daughter, and he became her son. And she called his name Moses: and she said, Because I drew him out of the water.

The next scene in this story can be compared to that of the Savior Jesus Christ. Just as Christ was rejected by his own people, Moses, who was in a great position to help the Hebrews as the adopted son of Pharaoh, ends up being sent into the wilderness because of the actions of his own people.

Exodus 2:11-15

11 And it came to pass in those days, when Moses was grown, that he went out unto his brethren, and looked on their burdens: and he spied an Egyptian smiting an Hebrew, one of his brethren.

MOSES AND THE EXODUS

> 12 And he looked this way and that way, and when he saw that there was no man, he slew the Egyptian, and hid him in the sand.
> 13 And when he went out the second day, behold, two men of the Hebrews strove together: and he said to him that did the wrong, Wherefore smitest thou thy fellow?
> 14 And he said, Who made thee a prince and a judge over us? intendest thou to kill me, as thou killedst the Egyptian? And Moses feared, and said, Surely this thing is known.
> 15 Now when Pharaoh heard this thing, he sought to slay Moses. But Moses fled from the face of Pharaoh, and dwelt in the land of Midian: and he sat down by a well.

Is not this the same question made to Jesus by the leaders of the Hebrews at the time of Christ's interrogation: "Who made thee a prince and a judge over us?" The answer is the same in both cases: the Lord God of Israel did it. While Moses is not crucified at this point, his banishment into the wilderness is still symbolic of Christ's departure from the world, seen following his death and resurrection. Moses goes to the land of Midian, where he marries one of the daughters of Jethro, the Priest of Midian. During his stay in the wilderness of Midian, we learn that the wicked Pharaoh that wanted to kill Moses has died, just like Herod died while Joseph, Mary, and Jesus were away. These similarities tie the two stories together. Moses is a type, symbolizing the mission of Jesus Christ.

> **Exodus 2:23-25**
> 23 And it came to pass in process of time, that the king of Egypt died: and the children of Israel sighed by reason of the bondage, and they cried, and their cry came up unto God by reason of the bondage.
> 24 And God heard their groaning, and God remembered his covenant with Abraham, with Isaac, and with Jacob.
> 25 And God looked upon the children of Israel, and God had respect unto them.

Moses now has his famous encounter with God at the burning bush. It is here that Moses receives his instructions from the Lord to return to Egypt.

> **Exodus 3:7-10**
> 7 And the LORD said, I have surely seen the affliction of my people which are in Egypt, and have heard their cry by reason of their taskmasters; for I know their sorrows;
> 8 And I am come down to deliver them out of the hand of the Egyptians, and to bring them up out of that land unto a good land and a large, unto a land flowing with milk and honey; unto the place of the Canaanites, and the Hittites, and the Amorites, and the Perizzites, and the Hivites, and the Jebusites.
> 9 Now therefore, behold, the cry of the children of Israel is come unto me: and I have also seen the oppression wherewith the Egyptians oppress them.
> 10 Come now therefore, and I will send thee unto Pharaoh, that thou mayest bring forth my people the children of Israel out of Egypt.

Moses obeys the voice of the Lord and returns to Egypt, and first goes to the elders of Israel. Aaron, Moses' brother, is assigned by the Lord as a spokesman for Moses, and thus Aaron relates to the people all that the Lord said and did before Moses in the Mount of Horeb. At this point, the people believe because of Aaron's report, and also by witnessing the signs that Moses and Aaron perform before them. However, when Moses and Aaron go to Pharaoh to request the release of the children of Israel, the first phase of resistance is felt. Evidently, the new Pharaoh is just as bad as his father who had sought to kill Moses.

THE LATTER RAIN

Exodus 5:1-9

1 AND afterward Moses and Aaron went in, and told Pharaoh, Thus saith the LORD God of Israel, Let my people go, that they may hold a feast unto me in the wilderness.
2 And Pharaoh said, Who is the LORD, that I should obey his voice to let Israel go? I know not the LORD, neither will I let Israel go.
3 And they said, The God of the Hebrews hath met with us: let us go, we pray thee, three days' journey into the desert, and sacrifice unto the LORD our God; lest he fall upon us with pestilence, or with the sword.
4 And the king of Egypt said unto them, Wherefore do ye, Moses and Aaron, let the people from their works? get you unto your burdens.
5 And Pharaoh said, Behold, the people of the land now are many, and ye make them rest from their burdens.
6 And Pharaoh commanded the same day the taskmasters of the people, and their officers, saying,
7 Ye shall no more give the people straw to make brick, as heretofore: let them go and gather straw for themselves.
8 And the tale of the bricks, which they did make heretofore, ye shall lay upon them; ye shall not diminish ought thereof: for they be idle; therefore they cry, saying, Let us go and sacrifice to our God.
9 Let there more work be laid upon the men, that they may labour therein; and let them not regard vain words.

There are two situations that develop. First, Pharaoh is annoyed that Moses and Aaron would even dare suggest that he let the Israelites go. He asks: "Who is the LORD, that I should obey his voice to let Israel go? I know not the LORD, neither will I let Israel go." This is not all. Pharaoh now increases the burdens on Israel by requiring them to make the same number of bricks as before, but without giving them straw. This shows the true character of this Pharaoh as a wicked tyrant. This increased labor now causes the second issue to occur. The children of Israel begin to question and doubt whether it is really such a good idea to listen to Moses after all. Even Moses himself starts to wonder if his meddling in the affairs of the people was such a good idea.

Exodus 5:20-23

20 And they met Moses and Aaron, who stood in the way, as they came forth from Pharaoh:
21 And they said unto them, The LORD look upon you, and judge; because ye have made our savour to be abhorred in the eyes of Pharaoh, and in the eyes of his servants, to put a sword in their hand to slay us.
22 And Moses returned unto the LORD, and said, Lord, wherefore hast thou so evil entreated this people? why is it that thou hast sent me?
23 For since I came to Pharaoh to speak in thy name, he hath done evil to this people; neither hast thou delivered thy people at all.

Now begins the stage in the story where the Lord shows forth his many mighty miracles and signs before Israel, Egypt, and Pharaoh. Moses first casts his staff on the ground before Pharaoh and it becomes a serpent, yet this does not convince Pharaoh. The Lord proceeds to send plagues on Egypt, which are done before the eyes of everyone. He separates the plagues so that they affect the Egyptians, but not the Israelites. The first plague is the turning of the waters of Egypt into blood (Exodus 7:14-18). The story proceeds with a continuous interaction between Moses and Pharaoh, in which the Lord sends forth plague

MOSES AND THE EXODUS

after plague. All the plagues sent forth by the hand of God show how hardened the heart of Pharaoh is, and how unwilling he is to let the children of Israel leave. The plagues are numerous:

1. Water turned to blood
2. Frogs overrun the Egyptian houses and are everywhere
3. Lice infest the Egyptians only
4. Flies get into the food and supplies of the Egyptians
5. Cattle die, while the cattle of the Hebrews are spared
6. Boils on the Egyptians
7. Hail and fire are called down from heaven, which destroy crops—Egyptians who are outside are killed, other damage occurs
8. Locusts come and infest the land of the Egyptians
9. Darkness for three days

With each of the proceeding plagues, Pharaoh appears to relent and concede to let the Hebrews leave Egypt. Moses stops every plague by entreating the Lord on Pharaoh's behalf. Each time the plague is stayed, Pharaoh reneges on his promise and again refuses to let them leave. After the last plague of darkness, Pharaoh again hardens his heart, but this time he also banishes Moses from his presence.

Exodus 10:28-29
28 And Pharaoh said unto him, Get thee from me, take heed to thyself, see my face no more; for in that day thou seest my face thou shalt die.
29 And Moses said, Thou hast spoken well, I will see thy face again no more.

This sets the stage for the final showdown between the Lord and Pharaoh. Ironically, the last plague to inflict Egypt is similar to the terrible act the previous Pharaoh had caused to occur at the time of Moses' birth. All the first-born males of the Egyptians are to be slain, and this goes for the least servant in the land all the way up to Pharaoh himself. The Hebrews are spared this plague if they strictly abide by the instructions given to them by the Lord through the prophet Moses. This becomes the institution of the Passover Feast.

Exodus 12:3-14
3 Speak ye unto all the congregation of Israel, saying, In the tenth day of this month they shall take to them every man a lamb, according to the house of their fathers, a lamb for an house:
4 And if the household be too little for the lamb, let him and his neighbour next unto his house take it according to the number of the souls; every man according to his eating shall make your count for the lamb.
5 Your lamb shall be without blemish, a male of the first year: ye shall take it out from the sheep, or from the goats:
6 And ye shall keep it up until the fourteenth day of the same month: and the whole assembly of the congregation of Israel shall kill it in the evening.
7 And they shall take of the blood, and strike it on the two side posts and on the upper door post of the houses, wherein they shall eat it.
8 And they shall eat the flesh in that night, roast with fire, and unleavened bread; and with bitter herbs they shall eat it.
9 Eat not of it raw, nor sodden at all with water, but roast with fire; his head with his legs, and with the purtenance thereof.

10 And ye shall let nothing of it remain until the morning; and that which remaineth of it until the morning ye shall burn with fire.
11 And thus shall ye eat it; with your loins girded, your shoes on your feet, and your staff in your hand; and ye shall eat it in haste: it is the LORD's passover.
12 For I will pass through the land of Egypt this night, and will smite all the firstborn in the land of Egypt, both man and beast; and against all the gods of Egypt I will execute judgment: I am the LORD.
13 And the blood shall be to you for a token upon the houses where ye are: and when I see the blood, I will pass over you, and the plague shall not be upon you to destroy you, when I smite the land of Egypt.
14 And this day shall be unto you for a memorial; and ye shall keep it a feast to the LORD throughout your generations; ye shall keep it a feast by an ordinance for ever.

This Passover Feast is a representation of the sacrifice of the Savior Jesus Christ. The lamb or goat used in the feast had to be the first-born, and it had to be without blemish. None of the bones were to be broken. When Christ is later crucified, the bones of the thieves that were killed along side of him were broken to hasten their deaths prior to the Passover Feast. However, Jesus was already dead; therefore, his bones were not broken.

Matthew 26:1-5
1 AND it came to pass, when Jesus had finished all these sayings, he said unto his disciples,
2 Ye know that after two days is the feast of the passover, and the Son of man is betrayed to be crucified.
3 Then assembled together the chief priests, and the scribes, and the elders of the people, unto the palace of the high priest, who was called Caiaphas,
4 And consulted that they might take Jesus by subtilty, and kill him.
5 But they said, Not on the feast day, lest there be an uproar among the people.

I do not believe that the leaders of the Jews were worried that the people would make the connection between the crucifixion of Jesus Christ and the symbolism portrayed in the Passover Feast. Rather, they just did not want his death to occur on the day of the Passover as it was a Holy Day. Just as they did no work on the Sabbath Day, they would not wish the people to see this act occur on the Passover either. In hindsight, it is hard not to recognize the great symbolism of this act as it unfolded and played out in the life of Jesus Christ.

John 19:31-33
31 The Jews therefore, because it was the preparation, that the bodies should not remain upon the cross on the sabbath day, (for that sabbath day was an high day,) besought Pilate that their legs might be broken, and that they might be taken away.
32 Then came the soldiers, and brake the legs of the first, and of the other which was crucified with him.
33 But when they came to Jesus, and saw that he was dead already, they brake not his legs:

When the Jews placed the blood of the Passover lamb on their door frames, this was a clear reference to the blood of Christ and his ability to pardon from sin. This act performed by the Hebrews on the eve of their departure from Egypt was a strong symbolic type of the ultimate sacrifice of the Son of God to pay the debt for the sins of all mankind. Direction was specifically given to the people by Moses to protect them from the destroying angel that was to come through

MOSES AND THE EXODUS

Egypt that night. Again, Moses serves as a type of Jesus Christ by instituting this saving ordinance among the Israelites, using the blood of the lamb as a marker for salvation.

Exodus 12:29-36
29 And it came to pass, that at midnight the LORD smote all the firstborn in the land of Egypt, from the firstborn of Pharaoh that sat on his throne unto the firstborn of the captive that was in the dungeon; and all the firstborn of cattle.
30 And Pharaoh rose up in the night, he, and all his servants, and all the Egyptians; and there was a great cry in Egypt; for there was not a house where there was not one dead.
31 And he called for Moses and Aaron by night, and said, Rise up, and get you forth from among my people, both ye and the children of Israel; and go, serve the LORD, as ye have said.
32 Also take your flocks and your herds, as ye have said, and be gone; and bless me also.
33 And the Egyptians were urgent upon the people, that they might send them out of the land in haste; for they said, We be all dead men.
34 And the people took their dough before it was leavened, their kneadingtroughs being bound up in their clothes upon their shoulders.
35 And the children of Israel did according to the word of Moses; and they borrowed of the Egyptians jewels of silver, and jewels of gold, and raiment:
36 And the LORD gave the people favour in the sight of the Egyptians, so that they lent unto them such things as they required. And they spoiled the Egyptians.

Over 400 years had passed from the time the Israelites first came to Egypt and the time that they were liberated by the Lord through the prophet Moses. This period of time spent in Egypt is a direct symbolic type that refers to the time between the falling away of the true Church of God shortly after the death and resurrection of Jesus Christ and its restoration to the earth—which is to occur sometime in these last days. On a macro-scale, Moses represents the Lord Jesus Christ who will reveal himself to some modern-day prophet, who will then begin the process of freeing the children of Israel from their captivity in Egypt, or man-made churches and institutions. Like in the case of Pharaoh just discussed, Satan will not easily allow the children of Israel to go forth out from their captivity. He will fight against Zion, but will do so in vain. Ultimately, the restored Zion will win over the hearts of those who recognize the voice of the Savior calling them out of the world.

On a micro-scale, Moses is again a symbolic type of Jesus Christ. He is in a position to help the Hebrews as the adopted son of the Pharaoh of Egypt. He is rejected by his own people, and sent to tarry in the wilderness for a season. For several years, Moses is lost to the knowledge of the children of Israel in Egypt, and they have no idea what he does in the land of Midian, or of his preparation for his divine mission to free them from captivity. This sojourn of Moses is a type of the Spiritual Famine period. After the record of Jesus' doings as contained in the New Testament, we really have no idea what he has been doing either. Jesus tells the Pharisees that he is going away, but they understood not.

John 7:32-36
32 The Pharisees heard that the people murmured such things concerning him; and the Pharisees and the chief priests sent officers to take him.
33 Then said Jesus unto them, Yet a little while am I with you, and then I go unto him that sent me.
34 Ye shall seek me, and shall not find me: and where I am, thither ye cannot come.

35 Then said the Jews among themselves, Whither will he go, that we shall not find him? will he go unto the dispersed among the Gentiles, and teach the Gentiles?
36 What manner of saying is this that he said, Ye shall seek me, and shall not find me: and where I am, thither ye cannot come?

In this statement to the Pharisees, Jesus is explaining that he will now depart from the world scene. Where will he be during this period of withdrawal from the earth? He will be with the Father. Of course, the wicked cannot go there. However, we learn in another scriptural reference that the righteous are able to go there.

John 14:1-4
1 LET not your heart be troubled: ye believe in God, believe also in me.
2 In my Father's house are many mansions: if it were not so, I would have told you. I go to prepare a place for you.
3 And if I go and prepare a place for you, I will come again, and receive you unto myself; that where I am, there ye may be also.
4 And whither I go ye know, and the way ye know.

The righteous need not fear. Those that trust in the Lord Jesus Christ will have a way prepared that they can go unto him in the house of his Father. We see that the Lord is leaving to go to the Father for a season. Moses' stay in the land of Midian is symbolic of this period of withdrawal. The return of Moses is symbolic of the return of Jesus Christ to the earth in the last days to enact the restoration of Zion to the earth. Not of his Second Coming, when all will see him at once, but his return to his servants the prophets.

The miracles and wonders performed by Moses in the eyes of the Egyptians are symbolic of the true doctrines of Zion that will be shown to the inhabitants of the earth in the latter times. Things will be revealed to the modern prophets that will be amazing to those that witness them. These events and tokens, when they occur, will demonstrate to the world that Jesus is the Christ, and that his Gospel has been restored to the earth again, in its perfect form. Over time, a crescendo effect will occur in that it will become more and more obvious that the restored Zion is indeed the true Church of the Lord Jesus Christ. Finally, a separation will occur between those that believe and those that do not. Let us examine this concept as it is portrayed in the story of Moses.

Exodus 14:5-12
5 And it was told the king of Egypt that the people fled: and the heart of Pharaoh and of his servants was turned against the people, and they said, Why have we done this, that we have let Israel go from serving us?
6 And he made ready his chariot, and took his people with him:
7 And he took six hundred chosen chariots, and all the chariots of Egypt, and captains over every one of them.
8 And the LORD hardened the heart of Pharaoh king of Egypt, and he pursued after the children of Israel: and the children of Israel went out with an high hand.
9 But the Egyptians pursued after them, all the horses and chariots of Pharaoh, and his horsemen, and his army, and overtook them encamping by the sea, beside Pi-hahiroth, before Baal-zephon.
10 And when Pharaoh drew nigh, the children of Israel lifted up their eyes, and, behold, the Egyptians marched after them; and they were sore afraid: and the children of Israel cried out unto the LORD.

MOSES AND THE EXODUS

11 And they said unto Moses, Because there were no graves in Egypt, hast thou taken us away to die in the wilderness? wherefore hast thou dealt thus with us, to carry us forth out of Egypt?
12 Is not this the word that we did tell thee in Egypt, saying, Let us alone, that we may serve the Egyptians? For it had been better for us to serve the Egyptians, than that we should die in the wilderness.

Despite the mighty miracles wrought in Egypt, the children of Israel still fear the armies of the Egyptians. They felt it would have been better to be in bondage to Pharaoh than to die in the wilderness. This is a symbolic representation of what happens as people join modern-day Zion. Despite the truths of the restored Gospel and even the testimony of the truth born to the heart of the individual through the Spirit, the influence of Egypt (the man-made institutions from whence they came), some of the people joining modern-day Zion will do so in fear. They will fear offending those they left behind. They will fear man more than God, and will be reticent to continue in the path of salvation. Many, in fact, will turn back to their old ways. Others will not even join the restored Church of God because of this fear of men. The faithful will ultimately see the mighty arm of the Lord revealed in their lives, leading to a mighty separation between those that believe and those that do not. It will be the duty of the servants of the Lord in that time to help reduce the fears of the children of Israel, and to bolster their faith in God's power to save them.

Exodus 14:13-22
13 And Moses said unto the people, Fear ye not, stand still, and see the salvation of the LORD, which he will shew to you to day: for the Egyptians whom ye have seen to day, ye shall see them again no more for ever.
14 The LORD shall fight for you, and ye shall hold your peace.
15 And the LORD said unto Moses, Wherefore criest thou unto me? speak unto the children of Israel, that they go forward:
16 But lift thou up thy rod, and stretch out thine hand over the sea, and divide it: and the children of Israel shall go on dry ground through the midst of the sea.
17 And I, behold, I will harden the hearts of the Egyptians, and they shall follow them: and I will get me honour upon Pharaoh, and upon all his host, upon his chariots, and upon his horsemen.
18 And the Egyptians shall know that I am the LORD, when I have gotten me honour upon Pharaoh, upon his chariots, and upon his horsemen.
19 And the angel of God, which went before the camp of Israel, removed and went behind them; and the pillar of the cloud went from before their face, and stood behind them:
20 And it came between the camp of the Egyptians and the camp of Israel; and it was a cloud and darkness to them, but it gave light by night to these: so that the one came not near the other all the night.
21 And Moses stretched out his hand over the sea; and the LORD caused the sea to go back by a strong east wind all that night, and made the sea dry land, and the waters were divided.
22 And the children of Israel went into the midst of the sea upon the dry ground: and the waters were a wall unto them on their right hand, and on their left.

This dramatic event recalls the image from Isaiah of a highway being provided by the Lord, leading out of Assyria. The way to truth and sound doctrine becomes clear to those who show their faith and trust in the Lord's ability to guide them.

Isaiah 35:8
8 And an highway shall be there, and a way, and it shall be called The way of holiness; the unclean shall not pass over it; but it shall be for those: the wayfaring men, though fools, shall not err therein.

THE LATTER RAIN

In our discussion of Isaiah, we showed that this highway was not only defined by the soundness of the doctrine of modern Zion, but also by the promptings of the Spirit to the seeker of truth and righteousness. Those that desire the Lord to be their God will have promptings leading them line upon line to the restored truth when it comes again upon the earth.

Isaiah 30:20-21
20 And though the Lord give you the bread of adversity, and the water of affliction, yet shall not thy teachers be removed into a corner any more, but thine eyes shall see thy teachers:
21 And thine ears shall hear a word behind thee, saying, This is the way, walk ye in it, when ye turn to the right hand, and when ye turn to the left.

The Lord promises to guide his children in a straight path to Zion through the promptings of his spirit. They will feel the truth in their hearts when they hear it from God's servants. The parting of the Red Sea is a great type of the Lord's ability to lead the modern-day children of Israel back to the restored truth of God. He will lead them out of apostasy and falsehood, which is represented by their being captive to Egypt and the wicked Pharaoh. In the Book of Isaiah, Israel was captive to Assyria and the wicked tyrant, the king of Assyria. Later, many of them fled to Egypt to escape, but the king of Assyria followed them to Egypt and overtook them there. The new Pharaoh, who knew not Joseph, represents this same event. An initial relief is received by the children of Israel, who flee the tyranny of the Assyrian-type churches and form their own churches of men. But soon, the Assyrian overtakes these institutions as well. The Assyrian conquering Egypt, and the new Pharaoh who knew not Joseph, both have the same symbolic meaning. Both kings represent the devil. Both resist the departure of their captives. Both are powerless against the Lord to stop the Exodus of Israel when it finally occurs.

Despite the power of God's word and the mighty evidences provided, Pharaoh sends his armies into the Red Sea after the Hebrews. While it is not certain from the scriptures whether Pharaoh himself accompanied them, or merely observed them as they went, the result is still the same. The children of Israel are saved and walk out of the Red Sea on dry ground, while the armies of the Egyptians are covered by the massive walls of water and drowned.

Exodus 14:23-31
23 And the Egyptians pursued, and went in after them to the midst of the sea, even all Pharaoh's horses, his chariots, and his horsemen.
24 And it came to pass, that in the morning watch the LORD looked unto the host of the Egyptians through the pillar of fire and of the cloud, and troubled the host of the Egyptians,
25 And took off their chariot wheels, that they drave them heavily: so that the Egyptians said, Let us flee from the face of Israel; for the LORD fighteth for them against the Egyptians.
26 And the LORD said unto Moses, Stretch out thine hand over the sea, that the waters may come again upon the Egyptians, upon their chariots, and upon their horsemen.
27 And Moses stretched forth his hand over the sea, and the sea returned to his strength when the morning appeared; and the Egyptians fled against it; and the LORD overthrew the Egyptians in the midst of the sea.
28 And the waters returned, and covered the chariots, and the horsemen, and all the host of Pharaoh that came into the sea after them; there remained not so much as one of them.

> 29 But the children of Israel walked upon dry land in the midst of the sea; and the waters were a wall unto them on their right hand, and on their left.
> 30 Thus the LORD saved Israel that day out of the hand of the Egyptians; and Israel saw the Egyptians dead upon the sea shore.
> 31 And Israel saw that great work which the LORD did upon the Egyptians: and the people feared the LORD, and believed the LORD, and his servant Moses.

In the last days, virtually the same struggle will exist, but it will be a spiritual struggle, not a physical battle as depicted in this both amazing and terrible event. Those attempting to leave the falsehood in favor of truth will be opposed by those who want to stop their progress, and to get them to return to their former beliefs. If the children of Israel exercise faith and push forward, it will be like "a wall unto them on their right hand, and on their left." It will be a wall of water, or a wall of sound doctrine and personal revelation. The scattered tribes of Israel during the Latter Rain period will proceed to the truth with confidence. They have been held captive for centuries, and "they shall wander from sea to sea, and from the north even to the east, they shall run to and fro to seek the word of the LORD, and shall not find it" (Amos 8:12). When the Lord returns in the last days and again establishes his Church, namely Zion, the men and women of Israel will find the true path. "The wayfaring men, though fools, shall not err therein."

The destruction of the Egyptians represents the same thing we saw in the other books we have analyzed thus far. In Isaiah, the armies of the Lord marched forth with the Word of the Lord to crush their enemies, the Assyrians. In Daniel, it was the stone cut out of the mountain without hands rolling forth to destroy the kingdoms of the earth as represented by the statue in Nebuchadnezzar's dream. The Lord will give us another testimony of this important message in the second part of Moses' story.

Journey to the Promised Land

The second phase of the story of Moses begins when the Israelites come forth out of the Red Sea. They have just witnessed the great miracle of salvation wrought by the Lord. They are safe from the Egyptians who sought to destroy them and bring them back into bondage. They see the drowned bodies of the Egyptian soldiers scattered on the shore, and their wrecked chariots. However, they are not yet in the Promised Land. They quickly begin to realize that they are in the wilderness, and the Red Sea has closed behind them so they cannot return to Egypt. Although they have witnessed many mighty miracles in the past weeks, they again begin to fear and this leads them to once again murmur against Moses and Aaron, and against the Lord as well.

> **Exodus 16:1-3**
>
> 1 AND they took their journey from Elim, and all the congregation of the children of Israel came unto the wilderness of Sin, which is between Elim and Sinai, on the fifteenth day of the second month after their departing out of the land of Egypt.
> 2 And the whole congregation of the children of Israel murmured against Moses and Aaron in the wilderness:
> 3 And the children of Israel said unto them, Would to God we had died by the hand of the LORD in the land of Egypt, when we sat by the flesh pots, and when we did eat bread to the full; for ye have brought us forth into this wilderness, to kill this whole assembly with hunger.

THE LATTER RAIN

In response to this murmuring by the children of Israel, the Lord does two things. First, he provides food for them in the form of manna from Heaven. Second, he has Moses smite the rock of Horeb, which causes water to come out so that they can drink. Both of these situations are the same from a symbolic perspective. They both represent the pure revelation from God to man, and they both show that even in the wilderness of affliction, the Lord God of Israel can and will provide nourishment and sustenance for those who seek him to be their God. This also represents the Former Rain period in which the children of God are led by prophets to the Promised Land.

> Exodus 16:4-8
>
> 4 Then said the LORD unto Moses, Behold, I will rain bread from heaven for you; and the people shall go out and gather a certain rate every day, that I may prove them, whether they will walk in my law, or no.
> 5 And it shall come to pass, that on the sixth day they shall prepare that which they bring in; and it shall be twice as much as they gather daily.
> 6 And Moses and Aaron said unto all the children of Israel, At even, then ye shall know that the LORD hath brought you out from the land of Egypt:
> 7 And in the morning, then ye shall see the glory of the LORD; for that he heareth your murmurings against the LORD: and what are we, that ye murmur against us?
> 8 And Moses said, This shall be, when the LORD shall give you in the evening flesh to eat, and in the morning bread to the full; for that the LORD heareth your murmurings which ye murmur against him: and what are we? your murmurings are not against us, but against the LORD.

Besides the institution of the manna, the above passage also demonstrates another interesting phenomenon relevant to the subject of prophets. The children of Israel blamed Moses and Aaron for their apparent plight. In verse seven, however, Moses says, "and what are we, that ye murmur against us?" meaning himself and Aaron. In the next verse, he clarified the issue: "and what are we? Your murmurings are not against us, but against the Lord." A prophet is really just the messenger. The prophet delivers the will of the Lord to the people, and they either accept it or reject it. Moses is making the point that, while they are murmuring against Moses and Aaron, they are really murmuring against the Lord himself. This same phenomenon occurred continually during the Former Rain period from Adam to Jesus Christ. The Lord's children continually resisted the Lord and his messengers, the prophets.

What is hard to understand, perhaps, is how the Israelites could have witnessed the miracle of the parting of the Red Sea, and then doubted that the Lord could provide for them food and water to sustain them in the wilderness. Miracles do not really convert an individual. Rather, it is the testimony of the Spirit of God to the heart that converts the individual and causes them to believe truth when it is received. Miracles only really help the faithful, and do very little for the unbelieving. By feeding the children of Israel through miraculous means, the Lord again emphasizes our dependence on Him for our survival, both temporally and spiritually.

> Exodus 16:9-15
>
> 9 And Moses spake unto Aaron, Say unto all the congregation of the children of Israel, Come near before the LORD: for he hath heard your murmurings.

MOSES AND THE EXODUS

10 And it came to pass, as Aaron spake unto the whole congregation of the children of Israel, that they looked toward the wilderness, and, behold, the glory of the LORD appeared in the cloud.
11 And the LORD spake unto Moses, saying,
12 I have heard the murmurings of the children of Israel: speak unto them, saying, At even ye shall eat flesh, and in the morning ye shall be filled with bread; and ye shall know that I am the LORD your God.
13 And it came to pass, that at even the quails came up, and covered the camp: and in the morning the dew lay round about the host.
14 And when the dew that lay was gone up, behold, upon the face of the wilderness there lay a small round thing, as small as the hoar frost on the ground.
15 And when the children of Israel saw it, they said one to another, It is manna: for they wist not what it was. And Moses said unto them, This is the bread which the LORD hath given you to eat.

If that were not enough, the children of Israel began to complain that they had no water. When they murmured, they always seemed to compare their current situation with that which they had experienced in Egypt.

Exodus 17:1-7
1 AND all the congregation of the children of Israel journeyed from the wilderness of Sin, after their journeys, according to the commandment of the LORD, and pitched in Rephidim: and there was no water for the people to drink.
2 Wherefore the people did chide with Moses, and said, Give us water that we may drink. And Moses said unto them, Why chide ye with me? wherefore do ye tempt the LORD?
3 And the people thirsted there for water; and the people murmured against Moses, and said, Wherefore is this that thou hast brought us up out of Egypt, to kill us and our children and our cattle with thirst?
4 And Moses cried unto the LORD, saying, What shall I do unto this people? they be almost ready to stone me.
5 And the LORD said unto Moses, Go on before the people, and take with thee of the elders of Israel; and thy rod, wherewith thou smotest the river, take in thine hand, and go.
6 Behold, I will stand before thee there upon the rock in Horeb; and thou shalt smite the rock, and there shall come water out of it, that the people may drink. And Moses did so in the sight of the elders of Israel.
7 And he called the name of the place Massah, and Meribah, because of the chiding of the children of Israel, and because they tempted the LORD, saying, Is the LORD among us, or not?

The Lord provided both food and water for the children of Israel while they were en route to the Promised Land and he did so in miraculous ways. Instead of giving thanks and maintaining a humble attitude toward the Lord, this faithless generation continued to ask, "Is the Lord among us, or not?" They continuously looked back to their previous existence in Egypt, and longed to return to it for security rather than rely on the arm of the Lord. This situation has relevance both on the individual level and for Israel as the chosen people of the Lord. Individually, we each have to learn to break out of our comfort zones, and free ourselves from the habits and attitudes that keep us bound by the arm of flesh. We must learn to rely on the pure promptings of the Lord and to act upon them. When enough of God's children are able to make this transition to where they rely on the arm of God rather than the arm of flesh, they begin as a whole to become a society based on faith and truth rather than worldly comfort and false tradition. The manna from Heaven and the water from the rock of Horeb are both symbolic of our dependence on the Lord for guidance and direction. This dependence is summarized by the Lord in Deuteronomy.

Deuteronomy 8:1-3

1 ALL the commandments which I command thee this day shall ye observe to do, that ye may live, and multiply, and go in and possess the land which the LORD sware unto your fathers.
2 And thou shalt remember all the way which the LORD thy God led thee these forty years in the wilderness, to humble thee, and to prove thee, to know what was in thine heart, whether thou wouldest keep his commandments, or no.
3 And he humbled thee, and suffered thee to hunger, and fed thee with manna, which thou knewest not, neither did thy fathers know; that he might make thee know that man doth not live by bread only, but by every word that proceedeth out of the mouth of the LORD doth man live.

The clear link is established between manna and revelation. In Exodus 20, the Lord reveals the Ten Commandments, although because of the wickedness of the children of Israel in constructing a Golden Calf to worship, the first set of tablets containing the Ten Commandments is destroyed.

Exodus 32:1-6

1 AND when the people saw that Moses delayed to come down out of the mount, the people gathered themselves together unto Aaron, and said unto him, Up, make us gods, which shall go before us; for as for this Moses, the man that brought us up out of the land of Egypt, we wot not what is become of him.
2 And Aaron said unto them, Break off the golden earrings, which are in the ears of your wives, of your sons, and of your daughters, and bring them unto me.
3 And all the people brake off the golden earrings which were in their ears, and brought them unto Aaron.
4 And he received them at their hand, and fashioned it with a graving tool, after he had made it a molten calf: and they said, These be thy gods, O Israel, which brought thee up out of the land of Egypt.
5 And when Aaron saw it, he built an altar before it; and Aaron made proclamation, and said, To morrow is a feast to the LORD.
6 And they rose up early on the morrow, and offered burnt offerings, and brought peace offerings; and the people sat down to eat and to drink, and rose up to play.

This turning back to worship idols, as was common among the Egyptians, suggests that many who encounter and embrace modern Zion will also have the tendency to turn back to their old ways and practices. They will prefer the falsehood of their former religion to the reality of true religion. The thought of a living God can be a scary concept. For, such a God is able to perceive our allegiance.

Exodus 32:7-10

7 And the LORD said unto Moses, Go, get thee down; for thy people, which thou broughtest out of the land of Egypt, have corrupted themselves:
8 They have turned aside quickly out of the way which I commanded them: they have made them a molten calf, and have worshipped it, and have sacrificed thereunto, and said, These be thy gods, O Israel, which have brought thee up out of the land of Egypt.
9 And the LORD said unto Moses, I have seen this people, and, behold, it is a stiffnecked people:
10 Now therefore let me alone, that my wrath may wax hot against them, and that I may consume them: and I will make of thee a great nation.

MOSES AND THE EXODUS

Moses pleads with God to spare the Israelites—to be patient with them. The golden calf is destroyed, and the main group of rebels that participated in this incident was destroyed. Eventually, Moses makes a new set of tablets and goes a second time to the mountain top to have the Lord again write the Ten Commandments thereon. For the rest of the time that the children of Israel were traveling in the wilderness, they are tried and tested of the Lord to see if they will keep these commandments. They are humbled and taught to live by "every word that proceedeth out of the mouth of the Lord." The symbols of food and water, as they relate to revelation from God, are repeated in the story of Moses as well.

The Lord also has Moses build a tabernacle for the Lord, which is basically a sacred habitation in which the Lord could come and dwell. Chapters 25 through 31 explain about the establishment of the Tabernacle of the Lord. It was in a sense a mobile temple, and the Lord assigned Aaron and his brethren from the tribe of Levi to administer the rites and ordinances pertaining to this holy structure. The Ark of the Covenant was constructed and placed in the Tabernacle. In the Ark of the Covenant were placed the tablets with the Ten Commandments given to Moses on the mount. The pattern for the construction, maintenance and function of the tabernacle and its various inner structures were also given to Moses through revelation. When the children of Israel were on the move, the Levite priests assigned to care for the Tabernacle were responsible for transporting the structure until the Lord indicated a new place for them to settle temporarily. At that time the Tabernacle would be set up again.

The Fearful Generation

The adult generation that came forth out of Egypt through the parting of the Red Sea did not immediately begin their wandering in the wilderness. The apparent intention of the Lord and Moses was to take them directly into the Land of Promise. Therefore, Moses leads them straight to the borders of the land of Canaan and promises to drive out the inhabitants of the land before them.

> Exodus 33:1-3
>
> 1 AND the LORD said unto Moses, Depart, and go up hence, thou and the people which thou hast brought up out of the land of Egypt, unto the land which I sware unto Abraham, to Isaac, and to Jacob, saying, Unto thy seed will I give it:
> 2 And I will send an angel before thee; and I will drive out the Canaanite, the Amorite, and the Hittite, and the Perizzite, the Hivite, and the Jebusite:
> 3 Unto a land flowing with milk and honey: for I will not go up in the midst of thee; for thou art a stiffnecked people: lest I consume thee in the way.

Verse three above is important to note. Here we learn that while the Lord is willing to go before the Israelites and drive their enemies out before them, he lets them know that because of their stiffneckedness, he will not dwell among them. I wish to emphasize that apparently the original intention of the Lord was to do just that—dwell among them! Had they been faithful and believing, the Lord might have dwelt in their midst. Had they not murmured and desired to return to Egypt, they would have known him personally. Had they not tempted the Lord with idolatry in worshiping the work of their own hands, then he might have actually revealed himself unto them. Instead, such a privilege is apparently reserved only for Moses, and later Joshua, in the confines of the Tabernacle.

Exodus 33:7-11

7 And Moses took the tabernacle, and pitched it without the camp, afar off from the camp, and called it the Tabernacle of the congregation. And it came to pass, that every one which sought the LORD went out unto the tabernacle of the congregation, which was without the camp.
8 And it came to pass, when Moses went out unto the tabernacle, that all the people rose up, and stood every man at his tent door, and looked after Moses, until he was gone into the tabernacle.
9 And it came to pass, as Moses entered into the tabernacle, the cloudy pillar descended, and stood at the door of the tabernacle, and the Lord talked with Moses.
10 And all the people saw the cloudy pillar stand at the tabernacle door: and all the people rose up and worshipped, every man in his tent door.
11 And the LORD spake unto Moses face to face, as a man speaketh unto his friend. And he turned again into the camp: but his servant Joshua, the son of Nun, a young man, departed not out of the tabernacle.

When the children of Israel arrived at the borders of the Promised Land, Moses sent twelve men, one from each of the Twelve Tribes of Israel, to spy out the land and return and give a report of their findings. Ten of these twelve spies brought back an evil report and expressed their fear of the people in the Land of Canaan. Only two gave a good report, and these two were Caleb and Joshua. (Note: Joshua was originally called Oshea).

Number 13:1-16

1 AND the LORD spake unto Moses, saying,
2 Send thou men, that they may search the land of Canaan, which I give unto the children of Israel: of every tribe of their fathers shall ye send a man, every one a ruler among them.
3 And Moses by the commandment of the LORD sent them from the wilderness of Paran: all those men were heads of the children of Israel.
4 And these were their names: of the tribe of Reuben, Shammua the son of Zaccur.
5 Of the tribe of Simeon, Shaphat the son of Hori.
6 Of the tribe of Judah, Caleb the son of Jephunneh.
7 Of the tribe of Issachar, Igal the son of Joseph.
8 Of the tribe of Ephraim, Oshea the son of Nun. [i.e. Joshua]
9 Of the tribe of Benjamin, Palti the son of Raphu.
10 Of the tribe of Zebulun, Gaddiel the son of Sodi.
11 Of the tribe of Joseph, namely, of the tribe of Manasseh, Gaddi the son of Susi.
12 Of the tribe of Dan, Ammiel the son of Gemalli.
13 Of the tribe of Asher, Sethur the son of Michael.
14 Of the tribe of Naphtali, Nahbi the son of Vophsi.
15 Of the tribe of Gad, Geuel the son of Machi.
16 These are the names of the men which Moses sent to spy out the land. And Moses called Oshea the son of Nun Jehoshua.

When we consider those that were chosen to go, the tribe of Levi was not represented in that group. Because of their duties and responsibilities with respect to the maintenance and function of the Tabernacle, and their performance of ordinances and sacrifices, they were apparently removed from the general organization of the Twelve Tribes of Israel. In their place, we see from the above passage that Joseph's two sons, Ephraim and Manasseh, were each represented as a separate tribe. The Tribe of Joseph, as predicted by Jacob, became two tribes, while the tribe of Levi was removed from the count and reserved for a special priesthood assignment. Let us now see the difference between the reports given by the men that went to spy out the land.

Numbers 13:26-33
26 And they went and came to Moses, and to Aaron, and to all the congregation of the children of Israel, unto the wilderness of Paran, to Kadesh; and brought back word unto them, and unto all the congregation, and shewed them the fruit of the land.
27 And they told him, and said, We came unto the land whither thou sentest us, and surely it floweth with milk and honey; and this is the fruit of it.
28 Nevertheless the people be strong that dwell in the land, and the cities are walled, and very great: and moreover we saw the children of Anak there.
29 The Amalekites dwell in the land of the south: and the Hittites, and the Jebusites, and the Amorites, dwell in the mountains: and the Canaanites dwell by the sea, and by the coast of Jordan.
30 And Caleb stilled the people before Moses, and said, Let us go up at once, and possess it; for we are well able to overcome it.
31 But the men that went up with him said, We be not able to go up against the people; for they are stronger than we.
32 And they brought up an evil report of the land which they had searched unto the children of Israel, saying, The land, through which we have gone to search it, is a land that eateth up the inhabitants thereof; and all the people that we saw in it are men of a great stature.
33 And there we saw the giants, the sons of Anak, which come of the giants: and we were in our own sight as grasshoppers, and so we were in their sight.

We see that the majority of those making their report were fearful and desired not to go in to possess the land. They feared man more than God. While they recognize the quality of the land, they felt they would be defeated by the men of the land because of their physical size and number. Despite Caleb's confident plea that they should go in and possess the land, the fearful and faithless opinion of the majority of the spies soon spread throughout the rest of the people who heard their report.

Exodus 14:1-5
1 AND all the congregation lifted up their voice, and cried; and the people wept that night.
2 And all the children of Israel murmured against Moses and against Aaron: and the whole congregation said unto them, Would God that we had died in the land of Egypt! or would God we had died in this wilderness!
3 And wherefore hath the LORD brought us unto this land, to fall by the sword, that our wives and our children should be a prey? were it not better for us to return into Egypt?
4 And they said one to another, Let us make a captain, and let us return into Egypt.
5 Then Moses and Aaron fell on their faces before all the assembly of the congregation of the children of Israel.

This generation certainly lacked the faith necessary to enter the Promised Land, even after all the miracles they had witnessed during their exodus from Egypt and their journeying in the wilderness. They again threatened to rebel against Moses and Aaron, and to appoint another leader to take them back to Egypt. While this may seem amazing to us as we read this account, remember that this story is a type and that it represents the calling of the children of Israel from out of the nations where they have been scattered. It is a type that specifically represents the rejection of the Lord when he came to the world in the flesh. Had Israel accepted Jesus Christ, they could have possessed the Church and Kingdom of God on the earth. They could have had the Lord Jesus Christ to dwell among them, to teach them and train them in the ways of salvation. Instead, they feared men rather than God, and they clung to their worldly traditions to the point of rejecting Jesus to be their God. Despite the miracles performed by Jesus and the pleas of the Lord's servants, the Apostles, after his death and resurrection, the Lord finally allowed them to be given up to wander in the wilderness of apostasy and tribulation among the nations.

Let us return now to the story of Moses and see how this lack of faith causes the children of Israel to be sent to wander in the wilderness for 40 years. The following account shows that Caleb was not alone in his attempt to change the mind of the people.

Numbers 14:6-10
6 And Joshua the son of Nun, and Caleb the son of Jephunneh, which were of them that searched the land, rent their clothes:
7 And they spake unto all the company of the children of Israel, saying, The land, which we passed through to search it, is an exceeding good land.
8 If the LORD delight in us, then he will bring us into this land, and give it us; a land which floweth with milk and honey.
9 Only rebel not ye against the LORD, neither fear ye the people of the land; for they are bread for us: their defence is departed from them, and the LORD is with us: fear them not.
10 But all the congregation bade stone them with stones. And the glory of the LORD appeared in the tabernacle of the congregation before all the children of Israel.

Caleb is joined by Joshua, the son of Nun, in his attempt to turn the opinion of the people. They both make the point that despite the physical size of the people who currently possess the Land of Promise, and despite their number, the Lord is able to fight their battles for them. They remind them that if the Lord be with Israel, they need not fear them at all. He will drive them out before his chosen people. Instead of accepting their argument, the people "bade stone them with stones." Despite the logic of the arguments put forth by these two servants of the Lord, the people would rather kill them than trust in their God to guide them safely into the Land of Promise. What may not be obvious about this situation is the identity of the tribes to which Caleb and Joshua belonged. Recall that Joshua's name had been Oshea, until Moses gave him the name Joshua.

Numbers 13:6,8
6 Of the tribe of Judah, Caleb the son of Jephunneh.
8 Of the tribe of Ephraim, Oshea the son of Nun.

Caleb is of the tribe of Judah and Joshua is of the tribe of Ephraim. This is extremely significant. It shows that Judah and Ephraim were the only two tribes that were accepted of the Lord because of their faith in this situation. It also explains again the concept of the narrowing of the tribes of Israel from the original twelve to just two families, Judah and Ephraim. The only exception to this concept is the tribe of the Levites, whose role in the last days will no doubt be clarified when the Lord brings again Zion. We saw the two families of Judah and Ephraim referred to in the books of Isaiah, Jeremiah and Ezekiel, and I maintain that Caleb and Joshua are again types of that which will ultimately occur in these latter times. Zion will be restored to the earth once more, and Ephraim and Judah eventually go in and possess it—but only after many years of wandering in the wilderness of confusion and falsehood.

Wandering in the Wilderness

From our study of the Book of Isaiah, we learned that "wandering in the wilderness" was a symbolic type indicating a period of time when prophets are not found on the earth. The second phase of the story of Moses reiterates the same thing we saw in the first phase of his life. In this case, however, the period of Spiritual Famine is represented by their wandering in the wilderness for forty years, rather than through Moses' sojourn with the Midianites and the bondage to Pharaoh.

Numbers 14:22-23

22 Because all those men which have seen my glory, and my miracles, which I did in Egypt and in the wilderness, and have tempted me now these ten times, and have not hearkened to my voice;
23 Surely they shall not see the land which I sware unto their fathers, neither shall any of them that provoked me see it:

Because of their lack of faith, the Lord decrees that none of the adults living in Israel will be allowed to enter into the Promised Land. The exceptions to this decree are Caleb and Joshua, who are promised that they will live to enter into the land of Canaan because of their faithfulness and their trust in the arm of God.

Numbers 14:26-39

26 And the LORD spake unto Moses and unto Aaron, saying,
27 How long shall I bear with this evil congregation, which murmur against me? I have heard the murmurings of the children of Israel, which they murmur against me.
28 Say unto them, As truly as I live, saith the LORD, as ye have spoken in mine ears, so will I do to you:
29 Your carcases shall fall in this wilderness; and all that were numbered of you, according to your whole number, from twenty years old and upward, which have murmured against me,
30 Doubtless ye shall not come into the land, concerning which I sware to make you dwell therein, save Caleb the son of Jephunneh, and Joshua the son of Nun.
31 But your little ones, which ye said should be a prey, them will I bring in, and they shall know the land which ye have despised.
32 But as for you, your carcases, they shall fall in this wilderness.
33 And your children shall wander in the wilderness forty years, and bear your whoredoms, until your carcases be wasted in the wilderness.
34 After the number of the days in which ye searched the land, even forty days, each day for a year, shall ye bear your iniquities, even forty years, and ye shall know my breach of promise.
35 I the LORD have said, I will surely do it unto all this evil congregation, that are gathered together against me: in this wilderness they shall be consumed, and there they shall die.
36 And the men, which Moses sent to search the land, who returned, and made all the congregation to murmur against him, by bringing up a slander upon the land,
37 Even those men that did bring up the evil report upon the land, died by the plague before the LORD.

> 38 But Joshua the son of Nun, and Caleb the son of Jephunneh, which were of the men that went to search the land, lived still.
> 39 And Moses told these sayings unto all the children of Israel: and the people mourned greatly.

This story is a symbolic representation of the unbelief of God's chosen people, the Jews, at the time of Christ's mortal ministry. Because they rejected Jesus Christ, the children of Israel were forced to endure a wilderness of another sort—the Spiritual Famine of hearing the words of the Lord. The story of Moses is telling us this same message again. The 40 years of wandering in the wilderness represents the period of apostasy spoken of by all the other prophets we have heretofore analyzed. While Moses is still with the children of Israel during this period, he is nonetheless helpless in changing the decree of the Lord against them. Hence, the Lord is not with them as before—at least with this faithless generation.

> **Numbers 14:40-43**
> 40 And they rose up early in the morning, and gat them up into the top of the mountain, saying, Lo, we be here, and will go up unto the place which the LORD hath promised: for we have sinned.
> 41 And Moses said, Wherefore now do ye transgress the commandment of the LORD? but it shall not prosper.
> 42 Go not up, for the LORD is not among you; that ye be not smitten before your enemies.
> 43 For the Amalekites and the Canaanites are there before you, and ye shall fall by the sword: because ye are turned away from the LORD, therefore the LORD will not be with you.

This 40-year period of wandering through the wilderness caused by the faithless generation of the children of Israel is representative of the longer period of Spiritual Famine that began shortly after the death of the Lord's Apostles and other servants, and shortly after the resurrection of Jesus Christ. The Great Spiritual Famine was also brought on by the wickedness of the generation who rejected Christ and his prophets. From that time forth, the inhabitants of the earth must subsist on the words of the prophets as contained in the Old and New Testaments. Except for this "manna," the Lord is nowhere to be found, and his prophets are withdrawn out of the camp. The children of Israel were left to wander to and fro in the earth seeking the word of God but not finding it (Amos 8:11).

Two separate accounts are contained in the Bible where Moses smites a rock with his rod, and water gushes out to provide moisture for the famished Israelites during their travels in the wilderness. The first is mentioned in Exodus 17, where Moses smites the rock at Horeb, and the second in Numbers 20, where Moses smites the rock at Meribah.

> **Exodus 17:5-6**
> 5 And the LORD said unto Moses, Go on before the people, and take with thee of the elders of Israel; and thy rod, wherewith thou smotest the river, take in thine hand, and go.
> 6 Behold, I will stand before thee there upon the rock in Horeb; and thou shalt smite the rock, and there shall come water out of it, that the people may drink. And Moses did so in the sight of the elders of Israel.

In this situation, Moses is humble. He asked the Lord what to do, and the Lord gave him direction through revelation indicating how to respond to the chiding of the people. This miracle occured on the way to the Promised Land before the people refused to go in and posses it. The second miracle occurred after the children of Israel were sent to wander in the wilderness for forty years.

> **Numbers 20:1-5**
> 1 THEN came the children of Israel, even the whole congregation, into the desert of Zin in the first month: and the people abode in Kadesh; and Miriam died there, and was buried there.
> 2 And there was no water for the congregation: and they gathered themselves together against Moses and against Aaron.
> 3 And the people chode with Moses, and spake, saying, Would God that we had died when our brethren died before the LORD!
> 4 And why have ye brought up the congregation of the LORD into this wilderness, that we and our cattle should die there?
> 5 And wherefore have ye made us to come up out of Egypt, to bring us in unto this evil place? it is no place of seed, or of figs, or of vines, or of pomegranates; neither is there any water to drink.

We see a similar situation as before. The children of Israel were thirsty and began to complain against Moses and Aaron. They again asked why the Lord had led them into the wilderness and not provided them with water to drink. We will see that while the Lord again commanded Moses to provide them water from a rock, this time Moses did so in a way that displeases the Lord.

> **Numbers 20:7-12**
> 7 And the LORD spake unto Moses, saying,
> 8 Take the rod, and gather thou the assembly together, thou, and Aaron thy brother, and speak ye unto the rock before their eyes; and it shall give forth his water, and thou shalt bring forth to them water out of the rock: so thou shalt give the congregation and their beasts drink.
> 9 And Moses took the rod from before the LORD, as he commanded him.
> 10 And Moses and Aaron gathered the congregation together before the rock, and he said unto them, Hear now, ye rebels; must we fetch you water out of this rock?
> 11 And Moses lifted up his hand, and with his rod he smote the rock twice: and the water came out abundantly, and the congregation drank, and their beasts also.
> 12 And the LORD spake unto Moses and Aaron, Because ye believed me not, to sanctify me in the eyes of the children of Israel, therefore ye shall not bring this congregation into the land which I have given them.

The mistake made by Moses and Aaron in the second event is what they said: "Must we fetch you water out of this rock?" instead of "Must the Lord fetch you water out of this rock?" They did not give credit to the Lord for performing the miracle and bringing forth the water from the rock. Instead, they acted as if they were the ones that were doing it, and this displeased the Lord to the point that he declared that neither Moses nor Aaron would be allowed to go in and possess the Land of Promise. It may seem like a harsh judgment, especially on Moses who had been so faithful. In both cases, the smiting of the rock and the gushing forth of the water is symbolic of the need for us to depend on the revelations and guidance from Jesus Christ. This same vivid image occurred when the Roman soldier smote the Lord Jesus Christ in his side with a spear while he hung on the cross (John 19:34). From the wound gushed forth water mixed with blood. Moses' action in smiting the rock at Horeb and later at Moribah suggests our dependence on revelation from the True Rock, Jesus Christ. However, Moses' taking of the glory unto himself is significant.

THE LATTER RAIN

The fact that this mistake in judgment made by Moses occurred during the 40-year banishment period is symbolic of the ministers who attempt to perform miracles in the name of the Lord without the proper authority, and without giving the glory to the Lord. Moses does not become a false priest in this situation, but his action serves as a type pointing to the false priests of the apostasy period. They take the honor unto themselves to get gain and glory of the world. This second miracle shows that while the children of Israel still need the water and nourishment from the Lord during the period of the Great Famine, they are receiving it from the false shepherds that take the honor to themselves as they interpret the word of God for their flock. While this meager nourishment keeps their hope in Christ alive, they continue to thirst for revelation, and hunger for sound doctrine.

Numbers 21:4-5

4 And they journeyed from mount Hor by the way of the Red sea, to compass the land of Edom: and the soul of the people was much discouraged because of the way.
5 And the people spake against God, and against Moses, Wherefore have ye brought us up out of Egypt to die in the wilderness? for there is no bread, neither is there any water; and our soul loatheth this light bread.

The manna from Heaven represents the meager diet provided by the words of the dead prophets during the period of the Great Famine. The people who wander through the wilderness of apostasy are forced to get nourishment and hope from the words contained in the Bible. They have no living prophets to interpret these words, or to give new direction and guidance as needed. While the scriptures in the Bible give them hope and encouragement, something is missing. The people want more. The answer to this dilemma is found in Jesus Christ. We are promised that if we truly seek him out, we will find him. Those that complain about the manna provided in the story of Moses are taught this same message in a dramatic fashion.

Numbers 21:6-9

6 And the LORD sent fiery serpents among the people, and they bit the people; and much people of Israel died.
7 Therefore the people came to Moses, and said, We have sinned, for we have spoken against the LORD, and against thee; pray unto the LORD, that he take away the serpents from us. And Moses prayed for the people.
8 And the LORD said unto Moses, Make thee a fiery serpent, and set it upon a pole: and it shall come to pass, that every one that is bitten, when he looketh upon it, shall live.
9 And Moses made a serpent of brass, and put it upon a pole, and it came to pass, that if a serpent had bitten any man, when he beheld the serpent of brass, he lived.

In this case, the fiery flying serpent placed on the staff represents the Lord Jesus Christ, who was placed on the cross and died as a sacrifice for the sins of all humanity. Those of us who look to him for a remission of our sins are made eligible for his forgiveness and mercy. We are spiritually healed. Those that believe not receive not of his intercession for sins, and become spiritually dead unto him. Satan is often referred to as a serpent with a negative connotation. We now see that the Lord Jesus Christ is also referred to as a serpent, but with a good connotation. This symbol of the serpent on the staff has been adopted by the medical profession symbolizing the power to heal. Isaiah also refers to the Savior as a serpent in this good sense.

> **Isaiah 14:29-30**
> 29 Rejoice not thou, whole Palestina, because the rod of him that smote thee is broken: for out of the serpent's root shall come forth a cockatrice, and his fruit shall be a fiery flying serpent.
> 30 And the firstborn of the poor shall feed, and the needy shall lie down in safety: and I will kill thy root with famine, and he shall slay thy remnant.

Here, the Prophet Isaiah is telling those that rejoiced when the Lord withdrew his presence from the earth that their rejoicing is but a temporary thing. The Lord Jesus Christ, the fiery flying serpent, will again visit the earth and restore Zion. When Jesus appears to prophets again in these last days, "the firstborn of the poor shall feed, and the needy shall lie down in safety." It will also mean the beginning of the end for Satan and his followers. Those that have taught falsehood will be vanquished by the power of the word of the Lord. The Lord will kill the root of the false ministers with famine and they will prosper no more.

Faithful Generation Finally Enters the Promised Land

As the last of the generation of faithless Israelites died off, the children of Israel again were brought to the borders of the Land of Promise. We know that Moses and Aaron would not be going into possess the land. Aaron has already died by this point in their journey, and now Moses takes the opportunity to counsel the rising generation as they prepare to go into the Land of Promise. One important counsel he gave them is to avoid the worship of idols and false gods.

> **Deuteronomy 4:21-24**
> 21 Furthermore the LORD was angry with me for your sakes, and sware that I should not go over Jordan, and that I should not go in unto that good land, which the LORD thy God giveth thee for an inheritance:
> 22 But I must die in this land, I must not go over Jordan: but ye shall go over, and possess that good land.
> 23 Take heed unto yourselves, lest ye forget the covenant of the LORD your God, which he made with you, and make you a graven image, or the likeness of any thing, which the LORD thy God hath forbidden thee.
> 24 For the LORD thy God is a consuming fire, even a jealous God.

Recall from Isaiah that the term "idol" not only means the worship of a statue or icon, but is also a symbolic type meaning anything man-made, as in a man-made church or any other organization that distracts one from the true Church and Kingdom of God. In giving this counsel, he is foreshadowing that eventually they will build unto themselves false doctrines and churches. Next, he tells them the consequence of this great evil against the Lord.

> **Deuteronomy 4:25-28**
> 25 When thou shalt beget children, and children's children, and ye shall have remained long in the land, and shall corrupt yourselves, and make a graven image, or the likeness of any thing, and shall do evil in the sight of the LORD thy God, to provoke him to anger:

> 26 I call heaven and earth to witness against you this day, that ye shall soon utterly perish from off the land whereunto ye go over Jordan to possess it; ye shall not prolong your days upon it, but shall utterly be destroyed.
> 27 And the LORD shall scatter you among the nations, and ye shall be left few in number among the heathen, whither the LORD shall lead you.
> 28 And there ye shall serve gods, the work of men's hands, wood and stone, which neither see, nor hear, nor eat, nor smell.

Our framework of symbols and types derived from our study of Isaiah helps us to understand the meaning of this prophecy given by Moses to the children of Israel. They will ultimately be driven and scattered, and removed from the Promised Land. They will be scattered among the nations and "shall worship gods, the work of men's hands." This refers to the false doctrines and incorrect philosophies of men that will fill the void created when the Lord withdraws his prophets and priesthood from the earth. The children of Israel will be scattered among the nations, and will be tangled up in these theories and tenants, not knowing where to find truth. This prophecy of Moses is specifically referring to the last days (meaning our day).

> **Deuteronomy 4:29-31**
> 29 But if from thence thou shalt seek the LORD thy God, thou shalt find him, if thou seek him with all thy heart and with all thy soul.
> 30 When thou art in tribulation, and all these things are come upon thee, even in the latter days, if thou turn to the LORD thy God, and shalt be obedient unto his voice;
> 31 (For the LORD thy God is a merciful God;) he will not forsake thee, neither destroy thee, nor forget the covenant of thy fathers which he sware unto them.

What is required to find the Lord? We must seek him with all our heart and with all our soul. Some are lost and do not even realize it. Others know they are lost and desire relief from their plight, but never appeal to the Lord directly. They seek comfort among the man-made solutions of the earth. But, these false organizations have not the power to save, nor satisfy. Only those who seek the Lord directly and call upon him in prayer will ultimately find him and his kingdom. He will guide them out from among the heathen through the promptings of his spirit, as if they were led by the hand.

But what manner of God do we seek? A man-made god is not real. "It cannot see, nor hear, nor eat, nor smell." What manner of God is the true and living God of Israel? He is a living being with all power. The Lord reminds the Israelites of this by asking them to consider the things he has done for them in bringing them up out of Egypt.

> **Deuteronomy 4:32-37**
> 32 For ask now of the days that are past, which were before thee, since the day that God created man upon the earth, and ask from the one side of heaven unto the other, whether there hath been any such thing as this great thing is, or hath been heard like it?
> 33 Did ever people hear the voice of God speaking out of the midst of the fire, as thou hast heard, and live?
> 34 Or hath God assayed to go and take him a nation from the midst of another nation, by temptations, by signs, and by wonders, and by war, and by a mighty hand, and by a stretched out arm, and by great terrors, according to all that the LORD your God did for you in Egypt before your eyes?

35 Unto thee it was shewed, that thou mightest know that the LORD he is God; there is none else beside him.
36 Out of heaven he made thee to hear his voice, that he might instruct thee: and upon earth he shewed thee his great fire; and thou heardest his words out of the midst of the fire.
37 And because he loved thy fathers, therefore he chose their seed after them, and brought thee out in his sight with his mighty power out of Egypt;

Therefore, I ask: what manner of God should we seek? One that can see and hear and eat and speak! He is tangible and real. He hears and answers prayers if we fear not his presence to be among us. Recall that the fear of the Lord's presence and the preference for Egypt and for the worship of idols are the only things that prevented the Lord from dwelling in the midst of Israel. If we seek him out today, we are promised that he will make himself known unto us in a way that will be sure and unmistakable.

Two situations prevent us from seeking him more fervently. First, we fear God because we are acutely aware of our unworthiness before him. We know the commandments and we do not keep them, and we are bound up in sin and lack the faith in his mercy. Second, like the Israelites of old, we prefer to worship according to our man-made doctrines which requires much less of us. We are so used to the routine that we do not want to give it up, even when deep down inside we know something is missing. It is much safer to leave the real God trapped in the pages of the Bible that describe his deeds and his works performed among the ancient patriarchs.

Just as in times past, it is the believing and faithful that will go in and posses the Land of Promise, or Zion. As we leave off our discussion of Moses, as contained in the Old Testament, we see that the mantle of authority is passed from Moses to Joshua, and it is Joshua that ultimately leads the children of Israel across the River Jordan into the land of Canaan. Caleb also goes in, but Joshua is the one that is chosen to lead.

Number 27:15-23

15 And Moses spake unto the LORD, saying,
16 Let the LORD, the God of the spirits of all flesh, set a man over the congregation,
17 Which may go out before them, and which may go in before them, and which may lead them out, and which may bring them in; that the congregation of the LORD be not as sheep which have no shepherd.
18 And the LORD said unto Moses, Take thee Joshua the son of Nun, a man in whom is the spirit, and lay thine hand upon him;
19 And set him before Eleazar the priest, and before all the congregation; and give him a charge in their sight.
20 And thou shalt put some of thine honour upon him, that all the congregation of the children of Israel may be obedient.
21 And he shall stand before Eleazar the priest, who shall ask counsel for him after the judgment of Urim before the LORD: at his word shall they go out, and at his word they shall come in, both he, and all the children of Israel with him, even all the congregation.
22 And Moses did as the LORD commanded him: and he took Joshua, and set him before Eleazar the priest, and before all the congregation:
23 And he laid his hands upon him, and gave him a charge, as the LORD commanded by the hand of Moses.

THE LATTER RAIN

How did God handle the procession of authority from one generation to another in ancient times? He called men through prophecy, and through the laying on of hands. Joshua was not selected because of his education, his means, or his outward appearance. The Lord made sure that the children of Israel were aware that the mantle of authority that had rested on Moses all those years was now being passed on to Joshua. It was Joshua, not Caleb, who ultimately led the children of Israel into the Promised Land. Moses is allowed to view the land from a mountaintop near by, but does not go in himself.

> **Deuteronomy 3:27-28**
> 27 Get thee up into the top of Pisgah, and lift up thine eyes westward, and northward, and southward, and eastward, and behold it with thine eyes: for thou shalt not go over this Jordan.
> 28 But charge Joshua, and encourage him, and strengthen him: for he shall go over before this people, and he shall cause them to inherit the land which thou shalt see.

Joshua leading the children of Israel to possess the Promised Land as described in the Book of Joshua is also symbolic of what will occur in the last days. Joshua was of the tribe of Ephraim, while Caleb was of the Tribe of Judah. It will be through the Tribe of Ephraim, the son of Joseph, that the great and last dispensation will be ushered in. The period of the Latter Rain will come through a prophet called from the loins of Ephraim. We see that both the story of Joseph in Egypt and the story of Moses are really symbolic messages telling us of things that will transpire in these, the last days.

The meaning of these stories is clarified by our framework of symbols and types that we gleaned from the Book of Isaiah. The main message that we should take away from both of these stories is that Jesus is the Christ. He is the predicted Savior and Messiah. There is no other but him. To make this point clear, we will now use the stories of Joseph and Moses as a means of transition into the New Testament. We will soon learn that the New Testament prophets understood this symbolism very well, and used it in their preaching as they attempted to convince their brethren of the divine calling of Jesus Christ as the Lord and Savior of the world. Let us now see how the apostles and disciples of the New Testament use the stories of Joseph and Moses as they preach of Christ.

CHAPTER ELEVEN

The New Testament

Before we begin to analyze any specific scriptures contained in the New Testament, I would first like to make some general comments about this amazing book. First of all, the New Testament was a new book of scripture added to the Old Testament. The books and epistles of the New Testament were assembled into a holy book several hundred years after the events occurred that are described therein. At the time that Christ was on the earth teaching people, ordaining apostles, and performing numerous miracles, there was no New Testament at all. When Christ instructed the learned elders of the Jews in the Temple of Jerusalem when he was twelve years old, he was reading to them scriptures contained in the Old Testament only. The events and situations mentioned in the New Testament were happening in real time. They were not fables or old wives' tales, but actual events. Only much later were these stories compiled into a document that became known as the New Testament.

While this may seem like a simple and perhaps obvious observation, it is not. Many people of today look at prophets and apostles, miracles and revelations, as things that happened in the past. They existed anciently, but not in our time. Sure, many people have had events in their lives such as the birth of a child after a long period of infertility, or the recovery of a loved one whom the doctors had expected to die. Such events are often referred to as miracles and attributed to the hand of the Lord in the lives of the individuals affected. These singular episodes, while important and meaningful, are not of the same magnitude as those described in the New Testament: the Lord appearing to the apostles after his resurrection, or Peter being led out of prison by an angel, or ancient prophets appearing to current priesthood holders as occurred on the Mount of Transfiguration. A difference exists between the Church as described in the New Testament and the countless Christian churches of today.

I recently read a book that was written by a Christian man who makes many sound points about the relationships between men and women. While I learned much from the book which I can apply to life, another issue is relevant to our current subject. The author would often refer to "the church" as if there were just one big Christian church. He did this several times throughout the text of his book. As I continued to encounter his references to "the church" several more times in his book, I ultimately found myself asking the question, "What church are you referring to?" There is no one Christian church. In fact, there are literally hundreds of them, each with a different interpretation of the doctrines contained in the Bible. He should have said instead "Christian churches of today" or "Christians" instead of "the church."

Rather than focus on the differences between the many different Christian denominations, I would prefer to look at what they all appear to have in common. The dominant similarity would be the belief in Jesus Christ as Savior of the world, and the basic idea being that Jesus Christ took upon him the sins of all the inhabitants that have or ever will live on the earth. Those that believe in him and repent of their sins and are baptized are thereby granted relief from the burden of their sins committed during mortality—given they continue to repent as needed. Christ thereby atones for their sins such that they are no longer held responsible for them. This doctrine is the main tenant of Christianity as a whole. It is the definitive concept that separates Christianity from other religions and non-Christian sects.

All other Christian doctrines and concepts are widely debated and vary greatly from one denomination to another. Who can and should hold the priesthood? How should baptism be performed (immersion versus sprinkling, as an infant or as a child or as an adult)? Grace versus works—which is more important in terms of obtaining one's salvation? All these ideas vary across the broad spectrum of beliefs that fall under the general category of religions known as "Christianity." My hope is that our analysis of the scriptures contained in the New Testament will do much to clarify the key doctrinal issues that should be present and looked for in the true Church of God.

A final observation about the New Testament concerns its source. It was written by the Apostles of the Lord Jesus Christ. We have already mentioned that the books of the New Testament were written after the death and resurrection of Jesus Christ. It is significant to note that Jesus Christ and his Apostles were Jews. Some might be tempted to say that the New Testament is the Stick of Joseph spoken of in Ezekiel 37, since it describes the conversion of Gentiles by the preaching of Paul and others. However, only after Peter received the revelation described in the Book of Acts was the Gospel of Jesus Christ extended to the Gentiles, or non-Jews. No mention is made of any Gentile converts being called as apostles within the time span covered by the New Testament writers. No books or epistles contained in the New Testament are attributed to converted Gentile writers. This is not to say that Gentiles could not have ultimately received callings in the Church, but it is never mentioned in the New Testament. The authors of the New Testament were all Jews, or as we have noted previously "of the tribe of Judah." The entire Bible, both Old Testament and New Testament, is a record that was preserved by and comes to us today by way of the Jews. I make this observation to point out the dependence of modern-day Christianity on ancient

Judaism. Furthermore, this interdependence between Judaism and Christianity seems to be an issue that must ultimately be resolved or explained by someone who really knows the answer, namely the Lord himself.

Having made these general observations, let us now begin to analyze various scriptures in the New Testament and see how they build the concepts derived from the Book of Isaiah. Since I noted that the definitive doctrine of modern Christianity pertains to the mission of the Lord Jesus Christ, let us first see how the New Testament prophets attempt to make a bridge from the Old Testament doctrines to that of Jesus Christ, the Savior and Redeemer.

Joseph and Moses Are Symbolic Types of Jesus Christ

In Acts, we find an interesting example of this type of transition. The narrative found in Acts, Chapter 7, is a great place to start our discussion of the New Testament scriptures. Acts 7 is an account of the preaching given by Stephen to the leaders of the Jews, which led to his being cast out of the city and stoned to death. The story is being told by Luke, author of the Book of Acts. This story reinforces our previous discussions concerning the figure of Joseph and the figure of Moses. Stephen is telling the leaders of the Jews that the story of Joseph and Moses are both types of something far greater than the actual stories that their lives represent. Listen to what Stephen tells the Jews about Joseph:

Acts 7:9-18
9 And the patriarchs, moved with envy, sold Joseph into Egypt: but God was with him,
10 And delivered him out of all his afflictions, and gave him favour and wisdom in the sight of Pharaoh king of Egypt; and he made him governor over Egypt and all his house.
11 Now there came a dearth over all the land of Egypt and Chanaan, and great affliction: and our fathers found no sustenance.
12 But when Jacob heard that there was corn in Egypt, he sent out our fathers first.
13 And at the second time Joseph was made known to his brethren; and Joseph's kindred was made known unto Pharaoh.
14 Then sent Joseph, and called his father Jacob to him, and all his kindred, threescore and fifteen souls.
15 So Jacob went down into Egypt, and died, he, and our fathers,
16 And were carried over into Sychem, and laid in the sepulchre that Abraham bought for a sum of money of the sons of Emmor the father of Sychem.
17 But when the time of the promise drew nigh, which God had sworn to Abraham, the people grew and multiplied in Egypt,
18 Till another king arose, which knew not Joseph.

Why does Stephen feel that this story is important? What is he trying to tell the leaders of the Jews, and why does this message anger Stephen's audience to the point of stoning him to death? He clearly reinforces types that we have already analyzed. We see that Joseph was separated from his brethren, and that he was able to rise to power in Egypt, and to thereby lay away food in storage having known of the impending "famine" through the interpretation of Pharaoh's dream. Joseph represents the "Savior" of his brethren, and is a type of Jesus Christ. Joseph also represents the whole tribe of Joseph or Ephraim, meaning the Northern Kingdom that was scattered years before. In this sense, he also represents the

Gentiles too. Stephen's story to the Jews points to the captivity in Egypt. He shows how it went okay at first, and the children of Egypt were blessed during the famine period and began to prosper. Eventually, however, a new pharaoh arises who "knew not Joseph."

> Acts 7:19-36
>
> 19 The same dealt subtilly with our kindred, and evil entreated our fathers, so that they cast out their young children, to the end they might not live.
> 20 In which time Moses was born, and was exceeding fair, and nourished up in his father's house three months:
> 21 And when he was cast out, Pharaoh's daughter took him up, and nourished him for her own son.
> 22 And Moses was learned in all the wisdom of the Egyptians, and was mighty in words and in deeds.
> 23 And when he was full forty years old, it came into his heart to visit his brethren the children of Israel.
> 24 And seeing one of them suffer wrong, he defended him, and avenged him that was oppressed, and smote the Egyptian:
> 25 For he supposed his brethren would have understood how that God by his hand would deliver them: but they understood not.
> 26 And the next day he shewed himself unto them as they strove, and would have set them at one again, saying, Sirs, ye are brethren; why do ye wrong one to another?
> 27 But he that did his neighbour wrong thrust him away, saying, Who made thee a ruler and a judge over us?
> 28 Wilt thou kill me, as thou diddest the Egyptian yesterday?
> 29 Then fled Moses at this saying, and was a stranger in the land of Madian, where he begat two sons.
> 30 And when forty years were expired, there appeared to him in the wilderness of mount Sina an angel of the Lord in a flame of fire in a bush.
> 31 When Moses saw it, he wondered at the sight: and as he drew near to behold it, the voice of the Lord came unto him,
> 32 Saying, I am the God of thy fathers, the God of Abraham, and the God of Isaac, and the God of Jacob. Then Moses trembled, and durst not behold.
> 33 Then said the Lord to him, Put off thy shoes from thy feet: for the place where thou standest is holy ground.
> 34 I have seen, I have seen the affliction of my people which is in Egypt, and I have heard their groaning, and am come down to deliver them. And now come, I will send thee into Egypt.
> 35 This Moses whom they refused, saying, Who made thee a ruler and a judge? the same did God send to be a ruler and a deliverer by the hand of the angel which appeared to him in the bush.
> 36 He brought them out, after that he had shewed wonders and signs in the land of Egypt, and in the Red sea, and in the wilderness forty years.

Stephen is using the life of a former prophet, in this case Moses, to demonstrate the mission of Jesus Christ. He is pointing out the similarity between the life of Moses and the life of Christ. Both were born at a time when there was a threat of death to the young males of the children of Israel. Both showed forth many mighty miracles and signs. Both Moses and Jesus Christ were rejected by their own brethren, but ultimately end up saving them from evil and tyranny. If we accept this comparison, Moses being a symbolic type of Jesus Christ, we must ask how it applies to our day and age. Let us look for the answers to this question in the following verses:

Acts 7:37-43

37 This is that Moses, which said unto the children of Israel, A prophet shall the Lord your God raise up unto you of your brethren, like unto me; him shall ye hear.
38 This is he, that was in the church in the wilderness with the angel which spake to him in the mount Sina, and with our fathers: who received the lively oracles to give unto us:
39 To whom our fathers would not obey, but thrust him from them, and in their hearts turned back again into Egypt,
40 Saying unto Aaron, Make us gods to go before us: for as for this Moses, which brought us out of the land of Egypt, we wot not what is become of him.
41 And they made a calf in those days, and offered sacrifice unto the idol, and rejoiced in the works of their own hands.
42 Then God turned, and gave them up to worship the host of heaven; as it is written in the book of the prophets, O ye house of Israel, have ye offered to me slain beasts and sacrifices by the space of forty years in the wilderness?
43 Yea, ye took up the tabernacle of Moloch, and the star of your god Remphan, figures which ye made to worship them: and I will carry you away beyond Babylon.

Here we see that Moses brings salvation to the children of Israel and leads them out of bondage and captivity. Instead of embracing the Gospel, they reject it and turn to their old ways. "As for this Moses, which brought us out of the land of Egypt, we wot not what is become of him." Could we not say the same thing today about Jesus Christ? As for Jesus Christ, we know not what is become of him? Furthermore, in verse 42, we see something we have seen before in the Old Testament scriptures: "Then God turned, and gave them up to worship the host of heaven." God gave them up. He left them and forsook them. Not because he desired to do so, but because they rejected him and his prophets. Finally, we see what really angers the Jews in Stephen's sermon. He links the wicked Israelites of the past with the current leaders of the Jews who he is now addressing in real life. And he does not spare their feelings.

Acts 7:51-60

51 Ye stiffnecked and uncircumcised in heart and ears, ye do always resist the Holy Ghost: as your fathers did, so do ye.
52 Which of the prophets have not your fathers persecuted? and they have slain them which shewed before of the coming of the Just One; of whom ye have been now the betrayers and murderers:
53 Who have received the law by the disposition of angels, and have not kept it.
54 When they heard these things, they were cut to the heart, and they gnashed on him with their teeth.
55 But he, being full of the Holy Ghost, looked up stedfastly into heaven, and saw the glory of God, and Jesus standing on the right hand of God,
56 And said, Behold, I see the heavens opened, and the Son of man standing on the right hand of God.
57 Then they cried out with a loud voice, and stopped their ears, and ran upon him with one accord,
58 And cast him out of the city, and stoned him: and the witnesses laid down their clothes at a young man's feet, whose name was Saul.
59 And they stoned Stephen, calling upon God, and saying, Lord Jesus, receive my spirit.
60 And he kneeled down, and cried with a loud voice, Lord, lay not this sin to their charge. And when he had said this, he fell asleep.

Stephen first demonstrates to the leaders of the Jews that Joseph and Moses were both types of the Messiah. The doctrine of a Messiah was not new to the Jews. Neither was the idea of Moses and Joseph being types of the Messiah. Stephen was showing them that Jesus Christ met all of the criteria set forth by the Old Testament prophets, and that he indeed was the Savior. He was the Son of God, sent to save the children of men from their sins. Stephen gets in trouble because he shows to the leaders of the Jews that they are just like the faithless generation of Israelites of old who slew the prophets. "Which of the prophets have not your fathers persecuted? and they have slain them which shewed before of the coming of the Just One; of whom ye have been now the betrayers and murderers:" Stephen was showing them that they had just killed the chosen Lamb of God. This was too much for them to take, and they took him out from the city and stoned him to death.

Stephen understood the types and symbols of the Old Testament scriptures. He not only understood them, but he used them in his preaching to convince his listeners of the authority and divinity of Jesus Christ. Jesus was indeed the Savior. Some of the people hearing the preaching of the apostles and disciples of Jesus Christ readily accepted the truth, and were converted and baptized into the Church of God. Many became angry at the true doctrine, and resisted the Spirit of the Lord. Despite the logic and reason associated with the arguments put forth by Stephen, Peter, Paul and others, those that rejected their message of salvation often did so with anger and hatred. Others rejected the message with shame and sorrow, not wanting to give up those things they felt were more important than this new life as a Christian. In both cases, had they humbled themselves enough to pray about it, they might have received clarification from the Spirit of God and been truly converted. Instead, they rejected it in favor of their current traditions, which they had become comfortable with. In our day, the truth could indeed come to us now, and we might reject it because we are too set in our ways and too proud to pray. Notice the reaction to Paul's preaching, given in Acts 26.

Acts 26:21-32
21 For these causes the Jews caught me in the temple, and went about to kill me.
22 Having therefore obtained help of God, I continue unto this day, witnessing both to small and great, saying none other things than those which the prophets and Moses did say should come:
23 That Christ should suffer, and that he should be the first that should rise from the dead, and should shew light unto the people, and to the Gentiles.
24 And as he thus spake for himself, Festus said with a loud voice, Paul, thou art beside thyself; much learning doth make thee mad.
25 But he said, I am not mad, most noble Festus; but speak forth the words of truth and soberness.
26 For the king knoweth of these things, before whom also I speak freely: for I am persuaded that none of these things are hidden from him; for this thing was not done in a corner.
27 King Agrippa, believest thou the prophets? I know that thou believest.
28 Then Agrippa said unto Paul, Almost thou persuadest me to be a Christian.
29 And Paul said, I would to God, that not only thou, but also all that hear me this day, were both almost, and altogether such as I am, except these bonds.

30 And when he had thus spoken, the king rose up, and the governor, and Bernice, and they that sat with them:
31 And when they were gone aside, they talked between themselves, saying, This man doeth nothing worthy of death or of bonds.
32 Then said Agrippa unto Festus, This man might have been set at liberty, if he had not appealed unto Caesar.

These verses, which are taken from the Book of Acts, emphasize the same point as before. In the above situation, Paul has King Agrippa nearly converted. In fact, King Agrippa himself admits he is close to conversion saying, "Almost thou persuadest me to be a Christian." What was it that had Agrippa almost converted? It was the fact that apparently King Agrippa was familiar with the prophets. He was well-studied in the scriptures of the Old Testament. Paul's arguments, which were well-founded in the Old Testament prophecies, had an amazing influence on the heart of King Agrippa. The only thing missing was prayer. While the king felt touched in his heart, he failed to consult with the Lord on the matter. He was, therefore, left to interpret things on his own, and was heavily swayed by the influence of his peers—and clearly it was not popular to embrace the Christian cause in those times.

Hebrews 3:1-19

1 Wherefore, holy brethren, partakers of the heavenly calling, consider the Apostle and High Priest of our profession, Christ Jesus;
2 Who was faithful to him that appointed him, as also Moses was faithful in all his house.
3 For this man was counted worthy of more glory than Moses, inasmuch as he who hath builded the house hath more honour than the house.
4 For every house is builded by some man; but he that built all things is God.
5 And Moses verily was faithful in all his house, as a servant, for a testimony of those things which were to be spoken after;
6 But Christ as a son over his own house; whose house are we, if we hold fast the confidence and the rejoicing of the hope firm unto the end.
7 Wherefore (as the Holy Ghost saith, To day if ye will hear his voice,
8 Harden not your hearts, as in the provocation, in the day of temptation in the wilderness:
9 When your fathers tempted me, proved me, and saw my works forty years.
10 Wherefore I was grieved with that generation, and said, They do alway err in their heart; and they have not known my ways.
11 So I sware in my wrath, They shall not enter into my rest.)
12 Take heed, brethren, lest there be in any of you an evil heart of unbelief, in departing from the living God.
13 But exhort one another daily, while it is called To day; lest any of you be hardened through the deceitfulness of sin.
14 For we are made partakers of Christ, if we hold the beginning of our confidence stedfast unto the end;
15 While it is said, To day if ye will hear his voice, harden not your hearts, as in the provocation.
16 For some, when they had heard, did provoke: howbeit not all that came out of Egypt by Moses.
17 But with whom was he grieved forty years? was it not with them that had sinned, whose carcases fell in the wilderness?
18 And to whom sware he that they should not enter into his rest, but to them that believed not?
19 So we see that they could not enter in because of unbelief.

THE LATTER RAIN

The Apostle Paul is addressing the Hebrews, or the Jews who had converted to Christ. He is talking to them, and reemphasizing the close comparison between Moses and Jesus. At the time that Paul sent this epistle to the Hebrews, Moses was highly revered by the Jews. The point Paul, Stephen and others make repeatedly in the New Testament is that it is easy to revere a dead prophet, but much more difficult to recognize a living prophet who comes to us in our day.

According to Paul, Jesus Christ is much greater than Moses, and should be revered accordingly. Paul is reminding the Hebrews that have accepted Christ that they must not harden their hearts and fall away from their faith by turning back to their former ways and practices, lest they become like unto the Israelites of old, who rejected Moses' counsel and were obliged to wander in the wilderness for forty years. They could have entered into the Promised Land, but by rejecting the Lord, they chose desolation and sorrow instead.

Paul, in the Epistle to the Hebrews, is warning the members of the Church of Christ that they must be vigilant and hold fast to the faith, otherwise they will experience a similar fate as the Israelites of old—that of wandering in the "wilderness." Applying our keys derived from Isaiah, we recall that references to "wilderness," "desolation," or "famine" are symbolic terms to describe periods when direct revelation is not available on the earth. Accepting the truth when it comes into one's life requires a great deal of faith, since opposition will always be present to dissuade the children of men from accepting the truth.

Hebrews 11:23-28

23 By faith Moses, when he was born, was hid three months of his parents, because they saw he was a proper child; and they were not afraid of the king's commandment.
24 By faith Moses, when he was come to years, refused to be called the son of Pharaoh's daughter;
25 Choosing rather to suffer affliction with the people of God, than to enjoy the pleasures of sin for a season;
26 Esteeming the reproach of Christ greater riches than the treasures in Egypt: for he had respect unto the recompence of the reward.
27 By faith he forsook Egypt, not fearing the wrath of the king: for he endured, as seeing him who is invisible.
28 Through faith he kept the passover, and the sprinkling of blood, lest he that destroyed the firstborn should touch them.

Here we see that even Moses, who was so highly revered by the Jews living at the time of Christ and his disciples, had to make sacrifices and decisions based on faith. Yet, he conferred with the Lord directly and received the strength to overcome the obstacles he faced. He saw the wisdom of God as being greater even than the riches of Egypt which were at his disposal. If we apply the keys from Isaiah, his forsaking of Egypt would also represent the forsaking of the arm of flesh in favor of the arm of the Lord. His life is symbolic of our need to forsake the doctrines of men in favor of the true doctrine of Christ.

Jeremiah 23:7-8

7 Therefore, behold, the days come, saith the LORD, that they shall no more say, The LORD liveth, which brought up the children of Israel out of the land of Egypt;

8 But, The LORD liveth, which brought up and which led the seed of the house of Israel out of the north country, and from all countries whither I had driven them; and they shall dwell in their own land.

These first scriptural references from the New Testament carry on the themes from the Old Testament, using them to demonstrate the divinity and authority of Jesus Christ as the prophesied Savior and Redeemer of mankind. They demonstrate how clearly the Jews at the time of Christ relied on Moses as a model and example for their conduct and belief. In the last days, people will find it even more miraculous that Christ was able to lead his chosen people out from among the heathen nations of the world, than the fact that he led the children of Israel out of Egypt in ancient times.

This ancient event is in fact a type for what must occur in the last days. While the New Testament is a "second testimony" of Jesus Christ, the disciples who wrote the New Testament are constantly reminding their audiences of the things written in the Old Testament that point to or testify of Jesus Christ. Both the current facts in real time as well as the ancient prophecies in the Old Testament both testify of the divine nature of Jesus Christ. All things point to Christ. Just as the Jews in the time of Christ resisted the new Gospel that came to them, today we too might resist that which is new, and that which requires us to let go of our established habits and traditions of worship. The key to discernment is prayer.

Lineage of David as a Sign of Jesus Christ's Divinity

Joseph and Moses have another interesting thing in common. Both were representative of royalty. Joseph was the first-born of Rachael, the beloved wife of Jacob, who received the birthright when his elder half-brother Reuben lost the birthright through transgression. Despite being sold into Egypt by his brethren, he was still the birthright son of Jacob, and heir to the power and authority of Jacob as the patriarch of the House of Israel. Likewise, Moses was raised as the son of Pharaoh, and thereby heir to the power and means afforded the Pharaohs of Egypt. While this power and authority was worldlier than that of Joseph, it was nonetheless symbolic of the royal right of Moses to lead and to reign.

The issue of royal lineage is actually the first subject addressed in the New Testament. The first chapter of the Gospel of Matthew starts out with a detailed account of the lineage of Jesus Christ through the patriarchs of Israel, starting with Abraham, who was the first patriarch of the covenant made with the Lord, separating Israel as a chosen people of God.

Matthew 1:1-2

1 The book of the generation of Jesus Christ, the son of David, the son of Abraham.
2 Abraham begat Isaac; and Isaac begat Jacob; and Jacob begat Judas and his brethren;

Bear in mind that the names in the New Testament are slightly different than those in the Old Testament in some instances. Judah from the Old Testament becomes Judas in the New Testament. The important point is that Matthew is citing the lineage of Jesus Christ, which includes Judah, Jesse, David the king, and so forth down to Joseph, the husband of Mary.

THE LATTER RAIN

Matthew 1:6, 16-17

6 And Jesse begat David the king; and David the king begat Solomon of her that had been the wife of Urias; [...]
16 And Jacob begat Joseph the husband of Mary, of whom was born Jesus, who is called Christ.
17 So all the generations from Abraham to David are fourteen generations; and from David until the carrying away into Babylon are fourteen generations; and from the carrying away into Babylon unto Christ are fourteen generations.

One should ask why this royal lineage was so important, and why it was the first thing cited by the Disciples of Christ in the New Testament? Even more significant than the cases of Joseph and Moses, Jesus Christ is shown to be an heir to the Israelite kings through Judah, Jesse, and David. Were Israel not under the control of the Roman Empire at the time of Jesus' birth, Joseph the husband of Mary would have been eligible to be king, and thus, Jesus would have also received this right as the firstborn son of Joseph. While it is true that Joseph was actually only Jesus' adoptive father due to the way Jesus was conceived of God, it is still no coincidence that Jesus is born in this royal lineage. When Pilate placed the plaque above the cross which read "King of the Jews," he was stating both a symbolic truth as well as a literal truth in terms of birthright. The educated and learned Jews of the time knew and expected the Messiah to be born through this royal line. When Jesus began to perform his many miracles and wonders before the people, it caused the chosen status of Jesus Christ to be brought into question.

Matthew 12:23

23 And all the people were amazed, and said, Is not this the son of David?

Luke 2:4

4 And Joseph also went up from Galilee, out of the city of Nazareth, into Judaea, unto the city of David, which is called Bethlehem; (because he was of the house and lineage of David:)

While many people knew that Christ was raised in Nazareth, his birthplace may not have been common knowledge. It was widely known that the Messiah would be born in Bethlehem, and that his lineage would be through the tribe of Judah and through the royal line of David the King.

Acts 2:29-38

29 Men and brethren, let me freely speak unto you of the patriarch David, that he is both dead and buried, and his sepulchre is with us unto this day.
30 Therefore being a prophet, and knowing that God had sworn with an oath to him, that of the fruit of his loins, according to the flesh, he would raise up Christ to sit on his throne;
31 He seeing this before spake of the resurrection of Christ, that his soul was not left in hell, neither his flesh did see corruption.
32 This Jesus hath God raised up, whereof we all are witnesses.
33 Therefore being by the right hand of God exalted, and having received of the Father the promise of the Holy Ghost, he hath shed forth this, which ye now see and hear.
34 For David is not ascended into the heavens: but he saith himself, The LORD said unto my Lord, Sit thou on my right hand,
35 Until I make thy foes thy footstool.
36 Therefore let all the house of Israel know assuredly, that God hath made that same Jesus, whom ye have crucified, both Lord and Christ.

> 37 Now when they heard this, they were pricked in their heart, and said unto Peter and to the rest of the apostles, Men and brethren, what shall we do?
> 38 Then Peter said unto them, Repent, and be baptized every one of you in the name of Jesus Christ for the remission of sins, and ye shall receive the gift of the Holy Ghost.

We see from the above verses how powerful the knowledge of Jesus Christ's lineage and royal position within the tribes of Israel was to those who finally realized this significance. It was a horrifying thought to them that they had directly or indirectly taken part in his crucifixion, leading to the concerned question: "Men and brethren, what shall we do?" To this humble question, Peter responded resoundly: "Repent, and be baptized every one of you in the name of Jesus Christ for the remission of sins, and ye shall receive the gift of the Holy Ghost." This exhortation from Peter reiterates the need for priesthood authority to perform necessary ordinances such as baptism, which we will discuss soon. Before we leave the lineage of Christ, however, let us look at two other scriptures that again support his royal standing and mission.

Revelation 5:1-5

> 1 And I saw in the right hand of him that sat on the throne a book written within and on the backside, sealed with seven seals.
> 2 And I saw a strong angel proclaiming with a loud voice, Who is worthy to open the book, and to loose the seals thereof?
> 3 And no man in heaven, nor in earth, neither under the earth, was able to open the book, neither to look thereon.
> 4 And I wept much, because no man was found worthy to open and to read the book, neither to look thereon.
> 5 And one of the elders saith unto me, Weep not: behold, the Lion of the tribe of Juda, the Root of David, hath prevailed to open the book, and to loose the seven seals thereof.

Revelation 22:16-17

> 16 I Jesus have sent mine angel to testify unto you these things in the churches. I am the root and the offspring of David, and the bright and morning star.
> 17 And the Spirit and the bride say, Come. And let him that heareth say, Come. And let him that is athirst come. And whosoever will, let him take the water of life freely.

John the Revelator is completely clear on the subject of Christ's lineage and right to rule. The Savior says through John in Revelation 22:16, "I am the root and the offspring of David, and the bright and morning star." From Revelation 5, we learn that while there was concern about who was worthy to open the book, it is shown that the Lamb of God, who was slain, is the only one that "prevailed to open the book." The Lion of the tribe of Juda is obviously referring to Jesus Christ, and these verses spell out the importance of his royal lineage and divine mission. Jesus Christ was indeed the ultimate figure of royalty in the eyes of the apostles, and they did much to explain this to the people living during their time. Not only did they use Joseph and Moses as types to explain this concept, they also demonstrated his literal connection to King David with the caveat that Jesus was greater than them all. "David is not ascended into the heavens: but he saith himself, The LORD said unto my Lord, Sit thou on my right hand, until I make thy foes thy footstool. Therefore let all the house of Israel know assuredly, that God hath made that same Jesus, whom ye have crucified, both Lord and Christ."

According to these statements, Jesus Christ is already resurrected, and already sitting on the right hand of God the Father in the Heavens. While David, the King of Israel, who defeated Goliath in 1 Samuel 16, is still a spirit, being dead, and is waiting for the time when his resurrection will occur.

The association of Jesus Christ with these ancient men was exceptionally poignant to the Jews living at the time of the apostles. The Jews who opposed the apostles held these three patriarchs, Joseph, Moses, and King David, in great honor. For the apostles to state that the Jewish leaders had crucified the very Messiah who their own great prophets had predicted would come forth must have been a huge blow to their conscience. The result was either a great feeling of guilt and remorse as in Acts 2, or anger and hatred as in the case where Stephen was stoned to death. The disciples of Christ who were preaching the Gospel at this time were definitely hitting a nerve. They were stating the truth in such a way that was well-understood by the Jews of the day. That knowledge either led to their conversion or to their condemnation.

CHAPTER TWELVE

The Mission of Jesus Christ

While many differences exist between the beliefs and doctrines of the many Christian churches of today, the overriding similarity of them all concerns the mission of Jesus Christ. While disagreement might exist among the different sects concerning what qualifies one for a remission of sins, most would agree that the principle mission of Jesus Christ was to be a sacrifice for the sins of all mankind. He is the way, the truth, and the light, leading us out of a state of corruption into a more perfect existence. Of all the treasures of the earth, forgiveness of one's sins is the greatest gift one can give, and only the Savior Jesus Christ had the right, power, and authority to give such a powerful gift. One of the first counsels we hear from Jesus Christ is to seek out that gift.

> Matthew 6:19-21, 33
> 19 Lay not up for yourselves treasures upon earth, where moth and rust doth corrupt, and where thieves break through and steal:
> 20 But lay up for yourselves treasures in heaven, where neither moth nor rust doth corrupt, and where thieves do not break through nor steal:
> 21 For where your treasure is, there will your heart be also.
> 33 But seek ye first the kingdom of God, and his righteousness; and all these things shall be added unto you.

With the pressures and concerns of modern life upon us, it is sometimes hard to make time for pondering such philosophical questions, but this first counsel of the Lord Jesus Christ is to do just that. Our best attempts to save for the future can easily be destroyed without really any fault of our own. Stock markets can collapse within hours. Our secure jobs can be lost and our life savings depleted. The one lasting truth in this life, according to the Savior, is to find his Kingdom and his righteousness. He is saying in the above verse that every man, woman, and child should see it as a lifelong quest to find the Lord's Kingdom on the earth, and to apply its teaching toward a more righteous existence. This implies an earnest attempt to seek out truth. We must pray for guidance and then be sensitive to the promptings of the spirit, as it descends upon our heart and mind. In this way, he is able to guide us, line upon line and precept upon precept, until we come to the point of discovering actual truth.

While some may find this challenge to be constraining or confining, it is really the only way to find truth. We should do so with faith, knowing that it is the intent of the Lord to help us along. His purpose is to bless and to save, but it is up to each individual to ask Him for help.

Luke 9:56

56 For the Son of man is not come to destroy men's lives, but to save them. And they went to another village.

Luke 11:9-13

9 And I say unto you, Ask, and it shall be given you; seek, and ye shall find; knock, and it shall be opened unto you.
10 For every one that asketh receiveth; and he that seeketh findeth; and to him that knocketh it shall be opened.
11 If a son shall ask bread of any of you that is a father, will he give him a stone? or if he ask a fish, will he for a fish give him a serpent?
12 Or if he shall ask an egg, will he offer him a scorpion?
13 If ye then, being evil, know how to give good gifts unto your children: how much more shall your heavenly Father give the Holy Spirit to them that ask him?

Whether a reader of the Bible or not, most people have heard the counsel from the Savior, "Ask, and it shall be given you," although most people just say, "Ask, and you shall receive." My mother had another variation on this wise counsel, which went like this, "You've got a mouth. Use it!" While my mother's counsel was aimed more at removing any timid nature from her son as he went forth to face the world, it is still the same advice. We must open our mouths and ask for the things that we want, whether temporal in nature, or spiritual in nature. It is the same. Blessings come to those that seek them out, and what the Lord is saying in these verses is that if we make the finding of his Kingdom our principle occupation, then he has promised us again and again that he will indeed help us obtain it.

This not only leads us to expect guidance in the form of inspiration and personal revelation, but it also suggests fairly clearly that indeed a Kingdom of God is available, or a Church, or as we have called it elsewhere, Zion. The Nation or Kingdom of God is known as Zion, and Jesus Christ is the head thereof. There is only one Zion, not many. Anyone who truly seeks for it is promised to find it, the only exception being those seeking it during the period of the Great Spiritual Famine. Still, even they will not be withheld the blessings of the Kingdom in the end. It is the petition of the humble seekers of truth that will ultimately cause the return of Zion to the earth in the last days.

Luke 12:27-34

27 Consider the lilies how they grow: they toil not, they spin not; and yet I say unto you, that Solomon in all his glory was not arrayed like one of these.
28 If then God so clothe the grass, which is to day in the field, and to morrow is cast into the oven; how much more will he clothe you, O ye of little faith?

29 And seek not ye what ye shall eat, or what ye shall drink, neither be ye of doubtful mind.
30 For all these things do the nations of the world seek after: and your Father knoweth that ye have need of these things.
31 But rather seek ye the kingdom of God; and all these things shall be added unto you.
32 Fear not, little flock; for it is your Father's good pleasure to give you the kingdom.
33 Sell that ye have, and give alms; provide yourselves bags which wax not old, a treasure in the heavens that faileth not, where no thief approacheth, neither moth corrupteth.
34 For where your treasure is, there will your heart be also.

Again the promise is repeated, and we are shown that as he cares for the lilies of the field, so shall he care for us. As we search for the Kingdom of Heaven, however, we should realize that anything worthwhile usually requires sacrifice and effort to obtain. It is not an easy quest, but it will be satisfying in the end. The opposition that we encounter as we seek for the Lord may often surprise us.

Luke 12:51-53
51 Suppose ye that I am come to give peace on earth? I tell you, Nay; but rather division:
52 For from henceforth there shall be five in one house divided, three against two, and two against three.
53 The father shall be divided against the son, and the son against the father; the mother against the daughter, and the daughter against the mother; the mother in law against her daughter in law, and the daughter in law against her mother in law.

Here we see that finding truth may actually lead to division in the short term. The members of one's own family may oppose the humble seeker in his quest. Let us bear this in mind as we press forward in our search for God's Kingdom, and realize again that "anger resteth in the bosom of fools." (Ecclesiastes 7:9) As we discover sound doctrine, be aware that one of the key indicators that we are on to something good is that opposition will invariably be present as well. Often simple tests of truth can be used to know if we are right, and if we push through the opposition and test the Lord on what we feel is right, he has promised to help us see it even more clearly.

John 3:14-21
14 And as Moses lifted up the serpent in the wilderness, even so must the Son of man be lifted up:
15 That whosoever believeth in him should not perish, but have eternal life.
16 For God so loved the world, that he gave his only begotten Son, that whosoever believeth in him should not perish, but have everlasting life.
17 For God sent not his Son into the world to condemn the world; but that the world through him might be saved.
18 He that believeth on him is not condemned: but he that believeth not is condemned already, because he hath not believed in the name of the only begotten Son of God.
19 And this is the condemnation, that light is come into the world, and men loved darkness rather than light, because their deeds were evil.
20 For every one that doeth evil hateth the light, neither cometh to the light, lest his deeds should be reproved.
21 But he that doeth truth cometh to the light, that his deeds may be made manifest, that they are wrought in God.

If the main aspect of the Savior's mission is his sacrifice for our sins, the main task of his disciples is to lead people to find out about this great offering. He established the way and now wants all to find it. Once we enter into the way, we learn of certain requirements of salvation; but, in the end, it is the Savior who decides who has been faithful, and who has not in finding his truth. He serves as the judge on the last day. This is another important component of the mission of Jesus Christ.

John 5:22

22 For the Father judgeth no man, but hath committed all judgment unto the Son:

1 Corinthians 6:1-3

1 Dare any of you, having a matter against another, go to law before the unjust, and not before the saints?
2 Do ye not know that the saints shall judge the world? and if the world shall be judged by you, are ye unworthy to judge the smallest matters?
3 Know ye not that we shall judge angels? how much more things that pertain to this life?

From these scriptures, we learn that not only has the Father given all judgment unto the Son, even the son can and will delegate some of this responsibility to his disciples. While to many this might indicate a feeling of superiority, we will see that in the Kingdom of Heaven, the exact opposite is expected of the true disciples of God.

John 13:12-17

12 So after he had washed their feet, and had taken his garments, and was set down again, he said unto them, Know ye what I have done to you?
13 Ye call me Master and Lord: and ye say well; for so I am.
14 If I then, your Lord and Master, have washed your feet; ye also ought to wash one another's feet.
15 For I have given you an example, that ye should do as I have done to you.
16 Verily, verily, I say unto you, The servant is not greater than his lord; neither he that is sent greater than he that sent him.
17 If ye know these things, happy are ye if ye do them.

Jesus shows that leadership in its truest form implies being a servant to one's followers. This is the complete opposite of the tyrannical nature of leadership that many people assume. The condescension of Jesus Christ is that he seeks us out on an individual basis, despite being all-powerful and able to destroy and to make alive. He leads us to light and truth. While he is the King of kings, he still serves us in many different ways. For example, he has served us by providing a means whereby we may be resurrected from the dead. Apparently, this gift from Christ is available to all living beings, whether we are righteous or wicked.

Acts 24:15

15 And have hope toward God, which they themselves also allow, that there shall be a resurrection of the dead, both of the just and unjust.

1 Corinthians 15:19-22

19 If in this life only we have hope in Christ, we are of all men most miserable.
20 But now is Christ risen from the dead, and become the firstfruits of them that slept.
21 For since by man came death, by man came also the resurrection of the dead.
22 For as in Adam all die, even so in Christ shall all be made alive.

THE MISSION OF JESUS CHRIST

A resurrection will occur for all persons born into this world, both the just and the unjust. All will eventually die, which is a point that few argue, but the idea that all will be resurrected from the dead is an issue that is not as clearly understood. According to the scriptures in the Bible, even the vilest persons that have lived on the earth will be resurrected and brought to stand judgment, having an immortal body of flesh and bone. They will not remain spirits but become living souls.

Let us now look at the scriptures that touch on this subject. The first person to be resurrected was Jesus Christ himself. The first person to witness the Resurrected Lord was Mary Magdalene, just outside the tomb where Christ had been placed after his crucifixion. As we examine this issue further, we will gain a clear understanding of the true nature of Jesus Christ, his form, body, and appearance as a resurrected being of flesh and bone.

> **John 20:11-18**
> 11 But Mary stood without at the sepulchre weeping: and as she wept, she stooped down, and looked into the sepulchre,
> 12 And seeth two angels in white sitting, the one at the head, and the other at the feet, where the body of Jesus had lain.
> 13 And they say unto her, Woman, why weepest thou? She saith unto them, Because they have taken away my Lord, and I know not where they have laid him.
> 14 And when she had thus said, she turned herself back, and saw Jesus standing, and knew not that it was Jesus.
> 15 Jesus saith unto her, Woman, why weepest thou? whom seekest thou? She, supposing him to be the gardener, saith unto him, Sir, if thou have borne him hence, tell me where thou hast laid him, and I will take him away.
> 16 Jesus saith unto her, Mary. She turned herself, and saith unto him, Rabboni; which is to say, Master.
> 17 Jesus saith unto her, Touch me not; for I am not yet ascended to my Father: but go to my brethren, and say unto them, I ascend unto my Father, and your Father; and to my God, and your God.
> 18 Mary Magdalene came and told the disciples that she had seen the Lord, and that he had spoken these things unto her.

Here we learn several things about the risen Lord. First, Mary Magdalene may have been the first person to see Jesus after his resurrection from the dead. She saw him even before he had ascended to his Father in Heaven. This shows that evidently God the Father was in another place, and that Jesus was going to see him soon after his encounter with Mary. Jesus felt it important to make this point to her and to not allow her to touch his resurrected body until he had first gone and presented himself to the Father.

Whether she touched him or not, the important point is that Jesus was not in Heaven while he was dead. For three days his spirit was outside of his body, which lay in the tomb. Jesus here demonstrated through his encounter with Mary Magdalene that when we die, we do not go directly to our Father in Heaven. That apparently only occurs after resurrection and judgment. Instead, we go to a place for the spirits of the dead. If Jesus was not with his Father in Heaven, then where did he go? What did he do? Recall what Jesus said to one of the two thieves that were also crucified with Jesus that day:

THE LATTER RAIN

Luke 23:39-43
39 And one of the malefactors which were hanged railed on him, saying, If thou be Christ, save thyself and us.
40 But the other answering rebuked him, saying, Dost not thou fear God, seeing thou art in the same condemnation?
41 And we indeed justly; for we receive the due reward of our deeds: but this man hath done nothing amiss.
42 And he said unto Jesus, Lord, remember me when thou comest into thy kingdom.
43 And Jesus said unto him, Verily I say unto thee, To day shalt thou be with me in paradise.

Many people view this situation as an example of death bed repentance. They feel that because Jesus said "To day shalt thou be with me in paradise," the repentant thief went with Jesus to heaven right away. However, we see from Jesus' encounter with Mary Magdalene outside the tomb that this was not really the case. Jesus went with the humble, repentant thief to another place known as paradise, but it was not where God the Father was. It was not Heaven.

1 Peter 3:18-20
18 For Christ also hath once suffered for sins, the just for the unjust, that he might bring us to God, being put to death in the flesh, but quickened by the Spirit:
19 By which also he went and preached unto the spirits in prison;
20 Which sometime were disobedient, when once the longsuffering of God waited in the days of Noah, while the ark was a preparing, wherein few, that is, eight souls were saved by water.

1 Peter 4:6
6 For for this cause was the gospel preached also to them that are dead, that they might be judged according to men in the flesh, but live according to God in the spirit.

From 1st Peter in the New Testament, we learn that Christ was not in Heaven during the time between his death and his subsequent resurrection. Instead, "he went and preached unto the spirits" of the dead. Christ was among the dead who were righteous and thus in a state of paradise. The repentant thief must have also joined him there as well. In this place, Jesus could then explain the Gospel to him. Now, it may be that a different place exists for those that die in their wickedness, and the other thief might have been sent there. Jesus Christ was not in Heaven during the time he was out of his body, and from the encounter with Mary Magdalene, it would seem that Jesus wanted us all to know this—to make the distinction. Bear this fact in mind as we now pick up again in John 20 and see what happens after Jesus' appearance to Mary Magdalene.

John 20:19-31
19 Then the same day at evening, being the first day of the week, when the doors were shut where the disciples were assembled for fear of the Jews, came Jesus and stood in the midst, and saith unto them, Peace be unto you.
20 And when he had so said, he shewed unto them his hands and his side. Then were the disciples glad, when they saw the Lord.
21 Then said Jesus to them again, Peace be unto you: as my Father hath sent me, even so send I you.
22 And when he had said this, he breathed on them, and saith unto them, Receive ye the Holy Ghost:

THE MISSION OF JESUS CHRIST

23 Whose soever sins ye remit, they are remitted unto them; and whose soever sins ye retain, they are retained.
24 But Thomas, one of the twelve, called Didymus, was not with them when Jesus came.
25 The other disciples therefore said unto him, We have seen the Lord. But he said unto them, Except I shall see in his hands the print of the nails, and put my finger into the print of the nails, and thrust my hand into his side, I will not believe.
26 And after eight days again his disciples were within, and Thomas with them: then came Jesus, the doors being shut, and stood in the midst, and said, Peace be unto you.
27 Then saith he to Thomas, Reach hither thy finger, and behold my hands; and reach hither thy hand, and thrust it into my side: and be not faithless, but believing.
28 And Thomas answered and said unto him, My Lord and my God.
29 Jesus saith unto him, Thomas, because thou hast seen me, thou hast believed: blessed are they that have not seen, and yet have believed.
30 And many other signs truly did Jesus in the presence of his disciples, which are not written in this book:
31 But these are written, that ye might believe that Jesus is the Christ, the Son of God; and that believing ye might have life through his name.

By the time that Jesus appeared unto all the apostles including Thomas, he must have already been to see the Father in Heaven. He was now willing to have them touch his body. He asked them to touch the prints of the nails in his hands and his feet and to thrust their hands into his side where he had been speared by the soldiers. Otherwise, he would have said the same thing to them as he said to Mary, "Touch me not." The first encounter with the apostles minus Thomas is also given in Luke, and there we see even more detail of how alive Jesus really was.

Luke 24:36-48
36 And as they thus spake, Jesus himself stood in the midst of them, and saith unto them, Peace be unto you.
37 But they were terrified and affrighted, and supposed that they had seen a spirit.
38 And he said unto them, Why are ye troubled? and why do thoughts arise in your hearts?
39 Behold my hands and my feet, that it is I myself: handle me, and see; for a spirit hath not flesh and bones, as ye see me have.
40 And when he had thus spoken, he shewed them his hands and his feet.
41 And while they yet believed not for joy, and wondered, he said unto them, Have ye here any meat?
42 And they gave him a piece of a broiled fish, and of an honeycomb.
43 And he took it, and did eat before them.
44 And he said unto them, These are the words which I spake unto you, while I was yet with you, that all things must be fulfilled, which were written in the law of Moses, and in the prophets, and in the psalms, concerning me.
45 Then opened he their understanding, that they might understand the scriptures,
46 And said unto them, Thus it is written, and thus it behoved Christ to suffer, and to rise from the dead the third day:
47 And that repentance and remission of sins should be preached in his name among all nations, beginning at Jerusalem.
48 And ye are witnesses of these things.

Here, Jesus makes it emphatically clear that he is not a spirit, "for a spirit hath not flesh and bones, as ye see me have." The Resurrected Lord allowed them to touch his body and see that he was a tangible being. He even ate in their presence. "And they gave him a piece of broiled fish, and of an honeycomb. And he took it, and did eat before them." These encounters show the true nature and being of Jesus Christ, the Lord and Savior of us all. Through these verses, we learn of his ability to appear to his disciples on the earth. He can come and go as he likes. Nothing in Heaven or earth can stop him from appearing to anyone he desires to visit. After the publication of the New Testament, why is it that he apparently chooses not to appear to anyone for thousands of years? At least, no records are available of such an occurrence. The Apostles of the Lord were set apart and called as "witnesses of these things." If indeed they were witnesses of the risen Lord, and they were meant to continue, why do the records of such appearances of Jesus to his disciples suddenly cease? It would not just stop unless his disciples were taken away as well. We will revisit this issue shortly, but for now let us finish our discussion of the resurrection.

Matthew 27:52-53
52 And the graves were opened; and many bodies of the saints which slept arose,
53 And came out of the graves after his resurrection, and went into the holy city, and appeared unto many.

The above scripture shows that Jesus was not the only one to come forth from the dead. Many bodies of the just people of the time arose from the dead and appeared unto many. This information was meant to be had by us. We are to see that the just people who had died were allowed to come forth after the resurrection of Jesus Christ. In other words, he conquered death and made it possible for all people to eventually receive the resurrection.

Law of Moses Fulfilled

Another interesting aspect of the New Testament is the cessation of the rituals practiced under the Law of Moses. The Law of Moses was instituted by the Lord through the prophet Moses, and entailed the practice of animal sacrifice for the remission of sins and for demonstrations of thanksgiving for blessings received of the Lord. The outward observances were laid out for the children of Israel by the Lord through Moses, and were performed by Aaron and the priests of Levi.

The Law of Moses and the practice of animal sacrifice was a symbolic type pointing toward the ultimate and last great sacrifice. The sacrifice of Jesus Christ on the Cross of Calvary and his atonement for sins in the Garden of Gethsemane represent the last great sacrifice, and thus fulfilled the Law of Moses. He was put to death for the sins of all mankind, just as the animals sacrificed in times past. The Law of Moses was given as a type. The animal sacrifices were performed for the remission of specific sins committed by the children of Israel. After the sacrifice of Jesus Christ, who was the first-born Lamb of God, animal sacrifice for the remission of sins was no longer needed.

The observance of the Passover supper was also a symbolic type, looking forward to the crucifixion of Jesus Christ. During Passover, the Jews would prepare a first-born lamb without any blemish or defect, and prepare it for dinner without breaking any of its bones. This was first practiced when the Lord had warned the children of Israel to put the blood of this lamb on their door frame so that the destroying angel would pass by them, or "pass over" them. The idea that Jesus Christ represented the fulfillment of this ritual practiced by the Jews has been debated for centuries. Let us look at some scriptures that shed light on both the practice of animal sacrifice and the observance of the Passover feast.

> **Luke 24:44-45**
>
> 44 And he said unto them, These are the words which I spake unto you, while I was yet with you, that all things must be fulfilled, which were written in the law of Moses, and in the prophets, and in the psalms, concerning me.
> 45 Then opened he their understanding, that they might understand the scriptures,

Recall the scripture we read to show that the Lord was able to appear to his disciples, and that he showed them his body and ate fish and honeycomb. We also learned that he enlightened their understanding at that time concerning the fulfillment of the Law of Moses. He showed unto them that he was indeed the Great and Last Sacrifice, and that the Law of Moses had an end in Christ. All the things that pointed forward to the Messiah had an end in Christ.

> **Hebrews 9:6-14**
>
> 6 Now when these things were thus ordained, the priests went always into the first tabernacle, accomplishing the service of God.
> 7 But into the second went the high priest alone once every year, not without blood, which he offered for himself, and for the errors of the people:
> 8 The Holy Ghost this signifying, that the way into the holiest of all was not yet made manifest, while as the first tabernacle was yet standing:
> 9 Which was a figure for the time then present, in which were offered both gifts and sacrifices, that could not make him that did the service perfect, as pertaining to the conscience;
> 10 Which stood only in meats and drinks, and divers washings, and carnal ordinances, imposed on them until the time of reformation.
> 11 But Christ being come an high priest of good things to come, by a greater and more perfect tabernacle, not made with hands, that is to say, not of this building;
> 12 Neither by the blood of goats and calves, but by his own blood he entered in once into the holy place, having obtained eternal redemption for us.
> 13 For if the blood of bulls and of goats, and the ashes of an heifer sprinkling the unclean, sanctifieth to the purifying of the flesh:
> 14 How much more shall the blood of Christ, who through the eternal Spirit offered himself without spot to God, purge your conscience from dead works to serve the living God?

The Apostle Paul is explaining to the Hebrew members of the Church that Christ, through his ultimate sacrifice for sins, is able to sanctify all those who humble themselves, and who accept his Gospel and partake of the saving ordinances. His audience, being Jews, is completely familiar with the practice of animal sacrifice, and some of them probably had a hard time letting go of those rituals. Paul is attempting to show them that the sacrifice of Jesus Christ not only sanctifies those that believe on him from sin, but also does away with the need for animal sacrifice. He is stressing the point that, in reality, the animal sacrifices performed in the past could not really redeem someone from their sins at all, but they were a type pointing to the ultimate and final sacrifice of the Lamb of God that finally could redeem a man from his sins.

THE LATTER RAIN

Hebrews 10:11-18
11 And every priest standeth daily ministering and offering oftentimes the same sacrifices, which can never take away sins:
12 But this man, after he had offered one sacrifice for sins for ever, sat down on the right hand of God;
13 From henceforth expecting till his enemies be made his footstool.
14 For by one offering he hath perfected for ever them that are sanctified.
15 Whereof the Holy Ghost also is a witness to us: for after that he had said before,
16 This is the covenant that I will make with them after those days, saith the Lord, I will put my laws into their hearts, and in their minds will I write them;
17 And their sins and iniquities will I remember no more.
18 Now where remission of these is, there is no more offering for sin.

"There is no more offering for sin." The ultimate sacrifice for sins performed by Jesus Christ in allowing himself to be lifted up on the cross fulfilled the law of Moses and the need for sin offerings in the way of animal sacrifice. Instead, the Lord requires that we offer up a broken heart and a contrite spirit and that we humble ourselves and believe on his name. We must not only believe, but also keep his commandments and take part in the saving ordinances of his Gospel as contained in his Church, and administered by those in authority to perform such ordinances. To summarize the mission of Christ, we can now see that it is indeed the remission of sins and the raising of the dead through the resurrection. He is the creator of all things and the finisher of our existence, for through him we will all be judged.

Hebrews 1:1-3
1 GOD, who at sundry times and in divers manners spake in time past unto the fathers by the prophets,
2 Hath in these last days spoken unto us by his Son, whom he hath appointed heir of all things, by whom also he made the worlds;
3 Who being the brightness of his glory, and the express image of his person, and upholding all things by the word of his power, when he had by himself purged our sins, sat down on the right hand of the Majesty on high;

God speaks to us through prophets, and Jesus Christ was indeed a prophet in that he relayed the will of God the Eternal Father to those living on the earth. He was much more than just a prophet, however, for he was also our Savior and Redeemer, and God the Son. He was appointed to atone for the sins of the world and to release the bands of death through the resurrection. We learn above that after he had performed his all-important mission for the inhabitants of the earth, he returned to be with the Father again, and "sat down on the right hand of the Majesty on high." Even after his great act of providing an escape from both death and hell, he still recognized the Father and gave all glory unto him.

Ephesians 1:17-23
17 That the God of our Lord Jesus Christ, the Father of glory, may give unto you the spirit of wisdom and revelation in the knowledge of him:
18 The eyes of your understanding being enlightened; that ye may know what is the hope of his calling, and what the riches of the glory of his inheritance in the saints,
19 And what is the exceeding greatness of his power to us-ward who believe, according to the working of his mighty power,

THE MISSION OF JESUS CHRIST

20 Which he wrought in Christ, when he raised him from the dead, and set him at his own right hand in the heavenly places,
21 Far above all principality, and power, and might, and dominion, and every name that is named, not only in this world, but also in that which is to come:
22 And hath put all things under his feet, and gave him to be the head over all things to the church,
23 Which is his body, the fulness of him that filleth all in all.

Here we learn that although Christ is restored to his former position on the right-hand of God the Father, he is still the "head over all things to the church." The true Church of Christ is, therefore, governed by Jesus Christ himself, a resurrected being, who gives inspiration and guidance to his disciples and followers through his servants, the prophets. Nothing restrains him from appearing again to his apostles, prophets, or to anyone he desires to visit. He has all power. Nothing could prevent him from instructing his disciples in person as he did in the account contained in Acts.

Colossians 1:16-18
16 For by him were all things created, that are in heaven, and that are in earth, visible and invisible, whether they be thrones, or dominions, or principalities, or powers: all things were created by him, and for him:
17 And he is before all things, and by him all things consist.
18 And he is the head of the body, the church: who is the beginning, the firstborn from the dead; that in all things he might have the preeminence.

Jesus Christ is the creator of heaven and earth. Through his atoning sacrifice, he purged our sins if we believe and accept him. He also loosed the bands of death, leading to the resurrection of all mankind. He has conquered both death and hell; death, in that he leads us to life everlasting through the resurrection. Hell, in that he has provided a means whereby all mankind may find a remission of their sins through obedience to the laws and ordinances of his Gospel and Church. His final role is to be our judge in that great and final day.

2 Corinthians 5:10
10 For we must all appear before the judgment seat of Christ; that every one may receive the things done in his body, according to that he hath done, whether it be good or bad.

A man will be judged for "the things done in his body," meaning during his mortal existence on earth. The Law of Moses was a guide to help the children of Israel live a proper life during this mortal state. Jesus Christ brought us the higher law. He taught us to follow the dictates of our own hearts, relying wholly on him and the Holy Ghost, which inspires all those who possess it to do good works. This does not mean that we must only believe on his name, but we must also take part in the saving ordinances of the Gospel (baptism, etc.), in order to be eligible for salvation in his Kingdom. This brings us to the subject of priesthood authority. Let us examine what the New Testament teaches concerning the priesthood of God.

CHAPTER THIRTEEN

Priesthood Authority

1 Corinthians 14:33
33 For God is not the author of confusion, but of peace, as in all churches of the saints.

Some might view the statement "in all churches of the saints" as an explanation of the current state of Christian belief (many different denominations with Christ guiding them all). I do not! I see it as one Church of Christ, with several congregations of that Church in different geographical locations—Ephesus, Corinth, Jerusalem, etc. The priesthood leadership of Peter and the other apostles guided these congregations through inspiration from the spirit as needed or prompted. This prevented confusion and dissension among the church members of that day. What about our day?

If God is not the author of confusion, how does one explain the current state of Christian belief? As previously stated, there are literally hundreds, if not thousands of different Christian sects, all claiming to be guided and directed by Jesus Christ through the interpretation of the Bible. They differ widely in opinion over the many different tenants and practices that appear in the Bible. Some baptize infants. Some wait until they are older to receive baptism. Some baptize by immersion in water, others sprinkle water to baptize. The method for calling church leaders also varies widely from church to church, and from denomination to denomination. This state of confusion is enough to cause a humble seeker of truth to throw his hands into the air and say, "Dear Lord, where can you be found?" It truly contradicts the idea of stability and consistency that we think of in a wise, all-knowing God. What he did in the past, he should do today.

Hebrews 13:8-12
8 Jesus Christ the same yesterday, and to day, and for ever.
9 Be not carried about with divers and strange doctrines. For it is a good thing that the heart be established with grace; not with meats, which have not profited them that have been occupied therein.
10 We have an altar, whereof they have no right to eat which serve the tabernacle.

PRIESTHOOD AUTHORITY

11 For the bodies of those beasts, whose blood is brought into the sanctuary by the high priest for sin, are burned without the camp.
12 Wherefore Jesus also, that he might sanctify the people with his own blood, suffered without the gate.

If Jesus Christ is "the same yesterday, and to day, and for ever," then we should hope to find a Church on the earth that takes the same form and functions as the Church first established by the Lord as recorded in the New Testament. There should be no confusion about it at all.

Ephesians 4:5-15
5 One Lord, one faith, one baptism,
6 One God and Father of all, who is above all, and through all, and in you all.
7 But unto every one of us is given grace according to the measure of the gift of Christ.
8 Wherefore he saith, When he ascended up on high, he led captivity captive, and gave gifts unto men.
9 (Now that he ascended, what is it but that he also descended first into the lower parts of the earth?
10 He that descended is the same also that ascended up far above all heavens, that he might fill all things.)
11 And he gave some, apostles; and some, prophets; and some, evangelists; and some, pastors and teachers;
12 For the perfecting of the saints, for the work of the ministry, for the edifying of the body of Christ:
13 Till we all come in the unity of the faith, and of the knowledge of the Son of God, unto a perfect man, unto the measure of the stature of the fulness of Christ:
14 That we henceforth be no more children, tossed to and fro, and carried about with every wind of doctrine, by the sleight of men, and cunning craftiness, whereby they lie in wait to deceive;
15 But speaking the truth in love, may grow up into him in all things, which is the head, even Christ:

Here we learn that there should be only one faith or church: "One Lord, one faith, one baptism." Can anything be clearer? Next, we learn that there was evidently a space of time allotted between the time Jesus died on the cross and the time he ascended up on high to rejoin his Father in Heaven. He was doing something among the spirits of the dead during this time, and then returned to Heaven after his encounter with Mary Magdalene outside the tomb.

We can also see in Ephesians that Jesus Christ is the head of the Church, and that he governs it from his throne on high. As in times past, when his Church is found on the earth, it will have prophets to guide her. "And he gave some, apostles; and some, prophets; and some, evangelists; and some, pastors and teachers; for the perfecting of the saints, for the work of the ministry, for the edifying of the body of Christ." Those that possess the priesthood of God, and are truly authorized of him and rightfully ordained to such callings, are in their positions to help the followers of Christ progress on their way back to Him. The priesthood holder has the authority to preach, teach, baptize, exhort, and so forth. He can do nothing save that which his office entitles him to do, and as moved upon by the Holy Spirit. Apparently, this is meant to help the member progress towards perfection, "till we all come in the unity of the faith, and of the knowledge of the Son of God, unto a perfect man, unto the measure of the stature of the fullness of Christ."

The leaders of Christ's Church and Kingdom on the earth are there to lead us to a perfect understanding of Christ. Why? Because of all the confusion that assails us otherwise. "That we henceforth be no more children, tossed to and fro, and carried about with every wind of doctrine, by the sleight of men, and cunning craftiness, whereby they lie in wait to deceive; but speaking the truth in love, may grow up into him in all things, which is the head, even Christ." Christ is the head, but he calls mortal men to administer the affairs of his Church, and to do so through inspiration and divine guidance directly from him. What types of men were called to such callings in the Priesthood of God, and what should they be like today?

Matthew 11:25
25 At that time Jesus answered and said, I thank thee, O Father, Lord of heaven and earth, because thou hast hid these things from the wise and prudent, and hast revealed them unto babes.

According to Matthew 11:25, God does not generally choose the wise and prudent men of the world to be his leaders. Rather, he reveals his teachings to the humble and the meek.

Luke 5:36-39
36 And he spake also a parable unto them; No man putteth a piece of a new garment upon an old; if otherwise, then both the new maketh a rent, and the piece that was taken out of the new agreeth not with the old.
37 And no man putteth new wine into old bottles; else the new wine will burst the bottles, and be spilled, and the bottles shall perish.
38 But new wine must be put into new bottles; and both are preserved.
39 No man also having drunk old wine straightway desireth new: for he saith, The old is better.

God will choose men to lead his Church that are not already heavily indoctrinated in another religious background—babes, so to speak. It is easier to teach someone the right way when they have not already learned a different way of doing things. In governing his Church, the Lord appears to choose men to lead in Zion who are not tainted or already saturated in the doctrines of incorrect faiths.

1 Corinthians 1:25-27
25 Because the foolishness of God is wiser than men; and the weakness of God is stronger than men.
26 For ye see your calling, brethren, how that not many wise men after the flesh, not many mighty, not many noble, are called:
27 But God hath chosen the foolish things of the world to confound the wise; and God hath chosen the weak things of the world to confound the things which are mighty;

God is able to take ordinary men and make them strong. He can inspire the simple and humble men he chooses to confound even the most eloquent and educated men on earth. Education, social standing, and relative wealth appear to have little to do with who God chooses to govern the affairs of his Church.

PRIESTHOOD AUTHORITY

We can see this in the selection of his Twelve Apostles as described in Matthew 10:2-4. They are: (1) Simon Peter, (2) James, (3) John, (4) Andrew, brother of Peter, (5) Philip, (6) Bartholomew, (7) Thomas, (8) Matthew, the Publican, (9) James, (10) Thaddaeus, (11) Simon, and (12) Judas Iscariot.

None of these men were taken from the current ruling body of the Jews, the Sanhedrin. Nor did they have any advantageous position in life that might have helped them in any particular way. These same men, however, were inspired and directed to withstand the opposition and argument of the wise men of the day. The point is that Jesus called Twelve Apostles to lead the affairs of his Church, and if he is the "same yesterday, and to day, and for ever," then one would expect to find Twelve Apostles today, leading and guiding his people and helping them progress toward perfection. If the Church of Christ were meant to continue through the centuries, then every time an apostle died or was removed, another one would need to be called in his stead.

Acts 1:23-26

23 And they appointed two, Joseph called Barsabas, who was surnamed Justus, and Matthias.
24 And they prayed, and said, Thou, Lord, which knowest the hearts of all men, shew whether of these two thou hast chosen,
25 That he may take part of this ministry and apostleship, from which Judas by transgression fell, that he might go to his own place.
26 And they gave forth their lots; and the lot fell upon Matthias; and he was numbered with the eleven apostles.

The body of men known as the Twelve Apostles was designed to continue as a governing body in the Church. "The lot fell upon Matthias; and he was numbered with the eleven." We must assume likewise, that when Herod slew James, another apostle was called to take his place as well, although who that was is not specified in the scriptures.

Acts 12:1-3

1 NOW about that time Herod the king stretched forth his hands to vex certain of the church.
2 And he killed James the brother of John with the sword.
3 And because he saw it pleased the Jews, he proceeded further to take Peter also. (Then were the days of unleavened bread.)

We know that Paul, the converted Jew who became the author of the majority of the epistles of the New Testament, must have been called as an apostle at some point. However, it is not clearly stated whose spot he took. In fact, neither Paul nor Barnabas is mentioned on the original list of Twelve Apostles found in Matthew 10:2-3, and yet they both eventually were ordained as apostles.

Acts 14:14

14 Which when the apostles, Barnabas and Paul, heard of, they rent their clothes, and ran in among the people, crying out,

According to the New Testament, the body of the Twelve Apostles should still exist today if the true Church that Jesus Christ established had remained intact on the earth. It did not! As predicted by the Old Testament, the prophets and apostles of the true Church of God were allowed to be overrun by the followers of Satan.

THE LATTER RAIN

Eventually, no one was left alive to govern the Church. Within a short time, no one held the priesthood of God. Not one stone was left standing upon another.

Opposition to the truth and to the prophets of God seems to have always existed. It continued during the time Christ was living and ministering among the children of Israel. In fact, such opposition and unbelief was greatest among those that knew Jesus personally as he was growing up in the city of Nazareth.

> **Matthew 13:54-58**
>
> 54 And when he was come into his own country, he taught them in their synagogue, insomuch that they were astonished, and said, Whence hath this man this wisdom, and these mighty works?
> 55 Is not this the carpenter's son? is not his mother called Mary? and his brethren, James, and Joses, and Simon, and Judas?
> 56 And his sisters, are they not all with us? Whence then hath this man all these things?
> 57 And they were offended in him. But Jesus said unto them, A prophet is not without honour, save in his own country, and in his own house.
> 58 And he did not many mighty works there because of their unbelief.
> (see also Mark 6:2-6)

Those closest to the Savior had the greatest trouble accepting him as the Messiah. They opposed him and did not believe. Therefore, he did no great miracles in their presence except for a few healings. Would not the same thing occur today if Jesus Christ were to again call prophets on the earth? We could expect such a prophet or prophets to be opposed by the doctrines of the world and by those that knew them in their youth.

> **Matthew 15:8-9**
>
> 8 This people draweth nigh unto me with their mouth, and honoureth me with their lips; but their heart is far from me.
> 9 But in vain they do worship me, teaching for doctrines the commandments of men.

Jesus describes a time when people "teach for doctrines the commandments of men." Likewise, we see why prophets and apostles were so important to the Church when we read Ephesians 4:14: "That we henceforth be no more children, tossed to and fro, and carried about with every wind of doctrine, by the sleight of men, and cunning craftiness, whereby they lie in wait to deceive." The pressure placed on the believers of Christ must have been great.

> **John 12:42-43**
>
> 42 Nevertheless among the chief rulers also many believed on him; but because of the Pharisees they did not confess him, lest they should be put out of the synagogue:
> 43 For they loved the praise of men more than the praise of God.

We see here how many people are hindered from accepting the truth because of the influence of the world and the praise of man. They seek things that are easy to believe and that are accepted by the world, rather than that which is true and authorized of God.

> **1 Thessalonians 2:4-6**
>
> 4 But as we were allowed of God to be put in trust with the gospel, even so we speak; not as pleasing men, but God, which trieth our hearts.

PRIESTHOOD AUTHORITY

5 For neither at any time used we flattering words, as ye know, nor a cloke of covetousness; God is witness:
6 Nor of men sought we glory, neither of you, nor yet of others, when we might have been burdensome, as the apostles of Christ.

Just as the strong doctrine of Jesus Christ amazed his neighbors and friends when he taught in the synagogue at Nazareth, the apostles and other disciples of Christ who taught by the spirit used not flattering words, but spoke with authority. They relied wholly on the revelations given them in the hour to convince their listeners and to transfer their message with power and great force. Those that believed felt the spirit of confirmation, while those that resisted the word usually became offended, angry, and ultimately enemies of God. Others merely went their way in shame, knowing the truth, but being unable to accept it because of what they perceived as the sacrifices required.

The Priesthood of God is the same yesterday, today and forever. Therefore, Zion or the Kingdom of God on the earth, his Church, should have the same administrative organization today as it did anciently. The offices and callings that existed then should exist now. If they do not exist today, these are evidences of a falling away from the truth. I showed in the first chapter of this book that the priesthood cannot be bought with money. Neither can it be acquired because of political position or worldly strength. It is passed down from one man to the other by inspiration and the laying on of hands. The force that energizes and activates this priesthood is the spirit of revelation given by Jesus Christ himself from his throne on high.

Matthew 16:13-20

13 When Jesus came into the coasts of Cæsarea Philippi, he asked his disciples, saying, Whom do men say that I the Son of man am?
14 And they said, Some say that thou art John the Baptist: some, Elias; and others, Jeremias, or one of the prophets.
15 He saith unto them, But whom say ye that I am?
16 And Simon Peter answered and said, Thou art the Christ, the Son of the living God.
17 And Jesus answered and said unto him, Blessed art thou, Simon Bar-jona: for flesh and blood hath not revealed it unto thee, but my Father which is in heaven.
18 And I say also unto thee, That thou art Peter, and upon this rock I will build my church; and the gates of hell shall not prevail against it.
19 And I will give unto thee the keys of the kingdom of heaven: and whatsoever thou shalt bind on earth shall be bound in heaven: and whatsoever thou shalt loose on earth shall be loosed in heaven.
20 Then charged he his disciples that they should tell no man that he was Jesus the Christ.

Revelation from God is the key characteristic that leads and guides his Church. Revelation from Jesus to his disciples following his resurrection is what would lead the Church and guide her onward. Peter told Jesus, "Thou art the Christ, the Son of the living God." And Jesus responded, "Blessed art though Simon Bar-jona: for flesh and blood hath not revealed it unto thee, but my Father which is in heaven." The most powerful way that God is able to guide his Church is not through what is written necessarily in the past and not what you learn from another person, but that which you receive by revelation in real time directly from God himself. It requires the spirit of prophecy to be active and alive in the teacher, and the spirit of revelation and discernment to occur for the listener. The rock upon which God will build his Church is the rock of revelation, and the gates of hell shall not prevail against it.

Some might be tempted to say that this last statement shows that the Church will not be prevailed against. In other words, it will not be taken from the earth. This statement is actually predicting that the gates of hell will encompass the Church for a season, but will not prevail in the end. Satan and his followers will appear to have conquered the Kingdom of God, but only because Christ allows it to occur, just as he allowed himself to be crucified to fulfill the will of the Father. Had he wanted, Jesus could have called forth legions of Angels to free him from the cross, and to conquer his abductors. He gave his life freely, and suffered it to be so in order to fulfill all righteousness, and to provide means for our escape from both death and hell. Likewise, Jesus Christ allowed his Church to be taken from the earth because of unrighteousness. He withdrew his prophets, leaving man to fend for himself among the many false doctrines and false beliefs swirling around throughout the ages.

Despite this apparent victory for Satan, in the end Zion will return. Christ will restore his Kingdom to the earth once more, and he will do so through the rock of revelation and through prophets, apostles and direction from on high. The period of the Latter Rain, when it comes again to the earth, will be a period of restoration in that the ordinance, offices, and callings within the Church will be reinstituted in the same form as they existed in the ancient Church. Once again, the rivers and rain of divine revelation will begin to flow on the earth. The servants of the Lord living at that time will be inspired to bring forth new doctrine and new teachings directly from God himself. All will be renewed, and little by little the kingdom of Assyria, or the kingdom of the devil, will be conquered and vanquished until the whole earth is filled with the knowledge of the Lord, and peace reigns. Before this happens, the devil is allowed by God to have dominion over the entire earth, and the prophets of the Lord are taken. During this time, men are left to themselves and though they seek for truth, they do not find it.

In the time of Christ, a similar phenomenon occurred concerning the Samaritans. The Samaritans were the people living in and around Samaria, which had formerly been the capital of the Great Kingdom of Israel and the Northern Ten Tribes. After these tribes were literally carried away captive and lost to the view of the world, those that lived in this area still attempted to practice the former religion, albeit mixed with beliefs and practices taken from the surrounding nations. They practiced an apostate religion that had "a form of godliness, but denied the power there of." They still did sacrifices of animals, and they still performed ordinances having priests and other leaders that assumed the roles without proper authority.

The Jews living during this time disdained the Samaritans, and feared to mingle with them because they did not want to corrupt their own religion with that of the Samaritans. The story of Christ's meeting with a Samaritan woman at a well near Samaria is quite instructive in showing the dynamic that existed between the Jews and the Samaritans. This story also demonstrates the concept of priesthood authority and divine revelation. As we examine this story, bear in mind that Samaria is a type representing Joseph and the Northern Ten Tribes of Israel which have already succumbed to the famine of hearing the word of the Lord, while Jerusalem represents Judah, or the Jews, who as predicted by the Old Testament prophets must shortly suffer a similar fate.

> **John 4:1-9**
> 1 WHEN therefore the Lord knew how the Pharisees had heard that Jesus made and baptized more disciples than John,
> 2 (Though Jesus himself baptized not, but his disciples,)
> 3 He left Judæa, and departed again into Galilee.
> 4 And he must needs go through Samaria.
> 5 Then cometh he to a city of Samaria, which is called Sychar, near to the parcel of ground that Jacob gave to his son Joseph.
> 6 Now Jacob's well was there. Jesus therefore, being wearied with his journey, sat thus on the well: and it was about the sixth hour.
> 7 There cometh a woman of Samaria to draw water: Jesus saith unto her, Give me to drink.
> 8 (For his disciples were gone away unto the city to buy meat.)
> 9 Then saith the woman of Samaria unto him, How is it that thou, being a Jew, askest drink of me, which am a woman of Samaria? for the Jews have no dealings with the Samaritans.

Here we see the relationship that existed between the Jews and the Samaritans. The Jews would normally not have anything to do with them. In this instance, however, the Lord uses this dynamic to teach many important principals concerning revelation and true religion. I find it interesting as well that he chooses to discuss the issue of revelation while seated at the well from which water is drawn. This symbolic setting reinforces our previous discussion concerning the relationship between water as mentioned in the scriptures and revelation as given to man from God.

> **John 4:10-14**
> 10 Jesus answered and said unto her, If thou knewest the gift of God, and who it is that saith to thee, Give me to drink; thou wouldest have asked of him, and he would have given thee living water.
> 11 The woman saith unto him, Sir, thou hast nothing to draw with, and the well is deep: from whence then hast thou that living water?
> 12 Art thou greater than our father Jacob, which gave us the well, and drank thereof himself, and his children, and his cattle?
> 13 Jesus answered and said unto her, Whosoever drinketh of this water shall thirst again:
> 14 But whosoever drinketh of the water that I shall give him shall never thirst; but the water that I shall give him shall be in him a well of water springing up into everlasting life.

The living water Christ is talking about is of course not actual water. What he is referring to is revelation, or his word. The water of revelation is the water of a true knowledge of the Gospel of Jesus Christ, and it comes from Jesus Christ himself through the Spirit. This passage reinforces our previous findings, since it makes a clear link between the two types of water: the liquid that nourishes plants and animals, and the divine water that inspires, directs, and comforts the soul. Both give life, one temporally and the other spiritually. To further demonstrate this point, let us examine another scripture from the Book of John.

> John 7:37-39
>
> 37 In the last day, that great day of the feast, Jesus stood and cried, saying, If any man thirst, let him come unto me, and drink.
> 38 He that believeth on me, as the scripture hath said, out of his belly shall flow rivers of living water.
> 39 (But this spake he of the Spirit, which they that believe on him should receive: for the Holy Ghost was not yet given; because that Jesus was not yet glorified.)

This scripture identifies the meaning of the living water of Christ as the Spirit. The Spirit is the medium through which the Lord transmits thoughts, ideas, and teachings to the receiver thereof. We see that it had not fallen on any of his disciples as yet, since Jesus was still in their presence. For this reason, many of his disciples might seem naïve or slow to catch on. Often, however, lessons we learn through the Spirit are taught through recollection of situations that might have occurred days, weeks, or even years before. Once the disciples of Christ received the gift of the Holy Ghost, the events and teachings of the Savior were clarified for them. The symbolic image of living water, therefore, must have been greatly reinforced as water actually gushed forth from the body of Jesus when the soldier stabbed him with the point of a spear after his death on the cross. In all these symbolic images, Christ is indicating that the spiritual water is actually the greatest of all, and like his disciples, the Samaritan woman at the well does not understand this point immediately.

> John 4:15-19
>
> 15 The woman saith unto him, Sir, give me this water, that I thirst not, neither come hither to draw.
> 16 Jesus saith unto her, Go, call thy husband, and come hither.
> 17 The woman answered and said, I have no husband. Jesus said unto her, Thou hast well said, I have no husband:
> 18 For thou hast had five husbands; and he whom thou now hast is not thy husband: in that saidst thou truly.
> 19 The woman saith unto him, Sir, I perceive that thou art a prophet.

The woman perceives him to be a prophet because he is able to tell her something about herself that she knows he would not know had the spirit not revealed it to him. Even this lowly Samaritan woman recognized that the spirit of prophecy was present in Jesus, and she understood him to be a prophet. This knowledge must have made her a bit defensive of her own religion, since she then goes on to justify it before Jesus.

> John 4:20-22
>
> 20 Our fathers worshipped in this mountain; and ye say, that in Jerusalem is the place where men ought to worship.
> 21 Jesus saith unto her, Woman, believe me, the hour cometh, when ye shall neither in this mountain, nor yet at Jerusalem, worship the Father.
> 22 Ye worship ye know not what: we know what we worship: for salvation is of the Jews.

This is an important scripture for several reasons. It is clearly an example of the difference between the unauthorized doctrines of men and the authorized doctrines of God. When the woman tells Jesus that her fathers worshipped in this mountain, Jesus responds to her: "Ye worship ye know not what: we know what we worship: for salvation is of the Jews." Said another way, I take this to mean: "You worship, but the religion you follow is not authorized nor is it sanctioned of the Father. Therefore, ye worship the doctrines of men mixed with bits and piece of the true faith which was lost long ago. However, we know what we worship, and the true and living priesthood of God is at this time had among the Jews. They have not yet been corrupted, and thus, salvation is of the Jews. You have to go through them for your ceremonies to count hereafter."

Of greater significance is what Jesus says in the middle of the above cited verses: "Woman, believe me, the hour cometh, when ye shall neither in this mountain, nor yet at Jerusalem, worship the Father." What does he mean by this? With our findings from Isaiah and the other Old Testament prophets clearly in hand, we know what he is saying. The priesthood of God is to be taken from the earth. He is saying that the hour cometh, when Zion will be taken from the earth. The time is coming when men will wander to and fro on the earth, seeking the word of God and not find it (Amos 8:11-12). The Savior, Jesus Christ, is predicting the withdrawal of the prophets from the earth, and the dark day of Spiritual Famine and dearth. If the prophets of old were truly inspired of God on this famine issue, we should expect to hear the same message from the Lord during his mortal ministry, and indeed we do.

John 4:23-26
23 But the hour cometh, and now is, when the true worshippers shall worship the Father in spirit and in truth: for the Father seeketh such to worship him.
24 God is a Spirit: and they that worship him must worship him in spirit and in truth.
25 The woman saith unto him, I know that Messias cometh, which is called Christ: when he is come, he will tell us all things.
26 Jesus saith unto her, I that speak unto thee am he.

Here the Savior tells the woman that, at that point in time, the true worshippers could indeed worship the Father in spirit and truth. Later it may not be available, but at that moment in time it was, and not only that, but the chosen Messiah was in fact the one speaking to her directly. What an amazing event this must have been! The woman knew that a Messiah was predicted to come, and she said incredibly, "When he is come, he will tell us all things." She means when he is come, he will clarify and tell us what we need to do to achieve salvation and eternal life. But it must have been quite a surprise for her to learn that the man addressing her at the well was the Savior she had been anticipating.

John 4:27-42
27 And upon this came his disciples, and marvelled that he talked with the woman: yet no man said, What seekest thou? or, Why talkest thou with her?
28 The woman then left her waterpot, and went her way into the city, and saith to the men,
29 Come, see a man, which told me all things that ever I did: is not this the Christ?
30 Then they went out of the city, and came unto him.
31 In the mean while his disciples prayed him, saying, Master, eat.
32 But he said unto them, I have meat to eat that ye know not of.
33 Therefore said the disciples one to another, Hath any man brought him ought to eat?
34 Jesus saith unto them, My meat is to do the will of him that sent me, and to finish his work.

35 Say not ye, There are yet four months, and then cometh harvest? behold, I say unto you, Lift up your eyes, and look on the fields; for they are white already to harvest.
36 And he that reapeth receiveth wages, and gathereth fruit unto life eternal: that both he that soweth and he that reapeth may rejoice together.
37 And herein is that saying true, One soweth, and another reapeth.
38 I sent you to reap that whereon ye bestowed no labour: other men laboured, and ye are entered into their labours.
39 And many of the Samaritans of that city believed on him for the saying of the woman, which testified, He told me all that ever I did.
40 So when the Samaritans were come unto him, they besought him that he would tarry with them: and he abode there two days.
41 And many more believed because of his own word;
42 And said unto the woman, Now we believe, not because of thy saying: for we have heard him ourselves, and know that this is indeed the Christ, the Saviour of the world.

We see that the meat that had filled Jesus was not temporal, but rather spiritual meat. He had been fed by the experience of encountering the woman at the well, but his disciples did not yet understand his meaning at that point. Neither did they understand why he would converse with a Samaritan woman in the first place. This brief encounter between Jesus and the Samaritan woman was undertaken by the Savior to teach us important doctrinal insights. Jesus told them to "Lift up your eyes, and look on the fields, for they are white already to harvest." The world was primed and ready to receive the pleasing word of Christ. The Samaritans, though not socially accepted of the Jews, were as ready to receive it as were the Jews. In contrast, like his neighbors and former friends from Nazareth, the Jews as a people were blinded to the coming of the Savior in their midst. "He came unto his own, and his own received him not" (John 1:11).

John 5:39-47

39 Search the scriptures; for in them ye think ye have eternal life: and they are they which testify of me.
40 And ye will not come to me, that ye might have life.
41 I receive not honour from men.
42 But I know you, that ye have not the love of God in you.
43 I am come in my Father's name, and ye receive me not: if another shall come in his own name, him ye will receive.
44 How can ye believe, which receive honour one of another, and seek not the honour that cometh from God only?
45 Do not think that I will accuse you to the Father: there is one that accuseth you, even Moses, in whom ye trust.
46 For had ye believed Moses, ye would have believed me: for he wrote of me.
47 But if ye believe not his writings, how shall ye believe my words?

Addressing the Jews, Jesus makes this point clear. Because they have not the love of God in them, they reject the great message of salvation, and the very Savior himself. He predicts that, instead of accepting the true gospel as the true worshipper would do, they will accept another who comes in his own name, and they will give him honor, but it will be worldly honor and not of God. Finally, he points out that even Moses will testify against them and against their works, though they look to Moses as a symbol of their faith. We can imagine that since these Jews he was addressing were not true seekers of truth, but seekers of gain and of the glory of the world, Jesus' statement about Moses must have incited anger within them rather than humility. Let us now see how the anger and persecution coming from the Jews and others is able to begin the ultimate process that leads to the extinction of the true and living Church from off the face of the earth. We must realize of course that the Lord was not only aware of it, but that he had inspired the Old Testament prophets to predict this great event many years before it actually occurred.

Persecution of and Opposition to the Church

We began our discussion of the New Testament by citing the martyrdom of Stephen, who was stoned to death by an angry mob of Jews. We learned that Paul, who would later become an apostle and a great missionary in the Church, actually held the coats for those that did the stoning of Stephen. We also saw from the message delivered by Stephen that what angered the Jews the most were his references to Moses, him being a type of Jesus Christ. In reality, the message of Stephen and the message of Jesus in John 5 is the same. They both suggest that a true believer in Moses should believe in Christ as well, since Moses looked forward to Christ. Even though it was the truth, it made them angry to the point of violence. Anyone who sincerely reads the New Testament cannot come away from it without getting the feeling that the Church of Christ was under constant attack from not only the Jews, but also from the Greeks, Romans, and others. It was not a happy time, temporally speaking. The Church was literally under siege.

Matthew 11:7-19

7 And as they departed, Jesus began to say unto the multitudes concerning John, What went ye out into the wilderness to see? A reed shaken with the wind?
8 But what went ye out for to see? A man clothed in soft raiment? behold, they that wear soft clothing are in kings' houses.
9 But what went ye out for to see? A prophet? yea, I say unto you, and more than a prophet.
10 For this is he, of whom it is written, Behold, I send my messenger before thy face, which shall prepare thy way before thee.
11 Verily I say unto you, Among them that are born of women there hath not risen a greater than John the Baptist: notwithstanding he that is least in the kingdom of heaven is greater than he.
12 And from the days of John the Baptist until now the kingdom of heaven suffereth violence, and the violent take it by force.
13 For all the prophets and the law prophesied until John.
14 And if ye will receive it, this is Elias, which was for to come.
15 He that hath ears to hear, let him hear.
16 But whereunto shall I liken this generation? It is like unto children sitting in the markets, and calling unto their fellows,
17 And saying, We have piped unto you, and ye have not danced; we have mourned unto you, and ye have not lamented.
18 For John came neither eating nor drinking, and they say, He hath a devil.
19 The Son of man came eating and drinking, and they say, Behold a man gluttonous, and a winebibber, a friend of publicans and sinners. But wisdom is justified of her children.

Here the Lord is upbraiding the Jews for not believing in John the Baptist when they had the chance. He is asking what it was that they went out to see. He goes on to explain that it could not have been a man clothed in fine raiment. No, but he knows that they went out to see him because he was filled with the spirit of prophecy, and recognized as a prophet. Jesus reminds them that despite their knowledge of John's prophetic character, the Pharisees still rejected him, saying he hath a devil. Neither did they accept Christ. He points out the foolishness of their rash judgments, which are based more on the fear of man than on the fear of God.

The important verse from the scripture cited above is verse 12: "And from the days of John the Baptist until now the Kingdom of Heaven suffereth violence, and the violent take it by force." The Lord indicates here that the true Kingdom of Heaven has always been opposed by the wicked, and it is their intention at this point in time (the time of Christ) to "take it by force."

We showed earlier that the apostles who died were replaced by new ones, but at some point in history we lose track of this succession. Within a few hundred years from the resurrection of Jesus Christ, a body of Twelve Apostles can no longer be found in any of the institutions or organizations on the earth claiming to be a Christian church. So, what happened to the apostles? As I pondered this question, I researched the historical record of the martyrs during the early Church period. In doing so, I stumbled across a book called Fox's Book of Martyrs. This book recounts the deaths of the apostles and other saints, and is readily accessible. The first section of the book is dedicated to those saints mentioned in the New Testament, describing how each was killed, including Stephen, James the Great, Phillip, Matthew, James the Less, Matthias, Andrew, Mark, Peter, Paul, Jude, Bartholomew, Luke, Thomas, Simon, John and Barnabus. For example, Peter is shown to have been crucified upside-down at his request, not feeling worthy to be crucified in the same manner as was the Savior.

While the accuracy of each of these accounts is questioned by many scholars, it is still instructive to show the demise of the leaders of the ancient Church of God. Something obviously happened to them. The recorded history of the leaders of the Lord's Church on the earth came to an end. This fact is entirely consistent with the idea of a withdrawal of the Lord's servants, the prophets, from the earth. Satan (the king of Assyria from the Book of Isaiah), was allowed by the Lord to overcome them because of their wickedness, leaving the world without revelation and direction.

I cite Fox's Book of Martyrs not to discuss the accuracy of the document. Instead, I want to show that persecution of the priesthood leaders of the early Church is a commonly accepted phenomenon. I welcome other opinions about the actual fate of the ancient Church leaders, but the point is that they did meet a fate, and were killed off. If the governing body of the Church known as the Twelve Apostles was indeed meant to remain, we would have a record of the succession of that body, and we should have a body of Twelve Apostles today. Instead, most of them were martyred for the cause of the Gospel. Even if they had all lived out their normal mortal lives, replacements should have been made regularly as they began to die of old age. Such records would have been had in the Church and even recorded as scripture. Instead, the knowledge of any newly-appointed leaders of the Church of Christ is lost completely. Why?

PRIESTHOOD AUTHORITY

The succession of the apostles and prophets of the Church of God was allowed to become extinct by the Lord himself. Without the apostles and prophets to guide and direct the affairs of the Church, and to keep it organized and in line with the will of the Lord, the remaining members of the Church were soon either led astray by the prevailing doctrines of men or became martyrs to the cause of Jesus as well. It is reasonable to make the assumption from the available evidence that the Church of Jesus Christ fled into the wilderness, thus ushering in the dark day of the Great Spiritual Famine spoken of in the Book of Amos. Let us now examine several scriptures that support this concept.

- Warnings to stay strong despite persecution

1 Peter 5:8-11
8 Be sober, be vigilant; because your adversary the devil, as a roaring lion, walketh about, seeking whom he may devour:
9 Whom resist stedfast in the faith, knowing that the same afflictions are accomplished in your brethren that are in the world.
10 But the God of all grace, who hath called us unto his eternal glory by Christ Jesus, after that ye have suffered a while, make you perfect, stablish, strengthen, settle you.
11 To him be glory and dominion for ever and ever. Amen.

- Warnings about evil persons entering the Church (Wolves in sheep's clothing)

Matthew 7:15-20
15 Beware of false prophets, which come to you in sheep's clothing, but inwardly they are ravening wolves.
16 Ye shall know them by their fruits. Do men gather grapes of thorns, or figs of thistles?
17 Even so every good tree bringeth forth good fruit; but a corrupt tree bringeth forth evil fruit.
18 A good tree cannot bring forth evil fruit, neither can a corrupt tree bring forth good fruit.
19 Every tree that bringeth not forth good fruit is hewn down, and cast into the fire.
20 Wherefore by their fruits ye shall know them.

Jesus Christ was warning the people that false prophets would come dressed in sheep's clothing. They would set themselves up as if they had authority and power from the Lord, although they did not. The Lord told how to discern between a good prophet and an unauthorized prophet. This advice is as valid today as it was then. We can tell by their fruits—that which they do and that which they say or write. Later, in the Gospel of Matthew, we see the Lord further clarify what he means by false prophets.

Matthew 15:1-9
1 THEN came to Jesus scribes and Pharisees, which were of Jerusalem, saying,
2 Why do thy disciples transgress the tradition of the elders? for they wash not their hands when they eat bread.
3 But he answered and said unto them, Why do ye also transgress the commandment of God by your tradition?
4 For God commanded, saying, Honour thy father and mother: and, He that curseth father or mother, let him die the death.
5 But ye say, Whosoever shall say to his father or his mother, It is a gift, by whatsoever thou mightest be profited by me;

6 And honour not his father or his mother, he shall be free. Thus have ye made the commandment of God of none effect by your tradition.
7 Ye hypocrites, well did Esaias prophesy of you, saying,
8 This people draweth nigh unto me with their mouth, and honoureth me with their lips; but their heart is far from me.
9 But in vain they do worship me, teaching for doctrines the commandments of men.

The false teachers and prophets are those that draw near unto God with their mouths, and honor him with their lips, but their hearts are far from him. They interpret the scriptures of God to their own advantage to get gain and to usurp power over the innocent and the just. They are indeed wolves in sheep's clothing. They act as if they know God, but in reality they are imposters, leading their followers away from the truth and into darkness and confusion. The Savior is not the only one that warns of such false prophets and teachers entering into the flock.

Acts 20:29-35
29 For I know this, that after my departing shall grievous wolves enter in among you, not sparing the flock.
30 Also of your own selves shall men arise, speaking perverse things, to draw away disciples after them.
31 Therefore watch, and remember, that by the space of three years I ceased not to warn every one night and day with tears.
32 And now, brethren, I commend you to God, and to the word of his grace, which is able to build you up, and to give you an inheritance among all them which are sanctified.
33 I have coveted no man's silver, or gold, or apparel.
34 Yea, ye yourselves know, that these hands have ministered unto my necessities, and to them that were with me.
35 I have shewed you all things, how that so labouring ye ought to support the weak, and to remember the words of the Lord Jesus, how he said, It is more blessed to give than to receive.

Is the Apostle Paul giving the disciples he is leaving behind any great hope for the continuation of the Church among them? No. On the contrary, he was warning them to stay strong in the faith, despite the forthcoming attack by false teachers and evil men from both inside and outside of the Church. It appears that he and the other leaders of the Church had been holding back a raging flood of falsehood, which was ready to be poured out over the whole earth as soon as they, the apostles, were taken away. He had been reminding them of this pending demise of the true Church for at least three years. It was not something that just came to him as he was going to Rome where he would be martyred. No. It was an event foretold by all the prophets before him, and the Spirit had been prompting him to preach about it during his entire ministry. Finally, he reminded his followers that his fruits were good and of God, that he had not sought after silver, gold, or fine apparel, but only to build up of the Kingdom of God in meekness and humility. Later he reiterated this same message again to his fellow servant, Timothy.

2 Timothy 4:1-4
1 I CHARGE thee therefore before God, and the Lord Jesus Christ, who shall judge the quick and the dead at his appearing and his kingdom;
2 Preach the word; be instant in season, out of season; reprove, rebuke, exhort with all longsuffering and doctrine.

PRIESTHOOD AUTHORITY

> 3 For the time will come when they will not endure sound doctrine; but after their own lusts shall they heap to themselves teachers, having itching ears;
> 4 And they shall turn away their ears from the truth, and shall be turned unto fables.

Here Paul reminds Timothy of the impending fate of the flock. He says that the time will come when they will no longer endure sound doctrine. They will turn away their ears from the truth, and shall be turned unto fables. He reminds Timothy to stay strong despite the frequent deaths and martyrdom occurring among the Church leadership.

It reminds me of the stark image of the last helicopter leaving Saigon at the end of the Vietnam conflict. You see the desperate attempts of people to hang on to the helicopter as it lifts off, knowing full well that those left behind would have to live through the oppression and hardship of the coming transition years. Likewise, Paul is warning Timothy that a dark period is beginning for all mankind—the Dark Ages are being ushered in!

Predictions About a Falling Away

> **2 Thessalonians 2:1-5**
>
> 1 NOW we beseech you, brethren, by the coming of our Lord Jesus Christ, and by our gathering together unto him,
> 2 That ye be not soon shaken in mind, or be troubled, neither by spirit, nor by word, nor by letter as from us, as that the day of Christ is at hand.
> 3 Let no man deceive you by any means: for that day shall not come, except there come a falling away first, and that man of sin be revealed, the son of perdition;
> 4 Who opposeth and exalteth himself above all that is called God, or that is worshipped; so that he as God sitteth in the temple of God, shewing himself that he is God.
> 5 Remember ye not, that, when I was yet with you, I told you these things?

The Apostle Paul again warns the people of an impending siege against them. He is addressing the Thessalonians, and tells them point-blank that, before the Second Coming, there will be a falling away first, and that man of sin be revealed, the son of perdition. Paul is stating the same thing we heard in the Book of Isaiah. Satan will conquer Israel and completely overrun her, such that none can escape. Paul not only tells them that the falling away is coming, but he tells them by whose hand it will come—the hand of Satan. Again, he asks the poor Thessalonians, "Remember ye not, that, when I was yet with you, I told you these things?" This was such an important message that he not only told them about it in person, but he later wrote them this epistle to remind them one more time.

> **Revelation 13:7**
>
> 7 And it was given unto him to make war with the saints, and to overcome them: and power was given him over all kindreds, and tongues, and nations.

In this passage, it is the Apostle John who is prophesying, not Paul, but his message is clear. It was given unto Satan to make war with the saints, and to overcome them. This matches exactly what we saw prophesied in the Old Testament, and yet it is contained in the New Testament.

THE LATTER RAIN

Isaiah 24:1-6

1 BEHOLD, the LORD maketh the earth empty, and maketh it waste, and turneth it upside down, and scattereth abroad the inhabitants thereof.
2 And it shall be, as with the people, so with the priest; as with the servant, so with his master; as with the maid, so with her mistress; as with the buyer, so with the seller; as with the lender, so with the borrower; as with the taker of usury, so with the giver of usury to him.
3 The land shall be utterly emptied, and utterly spoiled: for the LORD hath spoken this word.
4 The earth mourneth and fadeth away, the world languisheth and fadeth away, the haughty people of the earth do languish.
5 The earth also is defiled under the inhabitants thereof; because they have transgressed the laws, changed the ordinance, broken the everlasting covenant.
6 Therefore hath the curse devoured the earth, and they that dwell therein are desolate: therefore the inhabitants of the earth are burned, and few men left.

The Lord mourns because the earth is so defiled during these Dark Ages. Why is the earth spoiled? "Because they have transgressed the laws, changed the ordinance, broken the everlasting covenant. Therefore hath the curse devoured the earth, and they that dwell therein are desolate." Without the ordinances of salvation and the guidance of prophets, the inhabitants of the earth are burned up by the tyranny and falsehood of Satan and his ministers. Let us now return to what the Lord has to say about the impending fall into spiritual darkness.

- Parables of Jesus Christ Predicting a Falling Away

If a falling away from the truth was to occur, it would make sense that Jesus Christ would also predict such an event. Let us look for this in his parables, and see what should befall the earth prior to his return in glory.

Matthew 24:3-15

3 And as he sat upon the mount of Olives, the disciples came unto him privately, saying, Tell us, when shall these things be? and what shall be the sign of thy coming, and of the end of the world?
4 And Jesus answered and said unto them, Take heed that no man deceive you.
5 For many shall come in my name, saying, I am Christ; and shall deceive many.
6 And ye shall hear of wars and rumours of wars: see that ye be not troubled: for all these things must come to pass, but the end is not yet.
7 For nation shall rise against nation, and kingdom against kingdom: and there shall be famines, and pestilences, and earthquakes, in divers places.
8 All these are the beginning of sorrows.
9 Then shall they deliver you up to be afflicted, and shall kill you: and ye shall be hated of all nations for my name's sake.
10 And then shall many be offended, and shall betray one another, and shall hate one another.
11 And many false prophets shall rise, and shall deceive many.
12 And because iniquity shall abound, the love of many shall wax cold.
13 But he that shall endure unto the end, the same shall be saved.
14 And this gospel of the kingdom shall be preached in all the world for a witness unto all nations; and then shall the end come.
15 When ye therefore shall see the abomination of desolation, spoken of by Daniel the prophet, stand in the holy place, (whoso readeth, let him understand:)

What an amazing passage of scripture! First of all, it is given in response to a direct question from his disciples: "When shall these things be and what shall be the sign of thy coming, and of the end of the world?" They are asking what will happen prior to the Second Coming. And how does he respond? He says it will not come until "many come in his name, being false prophets, saying I am Christ, and deceive many." The idea of false prophets arising is consistent with the many other New Testament scriptures we have just cited showing a complete overthrow of the Church of God on the earth. Before the end, however, the Kingdom of God shall be restored again to the earth and preached throughout the world for a witness unto the nations, and then shall the end come. Even if Satan is given a temporary victory because God allowed it to be so, before the Second Coming of the Lord, the same gospel as the apostles preached before will once again be preached to the children of men and go to every nation, kindred, tongue and people. Hence, there is a Former Rain period followed by a Spiritual Famine period. Finally, the Latter Rain period comes upon the earth prior to the Second Coming, when the Lord appears in his glory before all the inhabitants of the earth!

Matthew 21:33-46

33 Hear another parable: There was a certain householder, which planted a vineyard, and hedged it round about, and digged a winepress in it, and built a tower, and let it out to husbandmen, and went into a far country:
34 And when the time of the fruit drew near, he sent his servants to the husbandmen, that they might receive the fruits of it.
35 And the husbandmen took his servants, and beat one, and killed another, and stoned another.
36 Again, he sent other servants more than the first: and they did unto them likewise.
37 But last of all he sent unto them his son, saying, They will reverence my son.
38 But when the husbandmen saw the son, they said among themselves, This is the heir; come, let us kill him, and let us seize on his inheritance.
39 And they caught him, and cast him out of the vineyard, and slew him.
40 When the lord therefore of the vineyard cometh, what will he do unto those husbandmen?
41 They say unto him, He will miserably destroy those wicked men, and will let out his vineyard unto other husbandmen, which shall render him the fruits in their seasons.
42 Jesus saith unto them, Did ye never read in the scriptures, The stone which the builders rejected, the same is become the head of the corner: this is the Lord's doing, and it is marvellous in our eyes?
43 Therefore say I unto you, The kingdom of God shall be taken from you, and given to a nation bringing forth the fruits thereof.
44 And whosoever shall fall on this stone shall be broken: but on whomsoever it shall fall, it will grind him to powder.
45 And when the chief priests and Pharisees had heard his parables, they perceived that he spake of them.
46 But when they sought to lay hands on him, they feared the multitude, because they took him for a prophet.

Compare the parable given by the Lord in Matthew 21 with the parable given by the Lord through the prophet Isaiah.

Isaiah 5:1-7

1 NOW will I sing to my wellbeloved a song of my beloved touching his vineyard. My wellbeloved hath a vineyard in a very fruitful hill:
2 And he fenced it, and gathered out the stones thereof, and planted it with the choicest vine, and built a tower in the midst of it, and also made a winepress therein: and he looked that it should bring forth grapes, and it brought forth wild grapes.

> 3 And now, O inhabitants of Jerusalem, and men of Judah, judge, I pray you, betwixt me and my vineyard.
> 4 What could have been done more to my vineyard, that I have not done in it? wherefore, when I looked that it should bring forth grapes, brought it forth wild grapes?
> 5 And now go to; I will tell you what I will do to my vineyard: I will take away the hedge thereof, and it shall be eaten up; and break down the wall thereof, and it shall be trodden down:
> 6 And I will lay it waste: it shall not be pruned, nor digged; but there shall come up briers and thorns: I will also command the clouds that they rain no rain upon it.
> 7 For the vineyard of the LORD of hosts is the house of Israel, and the men of Judah his pleasant plant: and he looked for judgment, but behold oppression; for righteousness, but behold a cry.

These are actually the same parable. The prophet Isaiah, however, clarifies the meaning of the one given by the Lord to the Jews. "For the vineyard of the LORD of hosts is the house of Israel, and the men of Judah his pleasant plant: and he looked for judgment, but behold oppression; for righteousness, but behold a cry."

It is amazing how the statements of the Lord caused such anger among the leaders of the Jews. Still, they did not take him immediately because they feared the people. They feared the people because the people took him for a prophet! The same type of anger will most likely occur when the Latter Rain period is finally ushered in upon the earth. The true Gospel will once again spring forth, but the leaders of the churches of the world will fight against it and incite anger in the hearts of men against the true doctrine of Christ.

In the latter times, unlike during the time just after the resurrection of the Lord, the Kingdom of Zion will prevail. "Whosoever shall fall on this stone shall be broken: but on whomsoever it shall fall, it will grind him to powder." Zion will no longer be moved out of its place, but will march forth from obscurity and conquer Satan and his dominion, crushing all nations (doctrines and falsehoods) that oppose it under the weight of the stone which the builders rejected, even Jesus Christ.

A Time of Retreat

During the time of the New Testament writings, we see a totally different set of circumstances unfolding. It was not a time of victory, but a time of retreat. We hear the voice of warning from Jesus Christ and subsequently from his Apostles that Zion will need to flee into the wilderness. We have seen the prediction of a falling away. Now let us see the order in which this falling away is proposed to occur by the Apostle Paul in his epistle to the Romans.

Romans 11:1-5

> 1 I SAY then, Hath God cast away his people? God forbid. For I also am an Israelite, of the seed of Abraham, of the tribe of Benjamin.
> 2 God hath not cast away his people which he foreknew. Wot ye not what the scripture saith of Elias? how he maketh intercession to God against Israel, saying,
> 3 Lord, they have killed thy prophets, and digged down thine altars; and I am left alone, and they seek my life.
> 4 But what saith the answer of God unto him? I have reserved to myself seven thousand men, who have not bowed the knee to the image of Baal.
> 5 Even so then at this present time also there is a remnant according to the election of grace.

PRIESTHOOD AUTHORITY

In these verses, Paul explains that while most of the Jews have rejected the Gospel of Jesus Christ, there were still a number of Jews that did not reject him. They believed on his words, accepted his baptism, and joined the true fold of God. He points to the case of Elijah the prophet, who felt like he was all alone in his belief in the true faith of the Lord. The Lord comes to him in the mouth of the cave and explains that there yet remained "seven thousand in Israel, all the knees which have not bowed unto Baal, and every mouth which hath not kissed him" (1 Kings 19:18).

Romans 11:9-15

9 And David saith, Let their table be made a snare, and a trap, and a stumbling block, and a recompence unto them:
10 Let their eyes be darkened, that they may not see, and bow down their back alway.
11 I say then, Have they stumbled that they should fall? God forbid: but rather through their fall salvation is come unto the Gentiles, for to provoke them to jealousy.
12 Now if the fall of them be the riches of the world, and the diminishing of them the riches of the Gentiles; how much more their fulness?
13 For I speak to you Gentiles, inasmuch as I am the apostle of the Gentiles, I magnify mine office:
14 If by any means I may provoke to emulation them which are my flesh, and might save some of them.
15 For if the casting away of them be the reconciling of the world, what shall the receiving of them be, but life from the dead?

Paul shows that while there might have been a few of the Jews that remained in the faith, the majority had fallen away from the true fold of God and become blinded from the correct doctrine. He quotes from the 69th Psalm, showing that even David the Psalmist predicted that his descendants, the Jews, would be taken by the snare and fall into a trap. He is counseling the Gentiles, or non-Jews, from Rome to resist the temptation to gloat over the fall of the Jews. He points out that his hope is still to "save some of them." Their fall may have opened the Gospel to the rest of the world, but it does not mean that we should not look for the return of Judah to its former position of favor in the eyes of the Lord. It is fairly clear from Paul's words in Romans 11, at that point in time the Jews had lost the mantle of authority they previously held after rejecting the Messiah. Recall what Jesus had explained to the Samaritan woman at the well:

John 4:21-22

21 Jesus saith unto her, Woman, believe me, the hour cometh, when ye shall neither in this mountain, nor yet at Jerusalem, worship the Father.
22 Ye worship ye know not what: we know what we worship: for salvation is of the Jews.

Jesus was telling this woman that at that moment in time, salvation was still of the Jews. But, it would soon occur that "ye shall neither in this mountain, nor yet at Jerusalem, worship the Father." None of the descendants of Joseph living in the region around Samaria had the priesthood or the power to perform the saving ordinances—They had already fallen away by this time. Jesus was saying that Judah would follow and soon thereafter fall away. "Neither in this mountain" means through Ephraim or the Gentiles—which was already in apostate form.

THE LATTER RAIN

"Nor at Jerusalem" means the Tribe of Judah—which would soon follow her sister into apostasy. With both of them gone, Zion is no longer available to the children of men.

> **Matthew 21:42-43**
>
> 42 Jesus saith unto them, Did ye never read in the scriptures, The stone which the builders rejected, the same is become the head of the corner: this is the Lord's doing, and it is marvellous in our eyes?
> 43 Therefore say I unto you, The kingdom of God shall be taken from you, and given to a nation bringing forth the fruits thereof.

After the rejection of Jesus Christ, the chief corner stone, the Kingdom of God was taken from the Jews and given to the Gentiles or non-Jews for a brief period of time. This occurred through the preaching of the apostles, who were themselves Jews, but Jews having a firm and immovable testimony of the Divine Mission of Jesus Christ as the Savior of the World. Some feel that this transition was a permanent change, and that the Jews should be hated and despised. In Romans 11, the Apostle Paul makes it clear that this is indeed a false doctrine. Instead, the true Church of God should do all that is in its power to redeem the Jews, and to reclaim them into the true olive tree, bringing them back from their spiritual death into a renewed state of life.

> **Romans 11:16-21**
>
> 16 For if the firstfruit be holy, the lump is also holy: and if the root be holy, so are the branches.
> 17 And if some of the branches be broken off, and thou, being a wild olive tree, wert graffed in among them, and with them partakest of the root and fatness of the olive tree;
> 18 Boast not against the branches. But if thou boast, thou bearest not the root, but the root thee.
> 19 Thou wilt say then, The branches were broken off, that I might be graffed in.
> 20 Well; because of unbelief they were broken off, and thou standest by faith. Be not highminded, but fear:
> 21 For if God spared not the natural branches, take heed lest he also spare not thee.

These verses act as a form of foreshadowing. Paul carefully counsels the Romans not to boast themselves as being better than the Jews who fell from grace due to their unbelief. "Because of unbelief they were broken off, and thou standest by faith." Then he gives a stark warning: "Be not highminded, but fear: For if God spared not the natural branches, take heed lest he also spare not thee." He is saying that the Gentiles might also be broken off, even though they were newly grafted into the true olive tree of the Lord. Paul reiterates this same warning in the very next verses of the same chapter.

> **Romans 11:22-26**
>
> 22 Behold therefore the goodness and severity of God: on them which fell, severity; but toward thee, goodness, if thou continue in his goodness: otherwise thou also shalt be cut off.
> 23 And they also, if they abide not still in unbelief, shall be graffed in: for God is able to graff them in again.
> 24 For if thou wert cut out of the olive tree which is wild by nature, and wert graffed contrary to nature into a good olive tree: how much more shall these, which be the natural branches, be graffed into their own olive tree?

25 For I would not, brethren, that ye should be ignorant of this mystery, lest ye should be wise in your own conceits; that blindness in part is happened to Israel, until the fulness of the Gentiles be come in.
26 And so all Israel shall be saved: as it is written, There shall come out of Sion the Deliverer, and shall turn away ungodliness from Jacob:

Here Paul makes a reference to a concept we must examine. He says that "Blindness in part is happened to Israel, until the fullness of the Gentiles be come in." I am referring to the phrase, "Fullness of the Gentiles." What does he mean by this? He mentions it while at the same time warning the Gentile converts not to boast lest they themselves be cut off like the Jews. As I pondered over the strangeness of these two extremes (being cut off versus having a fullness), I realized that, according to the Old Testament prophets we have already studied, when Zion is taken away, it will be all-encompassing. The priesthood and prophecy will be removed and withdrawn from the earth entirely. The devil is given full dominion over the inhabitants of the earth, and the good people of the earth are left to contend with persecution, injustice and tyranny in its vilest forms. If this were the case, and indeed it was, then the foreshadowing of Paul about the Gentiles being cut off like the Jews also must have already come to pass. If both the Jews and the Gentiles were cut off from the true faith, the "Fullness of the Gentiles" must refer to the Latter Rain period when Zion is restored again to the earth, and prophets are again called to lead Israel out of darkness and to guide the humble followers of truth to their end destination within the true fold of God.

It is especially telling when he says to them, "There shall come out of Sion the Deliverer, and shall turn away ungodliness from Jacob:" Now clearly, Jesus Christ is the Deliverer in the sense that he delivered us all from the penalty of sin, if we but repent, are baptized, and continue in the faith. This is further spelled out in the verse that follows:

Romans 11:27-32
27 For this is my covenant unto them, when I shall take away their sins.
28 As concerning the gospel, they are enemies for your sakes: but as touching the election, they are beloved for the fathers' sakes.
29 For the gifts and calling of God are without repentance.
30 For as ye in times past have not believed God, yet have now obtained mercy through their unbelief:
31 Even so have these also now not believed, that through your mercy they also may obtain mercy.
32 For God hath concluded them all in unbelief, that he might have mercy upon all.

We see that the Deliverer spoken of in Romans 11:26 is Jesus Christ the Redeemer from sin. However, in verse 27, it is talking about some future time—a time "when I shall take away their sins," meaning the sins of the Jews, when they begin to believe on him. In verse 31, the Gentiles received the Gospel from the Jews; in future times, the Jews will receive the Gospel from the Gentiles. The Gentiles received access to the Gospel due to the Jews having rejected Christ; even so, in the day of the restitution of all things, the Gentiles will receive a fullness of the Gospel once Zion is restored, and then shall be instruments in the hands of the Lord in bringing the Jews back into the true olive tree. The Jews will again be grafted in and restored to their former station and honor. First comes the period of unbelief and darkness. "For God hath concluded them all in unbelief, that he might have mercy upon all." If indeed all fall into a period of Spiritual Famine, all will need the mercy of the Lord to be restored again.

Matthew 20:16
16 So the last shall be first, and the first last: for many be called, but few chosen.

This oft-quoted verse has a direct application to the subject of our discussion. While it can have many different applications depending on the context, it also serves as a symbolic reference to the order in which God's children receive the full Gospel of Jesus Christ. In the Former Rain period, Jesus and his Apostles went first to the Jews. Only later was the Gospel preached to the Gentiles, after Peter was instructed to extend it to them as well. The Gentiles were the last, and the Jews the first during the Former Rain. In the Latter Rain period, the Gentiles should, therefore, be the first to receive the Gospel in its fullness, and only after some time will the Jews start to believe. The last (the Gentiles) shall be first and the first (the Jews) last in the final dispensation when prophets are again called upon the earth.

Recall that the term Gentile has slightly different meanings depending on the context and the time period in question. At first, it meant anyone that was a non-Israelite, a heathen, or an outsider. After the Northern Ten Tribes of Israel were literally carried away and scattered by Assyria, they mixed with the nations of the world, or with the Gentiles. This led to the Ten Lost Tribes being referred to as Gentiles as well. Judah to the south remained the only part of Israel's posterity with priesthood and prophets. Everyone else was known as a Gentile. Today everyone can thereby be classified as either a Jew (a member of the tribe of Judah) or a Gentile. Since the Northern Ten Tribes were associated with the Tribe of Ephraim or Joseph his father, references to Gentiles can also mean a reference to Joseph, Ephraim, or the Lost Ten Tribes.

What I want to make clear is this: the Gospel of Jesus Christ was taught first to the Jews and then to the Gentiles during the period of the Former Rain. In the latter times, we should expect the fullness of the Lord's Gospel to be reestablished on the earth through prophets called from the Northern Ten Tribes, as they are called out of obscurity into the Light of the Gospel. Thus, the last shall be first, and the first last. This concept also supports the idea of there being a middle period when no one has the priesthood authority to act in the name of God.

Matthew 10:5-6
5 These twelve Jesus sent forth, and commanded them, saying, Go not into the way of the Gentiles, and into any city of the Samaritans enter ye not:
6 But go rather to the lost sheep of the house of Israel.

During his mortal existence, the Lord not only confined his missionary work to the Jews, but he also limited the preaching of his Twelve Apostles to the house of Israel. The key point is the transition that occurred once he was completely rejected of the Jews, his ancient covenant people. Recall the parable of the

PRIESTHOOD AUTHORITY

vineyard cited previously, how the Lord asked the Jews what should be done to the wicked husbandmen.

> **Matthew 21:40-44**
>
> 40 When the lord therefore of the vineyard cometh, what will he do unto those husbandmen?
> 41 They say unto him, He will miserably destroy those wicked men, and will let out his vineyard unto other husbandmen, which shall render him the fruits in their seasons.
> 42 Jesus saith unto them, Did ye never read in the scriptures, The stone which the builders rejected, the same is become the head of the corner: this is the Lord's doing, and it is marvellous in our eyes?
> 43 Therefore say I unto you, The kingdom of God shall be taken from you, and given to a nation bringing forth the fruits thereof.
> 44 And whosoever shall fall on this stone shall be broken: but on whomsoever it shall fall, it will grind him to powder.

"The Kingdom of God shall be taken from you, and given to a nation bringing forth the fruits thereof." This statement has several important implications. First, it indicates that at the time the Lord was addressing the Jews in his mortal state, the power of the priesthood and the authority to administer the saving ordinances pertaining to the Kingdom of God was fully vested in the Jews. That is why Jesus said to the woman at the well of Jacob near Samaria, "Ye worship ye know not what, and salvation is of the Jews." The statement also clearly indicates that because they rejected and killed the prophets of God, and finally the Son of God himself, the Kingdom of God was taken from them and given to another nation. The nation spoken of is the Gentiles. In this context, it means the descendants of Joseph or the Ten Lost Tribes from the north, as well as those that are mingled with them, thus meaning the rest of humanity, or non-Jews. Before this transition occurred, the Lord sought to reclaim his own, those of the Tribe of Judah.

> **John 1:10-14**
>
> 10 He was in the world, and the world was made by him, and the world knew him not.
> 11 He came unto his own, and his own received him not.
> 12 But as many as received him, to them gave he power to become the sons of God, even to them that believe on his name:
> 13 Which were born, not of blood, nor of the will of the flesh, nor of the will of man, but of God.
> 14 And the Word was made flesh, and dwelt among us, (and we beheld his glory, the glory as of the only begotten of the Father,) full of grace and truth.

"He came unto his own, and his own received him not." When the wicked husbandmen rejected the Son and crucified him on the cross, he not only served as the fulfillment of the Law of Moses as the last great sacrifice for sin, but also as the last great act leading up to the rejection of Judah as a favored people of the Lord. When the Jews threatened Jesus' life in another instance, he tells them as much.

> **John 7:32-36**
>
> 32 The Pharisees heard that the people murmured such things concerning him; and the Pharisees and the chief priests sent officers to take him.
> 33 Then said Jesus unto them, Yet a little while am I with you, and then I go unto him that sent me.

> 34 Ye shall seek me, and shall not find me: and where I am, thither ye cannot come.
> 35 Then said the Jews among themselves, Whither will he go, that we shall not find him? will he go unto the dispersed among the Gentiles, and teach the Gentiles?
> 36 What manner of saying is this that he said, Ye shall seek me, and shall not find me: and where I am, thither ye cannot come?

Often the words of the wicked can actually turn out to be prophetic without their even knowing it. After the ascension of Jesus to the throne of the Father, the Gospel was opened up to the Gentiles and many of the Gentiles were gathered into the fold of God. What we must examine is whether this transition from the Jews to the Gentiles, or in other words from Judah to Joseph, was allowed to continue, or whether the Gentiles also fell away. Let us look at another interesting scripture on this subject.

John 10:14-18
> 14 I am the good shepherd, and know my sheep, and am known of mine.
> 15 As the Father knoweth me, even so know I the Father: and I lay down my life for the sheep.
> 16 And other sheep I have, which are not of this fold: them also I must bring, and they shall hear my voice; and there shall be one fold, and one shepherd.
> 17 Therefore doth my Father love me, because I lay down my life, that I might take it again.
> 18 No man taketh it from me, but I lay it down of myself. I have power to lay it down, and I have power to take it again. This commandment have I received of my Father.

Not only do these verses show that Jesus allowed himself to be put to death, and had the power to prevent it, they also show that he had the power to take his life up again. Just as he had raised others from the dead during his mortal ministry, he also had the power to take up his own life again. He became the first person in human history to be resurrected, although many others came forth shortly after him and were seen by many in and around Jerusalem.

Jesus Christ also says something else very curious to his disciples. "Other sheep I have which are not of this fold." What sheep is he referring to and what did he do among them when he went to them? We may combine this statement with the question posed by the Pharisees above: "Will he go unto the dispersed among the Gentiles, and teach the Gentiles?" This suggests that the Lord may have visited people from the dispersed Ten Lost Tribes (the Gentiles, or Ephraim).

What I am suggesting is that Jesus may have appeared to prophets and people living at that time in another part of the world separated from the known civilization of the day. This occurrence would then be hidden from the world, and not contained in the Bible. It poses an interesting question to consider. If the Lord is able to appear in his resurrected body to his disciples at Jerusalem, is there anything that would prevent him from appearing to other peoples and other nations if he so desired?

The question that remains is whether the scriptures indicate a falling away of the Gentiles as well. The transition of the Gospel from the Jews to the Gentiles appears fairly clear from the New Testament evidence. At first, it seems that the Church of Jesus Christ was meant to continue with the Gentiles. If we recall, however, what the Lord said about the temple of Jerusalem, we begin to see that this was not to last.

PRIESTHOOD AUTHORITY

Matthew 24:1-5

1 AND Jesus went out, and departed from the temple: and his disciples came to him for to shew him the buildings of the temple.
2 And Jesus said unto them, See ye not all these things? verily I say unto you, There shall not be left here one stone upon another, that shall not be thrown down.
3 And as he sat upon the mount of Olives, the disciples came unto him privately, saying, Tell us, when shall these things be? and what shall be the sign of thy coming, and of the end of the world?
4 And Jesus answered and said unto them, Take heed that no man deceive you.
5 For many shall come in my name, saying, I am Christ; and shall deceive many.

We cited this scripture earlier to show that Christ himself even predicted that false prophets and evil teachers would come in among the flock to deceive and lead away the hearts of men. I now cite it again in another context, to show that while he is predicting a falling away, he is also saying that it will be complete. When he refers to the temple in this manner, he is really referring to the Church or Kingdom of God. When he says, "There shall not be left one stone upon another, that shall not be thrown down," it includes both the Jews and the Gentiles. In other words, none of the disciples who possessed the true priesthood and authority from God will be left to administer the ordinances of salvation.

This idea first came to me when I was visiting Jerusalem and saw the Western Wall. At the time, I believed that this was the Western Wall of Solomon's ancient temple. Later I was corrected, and learned that the great Western Wall, or Wailing Wall as it is sometimes called, is more likely part of the Herod Temple Complex, rather than the Solomon Temple Complex. However, as I saw people praying in front of this structure, I realized that Christ was referring to the Church instead of the Temple itself. This would not be the first time that a reference to the Temple being destroyed was used to mean something else.

John 2:18-22

18 Then answered the Jews and said unto him, What sign shewest thou unto us, seeing that thou doest these things?
19 Jesus answered and said unto them, Destroy this temple, and in three days I will raise it up.
20 Then said the Jews, Forty and six years was this temple in building, and wilt thou rear it up in three days?
21 But he spake of the temple of his body.
22 When therefore he was risen from the dead, his disciples remembered that he had said this unto them; and they believed the scripture, and the word which Jesus had said.

In this situation, Jesus was referring to his body as a temple, that it would be rebuilt or resurrected after three days. When Jesus said: "There shall not be left here one stone upon another, that shall not be thrown down," he was then referring to the body of the Church. If we knew where to look, we could probably find a portion of the actual Temple of Solomon still intact. When Hiroshima was bombed with the first atomic weapon used in actual warfare, it obliterated buildings for miles around. Nonetheless, even at ground zero, buildings remained having at least some of their substructure intact. I cannot imagine that the destroying armies that sacked the temple of Solomon had the ability to undo each and every stone.

Therefore, reason tells me that another meaning was intended by the Savior, and the spirit confirms this idea.

Although Solomon's Temple was destroyed, rebuilt and then finally destroyed again, no one really knows for certain whether we might find a stone or two still lying one on top of the other. The excavation of Jerusalem has revealed many structures below the surface of the present city. Stones can be found that are left one upon another in many ruins from ancient times. The Western Wall is a vivid example, with many stones stacked up to form the wall. It is in the cracks of the Western Wall in Jerusalem people place bits of paper with prayers written on them. It is there that both Jews and Christians assemble to pray and worship, looking forward to the time when the temple will be rebuilt. While the Western Wall structure found today is not really part of the former Temple grounds, to many people who visit the site it represents the fallen greatness of Israel, and the destruction of the Temple of Solomon.

Jesus was referring to the Church—that it would be completely destroyed and taken from the earth! Had the Church of God continued, a new temple could have been built to replace the one that was destroyed. Without true prophets to guide the people in such an undertaking, the temple has remained in ruin. In the place of the authorized prophets came falsehood and apostasy. "For many shall come in my name, saying, I am Christ; and deceive many." What we should really be looking forward to is when the true Church of God will be rebuilt and the priesthood authority restored. As we now begin our examination of the Book of Revelation, let us look for signs or predictions of the falling away of not only the Jews, but also of the newly-converted Gentiles, who entered the Church of God through the preaching of Paul and the other apostles.

CHAPTER FOURTEEN

The Revelation of St. John the Divine

The Book of Revelation is a most interesting book indeed. Over the ages, the mysteries contained in Revelation have incited the curiosity of millions. Most people revere the Book of Revelation as a stern warning about things that will occur prior to the Second Coming of Christ. Think of all the movies and books that have taken their themes from this sacred book. Many plots derived from this book deal with the coming forth of a single great anti-Christ. Such movies and books show the birth of a child that will grow up to be the most evil man to ever live. Though he is opposed by many, he will use the supernatural powers of Satan to eliminate all enemies in his path. Also, he will have the mark of "666" as a distinguishing feature. Most of these stories show him as a ruthless and invincible tyrant. While the theme of predestined evil being unfolded through the life of this powerful anti-Christ is truly engaging, none of these dramatic stories ever seem to resolve how he is ultimately conquered and subdued by the Lord.

What I desire to demonstrate through scriptural analysis is that this personage is not a mortal being, and will never be born. He will never receive a body because he was cast down to earth as a spirit, and will remain a spirit forever. The Great Anti-Christ spoken of in the Book of Revelation is none other than Satan himself. The prediction of his ability to conquer the world through his evil powers and influence are descriptive of the events that occurred shortly after the Savior's mortal ministry. The scriptures point to his temporary reign, but ultimately he and his angels will be overcome once the Lord returns from his long withdrawal. Zion will once again spring forth on the earth. The identification of this beast figure as some future mortal, tyrannical leader that will take over the entire world through his evil supernatural powers is the same thing that has occurred with respect to the king of Assyria in the Book of Isaiah. Many have incorrectly associated this evil tyrant as being a future mortal being. To overcome such misconceptions, let us examine the Book of Revelation in light of our symbolic framework derived from Isaiah. I will start with a few general observations.

First of all, the very name of the book is significant—"Revelation." This has been the focus of our entire discussion from the beginning of this book. I have proposed that revelation would cease at some point in time leading to a great famine of hearing the words of the Lord. It is curious that the last book of the Bible is called Revelation. If the Lord's prophets were indeed withdrawn from the earth and his true priesthood removed, the Book of Revelation should give some indication of this event. We should see the same three distinct periods of time with respect to the presence of divine revelation on the earth.

In many languages, the title of this book is "Apocalypse," meaning the ultimate triumph of good over evil, and the destructive end of the world. In English, the title is "Revelation." Both are actually correct, in that it is a book of revelation concerning the things that will occur prior to the Second Coming of the Lord. Recall from the question posed by the disciples of the Lord in Matthew 24 what Jesus tells them will occur.

> **Matthew 24:3-5**
> 3 And as he sat upon the mount of Olives, the disciples came unto him privately, saying, Tell us, when shall these things be? and what shall be the sign of thy coming, and of the end of the world?
> 4 And Jesus answered and said unto them, Take heed that no man deceive you.
> 5 For many shall come in my name, saying, I am Christ; and shall deceive many.

If we combine these thoughts, we should look for a time when Satan and his followers will come in the name of the Lord, saying, "I am Christ; and shall deceive many." Let us keep this in mind as we go through the scriptures contained in this sacred work.

Symbolic Style

Another important characteristic of the Book of Revelation concerns the style in which it was written. Unlike the many other books of the New Testament, the Book of Revelation is more like the books of the Old Testament we previously analyzed. The things one reads in the Books of Revelation, Isaiah, Jeremiah, Ezekiel, and so forth, are all considered to be mysterious "prophecies." The mysteries of the Book of Revelation are cloaked in symbolism, as we saw in the Old Testament writings, while the rest of the books of the New Testament basically fall into three categories:

1. The Gospels, namely the Books of Matthew, Mark, Luke and John. These four books relate the story of the Lord Jesus Christ, namely that he is the Christ. He is the chosen Messiah and Savior of the world. Matthew, Mark, Luke, and John serve as witnesses to the world of the divinity of the Lord Jesus Christ.
2. The Acts of the Apostles, which is attributed to Luke as the author. This book describes the events and miracles performed by the apostles and the other disciples of Christ following his death and subsequent resurrection. The book, the Acts, is important in that it shows the continuation of the Lord's Church after his resurrection, and it gives a glimpse of the opposition the Church faced during this critical period after the Lord's departure.

THE REVELATION OF ST. JOHN THE DIVINE

3. The Epistles, meaning letters from the apostles either to certain congregations of the Lord's Church, or to specific individuals. These letters are instructive because they give the reader great insight into the opposition and challenges faced by the members of the Lord's Kingdom in that critical period of time. They are basically just what their name implies—letters. While many of these letters are filled with important morsels of doctrine and critical clarifications of right and wrong, they are still quite different in style from the more classical and prophetic books of the Bible.

In contrast to these three styles, the Book of Revelation returns the reader to the symbolic language characteristic of the Old Testament prophets. This book was written and prepared to reveal important information that would have otherwise been removed from the Bible by evil men wishing to thwart the progress of Zion and the salvation of God's children. The Book of Revelation was written by the Apostle John, who was also known as the Lord's Beloved. We have some evidence from the New Testament that John actually never tasted of death, but was rather allowed to tarry on the earth.

John 21:20-25
20 Then Peter, turning about, seeth the disciple whom Jesus loved following; which also leaned on his breast at supper, and said, Lord, which is he that betrayeth thee?
21 Peter seeing him saith to Jesus, Lord, and what shall this man do?
22 Jesus saith unto him, If I will that he tarry till I come, what is that to thee? follow thou me.
23 Then went this saying abroad among the brethren, that that disciple should not die: yet Jesus said not unto him, He shall not die; but, If I will that he tarry till I come, what is that to thee?
24 This is the disciple which testifieth of these things, and wrote these things: and we know that his testimony is true.
25 And there are also many other things which Jesus did, the which, if they should be written every one, I suppose that even the world itself could not contain the books that should be written. Amen.

The Apostle John, the Lord's Beloved Disciple or John the Revelator, may have been allowed to tarry on the earth without tasting of death. How this would be accomplished is not spelled out in the scriptures. Enough is said, however, that one comes away with the feeling that John might still be alive today, wandering the earth to fulfill the will of the Lord. This adds even more mystery to the Book of Revelation.

The above scripture from the Book of John is also significant because of the last verse cited. "And there are also many other things which Jesus did, the which, if they should be written every one, I suppose that even the world itself could not contain the books that should be written. Amen." This scripture is supportive of the open canon concept. It suggests that more of the acts of Jesus could have been written than those contained in the present Bible. Jesus did other things, and not just a few things, but many. This scripture suggests that other events might be recorded somewhere involving Jesus Christ, and that they might be forthcoming. The interesting aspect to this concept of additional scripture is what many believe is meant by a certain verse of scripture contained in the Book of Revelation itself.

THE LATTER RAIN

Revelation 22:18-19

18 For I testify unto every man that heareth the words of the prophecy of this book, If any man shall add unto these things, God shall add unto him the plagues that are written in this book:
19 And if any man shall take away from the words of the book of this prophecy, God shall take away his part out of the book of life, and out of the holy city, and from the things which are written in this book.

At first glance, this statement, which appears in the very last chapter of the Bible itself, might seem to suggest that the Lord's scriptures are complete, and there will be no more scripture added to the Bible. A closer analysis would tend to contradict such a suggestion. First of all we have seen what the very same author said about the acts of Jesus Christ in the last verse of the Book of John cited above—the works of Christ are endless, and could occupy countless books. If Christ did things on earth that were not included in the Bible, they would still have value to the children of men, and lead us closer to Christ. Rather than saying that no more scripture can be written, John is warning evil men not to mess with the text of his prophecy, specifically the Book of Revelation itself. He is concerned about the impending turnover of the sacred things of the Church to evil ministers who will pervert and alter the rites and ordinances of the true Gospel. A similar warning is given by Moses in Deuteronomy.

Deuteronomy 4:1-2

1 NOW therefore hearken, O Israel, unto the statutes and unto the judgments, which I teach you, for to do them, that ye may live, and go in and possess the land which the LORD God of your fathers giveth you.
2 Ye shall not add unto the word which I command you, neither shall ye diminish ought from it, that ye may keep the commandments of the LORD your God which I command you.

If one were to take this commandment from Moses literally, you should then not add to the words of Moses either. Therefore, the canon of scripture would end after the last book of Moses, which would be the book in which this was written (Deuteronomy). All of the scriptures, stories, and prophecies in the Bible after Deuteronomy would therefore be considered "adding to the word I command you." Moses had the same concern as John—that men would alter his words, statutes, and prophecies. The statement from John in the Book of Revelation really only warns men not to alter the text of the Book of Revelation, but it does not mean that nothing more about Christ will ever be written.

We already mentioned at the start of our discussion of the New Testament that at the time Jesus Christ was on the earth, and during the time when the New Testament apostles were active on the earth, there was no New Testament. There was a gap of about 400 years between the writing of the Book of Malachi and the Birth of the Savior. Many of the Jews at the time must have considered the Old Testament to be closed canon, and in some publications of the Old Testament it even states, "END OF THE PROPHETS," after the last verse of Malachi, Chapter 4. It follows that anyone visiting a Jewish synagogue today will find only the Torah, or the Old Testament as its Holy Text, with no mention at all of the New Testament works of Jesus Christ, nor those of his disciples.

THE REVELATION OF ST. JOHN THE DIVINE

If Jesus Christ could appear to Mary Magdalene, the Twelve Apostles, and others after his resurrection, why could he not appear today if he chose to do so? He could! He will when the time is right to restore his Kingdom again to the earth. When that great day arrives, it will be an event worthy of being recorded as a sacred work of scripture. The leaders of false doctrines and false priesthoods will complain in that day that God has finished his work, and will do no more. They turn his works into fables.

> **2 Timothy 4:3-4**
> 3 For the time will come when they will not endure sound doctrine; but after their own lusts shall they heap to themselves teachers, having itching ears;
> 4 And they shall turn away their ears from the truth, and shall be turned unto fables.

Let us now investigate the text of the Book of Revelation and see if indeed this process of falling away from the truth is also predicted by the Apostle John. Let us see if the symbols and types found in the Book of Isaiah are repeated in Revelation as well.

> **Revelation 1:1-3**
> 1 THE Revelation of Jesus Christ, which God gave unto him, to shew unto his servants things which must shortly come to pass; and he sent and signified it by his angel unto his servant John:
> 2 Who bare record of the word of God, and of the testimony of Jesus Christ, and of all things that he saw.
> 3 Blessed is he that readeth, and they that hear the words of this prophecy, and keep those things which are written therein: for the time is at hand.

The first thing we learn is that the Book of Revelation is a revelation or divine message from Jesus Christ of things which must shortly come to pass, and that this message was given through the servant John. The reader is admonished to "hear the words of this prophecy, and keep those things which are written therein: for the time is at hand." It would seem reasonable to view the things written in the Book of Revelation as things that are to occur after the ascension of Jesus Christ into Heaven, and before his Second Coming.

The Seven Remaining Candlesticks

> **Revelation 1:4-5**
> 4 JOHN to the seven churches which are in Asia: Grace be unto you, and peace, from him which is, and which was, and which is to come; and from the seven Spirits which are before his throne;
> 5 And from Jesus Christ, who is the faithful witness, and the first begotten of the dead, and the prince of the kings of the earth. Unto him that loved us, and washed us from our sins in his own blood,

John is addressing the disciples of the Church that are in the seven remaining congregations at the time the Book of Revelation was written. In fact, in verse 11 of Chapter 1 of Revelation, John is instructed by the Lord what to do:

> **Revelation 1:10-11**
> 10 I was in the Spirit on the Lord's day, and heard behind me a great voice, as of a trumpet,

> 11 Saying, I am Alpha and Omega, the first and the last: and, What thou seest, write in a book, and send it unto the seven churches which are in Asia; unto Ephesus, and unto Smyrna, and unto Pergamos, and unto Thyatira, and unto Sardis, and unto Philadelphia, and unto Laodicea.

The Lord indicates exactly which cities remain with members of his church: Ephesus, Smyrna, Pergamos, Thyatira, Sardis, Philadelphia, and Laodicea. He says nothing about Rome or Corinth or Galacia or the Hebrews in Jerusalem. Since the Book of Revelation was written some years after the events that occurred in the Gospels, the Acts, and the several Epistles, it would appear that the locations of the active congregations of the Lord's Church have been somewhat altered during the intervening years. If an active congregation still existed in Corinth, then I see no reason why the Lord would not have mentioned this city as well. These missing congregations must have already succumbed to the pressures and persecutions of the day, and their members fled to the remaining seven congregations, were killed, or fell away from the truth.

Many of the first congregations established by the apostles after the resurrection of Jesus Christ had already fallen away by the time Revelation was being written by the Apostle John on the Island of Patmos. The Book of Revelation is a warning to the remaining disciples and congregations to remain strong despite intense persecution and the spreading of lies and false doctrines by the false prophets of the day. Let us see what the Lord specifically tells the seven remaining congregations, starting with his message to the disciples in Ephesus:

> **Revelation 2:1-5**
> 1 UNTO the angel of the church of Ephesus write; These things saith he that holdeth the seven stars in his right hand, who walketh in the midst of the seven golden candlesticks;
> 2 I know thy works, and thy labour, and thy patience, and how thou canst not bear them which are evil: and thou hast tried them which say they are apostles, and are not, and hast found them liars:
> 3 And hast borne, and hast patience, and for my name's sake hast laboured, and hast not fainted.
> 4 Nevertheless I have somewhat against thee, because thou hast left thy first love.
> 5 Remember therefore from whence thou art fallen, and repent, and do the first works; or else I will come unto thee quickly, and will remove thy candlestick out of his place, except thou repent.

Right away, we see that the major trial facing the disciples at Ephesus is to resist those "which say they are apostles, and are not." As we saw before, many false prophets came among them teaching all manner of doctrines contrary to the Gospel of Christ, and it was all the members could do to resist them. In verse five, we see a strict warning from the Lord about what will happen if they are not patient, vigilant, and true: "I will come quickly, and will remove thy candlestick out of his place, except thou repent." This is a stark warning, and a form of foreshadowing unless they repent. At the very least, we should all agree that the Lord is not saying "All is well, don't worry about a thing." No, instead he is warning them to hang in there or their candlestick will also be snuffed out! This prediction is not limited to the congregation at Ephesus, but is given to each of the seven remaining groups of disciples.

THE REVELATION OF ST. JOHN THE DIVINE

Revelation 2:24-29
24 But unto you I say, and unto the rest in Thyatira, as many as have not this doctrine, and which have not known the depths of Satan, as they speak; I will put upon you none other burden.
25 But that which ye have already hold fast till I come.
26 And he that overcometh, and keepeth my works unto the end, to him will I give power over the nations:
27 And he shall rule them with a rod of iron; as the vessels of a potter shall they be broken to shivers: even as I received of my Father.
28 And I will give him the morning star.
29 He that hath an ear, let him hear what the Spirit saith unto the churches.

Here, the Lord counsels his disciples to remain faithful despite the persecutions of Satan and his ministers, and that he will ultimately overthrow the wicked nations of Satan, and "as the vessels of a potter shall they be broken to shivers." While Satan will advance temporarily, in the end he will be broken and defeated. In the meantime, the disciples of the remaining churches are counseled to try and remain strong despite opposition.

Revelation 6:9-11
9 And when he had opened the fifth seal, I saw under the altar the souls of them that were slain for the word of God, and for the testimony which they held:
10 And they cried with a loud voice, saying, How long, O Lord, holy and true, dost thou not judge and avenge our blood on them that dwell on the earth?
11 And white robes were given unto every one of them; and it was said unto them, that they should rest yet for a little season, until their fellowservants also and their brethren, that should be killed as they were, should be fulfilled.

In verse ten above, the martyrs of the cause of Jesus are asking the Lord, "How long, O Lord, holy and true, dost thou not judge and avenge our blood on them that dwell on the earth?" These are the good people of the earth—those that are killed by the wicked. They are the ones asking for justice to be administered upon their murderers. However, they must wait for a certain specified space of time, and "they should rest yet for a little season," and that during this time of waiting on the Lord, other martyrs would also be slain because they refuse the false doctrine of the devil.

The Seven Seals

The seven seals represent seven dispensations or millennia. Using the biblical perspective that man's existence on earth began about six thousand years ago, then the fifth seal would be from the birth of Jesus to about the year 1,000 AD. The martyrs under the altar are those that were killed during the Dark Ages. They include the apostles and prophets of the New Testament, and others killed for seeking truth. If we accept the seal/millennia perspective, we are now somewhere near the end of the 6th seal period and close to the ushering in of the 7th seal period, which would be the Millennium period after the Second Coming of Jesus Christ. This last period will be a time when the Lord will lead the righteous "unto living fountains of waters: and God shall wipe away all tears from their eyes."

THE LATTER RAIN

Revelation 7:13-17
13 And one of the elders answered, saying unto me, What are these which are arrayed in white robes? and whence came they?
14 And I said unto him, Sir, thou knowest. And he said to me, These are they which came out of great tribulation, and have washed their robes, and made them white in the blood of the Lamb.
15 Therefore are they before the throne of God, and serve him day and night in his temple: and he that sitteth on the throne shall dwell among them.
16 They shall hunger no more, neither thirst any more; neither shall the sun light on them, nor any heat.
17 For the Lamb which is in the midst of the throne shall feed them, and shall lead them unto living fountains of waters: and God shall wipe away all tears from their eyes.

The disciples that are given white robes to wear are those that are washed clean by the blood of the Savior Jesus Christ. "He that sitteth on the thrown shall dwell among them." The references to thirst, hunger, and water are also significant based on our study of Isaiah. "They shall hunger no more, neither thirst any more; neither shall the sun light on them, nor any heat. For the Lamb which is in the midst of the throne shall feed them, and shall lead them unto living fountains of waters." Those that suffered through the great period of prolonged Spiritual Famine on the earth will be rewarded in the end for their faithfulness. They shall all be recovered and none of them lost, even though they had to wade through a period of no revelation and no prophets. They were still judged to be faithful to the Lord, and a means will be provided to bring them into the Church and Kingdom of God, receiving their white robes at the time of their entering into the presence of the Lord.

Revelation 9:1-2
1 AND the fifth angel sounded, and I saw a star fall from heaven unto the earth: and to him was given the key of the bottomless pit.
2 And he opened the bottomless pit; and there arose a smoke out of the pit, as the smoke of a great furnace; and the sun and the air were darkened by reason of the smoke of the pit.

In Chapter 9 of Revelation, we are taught that a star fell from heaven to the earth, having the key of the bottomless pit. Clearly this is a reference to Satan and to his having dominion over hell, where the wicked will go after the final judgment. While it is my feeling and belief that the hell spoken of in the scriptures is not a literal caldron of lava designed to torture the wicked, it is rather a figurative burning of conscience that can never be quenched. Thus it is endless in its duration, knowing what they could have had, and what they gave up when they chose to follow Satan. As all men sin, and fall short, the only means of redeeming the children of men is through the atonement of Jesus Christ. Satan has as his purpose to thwart the Kingdom of God, and to tempt the would-be followers of Christ into the paths of falsehood and vanity, wickedness and sin.

Ephraim and Judah

Revelation 11:1-7
1 AND there was given me a reed like unto a rod: and the angel stood, saying, Rise, and measure the temple of God, and the altar, and them that worship therein.

THE REVELATION OF ST. JOHN THE DIVINE

2 But the court which is without the temple leave out, and measure it not; for it is given unto the Gentiles: and the holy city shall they tread under foot forty and two months.
3 And I will give power unto my two witnesses, and they shall prophesy a thousand two hundred and threescore days, clothed in sackcloth.
4 These are the two olive trees, and the two candlesticks standing before the God of the earth.
5 And if any man will hurt them, fire proceedeth out of their mouth, and devoureth their enemies: and if any man will hurt them, he must in this manner be killed.
6 These have power to shut heaven, that it rain not in the days of their prophecy: and have power over waters to turn them to blood, and to smite the earth with all plagues, as often as they will.
7 And when they shall have finished their testimony, the beast that ascendeth out of the bottomless pit shall make war against them, and shall overcome them, and kill them.

Many take this passage to mean that in the last days, two prophets will be raised up by the Lord and ultimately slain in the streets of Jerusalem. Their bodies will lay in the street for three and a half days while the wicked rejoice over them. Then will the Lord resurrect them in the view of all and call them up to him in heaven. While this may actually occur in a literal sense at some given time in the future, based on our previous insights gained from our study of both the Old and New Testaments, we can see another meaning in this great symbolic passage. Israel is often referred to as an olive tree, "and the children of Israel his pleasant fruit." We saw this from the Lord, from the apostles, and we now see it again in the Revelation of John. We saw from the earlier sections of Revelation that a reference to a candlestick meant a body of believers. In verse four, two olive trees are being described, Judah and Ephraim, which are like two candlesticks (or congregations of people) standing before the God of the earth.

When this idea ultimately occurred to me, verses six and seven suddenly had a meaning that fit well into the symbolic structure first defined through the study of Isaiah. The meaning rendered after the application of the symbols and types from Isaiah might read as follows: "These have power to shut heaven, and to end the former period of prophetic utterance. The waters of revelation are swallowed up in the blood of the prophets and the blood of the Lamb of God, and the earth is smitten with a great curse. When the prophets from Judah and the prophets from the Gentiles shall have finished their testimony to the world, Satan shall then be given power to overcome them both, and shall kill them and stop them from prophesying further."

Revelation 11:8-10

8 And their dead bodies shall lie in the street of the great city, which spiritually is called Sodom and Egypt, where also our Lord was crucified.
9 And they of the people and kindreds and tongues and nations shall see their dead bodies three days and an half, and shall not suffer their dead bodies to be put in graves.
10 And they that dwell upon the earth shall rejoice over them, and make merry, and shall send gifts one to another; because these two prophets tormented them that dwelt on the earth.

Time is not really relevant here. When it says three and a half days, it is figurative, not literal. It is a symbolic type, and what it means is that the bodies of Judah and Ephraim, or of fallen Israel, will lie in view of the people of the earth in the street of the great city, which spiritually is called Sodom and Egypt, where also our Lord was crucified. Well, this is a strange situation, since we would normally say that John is referring to Jerusalem, since that is where Christ was crucified. From our study of Isaiah, we see that whether the Bible writers say Sodom and Egypt, or Assyria and Egypt, they still represent the same set of entities—churches of the devil and churches of men. Thus, the bodies of the fallen people, Judah and Ephraim, are being rejoiced over by the leaders of the false churches of the devil and of men.

These false organizations, which profess to be of God, hold the inhabitants of the earth bound in sin and destined for hell if a means is not provided for their escape. When the Lord withdrew from these two branches of the true olive tree, they became spiritually dead to the eyes of the world. Satan and his followers are delighted by their apparent truimph over these two families of Israel during this great period of Spiritual Famine when the heavens are shut.

In the end, the inhabitants of the earth and the wicked ministers of false churches will all be surprised. For, at some point in time, the Lord God will breathe new life into these two fallen nations, Ephraim and Judah. Since in the Former Rain period it went from Judah to the Gentiles, in the Latter Rain period it will start with the Gentiles or Ephraim, and then finally back to Judah. Ultimately, they will both be alive again, and be grafted back into the true olive tree.

Isaiah 11:10-16
10 And in that day there shall be a root of Jesse, which shall stand for an ensign of the people; to it shall the Gentiles seek: and his rest shall be glorious.
11 And it shall come to pass in that day, that the Lord shall set his hand again the second time to recover the remnant of his people, which shall be left, from Assyria, and from Egypt, and from Pathros, and from Cush, and from Elam, and from Shinar, and from Hamath, and from the islands of the sea.
12 And he shall set up an ensign for the nations, and shall assemble the outcasts of Israel, and gather together the dispersed of Judah from the four corners of the earth.
13 The envy also of Ephraim shall depart, and the adversaries of Judah shall be cut off: Ephraim shall not envy Judah, and Judah shall not vex Ephraim.
14 But they shall fly upon the shoulders of the Philistines toward the west; they shall spoil them of the east together: they shall lay their hand upon Edom and Moab; and the children of Ammon shall obey them.
15 And the LORD shall utterly destroy the tongue of the Egyptian sea; and with his mighty wind shall he shake his hand over the river, and shall smite it in the seven streams, and make men go over dryshod.
16 And there shall be an highway for the remnant of his people, which shall be left, from Assyria; like as it was to Israel in the day that he came up out of the land of Egypt.

In the latter days, which days these are, the Gentiles will seek again to find the root of Jesse, which shall stand for an ensign of the people, even Jesus Christ—the Resurrected Lord. The Lord will finally restore Zion again to the earth, and he "shall set his hand again the second time to recover the remnant of his people, which shall be left from Assyria, and from Egypt." Sodom and Egypt, or Assyria and Egypt: they both mean the same thing. When the Lord restores Zion, the Gentiles, or descendants of Ephraim and Joseph will be the first to see it and the first to recognize it. This time, "the envy also of Ephraim shall depart, and the adversaries of Judah shall be cut off: Ephraim shall not envy Judah, and Judah shall not vex Ephraim." The contentions and divisions that existed between these two branches of Israel will be mended in the latter days, and they both shall be made alive again in the eyes of all the nations. A highway will be made for their return from Assyria and Egypt where they have been during the Dark Ages of spiritual dearth. Let us return to Revelation 11 to see this return predicted.

> **Revelation 11:11-19**
> 11 And after three days and an half the Spirit of life from God entered into them, and they stood upon their feet; and great fear fell upon them which saw them.
> 12 And they heard a great voice from heaven saying unto them, Come up hither. And they ascended up to heaven in a cloud; and their enemies beheld them.
> 13 And the same hour was there a great earthquake, and the tenth part of the city fell, and in the earthquake were slain of men seven thousand: and the remnant were affrighted, and gave glory to the God of heaven.
> 14 The second woe is past; and, behold, the third woe cometh quickly.
> 15 And the seventh angel sounded; and there were great voices in heaven, saying, The kingdoms of this world are become the kingdoms of our Lord, and of his Christ; and he shall reign for ever and ever.
> 16 And the four and twenty elders, which sat before God on their seats, fell upon their faces, and worshipped God,
> 17 Saying, We give thee thanks, O Lord God Almighty, which art, and wast, and art to come; because thou hast taken to thee thy great power, and hast reigned.
> 18 And the nations were angry, and thy wrath is come, and the time of the dead, that they should be judged, and that thou shouldest give reward unto thy servants the prophets, and to the saints, and them that fear thy name, small and great; and shouldest destroy them which destroy the earth.
> 19 And the temple of God was opened in heaven, and there was seen in his temple the ark of his testament: and there were lightnings, and voices, and thunderings, and an earthquake, and great hail.

After the period of time when the two great branches of Israel (Judah and Ephraim) are allowed to remain dead, the Spirit of Life from God suddenly enters into them again. They stand upon their feet, and great fear falls upon all those that had been rejoicing and making merry.

Remember how we discussed this great fear when we studied the words of Isaiah. The armies of the Lord will ride forth from place to place in a ruthless nature, and it will cause great fear to come upon the inhabitants of the earth. John is describing this same fear—The fear that comes upon the false ministers and false prophets, who draw near unto the Lord with their mouths, but their hearts are far from him. These are the ones that fear. Those that are held captive by Assyria and Egypt might also fear. They fear because they do not understand. They fear because they have been blinded and deceived by the works and vanities of the evil one.

The devil has created false doctrines and organizations to confuse and corrupt the right ways of the Lord. In this final dispensation, the Lord will once again speak from the heavens, and will gather his people unto himself. Ultimately, "the kingdoms of this world are become the kingdoms of our Lord, and of his Christ; and he shall reign for ever and ever." Once Zion is reestablished it will go forth and consume all false doctrines, and shall never be brought down again.

THE LATTER RAIN

The Church Flees into the Wilderness

Revelation 12:1-6

1 AND there appeared a great wonder in heaven; a woman clothed with the sun, and the moon under her feet, and upon her head a crown of twelve stars:
2 And she being with child cried, travailing in birth, and pained to be delivered.
3 And there appeared another wonder in heaven; and behold a great red dragon, having seven heads and ten horns, and seven crowns upon his heads.
4 And his tail drew the third part of the stars of heaven, and did cast them to the earth: and the dragon stood before the woman which was ready to be delivered, for to devour her child as soon as it was born.
5 And she brought forth a man child, who was to rule all nations with a rod of iron: and her child was caught up unto God, and to his throne.
6 And the woman fled into the wilderness, where she hath a place prepared of God, that they should feed her there a thousand two hundred and threescore days.

In light of our previous discussions, this passage of scripture should now become self-evident. The woman with a crown of twelve stars upon her head is Israel, Zion, or the Church and Kingdom of God. She has a crown of twelve stars, one for each of the tribes of Israel. The child that she bears is Jesus Christ, the Messiah. We see that Satan is waiting for the birth of the Savior to thwart it, and to stop God's eternal plans. The devil "stood before the woman which was ready to be delivered, for to devour her child as soon as it was born," which child should have ruled the nations, it being his right to do so. The identity of this child is clarified when it says that he was "caught up unto God, and to his throne," as was Jesus according to the testimony of the Twelve Apostles.

We learn that the woman, or the Church of God, "fled into the wilderness, where she hath a place prepared of God, that they should feed her there a thousand two hundred and threescore days." The exact time of this wilderness sojourn is not really that important. Days could mean years. What is important is that she went to the wilderness and waited. She was taken away by the Lord! Her son, the Holy One of Israel ascended up to the throne of his Father in Heaven. Who is left? The great red dragon, which drew away the third part of the stars of heaven, and did cast them to the earth. It is Satan, as is made clear in the following verses.

Revelation 12:7-12

7 And there was war in heaven: Michael and his angels fought against the dragon; and the dragon fought and his angels,
8 And prevailed not; neither was their place found any more in heaven.
9 And the great dragon was cast out, that old serpent, called the Devil, and Satan, which deceiveth the whole world: he was cast out into the earth, and his angels were cast out with him.
10 And I heard a loud voice saying in heaven, Now is come salvation, and strength, and the kingdom of our God, and the power of his Christ: for the accuser of our brethren is cast down, which accused them before our God day and night.
11 And they overcame him by the blood of the Lamb, and by the word of their testimony; and they loved not their lives unto the death.
12 Therefore rejoice, ye heavens, and ye that dwell in them. Woe to the inhabiters of the earth and of the sea! for the devil is come down unto you, having great wrath, because he knoweth that he hath but a short time.

THE REVELATION OF ST. JOHN THE DIVINE

Who is the dragon? "The great dragon is the one that was cast out, that old serpent, called the Devil, and Satan, which deceiveth the whole world." Satan is frantic to lead away the children of men because he knows that he only "hath but a short time."

Revelation 12:13-17

13 And when the dragon saw that he was cast unto the earth, he persecuted the woman which brought forth the man child.
14 And to the woman were given two wings of a great eagle, that she might fly into the wilderness, into her place, where she is nourished for a time, and times, and half a time, from the face of the serpent.
15 And the serpent cast out of his mouth water as a flood after the woman, that he might cause her to be carried away of the flood.
16 And the earth helped the woman, and the earth opened her mouth, and swallowed up the flood which the dragon cast out of his mouth.
17 And the dragon was wroth with the woman, and went to make war with the remnant of her seed, which keep the commandments of God, and have the testimony of Jesus Christ.

The woman, or the Church of God, flew into the wilderness, and in response, the serpent, or Satan, "cast out of his mouth water as a flood after the woman, that he might cause her to be carried away of the flood." From our analysis of Isaiah, we know that water is symbolic of revelation. In this specific case, it is Satan that is doing the inspiration. The leaders of churches and institutions claiming to be of Christ are inspired of the devil to torment and persecute the true saints of God (those that would have joined the Church of God were it present). They receive the full brunt of Satan's railings and tortures. Despite their suffering during the Spiritual Famine period, they ultimately receive a white robe in the presence of the Father, and all their tears are wiped away.

Note, that the earth itself helped the woman and saved her from this flood of false doctrine and tyranny. The earth opened up her mouth and swallowed up the flood which the dragon cast out of his mouth. Over time, more and more truth is brought forth and less and less evil is present. Tyranny too is eventually brought in check in preparation for a return of the Lord's Kingdom to the earth. In the meantime, Satan is given full reign over the earth, since the Church of the Savior fled into the wilderness. This same image is again repeated in Chapter 13 of Revelation.

The Two Beasts: Assyria and Egypt

Revelation 13:1-10

1 AND I stood upon the sand of the sea, and saw a beast rise up out of the sea, having seven heads and ten horns, and upon his horns ten crowns, and upon his heads the name of blasphemy.
2 And the beast which I saw was like unto a leopard, and his feet were as the feet of a bear, and his mouth as the mouth of a lion: and the dragon gave him his power, and his seat, and great authority.
3 And I saw one of his heads as it were wounded to death; and his deadly wound was healed: and all the world wondered after the beast.
4 And they worshipped the dragon which gave power unto the beast: and they worshipped the beast, saying, Who is like unto the beast? who is able to make war with him?

5 And there was given unto him a mouth speaking great things and blasphemies; and power was given unto him to continue forty and two months.
6 And he opened his mouth in blasphemy against God, to blaspheme his name, and his tabernacle, and them that dwell in heaven.
7 And it was given unto him to make war with the saints, and to overcome them: and power was given him over all kindreds, and tongues, and nations.
8 And all that dwell upon the earth shall worship him, whose names are not written in the book of life of the Lamb slain from the foundation of the world.
9 If any man have an ear, let him hear.
10 He that leadeth into captivity shall go into captivity: he that killeth with the sword must be killed with the sword. Here is the patience and the faith of the saints.

Who gives power to the beast? The dragon is the one that gives him his power, his seat, and great authority. Since the dragon is Satan, then we must assume that the beast spoken of is the church of the devil. In the end, "it was given unto him to make war with the saints, and to overcome them: and power was given him over all kindreds, and tongues, and nations." With the aid of our symbolic tools developed from the Old Testament and especially from the Book of Isaiah, it becomes clear what this means.

Satan, or the king of Assyria as he is called in Isaiah, is allowed by the Lord to have complete reign over the entire earth. Because of the wickedness of the children of Israel in killing the prophets, and also in crucifying the Son of God, they are finally given that which they desired. The Lord withdrew his prophets, his guidance, and his protection from the tribes of Israel, both Judah and Ephraim. They both lie dead in the street while the wicked of the world rejoice. "Here is the patience and the faith of the saints," (the good people that remain on the earth during the withdrawal period of the Church). They must endure hardships and deprivation at the hands of evil persons who usurp power over them without authority from God.

Now if this seems reasonable, I am curious as to the meaning of verse three above. "And I saw one of his heads as it were wounded to death; and his deadly wound was healed: and all the world wondered after the beast." I will address this issue later when we get to Chapter 17, where we gain new insight and understanding about this phenomenon.

Revelation 13:11-18

11 And I beheld another beast coming up out of the earth; and he had two horns like a lamb, and he spake as a dragon.
12 And he exerciseth all the power of the first beast before him, and causeth the earth and them which dwell therein to worship the first beast, whose deadly wound was healed.
13 And he doeth great wonders, so that he maketh fire come down from heaven on the earth in the sight of men,
14 And deceiveth them that dwell on the earth by the means of those miracles which he had power to do in the sight of the beast; saying to them that dwell on the earth, that they should make an image to the beast, which had the wound by a sword, and did live.
15 And he had power to give life unto the image of the beast, that the image of the beast should both speak, and cause that as many as would not worship the image of the beast should be killed.
16 And he causeth all, both small and great, rich and poor, free and bond, to receive a mark in their right hand, or in their foreheads:

17 And that no man might buy or sell, save he that had the mark, or the name of the beast, or the number of his name.
18 Here is wisdom. Let him that hath understanding count the number of the beast: for it is the number of a man; and his number is Six hundred threescore and six.

This second beast to come forth seems to the people as if he were a lamb, but he speaks like a dragon. He has a form of Godliness, but denies the power thereof. He seems to be a good thing coming forth, but he is still an imposter. In fact, despite his seemingly good intentions at first, he exercises all the power of the first beast before him. The second beast does virtually the same thing as the first beast. He deceives the children of men by the means of miracles and wonders. This beast, however, is also not of God, thou he appears to be so. He makes it so everyone has to have his mark on them or they can do no more commerce in the world. Everyone everywhere is in a sense signed up to join this beast and to worship the dragon that gives him his power and authority. Much fear and speculation has existed in books, movies, and popular culture concerning the mysterious number of the beast: 666. This feared mark is just a symbolic image, meaning that if you are affiliated with a church or institution that claims to be of God, but in reality is not, then your membership therein is like having the number "666" tattooed onto your right hand or onto your forehead. Those that are sealed up unto the resurrection of the just receive a symbolic mark in their forehead as well.

Revelation 7:2-3
2 And I saw another angel ascending from the east, having the seal of the living God: and he cried with a loud voice to the four angels, to whom it was given to hurt the earth and the sea,
3 Saying, Hurt not the earth, neither the sea, nor the trees, till we have sealed the servants of our God in their foreheads.

This concept of sealing a person to the church of the devil or sealing them to the Church of the Lamb of God has a symbolic meaning. It means that on judgment day, there will be no doubt who belongs to the Lord and who belongs to Satan. Even the individual being judged will know with a certainty which side he or she has chosen. It will be so clear—as if they were stamped with a seal from the Lord or from Satan. They merely look and see which mark they have.

This second beast represents a second wave of delusion that covers the earth. A second beast comes forth and possesses the power of the first. In Isaiah, this second wave of falsehood was represented as going to Egypt for help and then being overrun by the king of Assyria. Recall that in Isaiah, the children of Israel felt oppressed by Assyria (the kingdom of the devil), so they desired to flee away. However, instead of appealing to the Lord directly for aid and help, they sought help through the nation of Egypt. We learned from Isaiah that Egypt was a symbolic representation of the arm of flesh. In terms of churches and organizations, it represents the churches and organizations created by men to flee from the church of the devil. The second beast in Revelation 13 is also representative of the churches of men. Here in Revelation, the same situation is represented by this second beast that has two horns like a lamb, but speaks like a dragon. While these churches of men might appear to give refuge from the oppression of the first beast, in the end, Satan is allowed to overcome them as well, and the beast ends up exercising "all the power of the first beast before him." This second beast causes those that do not accept his false doctrines to be persecuted and ridiculed. The children of Israel and the good people of the earth are still held in bondage.

The Restoration

Revelation 14:1-5

1 AND I looked, and, lo, a Lamb stood on the mount Sion, and with him an hundred forty and four thousand, having his Father's name written in their foreheads.
2 And I heard a voice from heaven, as the voice of many waters, and as the voice of a great thunder: and I heard the voice of harpers harping with their harps:
3 And they sung as it were a new song before the throne, and before the four beasts, and the elders: and no man could learn that song but the hundred and forty and four thousand, which were redeemed from the earth.
4 These are they which were not defiled with women; for they are virgins. These are they which follow the Lamb whithersoever he goeth. These were redeemed from among men, being the firstfruits unto God and to the Lamb.
5 And in their mouth was found no guile: for they are without fault before the throne of God.

In verse two, we see an interesting link between a voice from heaven and the sound of many waters. It is similar to the analogy we found from the Old Testament, making the link between rain, water, dew, and the divine revelation from God to man on earth. The image we see in the beginning of this chapter is the Lamb of God, or Jesus Christ standing on Mount Zion, and with him a mighty array of righteous servants at his side. These 144,000 servants are servants that have a specific assignment concerning the gathering of Israel in the last days. The number 144,000 may be literal or figurative, but it is a multiple of twelve. Thus, they represent the Twelve Tribes of Israel.

In verse four, we read that "These were redeemed from among men, being the first fruits unto God and to the Lamb." They must be resurrected beings that are no longer living in mortality, or "among men," especially when we consider that they have stood before the throne of God. Recall that once Jesus was resurrected, he told Mary Magdalene that he was going to the Father. No mortal being could approach the throne of God or enter into Heaven without being resurrected and judged worthy to enter therein. Hence, the 144,000 with the seal of Heavenly Father written in their foreheads are special ministering angels in the form of resurrected beings. These servants of the Lord undoubtedly have been given the priesthood authority of the Lamb of God to perform their special function, which is to assist in the literal gathering of Israel in the last days, "for they are without fault before the throne of God." With Christ at their head, these resurrected beings assist the Lord in the work of the final dispensation—the Great Period of the Latter Rain.

Revelation 14:6-8

6 And I saw another angel fly in the midst of heaven, having the everlasting gospel to preach unto them that dwell on the earth, and to every nation, and kindred, and tongue, and people,

THE REVELATION OF ST. JOHN THE DIVINE

7 Saying with a loud voice, Fear God, and give glory to him; for the hour of his judgment is come: and worship him that made heaven, and earth, and the sea, and the fountains of waters.
8 And there followed another angel, saying, Babylon is fallen, is fallen, that great city, because she made all nations drink of the wine of the wrath of her fornication.

The "everlasting gospel" will once again be restored to the earth, having been lost for centuries. This everlasting gospel will be brought forth by the work of angels and resurrected servants of the Lord, just as the ancient prophets visited Jesus with Peter, James, and John present on the Mount of Transfiguration. The just saints of God who are set apart and sealed to come forth in these latter times will also appear unto the Lord's prophets, giving them guidance and direction directly from the throne of God. Once this final dispensation is ushered in, the great period of Spiritual Famine will have come to an end. The heavens will once again be open, and the Lord will speak again to his servants the prophets. Thus, "Babylon is fallen, is fallen that great city, because she made all nations drink of the wine of the wrath of her fornication."

The newly-restored doctrine will defeat the false traditions that abound and Babylon will eventually become extinct from the earth. While it may take years or even centuries before this transition is finally complete, the angel "flying in the midst of heaven" speaks as if it is done the moment it starts—the moment the Gospel is restored. But for sure, a key element of this final dispensation will be the preaching of the Gospel to the inhabitants of the earth, the ministering of angels to the just, and the freeing of them from the influence and power of the beast, or the church of the devil.

Revelation 14:9-20
9 And the third angel followed them, saying with a loud voice, If any man worship the beast and his image, and receive his mark in his forehead, or in his hand,
10 The same shall drink of the wine of the wrath of God, which is poured out without mixture into the cup of his indignation; and he shall be tormented with fire and brimstone in the presence of the holy angels, and in the presence of the Lamb:
11 And the smoke of their torment ascendeth up for ever and ever: and they have no rest day nor night, who worship the beast and his image, and whosoever receiveth the mark of his name.
12 Here is the patience of the saints: here are they that keep the commandments of God, and the faith of Jesus.
13 And I heard a voice from heaven saying unto me, Write, Blessed are the dead which die in the Lord from henceforth: Yea, saith the Spirit, that they may rest from their labours; and their works do follow them.
14 And I looked, and behold a white cloud, and upon the cloud one sat like unto the Son of man, having on his head a golden crown, and in his hand a sharp sickle.
15 And another angel came out of the temple, crying with a loud voice to him that sat on the cloud, Thrust in thy sickle, and reap: for the time is come for thee to reap; for the harvest of the earth is ripe.
16 And he that sat on the cloud thrust in his sickle on the earth; and the earth was reaped.
17 And another angel came out of the temple which is in heaven, he also having a sharp sickle.
18 And another angel came out from the altar, which had power over fire; and cried with a loud cry to him that had the sharp sickle, saying, Thrust in thy sharp sickle, and gather the clusters of the vine of the earth; for her grapes are fully ripe.
19 And the angel thrust in his sickle into the earth, and gathered the vine of the earth, and cast it into the great winepress of the wrath of God.

THE LATTER RAIN

20 And the winepress was trodden without the city, and blood came out of the winepress, even unto the horse bridles, by the space of a thousand and six hundred furlongs.

Verses 9-13 show that anyone still wearing the mark of the beast on judgment day will be excluded from entering into the presence of God. They will be damned for ever, or in other words, their progress stopped. In contrast, those who keep the commandments of God, and demonstrate faith in the true Gospel of Jesus Christ, are allowed access to God throughout all eternity. The challenge for the disciples of Jesus living after the restoration of the Gospel to the earth is to reap the earth, and bring as many as possible to the knowledge of the Lord. Through faith in Jesus Christ, repentance, baptism through the restored authority, and by following the Holy Spirit, the disciples of the Latter Rain period will continue to build up Zion until she, the woman from Revelation 12, fills the whole earth. The commandment is given in verse 18 above: "Thrust in thy sharp sickle, and gather the clusters of the vine of the earth; for her grapes are fully ripe." But, instead of the wine coming forth, "blood came out of the winepress, even unto the horse bridles, by the space of a thousand and six hundred furlongs." This same concept of wine becoming blood or water becoming blood is seen again in the following passage.

Revelation 16:3-6
3 And the second angel poured out his vial upon the sea; and it became as the blood of a dead man: and every living soul died in the sea.
4 And the third angel poured out his vial upon the rivers and fountains of waters; and they became blood.
5 And I heard the angel of the waters say, Thou art righteous, O Lord, which art, and wast, and shalt be, because thou hast judged thus.
6 For they have shed the blood of saints and prophets, and thou hast given them blood to drink; for they are worthy.

This also brings to mind the miracle we already discussed of the Lord changing water into wine at a marriage feast. The symbolism here is that the revelation coming forth in the Latter Rain period will be strengthened by the blood of the Lamb. His infinite sacrifice for the sins of the world will come as a vivid reminder to the wicked of their guilt before God. "For they have shed the blood of saints and prophets, and thou hast given them blood to drink; for they are worthy." The humble seekers of truth will see the new doctrine springing forth, and will be drawn to it. It will be the new wine in new bottles, made miraculously available to them by the Lord, and this new revelation will fill their souls with joy and happiness and hope.

As in Isaiah, we see that the Apostle John also repeats messages in different chapters with different symbolic images to depict the same thing. In Chapter 12, John used a mother in travail as a symbol of the Church of God, and we saw that when she was delivered, she fled into the wilderness for a space of time. Likewise, we saw that her son, when he was delivered, was taken up to the throne of God. Thus the woman spoken of in Revelation 12 was the Church of God, and she escaped into the wilderness for a time.

THE REVELATION OF ST. JOHN THE DIVINE

The Mother of Harlots

Revelation 17:1-6

1 AND there came one of the seven angels which had the seven vials, and talked with me, saying unto me, Come hither; I will shew unto thee the judgment of the great whore that sitteth upon many waters:
2 With whom the kings of the earth have committed fornication, and the inhabitants of the earth have been made drunk with the wine of her fornication.
3 So he carried me away in the spirit into the wilderness: and I saw a woman sit upon a scarlet coloured beast, full of names of blasphemy, having seven heads and ten horns.
4 And the woman was arrayed in purple and scarlet colour, and decked with gold and precious stones and pearls, having a golden cup in her hand full of abominations and filthiness of her fornication:
5 And upon her forehead was a name written, MYSTERY, BABYLON THE GREAT, THE MOTHER OF HARLOTS AND ABOMINATIONS OF THE EARTH.
6 And I saw the woman drunken with the blood of the saints, and with the blood of the martyrs of Jesus: and when I saw her, I wondered with great admiration.

In Chapter 13, we were introduced to her opposite, or the church of the devil, only in that chapter she was symbolized as a beast having seven heads and ten horns, and her power came from the Dragon, who is the devil. Now we see that in Chapter 17, John ultimately uses the symbol of a woman to again describe a church. This time it is the church of the devil, not the Church of Christ. Instead of being a righteous woman like the one in Chapter 12 who was given wings "that she might fly into the wilderness;" the woman in Chapter 17 is represented as a whore. In fact, she is called "the Mother of Harlots and Abominations of the earth." She is "drunken with the blood of the saints, and with the blood of the martyrs of Jesus." Thus, John uses the symbol of a woman both for the good church and the evil church.

The connection between the Mother of Harlots in Chapter 17 and the seven-headed beast from Chapter 13 occurs in verse three above. The woman representing the church of the devil is sitting on a scarlet-colored beast, full of the names of blasphemy, "having seven heads and ten horns." This link shows that even though John has changed symbols from the beast to a woman, it is still the same reference—the church of the devil. She represents the churches of men, while the scarlet beast represents the churches of the devil that formed early in the Dark Ages of the Great Spiritual Famine. Just as Assyria eventually overran Israel when it fled to Egypt for refuge in our study of Isaiah, so too, the woman is ultimately shown to be riding the same beast as before—even Satan or the devil. She deceives the children of men, having a form of godliness, but denying the power and priesthood authority thereof. In the end, there are but two churches only: the Church of the Lamb of God, and the church of the devil.

Revelation 17:7-8

7 And the angel said unto me, Wherefore didst thou marvel? I will tell thee the mystery of the woman, and of the beast that carrieth her, which hath the seven heads and ten horns.
8 The beast that thou sawest was, and is not; and shall ascend out of the bottomless pit, and go into perdition: and they that dwell on the earth shall wonder, whose names were not written in the book of life from the foundation of the world, when they behold the beast that was, and is not, and yet is.

THE LATTER RAIN

In Chapter 13, the dragon gave power to the beast, meaning that Satan gave power to the church of the devil. The woman riding on the beast in Chapter 17 appears to have an advantage over the beast, and thus attracts many to follow after her. Ultimately, she too gets her power from the devil and cannot save men from their sins. She deceives many, and lulls them away into a false since of security. John the Revelator conveys the same message as contained in the Book of Isaiah, but with slightly different symbolic types. We saw the use of many different types to convey this same message in the other books of the Old Testament already discussed.

Revelation 17:9
9 And here is the mind which hath wisdom. The seven heads are seven mountains, on which the woman sitteth.

In verse nine above, we are given a hint at the meaning of the seven heads of the beast. "The seven heads are seven mountains, on which the woman sitteth." In taking this concept one step further, we may conclude that the seven mountains are seven continents—or the whole earth. This link comes from our understanding of Isaiah that Satan would have dominion over the entire earth. Since the earth has seven different continents, it means that the church of the devil is found throughout the entire earth and on every land mass.

Now let us revisit the meaning of the verse in Revelation 13:3 mentioned earlier: "And I saw one of his heads as it were wounded to death; and his deadly wound was healed: and all the world wandered after the beast." The seven heads represent the presence of the church and kingdom of the devil on every continent of the earth. A healthy living head would mean that the church of the devil is thriving there at that particular location and at that particular time. In contrast, a wounded head, and especially one that is wounded to death, would be a place or location on the earth where the kingdom of the devil, his church and his ministers, have no more power over the righteous. It would be a perfect Zion society, where the citizens of such a place are all keeping the commandments of God, and are guided by the spirit of God personally.

The dilemma is that no such place is ever mentioned in the Bible, neither before the resurrection of the Lord or after. However, my interpretation of verse three of Revelation 13 is that a head wounded to death represents a time when the righteousness of the people is so great that Satan has no power over them at all. The healing of that head or place, therefore, would mean that the righteous people were either finally corrupted, or somehow removed from that place. When the head was healed, it meant that the church of the devil was reestablished there as before.

That is the only conclusion I can draw about this curious verse. When "his deadly wound was healed," the church of the devil recovered its foothold on that continent again and began to thrive as before. That faithful society, if it did exist, was ultimately either removed, killed off, or finally contaminated such that the power of Satan was again active among them. A living prophet might be able to clarify this point by inquiring of the Lord once the Latter Rain period is ushered

THE REVELATION OF ST. JOHN THE DIVINE

in. The more important conclusion from the discussion of the seven heads of the beast, and the fact that the Mother of Harlots or whore "sitteth upon many waters," is that both of these symbols are consistent with Isaiah. They both point to the fact that at some point shortly after the resurrection of Jesus Christ, the Lord withdrew his apostles, prophets and disciples, and with them their authority and priesthood. The Church of the Lamb of God flew into the wilderness and the Lord Jesus Christ was taken up to the throne of the Father for a time. Satan was given free reign over the entire earth.

> **Revelation 17:10-15**
> 10 And there are seven kings: five are fallen, and one is, and the other is not yet come; and when he cometh, he must continue a short space.
> 11 And the beast that was, and is not, even he is the eighth, and is of the seven, and goeth into perdition.
> 12 And the ten horns which thou sawest are ten kings, which have received no kingdom as yet; but receive power as kings one hour with the beast.
> 13 These have one mind, and shall give their power and strength unto the beast.
> 14 These shall make war with the Lamb, and the Lamb shall overcome them: for he is Lord of lords, and King of kings: and they that are with him are called, and chosen, and faithful.
> 15 And he saith unto me, The waters which thou sawest, where the whore sitteth, are peoples, and multitudes, and nations, and tongues.

This means everyone! When it mentions kings, it means the individual leaders of churches that flood the earth as a result of the loss of the true Gospel. One follows the other, but each one of them makes war with the Lamb eventually. In the last days, the "Lamb shall overcome them: for he is the Lord of lords, and King of kings: and they that are with him are called, and chosen, and faithful." Ultimately, the Lord with his disciples by him will invade each of the seven continents and begin the work of the gathering of Israel. They will reap the fruit and bring it into the garners of the Lord. As good shepherds, they will call to the Lost Sheep of the House of Israel, who shall hear his voice and come into the fold of God. We see this process occurring in the first verses of Chapter 18 of Revelation.

> **Revelation 18:1-4**
> 1 AND after these things I saw another angel come down from heaven, having great power; and the earth was lightened with his glory.
> 2 And he cried mightily with a strong voice, saying, Babylon the great is fallen, is fallen, and is become the habitation of devils, and the hold of every foul spirit, and a cage of every unclean and hateful bird.
> 3 For all nations have drunk of the wine of the wrath of her fornication, and the kings of the earth have committed fornication with her, and the merchants of the earth are waxed rich through the abundance of her delicacies.
> 4 And I heard another voice from heaven, saying, Come out of her, my people, that ye be not partakers of her sins, and that ye receive not of her plagues.

The Lord finally remembers his people, yet they are all entangled in the snares of the Mother of Harlots, who has dominion over the entire earth. They must be drawn out of her, out of Babylon the Great. "Come out of her, my people, that ye be not partakers of her sins, and that ye receive not of her plagues." Once Zion is restored, and the true Gospel begins to roll forward like the rock cut out of a mountain without hands as in the Book of Daniel, then shall the inhabitants of the earth be given a choice. They must either cling to the vanities of Babylon, or come unto Zion and feast at the table of the Lord. Those that are afraid to flee Babylon, and thus cling to false doctrines of devils and men, will be forced to reap the rewards of their choice. They will taste of the plagues that will be dished out upon the great whore.

> **Revelation 18:5-10**
>
> 5 For her sins have reached unto heaven, and God hath remembered her iniquities.
> 6 Reward her even as she rewarded you, and double unto her double according to her works: in the cup which she hath filled fill to her double.
> 7 How much she hath glorified herself, and lived deliciously, so much torment and sorrow give her: for she saith in her heart, I sit a queen, and am no widow, and shall see no sorrow.
> 8 Therefore shall her plagues come in one day, death, and mourning, and famine; and she shall be utterly burned with fire: for strong is the Lord God who judgeth her.
> 9 And the kings of the earth, who have committed fornication and lived deliciously with her, shall bewail her, and lament for her, when they shall see the smoke of her burning,
> 10 Standing afar off for the fear of her torment, saying, Alas, alas, that great city Babylon, that mighty city! for in one hour is thy judgment come.

The colorful description in Chapter 18 above shows that Babylon the Great is indeed fallen. John the Revelator uses great literary descriptions to emphasize the greatness of her fall. He shows how some will mourn her demise because they are merchants on the sea who were made rich by her. These are the false ministers and false pastors who have profited on the innocent—who have promoted the whore to get gain and glory of the world. "Alas, alas, that great city, wherein were made rich all that had ships in the sea by reason of her costliness! For in one hour is she made desolate." All those that profited from her vanities and abused the naïve and the innocent for reward will view the demise of the great church of the devil with remorse and solace. In contrast, however, the true disciples of the lamb will rejoice!

> **Revelation 18:20-24**
>
> 20 Rejoice over her, thou heaven, and ye holy apostles and prophets; for God hath avenged you on her.
> 21 And a mighty angel took up a stone like a great millstone, and cast it into the sea, saying, Thus with violence shall that great city Babylon be thrown down, and shall be found no more at all.
> 22 And the voice of harpers, and musicians, and of pipers, and trumpeters, shall be heard no more at all in thee; and no craftsman, of whatsoever craft he be, shall be found any more in thee; and the sound of a millstone shall be heard no more at all in thee;
> 23 And the light of a candle shall shine no more at all in thee; and the voice of the bridegroom and of the bride shall be heard no more at all in thee: for thy merchants were the great men of the earth; for by thy sorceries were all nations deceived.
> 24 And in her was found the blood of prophets, and of saints, and of all that were slain upon the earth.

Here again we see the same things that we saw described in the Book of Isaiah. When the Lord finally comes out against the kingdom of Assyria, he will leave it completely desolate. With no more members in those false churches and institutions, none of the usual activities will occur there either—no more weddings, no more burning of candles, no more ornate craftsmanship. All of the heads of the beast will be wounded to death. This time, however, they will not heal but remain dead forever more. The kingdom of the devil will remain desolate for all time. It is a kingdom that was, and is not, and yet is. It had its day when it ruled over all the earth, but for the true disciples of Christ, it will be as if it "is not." Those sealed to the fate of that great whore (having the mark of the beast on judgment day) will live through the rest of eternity with the regret of their allegiance to the beast. For them, "it yet is."

Revelation 19:1-8
1 AND after these things I heard a great voice of much people in heaven, saying, Alleluia; Salvation, and glory, and honour, and power, unto the Lord our God:
2 For true and righteous are his judgments: for he hath judged the great whore, which did corrupt the earth with her fornication, and hath avenged the blood of his servants at her hand.
3 And again they said, Alleluia. And her smoke rose up for ever and ever.
4 And the four and twenty elders and the four beasts fell down and worshipped God that sat on the throne, saying, Amen; Alleluia.
5 And a voice came out of the throne, saying, Praise our God, all ye his servants, and ye that fear him, both small and great.
6 And I heard as it were the voice of a great multitude, and as the voice of many waters, and as the voice of mighty thunderings, saying, Alleluia: for the Lord God omnipotent reigneth.
7 Let us be glad and rejoice, and give honour to him: for the marriage of the Lamb is come, and his wife hath made herself ready.
8 And to her was granted that she should be arrayed in fine linen, clean and white: for the fine linen is the righteousness of saints.

In verse two, "for he hath judged the great whore, which did corrupt the earth with her fornication, and hath avenged the blood of his servants at her hand." The whole human plot that has played out through history has been designed to test the spirits of men and women in this mortal state. All are born, and all must die. But it is the way we live and the choices we make that define our lives. We are given opposition from the devil and his followers, and are also given guidance and direction from the Lord and his servants. We are free to choose. When the curtain falls and the final act is complete, it will be obvious to the Lord, and even obvious to ourselves, who we have served and where we belong.

The important symbolic image in this section is the wife of the Lamb. Recall in Chapter 12 of Revelation, the Church of God was represented as a woman, albeit as a mother. Here in Chapter 19, verse seven, the Church of God is represented as a wife or as a bride to the Lord. "For the marriage of the Lamb is come; and his wife hath made herself ready." She hath been restored and hath gathered in the dispersed of Israel. She is arrayed in fine linen, which is "the righteousness of the saints." Here the word "saints" represents the members of the Church of God. She is a pleasant and beautiful bride because she is arrayed with the righteous followers of Jesus that have accepted baptism and entered into the straight gate.

Revelation 19:9-10
9 And he saith unto me, Write, Blessed are they which are called unto the marriage supper of the Lamb. And he saith unto me, These are the true sayings of God.

THE LATTER RAIN

10 And I fell at his feet to worship him. And he said unto me, See thou do it not: I am thy fellowservant, and of thy brethren that have the testimony of Jesus: worship God: for the testimony of Jesus is the spirit of prophecy.

We started out this book with a discussion of the spirit of prophecy, and here it is defined for us nicely by the Apostle John. The spirit of prophecy is the testimony of Jesus. All those that truly have a testimony of Jesus will receive the spirit of prophecy and be shown the way, like a plane guided by a homing beacon to its final destination. This must be a testimony of the real living Jesus as compared to the mythological Jesus that has no power any more. The sheep of the Good Shepherd will know his voice and the voice of his servants, and will come and partake at the marriage supper of the Lamb. In contrast, those who are hardened in their hearts and are not open to the new wine of the Lord will fail to recognize the truth when it comes to them. They will miss the new thing that he will do among them. They will be unprepared when the Lord calls them. The key is to call upon the Lord and trust no one without first feeling the spirit of confirmation from the Lord himself. In this manner, we may discern whether the message we are receiving is from God or from men.

Revelation 19:11-13
11 And I saw heaven opened, and behold a white horse; and he that sat upon him was called Faithful and True, and in righteousness he doth judge and make war.
12 His eyes were as a flame of fire, and on his head were many crowns; and he had a name written, that no man knew, but he himself.
13 And he was clothed with a vesture dipped in blood: and his name is called The Word of God.

John repeats the same thing over again, but with a slightly different symbolic image. A rider on a white horse comes out from heaven, and his name is Faithful and True. This rider is the Lord Jesus Christ. In verse 13, we see that he is clothed with a vesture dipped in blood: and his name is called the Word of God. This also means Jesus Christ, as we might ascertain from the Gospel of John.

John 1:1-14
1 IN the beginning was the Word, and the Word was with God, and the Word was God.
2 The same was in the beginning with God.
3 All things were made by him; and without him was not any thing made that was made.
4 In him was life; and the life was the light of men.
5 And the light shineth in darkness; and the darkness comprehended it not.
6 There was a man sent from God, whose name was John.
7 The same came for a witness, to bear witness of the Light, that all men through him might believe.
8 He was not that Light, but was sent to bear witness of that Light.
9 That was the true Light, which lighteth every man that cometh into the world.
10 He was in the world, and the world was made by him, and the world knew him not.
11 He came unto his own, and his own received him not.
12 But as many as received him, to them gave he power to become the sons of God, even to them that believe on his name:
13 Which were born, not of blood, nor of the will of the flesh, nor of the will of man, but of God.
14 And the Word was made flesh, and dwelt among us, (and we beheld his glory, the glory as of the only begotten of the Father,) full of grace and truth.

THE REVELATION OF ST. JOHN THE DIVINE

Verse 14 sums it up nicely: the Word of God is Jesus Christ the Son, by whom the world was created, and by whom also the kingdom of the devil will be conquered in the last days. This rider is a symbolic representation of the Lord Jesus Christ.

Revelation 19:14-16

14 And the armies which were in heaven followed him upon white horses, clothed in fine linen, white and clean.
15 And out of his mouth goeth a sharp sword, that with it he should smite the nations: and he shall rule them with a rod of iron: and he treadeth the winepress of the fierceness and wrath of Almighty God.
16 And he hath on his vesture and on his thigh a name written, KING OF KINGS, AND LORD OF LORDS.

John now makes it even more obvious who the rider of the first white horse is: he is "KING OF KINGS, AND LORD OF LORDS." The Lord Jesus Christ is accompanied by many others, as was the case in the Book of Isaiah narrative. These may include the 144,000 faithful servants described in Revelation 14, who are already resurrected and present at the throne of God. They may also include those born in the Latter Rain period; those who are righteous disciples of the Church and Kingdom of God. We know that these other riders of white horses are clothed in fine linen, white and clean. If we recall from Revelation 19:8, "for the fine linen is the righteousness of saints." Thus, these holy warriors come forth to the battle clothed in righteousness and the power of the Lord.

As in the Book of Isaiah, the weapon used by these warriors is not a conventional weapon, like a sword of steel. The Sword of the Lord is his word. When the sharp sword comes out of his mouth and begins to smite the nations, it means that his Gospel is restored to the earth and begins to be preached to the people living on the earth at that time. Let us now see the end result.

Revelation 19:17-21

17 And I saw an angel standing in the sun; and he cried with a loud voice, saying to all the fowls that fly in the midst of heaven, Come and gather yourselves together unto the supper of the great God;
18 That ye may eat the flesh of kings, and the flesh of captains, and the flesh of mighty men, and the flesh of horses, and of them that sit on them, and the flesh of all men, both free and bond, both small and great.
19 And I saw the beast, and the kings of the earth, and their armies, gathered together to make war against him that sat on the horse, and against his army.
20 And the beast was taken, and with him the false prophet that wrought miracles before him, with which he deceived them that had received the mark of the beast, and them that worshipped his image. These both were cast alive into a lake of fire burning with brimstone.
21 And the remnant were slain with the sword of him that sat upon the horse, which sword proceeded out of his mouth: and all the fowls were filled with their flesh.

The kingdom of the devil is ultimately vanquished by the armies of the Lord Jesus Christ and by the preaching of his disciples in the last days. Little by little, the wicked that pervert the ways of the Lord are gathered out of Babylon and come repenting into Zion, or they are sealed up to condemnation at the Day of Judgment. In either case, the Lord has extended his arm of mercy and tried to reclaim all of God's children. The justice of God allows each of us to choose for ourselves and, in the end, many will fall short of the blessing of eternal life in the Kingdom of God because they are deceived by the cunning works of the devil. Still others are too caught up in the vain things of this world that they never stop to call upon God or ask for his spirit to guide them home. They just take life as it comes and are lead merrily along until they awake in the hereafter, unprepared to meet their maker.

> **Isaiah 29:7-8**
>
> 7 And the multitude of all the nations that fight against Ariel, even all that fight against her and her munition, and that distress her, shall be as a dream of a night vision.
> 8 It shall even be as when an hungry man dreameth, and, behold, he eateth; but he awaketh, and his soul is empty: or as when a thirsty man dreameth, and, behold, he drinketh; but he awaketh, and, behold, he is faint, and his soul hath appetite: so shall the multitude of all the nations be, that fight against mount Zion.

It will be an awful discovery for the unjust and the unprepared. The guilt felt by these will be as a lake of fire and brimstone burning for ever in their hearts and souls. Hopefully, we are taken by the sword of the Lord and carried away safe into Zion. The state of the soul after the resurrection and the judgment are again described in Chapter 20 of Revelation as well.

> **Revelation 20:1-6**
>
> 1 AND I saw an angel come down from heaven, having the key of the bottomless pit and a great chain in his hand.
> 2 And he laid hold on the dragon, that old serpent, which is the Devil, and Satan, and bound him a thousand years,
> 3 And cast him into the bottomless pit, and shut him up, and set a seal upon him, that he should deceive the nations no more, till the thousand years should be fulfilled: and after that he must be loosed a little season.
> 4 And I saw thrones, and they sat upon them, and judgment was given unto them: and I saw the souls of them that were beheaded for the witness of Jesus, and for the word of God, and which had not worshipped the beast, neither his image, neither had received his mark upon their foreheads, or in their hands; and they lived and reigned with Christ a thousand years.
> 5 But the rest of the dead lived not again until the thousand years were finished. This is the first resurrection.
> 6 Blessed and holy is he that hath part in the first resurrection: on such the second death hath no power, but they shall be priests of God and of Christ, and shall reign with him a thousand years.

The souls of the just come forth in the first resurrection, which occurs at the Second Coming of Christ. These will live with the Lord on the earth for a thousand years, during which time Satan will be bound, having no power over the hearts of men. My feeling is that Satan is bound because the just are not influenced by him, and thus he has no power over them. The rest of the dead are the unjust souls that are only resurrected after the millennium has ended. At that point, Satan again has power for a short season to influence people toward wickedness. After that period, comes the final judgment.

> **Revelation 20:7-15**
>
> 7 And when the thousand years are expired, Satan shall be loosed out of his prison,

THE REVELATION OF ST. JOHN THE DIVINE

8 And shall go out to deceive the nations which are in the four quarters of the earth, Gog and Magog, to gather them together to battle: the number of whom is as the sand of the sea.
9 And they went up on the breadth of the earth, and compassed the camp of the saints about, and the beloved city: and fire came down from God out of heaven, and devoured them.
10 And the devil that deceived them was cast into the lake of fire and brimstone, where the beast and the false prophet are, and shall be tormented day and night for ever and ever.
11 And I saw a great white throne, and him that sat on it, from whose face the earth and the heaven fled away; and there was found no place for them.
12 And I saw the dead, small and great, stand before God; and the books were opened: and another book was opened, which is the book of life: and the dead were judged out of those things which were written in the books, according to their works.
13 And the sea gave up the dead which were in it; and death and hell delivered up the dead which were in them: and they were judged every man according to their works.
14 And death and hell were cast into the lake of fire. This is the second death.
15 And whosoever was not found written in the book of life was cast into the lake of fire.

Ultimately, all will be brought before the bar of God to be judged for the things that they did in their life, whether they be good or evil. "And whosoever was not found written in the book of life was cast into the lake of fire." Now, I personally do not ascribe to the theory that this lake of fire and brimstone is a literal lake of lava. That notion is another concoction of men. The lake of fire and brimstone is a representation of the endless and unquenchable guilt that one will feel when he or she knows that they had the opportunity to choose life eternal, but loved evil instead. They were overcome by the temptations of the devil and, instead of calling on the Father for help, they allowed themselves to be carefully led away, never repenting of their sins. The saddest thing of all is that they can never make it right again. The time for second chances has ended. Thus, this punishment and remorse is endless and eternal, while the joy and happiness of the righteous will be just as endless and eternal.

Revelation 21:1-8

1 AND I saw a new heaven and a new earth: for the first heaven and the first earth were passed away; and there was no more sea.
2 And I John saw the holy city, new Jerusalem, coming down from God out of heaven, prepared as a bride adorned for her husband.
3 And I heard a great voice out of heaven saying, Behold, the tabernacle of God is with men, and he will dwell with them, and they shall be his people, and God himself shall be with them, and be their God.
4 And God shall wipe away all tears from their eyes; and there shall be no more death, neither sorrow, nor crying, neither shall there be any more pain: for the former things are passed away.
5 And he that sat upon the throne said, Behold, I make all things new. And he said unto me, Write: for these words are true and faithful.
6 And he said unto me, It is done. I am Alpha and Omega, the beginning and the end. I will give unto him that is athirst of the fountain of the water of life freely.
7 He that overcometh shall inherit all things; and I will be his God, and he shall be my son.
8 But the fearful, and unbelieving, and the abominable, and murderers, and whoremongers, and sorcerers, and idolaters, and all liars, shall have their part in the lake which burneth with fire and brimstone: which is the second death.

As we know from our previous discussions, the water of life is revelation. When the Lord says that he will give to him that is athirst of the fountain of the water of life freely, he means that he will inspire and direct those that call on his name.

Those that pass through the resurrection of the just will have this gift forever and always. They can grow and develop and learn directly from the Lord himself until they too understand all things. From verses one and two, we learn that the earth and the heavens will pass away, and be made new again. All the earth will be changed into a different type of planet. Those that prove worthy and are found on the right hand of God will come down from heaven to possess the earth and receive the renewed glory thereof. No more tears will be shed and no more pain will be felt, for these things will be done away. The joy of the Lord and his chosen people will continue forever.

The fearful and the wicked will be cast into "the lake which burneth with fire and brimstone: which is the second death." They are cast out of the presence of God. Do they cease to exist? No. They are alive in body, having been resurrected from the dead. Do they dwell on the earth in the presence of God? No, they do not. If physical death is the separation of the spirit from the body, then spiritual death (or the second death) is the separation of our souls from the presence of God. The rest of Revelation 21 is an elaborate description of the celestial state of Jerusalem, that great city, which is brought down out of heaven. While the descriptive language is impressive, the more important doctrine is the fact that the need for a temple will cease.

The Water of Revelation

> Revelation 21:22-23
>
> 22 And I saw no temple therein: for the Lord God Almighty and the Lamb are the temple of it.
> 23 And the city had no need of the sun, neither of the moon, to shine in it: for the glory of God did lighten it, and the Lamb is the light thereof.

We know from the scriptures that the temple was a place where the Lord could come. It was like a holy building or tabernacle that was kept separated from the uncleanness of the world. The Temple ceased to exist shortly after the New Testament events occurred. Solomon's Temple in Jerusalem served as the House of the Lord on the earth for centuries till it was ultimately destroyed, and the knowledge of its function and purpose was lost with the withdrawal of the Lord's servants, the prophets. All we know from the Bible is that it was a place that was different from the synagogue or chapel, yet it was visited regularly by the Jews and also by the Lord during his time in mortality. We can only hope that when the Gospel of Jesus Christ is restored to the earth that the knowledge of the temple, its use and purpose, will also be restored and understood at that time.

It is clear from the scriptures that the temple was a place where the Lord could come—a place of holiness. The wicked were excluded, and only those worthy of entry were allowed inside its walls. The point made in Revelation 21 is that when Jerusalem becomes a celestial city, all of the inhabitants will be righteous; therefore, temples will no longer be needed, "For the Lord God Almighty and the Lamb are the temple of it." The righteous will have the blessings of the presence of the Lord, which was the purpose of the temple in the first place. The need to build a structure to gain access to the Lord will be unnecessary.

THE REVELATION OF ST. JOHN THE DIVINE

Revelation 22:1-5

1 AND he shewed me a pure river of water of life, clear as crystal, proceeding out of the throne of God and of the Lamb.
2 In the midst of the street of it, and on either side of the river, was there the tree of life, which bare twelve manner of fruits, and yielded her fruit every month: and the leaves of the tree were for the healing of the nations.
3 And there shall be no more curse: but the throne of God and of the Lamb shall be in it; and his servants shall serve him:
4 And they shall see his face; and his name shall be in their foreheads.
5 And there shall be no night there; and they need no candle, neither light of the sun; for the Lord God giveth them light: and they shall reign for ever and ever.

God the Father and the Son are the light. The pure river, the water of life, will flow freely there, proceeding out of the throne of God and of the Lamb. If this symbol is the same as we have already defined, we can take it to mean that the inspiration and revelation of God will flow freely to all those that dwell therein. At some point, revelation becomes knowledge. The men and women living in this celestial state will commune openly with the Lord, and they will become one with him, as his Spirit will flow to them directly with no hindrance whatsoever.

Revelation 22:6-17

6 And he said unto me, These sayings are faithful and true: and the Lord God of the holy prophets sent his angel to shew unto his servants the things which must shortly be done.
7 Behold, I come quickly: blessed is he that keepeth the sayings of the prophecy of this book.
8 And I John saw these things, and heard them. And when I had heard and seen, I fell down to worship before the feet of the angel which shewed me these things.
9 Then saith he unto me, See thou do it not: for I am thy fellowservant, and of thy brethren the prophets, and of them which keep the sayings of this book: worship God.
10 And he saith unto me, Seal not the sayings of the prophecy of this book: for the time is at hand.
11 He that is unjust, let him be unjust still: and he which is filthy, let him be filthy still: and he that is righteous, let him be righteous still: and he that is holy, let him be holy still.
12 And, behold, I come quickly; and my reward is with me, to give every man according as his work shall be.
13 I am Alpha and Omega, the beginning and the end, the first and the last.
14 Blessed are they that do his commandments, that they may have right to the tree of life, and may enter in through the gates into the city.
15 For without are dogs, and sorcerers, and whoremongers, and murderers, and idolaters, and whosoever loveth and maketh a lie.
16 I Jesus have sent mine angel to testify unto you these things in the churches. I am the root and the offspring of David, and the bright and morning star.
17 And the Spirit and the bride say, Come. And let him that heareth say, Come. And let him that is athirst come. And whosoever will, let him take the water of life freely.

In this final chapter, we have the wrap-up of the Book of Revelation. John receives a vision of these things and is also instructed about them by an angel, who is his fellow servant. This angel was also apparently a former prophet of the Lord. While this angel's exact identity is not known, he does not put himself above John and forbids John from worshipping him. In verse 16, however, the Lord makes reference to his own identity. He calls himself the root and offspring of David, and the bright and morning star. In this celestial state, the Lord Jesus Christ will finally take his place of royalty as the offspring of David, and assume his rightful throne to rule and reign in righteousness forever.

We see again the reference to "revelation" in the Book of Revelation, as it is linked to the symbolic type of water. "Come, And let him that is athirst come. And whosoever will, let him take the water of life freely." Here the Lord is inviting all his children to call upon his name in prayer. He wants us to do so without fear, but rather with faith, believing whole-heartedly in his power to give us revelation and inspiration, and to ultimately lead us to his Kingdom on earth, to commune with his servants and be guided by his prophets. May we all be willing and able to abide his call, and to follow this wise counsel.

Protecting the Message

Revelation 22:18-21

18 For I testify unto every man that heareth the words of the prophecy of this book, If any man shall add unto these things, God shall add unto him the plagues that are written in this book:
19 And if any man shall take away from the words of the book of this prophecy, God shall take away his part out of the book of life, and out of the holy city, and from the things which are written in this book.
20 He which testifieth these things saith, Surely I come quickly. Amen. Even so, come, Lord Jesus.
21 The grace of our Lord Jesus Christ be with you all. Amen.
THE END

Now we come full circle in our discussion of this warning at the end of the Book of Revelation. It should be much clearer why the Apostle John made the statement in verse 19 above. He was warning the wicked men of the Great Famine period not to mess with his prophecy, but to let it pass through. We can now also see why this Book of Revelation was written like the books of the Old Testament, with many symbolic types to obscure the meaning thereof. If John had spoken plainly and clearly, and spelled out exactly what each of these symbols stood for, the Book of Revelation would not have survived the Dark Ages. It would have been taken out, and destroyed. But it did survive, and, with the help of the insights derived from Isaiah and the other scriptures contained in the Bible, we are able to discern more clearly the meaning of this great book. Again, I reiterate that the Apostle John made this warning to protect the contents of this book and not to suggest the end of revelation. Divine revelation is an eternal component of God's plan of salvation. Revelation is God's means of communicating truth and giving direction to those seeking the light of the Gospel and eternal life in his presence.

Since the Book of Revelation did pass through the Dark Ages, what did Satan do to cloak its meaning from the righteous, who would have otherwise discovered its meaning and sought to find their God more fervently? First, he tried to make it unavailable to the children of men. We know that over time, these attempts to withhold the Bible from the people were unsuccessful. The invention of the printing press and other advances in science and technology made the scriptures more readily available to men and women everywhere. As the Renaissance Period brought more openness of thought and freedom of thinking, the Bible became more available still. Men and women began to contemplate the messages contained in the Bible for themselves. "And the serpent cast out of his mouth water as a flood after the woman, that he might cause her to be carried away of the flood. And the earth opened her mouth, and swallowed up the flood which the dragon cast out of his mouth." The men and women of the earth began to be less susceptible to every wind of doctrine designed to deceive them, because they were able to read the scriptures for themselves.

To frighten the reader away from the message contained in the Book of Revelation, Satan has inspired men to invent alternate interpretations which scare the reader and cause him to put the book away. Popular culture has devised many such tales in books, movies, plays and other formats. The focus is always on the scary and terrifying thought that perhaps the young child we just laid down to rest in the crib might be the dreaded anti-Christ, possessing supernatural evil powers and destined to take over the entire world. This is false! We should not expect a single mortal anti-Christ, but many. Satan is the only being that truly fits this description, for he is the author of confusion and the purveyor of lies. He is not a mortal being, but a being of spirit. He is the great anti-Christ of the Book of Revelation. It is his design to lead the reader of Revelation away from the true meaning of the book and its symbols, and turn them into fables. Satan is also the master of fear. He wants us all to fear calling on God, and fear seeking help directly from the Lord through prayer and the study of the scriptures. If he can conjure up in our minds a God who is ruthless and scary in nature, we will not want to study it out in our minds, and we will lay it aside as a thing of naught.

Now, this is not to say that the Book of Revelation is not scary, even with the interpretation that I have laid forth. We still might not want to read it to our three-year-old daughter as we lay her down to sleep at night—talk of beasts and blood and dragons. However, we should not fear the Lord, nor fear his ability to clarify seemingly difficult questions in the scriptures. If we humbly seek his help and admit our own weakness and lack of understanding, he can help us see the truth of his word.

Matthew 6:33

33 But seek ye first the kingdom of God, and his righteousness; and all these things shall be added unto you.

If we take the counsel from this scripture to heart, we should all have as our first goal in life to seek out the Kingdom of God. Zion must at some point be restored to the earth through prophets and the administration of angels. It must be restored to the same form as it existed anciently, with the power and authority of the priesthood of God for the accomplishment of the essential ordinances of salvation. Our final chapter, therefore, will be devoted to an analysis of what we might look for in such a restored Zion.

Before we move on to a discussion of the restoration of Zion, let me conclude and summarize our discussion of the New Testament. We have seen that much evidence is indeed contained in the New Testament that supports the idea of a falling away. The members of the Church of Christ described in the New

Testament were not living during a joyful time. Rather, they were under siege from within the Church and from outside. False prophets were found among them, and persecutions in the vilest forms. We have shown that the apostles and prophets leading the Church were suffering death and persecution such that the priesthood lineage appears to have been lost. Scripture writing ceased with the writings of John in the Book of Revelation, and knowledge of the Twelve Apostles and their succession was also lost to historical record.

Finally, the symbols and types derived from our study of Isaiah are also prevalent in the New Testament, as they were in the Old Testament. We saw that Jesus Christ himself taught that the water that he offered his disciples was a type of water that eradicated thirst entirely. This water is the water of revelation, which comes to us through his Spirit, the Holy Ghost. When Jesus was given gall to drink on the cross, this was symbolic of the type of revelations that would be given to men during the great period of Spiritual Famine. The New Testament continues to support the prophecies found in the Book of Isaiah. While all of the children of God can find comfort from reading the scriptures, more is required than belief alone. We must all partake of the basic saving ordinances, which can only be performed by authorized servants of the Lord possessing the priesthood of God. Let us now see what we might expect to find if and when Zion is restored to the earth.

CHAPTER FIFTEEN

The Latter Rain

We have just completed a fairly extensive analysis of many books of the Bible, with the purpose of applying the symbols and types found in Isaiah to interpret the overall meaning of the scriptures. We have seen that the imagery of water, rain, dew, rivers, light, bread, and prosperity have repeated themselves over and over again throughout the scriptures. Their opposites, famine, dearth, wilderness, desolation, and darkness, have also been seen throughout the scriptures. The message from this extensive analysis is that the God of all humanity has divided his dealings with his children on the earth into two great periods: the Former Rain period, and the Latter Rain period. Even more significant, we have learned that the period in between these eras is a period of Spiritual Famine—a period when no prophets are found on the earth. The Lord has done nothing during this period. This famine period is void of true religion, having no priesthood power to perform the essential ordinances of salvation.

The last remaining questions, however, have to do with the Latter Rain period. When will this period begin? How will it be ushered in? How can we discern the restored Gospel from the traditions of men? It should be clear by now what is meant by the term Latter Rain. It is the period spoken of in the Book of Acts, when prophets shall again be called upon the earth.

Acts 3:20-21
20 And he shall send Jesus Christ, which before was preached unto you:
21 Whom the heaven must receive until the times of restitution of all things, which God hath spoken by the mouth of all his holy prophets since the world began.

Some may view this scripture as a reference to the great Second Coming when the Lord Jesus Christ will appear in his glory for all mankind to see. To them, it refers to the time known as the Rapture, when the righteous inhabitants of the earth, and those that have slept in the paradise of God, will rise and be called up to meet the Lord in the clouds, and then go on to possess the earth during the millennium period. This is incorrect.

THE LATTER RAIN

The Lord will appear much sooner to those who are once again called to his true ministry and priesthood. He will appear to and call forth prophets again upon the earth. Likewise, angels shall once again become active and come forth, many of them prophets from previous dispensations. Through the Lord, and through his ministering angels, all of the keys, power, and authority of God will once again be restored to the earth in its fullness.

Jesus Christ shall appear again. If he could appear to Mary Magdalene, the Twelve Apostles, and others after his resurrection in Jerusalem, he is in no way constrained from appearing to a prophet in this day and age. In fact, the scriptures testify that indeed he will.

The Lord Appears in his Glory

Psalm 102:16-17

16 When the LORD shall build up Zion, he shall appear in his glory.
17 He will regard the prayer of the destitute, and not despise their prayer.

When I first read this simple scripture found in the Psalms, I was amazed at its clarity and bold prediction. Recall that Jesus Christ predicted the destruction of the temple, and I said he was referring to the Church rather than the physical building of the temple itself. He said that "not one stone shall remain on top of another" (Matthew 24:2). If the Lord was referring to his Church, his priesthood, and his kingdom on the earth, then this prophecy in Psalm 102 makes even more sense. We can see that "When the LORD shall build up Zion" from the above scripture, it not only indicates that the Lord will rebuild Zion again, but it also indicates that it must at one point have been knocked down and destroyed.

A curious fact to note about this particular scripture is found in the German Einheitsübersetzung version of the same verses. While the verses are shifted down by one verse (17 and 18 instead of 16 and 17), the message is the same except for one critical word:

Psalm 102:17-18

17 Denn der Herr baut Zion wieder auf und erscheint in all seiner Herlichkeit.
18 Er wendet sich dem Gebet der Verlassenen zu, irhe Bitten verschmäht er nicht.

Literally translated it says, "When the Lord builds Zion *again*, and appears in all his glory, he will regard the prayer of the destitute, and will not despise their pleas." I have placed italics on the word "again" because it shows a critical aspect that is not had in the English version of this scripture. The word "wieder" means "again." While the English verse is still meaningful since it foretells that the Lord God of Israel shall appear when he builds up Zion, the German verses stipulate more clearly that it will be a second time for him to build it up.

Isaiah 41:24-25

24 Behold, ye are of nothing, and your work of nought: an abomination is he that chooseth you.
25 I have raised up one from the north, and he shall come: from the rising of the sun shall he call upon my name: and he shall come upon princes as upon morter, and as the potter treadeth clay.

THE LATTER RAIN

Here we see that, at some point, the Lord will raise up "one from the *north*, and he shall come: from the rising of the sun shall he *call upon my name*." I have emphasized two things in these verses. Firstly, this initial servant of the Latter Rain period will be raised up from the "north." Applying our symbolic understanding from Isaiah, we see that "north" could be referring to a servant from the Northern Ten Tribes that were lost and literally dispersed by the ancient kingdom of Assyria. While they were scattered among all nations and never recovered as a recognized people, the Lord knows where they have gone and he knows their doings, both anciently and today. They represent the tribe of Ephraim, the Son of Joseph; namely, the Joseph who was sold into Egypt. The first "Latter Rain" prophet will be associated with these lost tribes, and he will be identified as being from Ephraim, as opposed to Judah or the Jews. Secondly, he will pray to God directly.

This idea also makes sense in that "the first shall be last and the last shall be first." The Gospel of Jesus Christ first went to the Jews or Judah, and then was carried to the Gentiles (or Ephraim) by Peter, Paul, and the other disciples during the New Testament era. After the Gospel was taken from the earth, it should now go first to the Gentiles or Ephraim, and then later be preached to the Jews. Recall what the Lord said to the woman at the well in Samaria:

John 4:21-22
21 Jesus saith unto her, Woman, believe me, the hour cometh, when ye shall neither in this mountain, nor yet at Jerusalem, worship the Father.
22 Ye worship ye know not what: we know what we worship: for salvation is of the Jews.

Recall that the Jews held the priesthood and were authorized to administer the essential ordinances of salvation. They were sanctioned of the Lord at that time. From verse 21, we see that "the hour cometh, when ye shall neither in this mountain, nor yet at Jerusalem, worship the Father." I showed that this was a direct reference by the Savior to the great period of Spiritual Famine which would soon envelope the earth. He was saying that soon, no one would have the divine priesthood, and prophets would cease, being withdrawn from the earth by the Lord. No one would then be able to worship the Father in truth. Though individually, our Father in Heaven may still answer prayers or bless those that yearn for righteousness, as a whole, true religion would be unavailable to anyone. At the time Jesus addresses the woman at the well, however, the Jews held the authority and the Gentiles of Samaria did not. Judah had it, and not Ephraim. Only later was it extended to the Gentiles, for a brief period, and soon it was lost completely. In the last days, the scriptures clearly indicate that Zion will be restored again to the earth through the Gentiles first, or in other words through the Ten Lost Tribes to the north.

The Prophet From the North

Now, if and when such a prophet is raised up from the north, how will we be able to recognize that he is a true prophet? First of all, the Lord Jesus Christ will appear to him in all his glory, as we read in Psalm 102:16. He will appear to him and converse with him just as he did with the Twelve Apostles as recorded in Luke in the New Testament.

THE LATTER RAIN

Luke 24:36-43
36 And as they thus spake, Jesus himself stood in the midst of them, and saith unto them, Peace be unto you.
37 But they were terrified and affrighted, and supposed that they had seen a spirit.
38 And he said unto them, Why are ye troubled? and why do thoughts arise in your hearts?
39 Behold my hands and my feet, that it is I myself: handle me, and see; for a spirit hath not flesh and bones, as ye see me have.
40 And when he had thus spoken, he shewed them his hands and his feet.
41 And while they yet believed not for joy, and wondered, he said unto them, Have ye here any meat?
42 And they gave him a piece of a broiled fish, and of an honeycomb.
43 And he took it, and did eat before them.

Jesus makes it emphatically clear that he is not a gaseous cloud or nebulas form. He has a resurrected body of flesh and bone. He is not just a spirit. The apostles were able to handle his body and feel the prints of the nails in his hands and his feet. Christ even ate in front of them. If Jesus Christ is "the same yesterday, and to day, and for ever" (Hebrews 13:8), then he can certainly appear to people in our day as easily as he could appear to one in ancient times. Nothing restrains him from doing whatever he chooses. The first sign of this restoring prophet when he comes forth will be that he will have communed with the Lord personally in some manner, and will probably testify to the fact, just as the disciples of old testified of his appearances to them.

Matthew 7:15-20
15 Beware of false prophets, which come to you in sheep's clothing, but inwardly they are ravening wolves.
16 Ye shall know them by their fruits. Do men gather grapes of thorns, or figs of thistles?
17 Even so every good tree bringeth forth good fruit; but a corrupt tree bringeth forth evil fruit.
18 A good tree cannot bring forth evil fruit, neither can a corrupt tree bring forth good fruit.
19 Every tree that bringeth not forth good fruit is hewn down, and cast into the fire.
20 Wherefore by their fruits ye shall know them.

While we used this scripture earlier in our discussion to show that Jesus Christ was warning his disciples about the impending period of darkness to cover the entire earth, we may also understand that he is telling us how to recognize a true prophet as well. We recognize them by their fruits. If that which the prophet says, or does, or writes is good and testifies of Jesus Christ, he must be a true prophet. It is by the fruits of the prophet that we can recognize him. For instance, when we read the Bible and feel the spirit that accompanies it, we can feel that it is a holy book. We can therefore believe in our hearts that the authors of the books in the Bible were indeed true prophets. Few people today would argue that Moses was not a true prophet, nor Isaiah, nor Matthew, nor John. However, at the time of Christ, the leaders of the Jews believed in Moses, but not in John the Baptist or Jesus Christ. When a prophet is actually alive on the earth, many reject his message. This was especially true of the Lord Jesus Christ during his mortal ministry.

THE LATTER RAIN

John 1:10-11
10 He was in the world, and the world was made by him, and the world knew him not.
11 He came unto his own, and his own received him not.

Jesus came unto the Jews, and was a Jew himself. In fact, according to his lineage as recorded in the first chapter of Matthew, Jesus Christ was a direct descendant of King David, and thus an heir to both the temporal throne as well as the spiritual throne. Despite the signs and wonders that accompanied his birth and actions in life, the miracles and power of his speech, he was nonetheless rejected by those he sought to gather.

In the present day, would it be any easier for Jesus Christ to call a new prophet to be upon the earth? Would the world suddenly believe in a living prophet that appeared on the scene—especially if he said he had seen the risen Lord? Another sign of a true prophet is that opposition and tribulation will be ever-present in his life. The one difference between the Latter Rain period and the ancient times is that in the last days, once Zion is reestablished, she will never again be taken from the earth. Therefore, the first prophet or prophets of the Latter Rain period will meet opposition from the world, but will overcome it. They will establish the Lord's Church and it will remain intact forever more. The scriptures foretell the coming forth of Zion again. The fruits of the first prophets called by Jesus Christ in the Latter Rain period will be strong evidences of the truthfulness of his restored Gospel.

The Lord Calls to the Children of Israel

Isaiah 52:1-2
1 AWAKE, awake; put on thy strength, O Zion; put on thy beautiful garments, O Jerusalem, the holy city: for henceforth there shall no more come into thee the uncircumcised and the unclean.
2 Shake thyself from the dust; arise, and sit down, O Jerusalem: loose thyself from the bands of thy neck, O captive daughter of Zion.

After reading the many evidences of the Great Famine period, the above verses have renewed significance. We now see more clearly that the Lord is calling out to Israel through the prophet Isaiah to shake itself from the dust; to arise, and sit down. He tells them to "loose thyself from the bands of thy neck, O captive daughter of Zion." He is calling out to each living soul to regard the beliefs of their fathers with suspicion. Hold on to that which is good, but seek the Kingdom of God and his righteousness with all your heart. If we do this, he promises to help us return to Zion as in the days of old.

Isaiah 51:9-11
9 Awake, awake, put on strength, O arm of the LORD; awake, as in the ancient days, in the generations of old. Art thou not it that hath cut Rahab, and wounded the dragon?
10 Art thou not it which hath dried the sea, the waters of the great deep; that hath made the depths of the sea a way for the ransomed to pass over?
11 Therefore the redeemed of the LORD shall return, and come with singing unto Zion; and everlasting joy shall be upon their head: they shall obtain gladness and joy; and sorrow and mourning shall flee away.

THE LATTER RAIN

We are herein commanded of the Lord to "awake, as in the ancient days, in the generations of old." This same theme of waking up from a deep sleep is also reiterated with even more urgency in Isaiah 29.

Isaiah 29:9-14

9 Stay yourselves, and wonder; cry ye out, and cry: they are drunken, but not with wine; they stagger, but not with strong drink.
10 For the LORD hath poured out upon you the spirit of deep sleep, and hath closed your eyes: the prophets and your rulers, the seers hath he covered.
11 And the vision of all is become unto you as the words of a book that is sealed, which men deliver to one that is learned, saying, Read this, I pray thee: and he saith, I cannot; for it is sealed:
12 And the book is delivered to him that is not learned, saying, Read this, I pray thee: and he saith, I am not learned.
13 Wherefore the Lord said, Forasmuch as this people draw near me with their mouth, and with their lips do honour me, but have removed their heart far from me, and their fear toward me is taught by the precept of men:
14 Therefore, behold, I will proceed to do a marvellous work among this people, even a marvellous work and a wonder: for the wisdom of their wise men shall perish, and the understanding of their prudent men shall be hid.

In verses nine and ten, we see that the Lord has poured out the spirit of deep sleep, and covered the prophets and rulers of the people. This idea we have seen repeated over and over again throughout the Bible. As we now discuss the Latter Rain period, I want to pay attention to the last two verses above (13 and 14). The Lord tells us through the Prophet Isaiah that because our hearts are so far removed from him, and our fear toward him is taught by the precepts of men, he will now do something amazing for us. He calls it a "marvelous work and a wonder." This thing that he does will cause the wisdom of wise men to perish, and the understanding of prudent men to be hid.

Another sign of this first prophet of the Latter Rain dispensation is that he will not be called from among the leaders of the religions or philosophies of the day. As in ancient times, the Lord will call forth a prophet that is weak by the standards of the world, but he will pour out his spirit upon him and build him up and make him mighty. Recall the phrase in Psalm 102:17, "He will regard the prayer of the destitute." The prophet that ushers in the last dispensation will most likely be a man of meager means. He will not only lack wisdom as to the wisdom of the world, but he will probably not be very wealthy or politically strong either. This would be consistent with the Lord's choice of men in past dispensations.

1 Corinthians 1:20-31

20 Where is the wise? where is the scribe? where is the disputer of this world? hath not God made foolish the wisdom of this world?
21 For after that in the wisdom of God the world by wisdom knew not God, it pleased God by the foolishness of preaching to save them that believe.
22 For the Jews require a sign, and the Greeks seek after wisdom:
23 But we preach Christ crucified, unto the Jews a stumblingblock, and unto the Greeks foolishness;
24 But unto them which are called, both Jews and Greeks, Christ the power of God, and the wisdom of God.

25 Because the foolishness of God is wiser than men; and the weakness of God is stronger than men.
26 For ye see your calling, brethren, how that not many wise men after the flesh, not many mighty, not many noble, are called:
27 But God hath chosen the foolish things of the world to confound the wise; and God hath chosen the weak things of the world to confound the things which are mighty;
28 And base things of the world, and things which are despised, hath God chosen, yea, and things which are not, to bring to nought things that are:
29 That no flesh should glory in his presence.
30 But of him are ye in Christ Jesus, who of God is made unto us wisdom, and righteousness, and sanctification, and redemption:
31 That, according as it is written, He that glorieth, let him glory in the Lord.

The Apostle Paul explains to the Corinthians that the wisdom of the world is foolishness to God. For this reason, the first prophets of the Latter Rain period will not be called from the learned men of the world. Instead, they will be New Bottles, which are able to bear the New Wine which will distill upon their minds and in their hearts (Matthew 9:14-17). Otherwise, they would be tainted by false doctrines that were already firmly established in their minds. They will be spiritual men seeking to know the truth. The Lord prefers a clean slate when delivering his message, as explained in the verses just cited.

What might be the fruits of such a Latter Rain prophet? He should have fruits similar to those given to the prophets of old. He should do mighty works and they would be recorded. He might also write, and his testimony would become scripture, for this is how it was done of old. Finally, he would probably be taught by ancient prophets, who have the authority of the Gospel and can restore it to the new prophet. The idea of ancient prophets visiting mortal prophets is consistent with what we have seen in our study of the Bible. For example, ancient prophets appeared to Jesus and his disciples, Peter, James, and John, on the Mount of Transfiguration.

Mark 9:2-8
2 And after six days Jesus taketh with him Peter, and James, and John, and leadeth them up into an high mountain apart by themselves: and he was transfigured before them.
3 And his raiment became shining, exceeding white as snow; so as no fuller on earth can white them.
4 And there appeared unto them Elias with Moses: and they were talking with Jesus.
5 And Peter answered and said to Jesus, Master, it is good for us to be here: and let us make three tabernacles; one for thee, and one for Moses, and one for Elias.
6 For he wist not what to say; for they were sore afraid.
7 And there was a cloud that overshadowed them: and a voice came out of the cloud, saying, This is my beloved Son: hear him.
8 And suddenly, when they had looked round about, they saw no man any more, save Jesus only with themselves.

Now the identity of Moses is quite clear. Moses appeared to Jesus Christ while the Lord was in his mortal state. Moses had died, or was transfigured, but he had departed from the mortal state. Despite having passed on, he was able to appear to the Lord and commune with him. Likewise, this other prophet, Elias, was also present. The identity of this prophet might be the subject of debate, since many of the names given to prophets in the Old Testament are changed in the New

Testament. It was most likely Elijah the Tishbite. The General Epistle of James, Chapter 5, shows why.

> **James 5:16-18**
>
> 16 Confess your faults one to another, and pray one for another, that ye may be healed. The effectual fervent prayer of a righteous man availeth much.
> 17 Elias was a man subject to like passions as we are, and he prayed earnestly that it might not rain: and it rained not on the earth by the space of three years and six months.
> 18 And he prayed again, and the heaven gave rain, and the earth brought forth her fruit.

Here again we see the mention of the name Elias. However, we know from the context with a great deal of certainty that James is referring to the prophet Elijah. Elijah is the prophet that prayed to the Lord, and the heavens were shut for the space of three years and six months that it rained not. We can see the story of this mighty work in the 17th and 18th Chapters of 1st Kings in the Old Testament. Therefore, this other prophet was probably Elijah. He also communed with the Lord. John the Revelator also communed with an ancient prophet, as seen in our study of the Book of Revelation. It would be completely consistent for the same thing to occur in the last days when the Latter Rain dispensation is ushered in. While ancient prophets might indeed appear to the prophets of the last days, they might also speak out of the dust in the form of scriptures that might have been lost. What about the concept of new scripture? What form would it take, and what evidence is there in the Bible that such writings will come forth?

> **Isaiah 29:1-4**
>
> 1 WOE to Ariel, to Ariel, the city where David dwelt! add ye year to year; let them kill sacrifices.
> 2 Yet I will distress Ariel, and there shall be heaviness and sorrow: and it shall be unto me as Ariel.
> 3 And I will camp against thee round about, and will lay siege against thee with a mount, and I will raise forts against thee.
> 4 And thou shalt be brought down, and shalt speak out of the ground, and thy speech shall be low out of the dust, and thy voice shall be, as of one that hath a familiar spirit, out of the ground, and thy speech shall whisper out of the dust.

These verses give the impression of someone from ancient times trying to communicate to us in our day. "Thy voice shall be, as of one that hath a familiar spirit, out of the ground, and thy speech shall whisper out of the dust." These ancient prophets will talk to us from the past. Many of the deeds and actions of holy men from the past might one day be brought forth for our view. But where might these scriptures be recorded?

The Words of the Book

> **Isaiah 29:18**
>
> 18 And in that day shall the deaf hear the words of the book, and the eyes of the blind shall see out of obscurity, and out of darkness.

At first glance, we might be tempted to say that this verse is referring to the Bible. The problem with that assumption is that the writings found in the Bible have existed all the way through the Dark Ages of the Great Spiritual Famine period.

THE LATTER RAIN

The Bible is a collection of revelations from the old pool of water (Isaiah 22:11) or the Former Rain period. The stories in the Bible are the manna that fed the true seekers of knowledge as they wandered through the wilderness and were held captive by the doctrines and philosophies of men. If there was an old pool, there must be another book, or new pool, to come forth at some point near the beginning of the Latter Rain period. The new book will clarify things found in the Bible such that "the deaf shall hear the words of the book, and the eyes of the blind shall see out of obscurity, and out of darkness." Seeing out of obscurity suggests that it will confound the conventional wisdom of the day, and will be a new work—a marvelous work and a wonder! Furthermore, it will be the word of God unto man such that it will cut to the very soul. It will be a fruit of the Latter Rain prophet or prophets that bring it forth. This new book spoken of in Isaiah will come from the Tribe of Ephraim—the descendants of Joseph that were scattered and lost.

Ezekiel 37:15-23
15 The word of the LORD came again unto me, saying,
16 Moreover, thou son of man, take thee one stick, and write upon it, For Judah, and for the children of Israel his companions: then take another stick, and write upon it, For Joseph, the stick of Ephraim, and for all the house of Israel his companions:
17 And join them one to another into one stick; and they shall become one in thine hand.
18 And when the children of thy people shall speak unto thee, saying, Wilt thou not shew us what thou meanest by these?
19 Say unto them, Thus saith the Lord GOD; Behold, I will take the stick of Joseph, which is in the hand of Ephraim, and the tribes of Israel his fellows, and will put them with him, even with the stick of Judah, and make them one stick, and they shall be one in mine hand.
20 And the sticks whereon thou writest shall be in thine hand before their eyes.
21 And say unto them, Thus saith the Lord GOD; Behold, I will take the children of Israel from among the heathen, whither they be gone, and will gather them on every side, and bring them into their own land:
22 And I will make them one nation in the land upon the mountains of Israel; and one king shall be king to them all: and they shall be no more two nations, neither shall they be divided into two kingdoms any more at all:
23 Neither shall they defile themselves any more with their idols, nor with their detestable things, nor with any of their transgressions: but I will save them out of all their dwellingplaces, wherein they have sinned, and will cleanse them: so shall they be my people, and I will be their God.

While the Kingdom of Israel was united for a brief period under the reign of King David, and then under his son, Solomon, for the most part, Israel existed as a kingdom divided into two subgroups as we have shown many times. While it may seem redundant to mention this again, it is such an important issue that it bears repeating. I would rather mention it too much than have it misunderstood. Ephraim, Joseph, Israel, and Gentile, all four of these terms are references to the descendants of the Ten Tribes of Israel to the north. The Ten Tribes are condensed into one, and are referred to as a single group from then on, with the only exception being the Sons of Levi, who have some special calling based on lineage with respect to officiating in the Temple of God. Nonetheless, we can always link references to Ephraim to the dispersed Ten Tribes of Israel to the north. This is the case here in the verses from the Book of Ezekiel.

THE LATTER RAIN

We see in this citation that the Lord asks Ezekiel to take not just one stick and write upon it, but to take two sticks. This does not mean that Ezekiel will be the author himself, but it is a symbolic type indicating two books or two witnesses: one is for Judah and one for Ephraim. These two books will become one in the hand. They will be shown unto the children of Israel who will ask: "Wilt thou not shew us what thou meanest by these?" These two books brought together in the hand will cause curiosity to be developed in the mind of the dispersed of Israel. The purpose of the two books is made clear in verse 21: "Behold, I will take the children of Israel from among the heathen, whither they be gone, and will gather them on every side, and bring them into their own land." The purpose of these books is to lead the children of Israel out of obscurity and into the light of the true and restored Gospel.

While the stick of Judah is fairly easy to identify, the stick of Ephraim is a new concept. The Jews of today use the Torah, or the Old Testament, in their synagogues. It is accepted as scripture. We have also shown that the New Testament was written by the disciples of Jesus Christ, who were all Jews themselves. We can, therefore, say with a high degree of certainty that the "stick of Judah" spoken of is a book that comes to us from the Jews—namely the Holy Bible, including the Old and New Testament. However, the "stick of Ephraim" is not the Bible. It is a work of scripture written by prophets from the Northern Kingdom (the Lost Ten Tribes, or Ephraim). But, it should help clarify the writings contained in the Bible, leading the lost children of Israel to truth.

From the Babylonian conquest, we know that living prophets from Judah were taken captive with the rest of the Jews and carried away into Babylon. Some of them, like Daniel, became counselors to the king of Babylon. The point I wish to make is that the Spirit of Prophecy was alive and well even during this captivity period, and many books of the Bible were written and later included in the Bible as a result. While they may have been lost to the sight of the world, the prophets of the Northern Ten Tribes, and perhaps their descendants, were also able to perform mighty works and to record those stories in written form. Unlike the works of Daniel, which are recorded in the Bible, the stories and prophecies of the prophets from Ephraim are held from the view of the world by the Lord in his wisdom. They have been reserved to come forth in the dispensation of the fullness of times, or, as we have come to call it in this book: the Latter Rain period. Thus, another great defining aspect of modern-day Zion will be the coming forth of a new book containing the works and deeds of dead prophets from the Tribe of Ephraim. This new book will become one in the hand of the disciple of Christ and will be shown unto many who will declare: "Wilt thou not shew us what thou meanest by these?" Let us re-examine a scripture with respect to this new book from Ephraim.

John 10:16

16 And other sheep I have, which are not of this fold: them also I must bring, and they shall hear my voice; and there shall be one fold, and one shepherd.

Could it be that the other fold is the Tribe of Ephraim? It would make sense in light of the things written in Ezekiel 37. If it is true, we should expect an account of such a visit when the stick of Ephraim springs into view. This new book should describe an event where "they shall hear my voice." This means that Christ will have visited the descendants of Joseph in a place where they were dispersed. Remember the question posed by the Pharisees in John 7:

> **John 7:32-36**
> 32 The Pharisees heard that the people murmured such things concerning him; and the Pharisees and the chief priests sent officers to take him.
> 33 Then said Jesus unto them, Yet a little while am I with you, and then I go unto him that sent me.
> 34 Ye shall seek me, and shall not find me: and where I am, thither ye cannot come.
> 35 Then said the Jews among themselves, Whither will he go, that we shall not find him? will he go unto the dispersed among the Gentiles, and teach the Gentiles?
> 36 What manner of saying is this that he said, Ye shall seek me, and shall not find me: and where I am, thither ye cannot come?

Pay specific attention to verse 35: "Whither will he go, that we shall not find him? Will he go unto the dispersed among the Gentiles, and teach the Gentiles?" The Pharisees were referring to the Northern Ten Tribes that were "dispersed among the Gentiles" and lost. They were suggesting the same thing that seems to be presented in John 10:16. Other sheep will hear the voice of the Lord which are not of "this fold," meaning Judah. Remember that at no time during his mortal life did Jesus send his disciples to teach the Gentiles. Nor did the Savior teach them himself, with the exception of the Samaritan woman and her relatives. The Gentiles living in the known world at the time were only taught by the Apostles of Christ, following the Lord's ascension to the Father.

As a resurrected being, Jesus can appear to anyone at any time. If he has "other sheep which are not of this fold" (Judah), why would he not go and visit them? If such an event occurred, it would be recorded by the people who witnessed it. This account will be in the stick of Ephraim when it comes forth among us. This would be consistent with the symbolic story of Joseph who was sold into Egypt. The Lord, through the Lost Ten Tribes from the north, would thus be storing up spiritual nourishment in the form of scripture. It would ultimately come forth in the last days to save the dispersed children of Israel from the famine of hearing the words of the Lord. Using Joseph's life story as a symbolic type, the spiritual nourishment stored up by the Lost Ten Tribes in the form of scripture during the Former Rain period will be instrumental in leading all the House of Israel out of the Great Spiritual Famine.

The Water of Revelation

> **Isaiah 22:8-11**
> 8 And he discovered the covering of Judah, and thou didst look in that day to the armour of the house of the forest.
> 9 Ye have seen also the breaches of the city of David, that they are many: and ye gathered together the waters of the lower pool.
> 10 And ye have numbered the houses of Jerusalem, and the houses have ye broken down to fortify the wall.
> 11 Ye made also a ditch between the two walls for the water of the old pool: but ye have not looked unto the maker thereof, neither had respect unto him that fashioned it long ago.

THE LATTER RAIN

Adhering to the analogy between water and revelation that we derived from Isaiah, we see that, prior to the Spiritual Famine period, revelation was gathered by the Jews from the old pool and it has been used throughout the dark time to sustain the belief in and knowledge of the Savior Jesus Christ. This old pool corresponds to the Bible, or the stick of Judah. While many people in the world respect the Bible teachings, they do not look unto the "maker thereof, neither had respect unto him that fashioned it long ago." The Jews are not thanked for the Bible, but rather they have been persecuted and driven and killed.

Throughout history, it has been the general tendency for people to easily accept old scripture and deceased prophets, but not those that are living. The stick of Ephraim would represent such a book of scripture, and be considered a new pool of water when it finally comes forth. Just as the Jews rejected the authority of Jesus Christ and of the apostles, which came to be recorded in the New Testament, many might reject a new work of scripture if it came forth in our day. For the humble seeker of truth, the combination of old scripture brought together with new scripture, enhanced by personal revelation, in a sense creates a sure path to the true and restored Gospel. We saw this concept first described in our analysis of the Book of Isaiah, and it bears repeating given our fresh insights.

Isaiah 11:16

16 And there shall be an highway for the remnant of his people, which shall be left, from Assyria; like as it was to Israel in the day that he came up out of the land of Egypt.

We saw in the verses cited from Ezekiel 37 that the purpose of the two books was to lead the children of Israel to Zion. "Thus saith the Lord GOD; Behold, I will take the children of Israel from among the heathen, whither they be gone, and will gather them on every side, and bring them into their own land." Now we see from Isaiah 11:16 that this sure doctrine of multiple witnesses acts as a holy highway leading out of falsehood and confusion. The children of Israel are guided by the spirit that will testify of the truthfulness of these marvelous and wonderful things.

Isaiah 30:21

21 And thine ears shall hear a word behind thee, saying, This is the way, walk ye in it, when ye turn to the right hand, and when ye turn to the left.

The path to Zion is made so sure for the children of Israel that it will be as though a voice is speaking in their ears telling them what to do. In reality, they will. The voice of the Lord will whisper directions to each individual who undertakes the trail to Zion. In this manner, they will flee the kingdom of Assyria and the false doctrines of the world.

A New Path to Zion

Isaiah 42:16

16 And I will bring the blind by a way that they knew not; I will lead them in paths that they have not known: I will make darkness light before them, and crooked things straight. These things will I do unto them, and not forsake them.

Again we see the idea of Israel being lead by a new path, a sure path. And it is a way that they knew not. It is a new path found only during the period of the Latter Rain.

Isaiah 43:18-21
18 Remember ye not the former things, neither consider the things of old.
19 Behold, I will do a new thing; now it shall spring forth; shall ye not know it? I will even make a way in the wilderness, and rivers in the desert.
20 The beast of the field shall honour me, the dragons and the owls: because I give waters in the wilderness, and rivers in the desert, to give drink to my people, my chosen.
21 This people have I formed for myself; they shall shew forth my praise.

Here the Lord counsels us to forget the former things. Instead of relying on the old things, he will do a new thing. "It shall spring forth, shall ye not know it?" Again, we see the concept of a highway being laid before us leading us to the true Kingdom of God. The water/revelation concept is repeated in that he will cause rivers to spring up in the desert—or revelation to come where there has been none. This revelation spoken of through these symbolic types refers to both the revelations of the newly-called and living prophets that will usher in the Latter Rain period as well as new scriptures from the Tribe of Ephraim or Joseph, which will be just like we saw in the story of Joseph, who was sold into Egypt. The works of the prophets of the Lost Ten Tribes from the north will spring forth. The human family has considered them to be dead and gone, as Joseph's family considered him to be dead. However, in an amazing way, the Lord will have stored up spiritual food and nourishment during the Great Famine period which will ultimately feed his children and lead them again to Zion. The image of this migration toward Zion is eloquently expressed in Isaiah 35.

Isaiah 35:3-10
3 Strengthen ye the weak hands, and confirm the feeble knees.
4 Say to them that are of a fearful heart, Be strong, fear not: behold, your God will come with vengeance, even God with a recompence; he will come and save you.
5 Then the eyes of the blind shall be opened, and the ears of the deaf shall be unstopped.
6 Then shall the lame man leap as an hart, and the tongue of the dumb sing: for in the wilderness shall waters break out, and streams in the desert.
7 And the parched ground shall become a pool, and the thirsty land springs of water: in the habitation of dragons, where each lay, shall be grass with reeds and rushes.
8 And an highway shall be there, and a way, and it shall be called The way of holiness; the unclean shall not pass over it; but it shall be for those: the wayfaring men, though fools, shall not err therein.
9 No lion shall be there, nor any ravenous beast shall go up thereon, it shall not be found there; but the redeemed shall walk there:
10 And the ransomed of the LORD shall return, and come to Zion with songs and everlasting joy upon their heads: they shall obtain joy and gladness, and sorrow and sighing shall flee away.

Revelation shall spring up where there was none before. The Lord will call new prophets in the Latter Rain period that will guide the children of Israel home to Zion on a sure path of sound doctrine and authorized priesthood. With the calling of new prophets in the Latter Rain period, we should also look for the same organization that existed previously. We should find a governing body of Twelve Apostles reestablished. While the original Apostles of Jesus Christ were killed off, when Zion is reestablished, this same form of organization should be put back in place as well.

These modern-day apostles will have to receive the priesthood authority again in order to perform such ordinances as baptism, giving the Holy Ghost through the laying on of hands, and other essential ordinances of salvation. The explanation of how this occurs will be another sign of a true and restored Zion. Authority by education, political or financial means should have nothing to do with who receives this power. It can only be passed on from one man to the next by the laying on of hands as was done in ancient times. Since the priesthood had been lost, a means will be necessary to transfer the priesthood authority held by the ancient prophets to those of this final dispensation. The very prophets that held the priesthood keys will be the ones to appear to the modern prophets to ordain them to the everlasting priesthood of God. Angels from heaven will be sent to restore the ordinations during the final dispensation, which is symbolically represented by a downpour of spiritual rain and divine revelation.

Once the Church of Christ is restored to the earth, prophets called, and the priesthood of God reestablished, a true sign of Zion will be the sending of messengers throughout the world to tell of these special events. Just as the apostles preached the Gospel to the world following the resurrection of Christ, the harvest of souls that began then will continue in the final period of activity for the Lord on the earth. He will send his armies (his humble disciples) to reclaim the dispersed of Israel where they are held captive. Remember that the sword of the Lord is his word. His armies are his missionaries and disciples that preach this restored Gospel, this new thing, including the Holy Bible and a new book from Ephraim in their hand. They will go throughout the earth and reclaim the lost children of Israel.

Isaiah 10:24-27

24 Therefore thus saith the Lord GOD of hosts, O my people that dwellest in Zion, be not afraid of the Assyrian: he shall smite thee with a rod, and shall lift up his staff against thee, after the manner of Egypt.
25 For yet a very little while, and the indignation shall cease, and mine anger in their destruction.
26 And the LORD of hosts shall stir up a scourge for him according to the slaughter of Midian at the rock of Oreb: and as his rod was upon the sea, so shall he lift it up after the manner of Egypt.
27 And it shall come to pass in that day, that his burden shall be taken away from off thy shoulder, and his yoke from off thy neck, and the yoke shall be destroyed because of the anointing.

The false doctrines that exist in the world will eventually be put down by the servants of the Lord who carry the restored Gospel to every people. While the nations fear them and desire to flee, the doctrines of the Lord's Zion will ultimately overcome them all. "And it shall come to pass in that day, that his burden shall be taken away from off thy shoulder, and his yoke from off thy neck, and the yoke shall be destroyed because of the anointing." This symbolic language describes the powerful effect that the restored Gospel will have on those clinging to false notions and the traditions of men. They will ultimately become helpless to defend themselves. With time, the Lord of Hosts will put all his enemies under his feet.

The Temple of the Lord

Finally, a true sign of the restored Gospel would be the restoration of a temple and the ordinances performed therein. While very little is known about the function of temples from the Bible, it is clear from the Bible that they did exist. They were an important part of the worship of God in ancient times. We know that God dwelt first in the Tabernacle, which was a portable temple. It was in essence a Holy Tent, but it was still a place where God could come and fill it with his presence. The Tabernacle was constructed by the Jews as they wandered in the wilderness on their way to the Promised Land. It was built according to revelations given through the prophet Moses. The Lord was known to bring his presence into the Tabernacle and there commune with Moses and others. Later, Solomon was commanded to build a House for the Lord, which became the Great Temple of Solomon that now lies in ruins somewhere in the city of Jerusalem

Jesus frequented the Temple of Solomon when he lived on the earth. He drove the money changers from the outer courts of the temple, because he felt they were defiling it with their lust for lucre and their lack of reverence. Paul and the apostles also went to the temple. What they did therein remains a mystery that was lost when the Lord withdrew his apostles and prophets from the earth. The last chapters of Ezekiel are dedicated entirely to a description of the temple. In Ezekiel 47, for example, the prophet describes the issuing forth of water not from the side of Jesus, but from the east side of the temple, and they flow down and heal the Dead Sea. This symbolism shows the critical importance of the temple as a place of revelation. From the temple flows the Spirit of God.

> **Ezekiel 47:1,8**
> 1 AFTERWARD he brought me again unto the door of the house; and, behold, waters issued out from under the threshold of the house eastward: for the forefront of the house stood toward the east, and the waters came down from under from the right side of the house, at the south side of the altar.
> 8 Then said he unto me, These waters issue out toward the east country, and go down into the desert, and go into the sea: which being brought forth into the sea, the waters shall be healed.

The Book of Revelation culminates with John's description of the earth after it is renewed, saying in Revelation 21:22, "And I saw no temple therein: for the Lord God Almighty and the Lamb are the temple of it." Until the earth is renewed and the wicked banished, temples are required to exist on the earth. When the earth is cleansed, the planet itself will become a temple, allowing for the presence of God to come and exist therein. In the meantime, buildings are necessary to keep the unclean out from the presence of God when he comes into his temple. While the exact qualifications of those entering the temple have been lost to historical record, the Pharisees seemed to be outraged when the Apostle Paul brought Greek men into the Temple of Jerusalem.

THE LATTER RAIN

Acts 21:26-28

26 Then Paul took the men, and the next day purifying himself with them entered into the temple, to signify the accomplishment of the days of purification, until that an offering should be offered for every one of them.
27 And when the seven days were almost ended, the Jews which were of Asia, when they saw him in the temple, stirred up all the people, and laid hands on him,
28 Crying out, Men of Israel, help: This is the man, that teacheth all men every where against the people, and the law, and this place: and further brought Greeks also into the temple, and hath polluted this holy place.

The leaders of the Jews were outraged that these Greek men had entered the temple, not realizing that they had been sanctified and brought into the true fold of God. While little is known through the Bible about the function of the temple, it evidently was an exclusive place only for those worthy of entry. What we do know is that the temple is a Holy House of the Lord, and the loss of the temple understanding is another sign of the Great Spiritual Famine and of the falling away of the true Gospel. An understanding of the temple and its function will be a distinguishing mark of the restored Zion of the Latter Rain period.

Jesus Christ is the True Messiah

The purpose of this book has been to establish truth using the symbols and types derived from an analysis of the Book of Isaiah. We used Isaiah's writings to elucidate truth and derive knowledge from the other books of the Holy Bible. As a result, we see that the ancient prophets who wrote the books of the Bible are warning its readers of an impending dark period in the course of human history.

Through scriptural analysis, we learned that this period of Spiritual Famine would be characterized by the lack of prophets, revelation, and authorized priesthood to perform the essential ordinances of the Lord's Church and Kingdom. The Church of God was taken from the earth shortly after the ascension of the Lord Jesus Christ to take his rightful place on the right hand of his Father's throne. Thus, the Dark Ages of history began, and the Lord ceased his interactions with his children on earth for a season. While this was a punishment based on the wickedness of ancient Israel and Judah, this withdrawal was enacted by the Lord with much regret and remorse.

Jeremiah 13:16-17

16 Give glory to the LORD your God, before he cause darkness, and before your feet stumble upon the dark mountains, and, while ye look for light, he turn it into the shadow of death, and make it gross darkness.
17 But if ye will not hear it, my soul shall weep in secret places for your pride; and mine eye shall weep sore, and run down with tears, because the LORD's flock is carried away captive.

Through scriptural analysis we identified the attributes that should be present in the Lord's restored Church, to be consistent with the Holy Church that existed anciently.

John 10:24-27

24 Then came the Jews round about him, and said unto him, How long dost thou make us to doubt? If thou be the Christ, tell us plainly.

25 Jesus answered them, I told you, and ye believed not: the works that I do in my Father's name, they bear witness of me.
26 But ye believe not, because ye are not of my sheep, as I said unto you.
27 My sheep hear my voice, and I know them, and they follow me:

"My sheep hear my voice, and I know them, and they follow me." The main challenge for each and every reader of this book is to call on Heavenly Father directly in prayer. Ask him specifically if the things presented herein are true. More than anything else, I desire all to know that Jesus is the true Messiah—there is no other Messiah!

I also desire that each of us might develop a personal relationship with Heavenly Father through Jesus Christ, the Great Mediator. I know that he lives. He hears and answers prayers. He will answer anyone who asks in faith, and will lead them to truth.

Matthew 7:7-8
7 Ask, and it shall be given you; seek, and ye shall find; knock, and it shall be opened unto you:
8 For every one that asketh receiveth; and he that seeketh findeth; and to him that knocketh it shall be opened.

Ask Heavenly Father directly, believing that he can and will answer your prayer. Without consulting with God, we are left subject to every wind of doctrine floating in the sea of philosophical confusion. I have introduced concepts and ideas from the Prophet Isaiah and other writers of the Bible that are relevant for our day. They are not my words, but those of the ancient prophets, and of the Lord himself. My conclusion is that God will bring again Zion, and it will roll forth and consume all the false doctrines the world has to offer. While I leave it to each individual to decide about these things for themselves, I am completely certain for myself that they are true.

Daniel 2:45
45 Forasmuch as thou sawest that the stone was cut out of the mountain without hands, and that it brake in pieces the iron, the brass, the clay, the silver, and the gold; the great God hath made known to the king what shall come to pass hereafter: **and the dream is certain, and the interpretation thereof sure.**

LaVergne, TN USA
10 November 2010
204415LV00002B/2/P